Early prevention of adult antisocial behaviour

This book presents a comprehensive and up-to-date summary of how adult crime, antisocial behaviour and antisocial personality disorder can be prevented by interventions applied early in life. It reviews important childhood risk and protective factors for these adult outcomes. Alternative strategies of primary prevention (targeting the whole community) and secondary prevention (targeting persons identified as high-risk) are also discussed. The book also contains extensive information about prevention programmes in pregnancy and infancy, preschool programmes, parent education and training programmes, and school programmes (including the prevention of bullying). There is special emphasis on preventing the intergenerational transmission of antisocial behaviour by focusing on family violence, and a special review of whether risk factors and prevention programmes have different effects for females compared to males. Cost–benefit analyses of early prevention programmes are also reviewed, leading to the conclusion that adult antisocial behaviour can be prevented both effectively and cost-efficiently.

DAVID P. FARRINGTON is Professor of Psychological Criminology at the Institute of Criminology, Cambridge University. He has published extensively on criminological and psychological topics including twenty-eight books and monographs, one of which, *Understanding and Controlling Crime* (1986), won the prize for distinguished scholarship of the American Sociological Association Criminology Section.

JEREMY W. COID is Professor of Forensic Psychiatry at St Bartholomew's and the Royal London School of Medicine and Dentistry, Queen Mary College, University of London. His area of research is epidemiology of antisocial and high risk behaviour, with a special interest in personality disorder. He is the author of *Psychopathic and Antisocial Personality Disorders: Treatment and Research Issues* (with B. Dolan, 1993).

Cambridge Studies in Criminology

Edited by
Alfred Blumstein, *H. John Heinz School of Public Policy and Management, Carnegie Mellon University*
and David P. Farrington, *Institute of Criminology, University of Cambridge*

The Cambridge Studies in Criminology series aims to publish the highest quality research on criminology and criminal justice topics. Typical volumes report major quantitative, qualitative, and ethnographic research, or make a substantial theoretical contribution. There is a particular emphasis on research monographs, but edited collections may also be published if they make an unusually distinctive offering to the literature. All relevant areas of criminology and criminal justice are included, for example, the causes of offending, juvenile justice, the development of offenders, measurement and analysis of crime, victimisation research, policing, crime prevention, sentencing, imprisonment, probation, and parole. The series is global in outlook, with an emphasis on work that is comparative or holds significant implications for theory or policy.

Other books in the series

Life in the Gang: Family, Friends, and Violence, by Scott H. Decker and Barrik Van Winkle
Delinquency and Crime: Current Theories, edited by J. David Hawkins
Recriminalizing Delinquency: Violent Juvenile Crime and Juvenile Justice Reform, by Simon I. Singer
Mean Streets: Youth Crime and Homelessness, by John Hagan and Bill McCarthy
The Framework of Judicial Sentencing: A Study in Legal Decision Making, by Austin Lovegrove
The Criminal Recidivism Process, by Edward Zamble and Vernon L. Quinsey
Violence and Childhood in the Inner City, by Joan McCord
Judicial Policy Making and the Modern State: How the Courts Reformed America's Prisons, by Malcolm M. Feeley and Edward L. Rubin
Schools and Delinquency, by Denise C. Gottfredson
The Crime Drop in America, edited by Alfred Blumstein and Joel Wallman
Delinquent-Prone Communities, by Don Weatherburn and Bronwyn Lind
White-Collar Crime and Criminal Careers, by David Weisburd and Elin Waring, with Ellen F. Chayet
Sex Differences in Antisocial Behaviour: Conduct Disorder, Delinquency, and Violence in the Dunedin Longitudinal Study, by Terrie Moffitt, Avshalom Caspi, Michael Rutter, and Phil A. Silva
Delinquent Networks: Youth Co-Offending in Stockholm, by Jerzy Sarnecki
Criminality and Violence among the Mentally Disordered: The Stockholm Metropolitan Project, by Sheilagh Hodgins and Carl-Gunnar Janson
Why Corporations Obey the Law: Assessing Criminalization and Cooperative Models of Crime Control, by Sally S. Simpson
Situational Prison Control: Crime Control in Correctional Institutions, by Richard Wortley
Companions in Crime, by Mark Warr
The Criminal Career, by Britta Kyvsgaard
Gangs and Delinquency in Developmental Perspective, by Terence P. Thornberry et al.

Early Prevention of Adult Antisocial Behaviour

Edited by
David P. Farrington
University of Cambridge
Jeremy W. Coid
St Bartholomew's and the Royal London School of Medicine and Dentistry

CAMBRIDGE UNIVERSITY PRESS
Cambridge, New York, Melbourne, Madrid, Cape Town, Singapore, São Paulo

Cambridge University Press
The Edinburgh Building, Cambridge CB2 2RU, UK

Published in the United States of America by Cambridge University Press, New York

www.cambridge.org
Information on this title: www.cambridge.org/9780521651943

First published 2003
Third printing 2004
This digitally printed first paperback version 2006

A catalogue record for this publication is available from the British Library

ISBN-13 978-0-521-65194-3 hardback
ISBN-10 0-521-65194-8 hardback

ISBN-13 978-0-521-03079-3 paperback
ISBN-10 0-521-03079-X paperback

Contents

Figures

Tables

Contributors

Doris Bender Institute of Psychology, University of Erlangen-Nuremberg, Germany.

Avshalom Caspi, Social, Genetic and Developmental Psychiatry Research Centre, Institute of Psychiatry, King's College London, UK.

Jeremy W. Coid, Department of Psychological Medicine, St Bartholomew's and the Royal London School of Medicine and Dentistry, London, UK.

David P. Farrington, Institute of Criminology, University of Cambridge, UK.

Deborah Gorman-Smith, Institute for Juvenile Research, Department of Psychiatry, University of Illinois at Chicago, USA.

Stephanie M. Green, Western Psychiatric Institute and Clinic, University of Pittsburgh, USA.

J. David Hawkins, Social Development Research Group, University of Washington, Seattle, USA.

Todd I. Herrenkohl, Social Development Research Group, University of Washington, Seattle, USA.

Christa Japel, GRIP, University of Montreal, Canada.

Benjamin B. Lahey, Department of Psychiatry, University of Chicago, USA.

Rolf Loeber, Western Psychiatric Institute and Clinic, University of Pittsburgh, USA.

Friedrich Lösel, Institute of Psychology, University of Erlangen-Nuremberg, Germany.

Terrie E. Moffitt, Social, Genetic and Developmental Psychiatry Research Centre, Institute of Psychiatry, King's College London, UK.

Richard E. Tremblay, GRIP, University of Montreal, Canada.

David Utting, Joseph Rowntree Foundation, York, UK.

Brandon C. Welsh, Department of Criminal Justice, University of Massachusetts-Lowell, USA.

Preface

The origins of this book lie in a Network on the Primary Prevention of Adult Antisocial Behaviour that was established by the High Security Psychiatric Services Commissioning Board of the UK Department of Health. Dilys Jones was instrumental in creating this network, and we were chosen to chair it. In light of the relative paucity of information about this area, we decided to assemble a scholarly report summarising the current state of knowledge.

We invited international experts in the field, drawn from the United Kingdom, the United States, Canada and Germany, to write chapters on particular topics and to present their conclusions at a large Network conference held in London. We also invited discussants to comment (both verbally and later in writing) on each chapter, and we are very grateful to Avshalom Caspi, Jonathan Hill, Israel Kolvin, Barbara Maughan, Gillian Mezey, Mark Perfect, Stephen Scott, Kathy Silva, Michael Wadsworth and Donald West for their helpful comments. All authors subsequently revised and updated their chapters in light of all comments from discussants and from ourselves as editors.

We are very grateful to the UK Department of Health for funding the Network activities that led to this book. Since there is no other volume exactly on this topic, we hope that this book will simultaneously summarise what has been learned and also stimulate more research, especially on the early prevention of adult antisocial personality and psychopathy.

DAVID P. FARRINGTON
JEREMY W. COID

1 Advancing knowledge about the early prevention of adult antisocial behaviour

David P. Farrington

The main aims of this book are to review what is known about the causes and prevention of adult antisocial behaviour. The book aims to specify what we know, what we do not know, and what we need to know, recommending priority research that would address key questions and fill key gaps in knowledge. The main aim of this introductory chapter is to set the scene for the more detailed chapters that follow by outlining some of the key topics, issues and questions arising in the early prevention of adult antisocial behaviour. This chapter defines the territory by briefly reviewing epidemiology, development, risk and protective factors, and prevention programmes.

Four types of prevention can be distinguished (Tonry and Farrington, 1995). Criminal justice prevention refers to traditional deterrence, incapacitation and rehabilitation strategies operated by law enforcement and criminal justice agencies. Situational prevention refers to interventions designed to reduce the opportunities for antisocial behaviour and to increase the risk and difficulty of committing antisocial acts. Community prevention refers to interventions designed to change the social conditions and social institutions (e.g. community norms and organisations) that influence antisocial behaviour in communities. Developmental prevention refers to interventions designed to inhibit the development of antisocial behaviour in individuals, by targeting risk and protective factors that influence human development (see Farrington, 2000a).

This book concentrates on early developmental prevention programmes, including those implemented in pregnancy and infancy, parenting programmes, preschool programmes, individual skills training, and school programmes. Many of these involve primary prevention, targeting unselected individuals in the whole community, but secondary prevention programmes targeting children at risk are also reviewed. The focus of the book is on risk factors and early prevention in childhood and adolescence; for reviews of risk factors and early interventions for conduct disorder and delinquency, see Farrington (1999) and Rutter, Giller and Hagell (1998).

Definition and measurement

Definition of antisocial behaviour

There is clearly a syndrome of adult antisocial behaviour defined by a cluster of antisocial symptoms. This syndrome is given different names in different countries and different classification systems: antisocial personality disorder in DSM-IV (American Psychiatric Association, 1994), dissocial personality disorder in ICD-10 (World Health Organisation, 1992) and psychopathic disorder in the English Mental Health Act 1983, for example.

Both types of behaviour and features of personality are included in the antisocial behaviour syndrome. Types of behaviour include property crimes such as burglary, violent crimes, drug use, heavy drinking, drunk or reckless driving, sexual promiscuity or risky sex behaviour, divorce/separation or unstable sexual relationships, spouse or partner abuse, child abuse or neglect, unemployment or an unstable employment history, debts, dependence on welfare benefits, heavy gambling, heavy smoking, and repeated lying and conning. Personality features include impulsiveness and lack of planning, selfishness and egocentricity, callousness and lack of empathy, lack of remorse or guilt feelings, low frustration tolerance and high aggressiveness.

An important question is the relative importance of behavioural and personality symptoms in defining antisocial personality disorder. Hare and his colleagues (e.g. Hare, Hart and Harpur, 1991) have consistently criticised the DSM criteria for antisocial personality as too behavioural and insufficiently concerned with personality features. Hare's Psychopathy Checklist (PCL-R) distinguishes two factors. Factor 1 consists of personality features such as egocentricity, lack of remorse, and callousness, while factor 2 describes an impulsive, antisocial, and unstable lifestyle. The problem is that some features of an antisocial lifestyle (e.g. unemployment and dependence on welfare benefits) may either reflect an antisocial personality or may be caused by circumstances outside the person's own control. Because of this, it is desirable to include both behavioural and personality features in the definition of antisocial personality.

Another important question is whether individuals differ qualitatively (in kind) or quantitatively (in degree) in antisocial personality (Clark, Livesley and Morey, 1997). People can be scored according to their number of symptoms. For example, Robins and her colleagues (e.g. Robins and Price, 1991) have consistently argued that the number of childhood conduct disorder symptoms predicts the number of adult antisocial behaviour symptoms, rather than any specific childhood behaviour predicting a specific adult behaviour. The key problem is where to set the boundary between normal and pathological, or between health and illness. Existing boundaries depend largely on clinical judgement. For example, according to DSM-IV, 'only when antisocial personality traits are inflexible, maladaptive and persistent and cause significant functional impairment or subjective distress do they constitute Antisocial Personality Disorder' (American Psychiatric Association, 1994, p. 649). Far more is known about the early prevention of particular types of antisocial behaviour than about the early prevention of antisocial personality disorder or psychopathy.

Measurement of antisocial behaviour

Antisocial behaviour can be measured in a variety of ways. Interviews by psychiatrists are necessary to yield psychiatric diagnoses in Great Britain, where explicit diagnostic criteria are not as widely used as in North America. However, psychiatrist interviews are not very practical for large-scale epidemiological studies. One possible strategy is to use a two-stage procedure in which the population is initially screened using brief symptom questionnaires (e.g. Bebbington *et al.*, 1981). Then, more intensive clinical interviews can be given to all those with high symptom scores and to a representative sample of those with low scores.

Another possible method is to use an interview designed for non-clinicians, such as the NIMH Diagnostic Interview Schedule used in the Epidemiological Catchment Area project (Robins and Regier, 1991). Ratings or checklists completed by informants such as institutional staff can also be used, based on interviews and records, as in the case of the PCL-R (Hare, 1991). Alternatively, semi-structured interviews with informants such as relatives or close friends can be used, as with the Standardized Assessment of Personality (Pilgrim and Mann, 1990), or psychological tests and self-completion questionnaires can be used (e.g. Blackburn, 1975).

It is important with all measurement techniques to assess validity and reliability. However, one problem in assessing validity is that the external criterion for antisocial personality disorder or psychopathy is often based on psychiatric diagnoses, which may have low reliability (Malgady, Rogler and Tryon, 1992). It is especially important to measure the predictive validity of instruments given at a relatively early age or stage of development.

In this chapter, I will refer to results obtained in the Cambridge Study in Delinquent Development, which is a prospective longitudinal survey of 411 South London males from age 8 to age 46 (Farrington, 1995,

2002c). At age 32, a measure of antisocial personality was devised, based on the following twelve items: convicted in the last five years, self-reported offender, involved in fights, drug-taker, heavy drinker, poor relationship with parents, poor relationship with wife/cohabitee, divorced/child living elsewhere, frequent unemployment, anti-establishment attitude, tattooed, and impulsive (Farrington, 1991). These were measured in a structured social interview. The reliability of this scale was 0.71, and the worst quarter of the males had four or more adverse features out of twelve.

Inter-relationships between behaviours

In general, all the behavioural and personality symptoms listed above tend to be intercorrelated, since people who show one of them have an increased risk of also showing any other. For example, the two factor scores of the PCL-R are highly intercorrelated (over 0.5: Hare *et al.*, 1991), and the total PCL-R score is highly correlated with the diagnosis of antisocial personality disorder (0.67 in Hare, 1985). Comorbidity is a common finding, and it is assumed that all of the symptoms reflect the same underlying theoretical construct. However, it is important to quantify the degree of versatility in antisocial behaviour, and to assess whether it is more reasonable to assume two or more underlying constructs rather than only one. Another important question is whether conclusions are different with continuous as opposed to dichotomous measures of symptoms.

To the extent that intercorrelated clusters of symptoms are identified within the general category of antisocial behaviour, it may be useful to distinguish typologies of individuals. For example, Moffitt (1993) distinguished between 'life-course-persistent' individuals, who began their antisocial behaviour at an early age and persisted for a long time, and 'adolescence-limited' ones who began later and desisted earlier. However, it is unclear how far these categories differ in degree rather than in kind.

Epidemiology and development

Epidemiology

It is important to establish the prevalence of antisocial symptoms, and of antisocial personality disorder, at different ages. It is useful to determine the peak ages of different types of antisocial behaviour, and the peak ages for acceleration and deceleration in prevalence. Information is also needed about the frequency and seriousness of behaviours at different ages. Other important questions centre on how prevalence, frequency and seriousness vary with gender, ethnicity, and geographical area, and over time. Perhaps the most extensive data on the epidemiology of antisocial behaviour was provided by the Epidemiological Catchment Area Project (Robins, Tipp and Przybeck, 1991). For example, the estimated life-time prevalence of antisocial personality disorder in the USA was 7.3 per cent of males and 1.0 per cent of females. Similarly, Bland, Orn and Newman (1988) estimated that the life-time prevalence was 7 per cent of males in Edmonton, Canada. However, in Great Britain, the current prevalence of antisocial personality disorder was 1 per cent of males and 0.2 per cent of females in a national survey (Singleton *et al.*, 2002). The epidemiology of antisocial personality disorder has been most extensively reviewed by Moran (1999). In chapter 2, Jeremy Coid reviews epidemiological data and its implications for early prevention.

Another important epidemiological question concerns how far antisocial behaviour is concentrated among a small segment of the population. For example, in the Cambridge Study in Delinquent Development, about 6 per cent of the cohort males accounted for half of all the convictions up to age 32 (Farrington and West, 1993). These 'chronic offenders' were particularly likely to show other symptoms of antisocial personality, such as an unstable employment record, spouse assault, involvement in fights, drug-taking, heavy drinking, and anti-establishment attitudes. It is useful to quantify the degree of concentration of antisocial behaviour using the Lorenz curve and the Gini coefficient (Wikström, 1991, p.29).

Development

It is important not only to establish the prevalence of antisocial behaviour but also key features of antisocial careers such as the age of onset, the probability of persistence after onset, the duration of antisocial behaviour, and the age of desistance. According to Robins (1978), most boys who eventually developed antisocial personality disorder showed signs of conduct disorder (truancy, stealing and classroom disciplinary problems) as soon as they began attending school. This suggests that the antisocial syndrome has a very early age of onset, and conversely that early prevention is useful. Many other features of antisocial careers could be measured, such as acceleration and deceleration in the frequency of committing antisocial behaviour, escalation and de-escalation in seriousness, diversification, switching, and stabilisation (Loeber and LeBlanc, 1990). It may be difficult to distinguish between true desistance and intermittency or periods of remission.

More is known about criminal careers than about more general antisocial careers. For example, in the Cambridge Study up to age 40, the average age of the first conviction was 18.6, the average age of the last conviction was 25.8, the average length of the criminal career was 7.2 years, and the average number of offences leading to conviction was 4.6 (Farrington, Lambert and West, 1998). The males first convicted at the earliest ages (10–13) tended to become the most persistent offenders, committing an average 8.8 offences leading to convictions in an average criminal career spanning 9.9 years. It is generally true that an early onset of antisocial behaviour predicts a long and serious antisocial career.

It is important to study developmental sequences in antisocial careers, where one type of behaviour tends to be followed by another. Three types of sequences can be distinguished (Farrington, Loeber, Elliott *et al.*, 1990). First of all, different acts following each other may be different behavioural manifestations of the same underlying construct (e.g. antisocial personality) at different ages. Second, different acts may be different behavioural manifestations of the same or similar underlying constructs at different ages and also part of a developmental sequence, where one act is a stepping stone towards or facilitates another (e.g. where smoking cigarettes leads to marijuana use). Third, different acts may be indicators of different constructs and part of a causal sequence, where changes in an indicator of one construct cause changes in an indicator of a different construct (e.g. where low attainment leads to truancy). A further problem is that the same behaviour at different ages may reflect different underlying constructs (e.g. compare sexual intercourse at age 12, which is deviant, with sexual intercourse at age 25, which is normal).

Intragenerational continuity

It is important to assess the degree of continuity and stability in antisocial behaviour over time. Several researchers have reported that childhood conduct disorder tends to predict adult antisocial personality disorder. For example, in an Inner London study Zoccolillo *et al.* (1992) found that almost half of the males with three or more symptoms of conduct disorder at age 9–12 showed persistent antisocial behaviour after age 18 and fulfilled the criteria for adult antisocial personality disorder (see also Offord and Bennett, 1994; Rey *et al.*, 1995; Rutter *et al.*, 1994; Storm-Mathisen and Vaglum, 1994). In the Cambridge Study, the antisocial personality score at age 8–10 correlated 0.38 with the score at age 18, and the score at age 18 correlated 0.55 with the score at age 32 (Farrington, 1991).

These correlations help to quantify the degree of stability in the relative ordering of individuals as opposed to the degree of change. They do not indicate absolute stability in antisocial behaviour. For example, in the Cambridge Study the prevalence of marijuana use decreased significantly between ages 18 and 32, but there was a significant tendency for the users at age 18 also to be users at age 32 (Farrington, 1990). Conversely, binge drinking increased significantly between ages 18 and 32, and there was again significant consistency over time. Hence, relative stability often coincided with absolute change. It may be that stability varies according to the initial level of antisocial behaviour; for example, the most antisocial people may be the most stable.

Continuity refers to relationships between different behavioural manifestations over time. For example, hyperactivity at age 2 may predict cruelty to animals at age 6, which in turn predicts conduct disorder at age 10, which in turn predicts burglary at age 14, violence at age 18, partner abuse in the 20s and child abuse in the 30s. The major problem is how to establish that one behaviour leads to another in some way, since any behaviour A tends to be followed by many other behaviours (B, C, D...) with varying probabilities after varying time intervals.

Intergenerational continuity

Antisocial parents tend to have antisocial children. For example, in the Cambridge Study, 63 per cent of boys with convicted fathers were themselves convicted (odds ratio = 3.9), as were 61 per cent of boys with convicted mothers (odds ratio = 2.8). Convictions were highly concentrated in families; about 6 per cent of the cohort families accounted for about half of all the convictions of all family members (Farrington, Barnes and Lambert, 1996). Having a convicted parent at age 10 was the best single predictor of antisocial personality at age 32 (Farrington, 2000b).

It is unclear how far there is specific transmission of types of antisocial behaviour as opposed to general transmission of antisocial tendencies. For example, it is not clear that violent parents tend specifically to have violent children, or that drug-using parents tend specifically to have drug-using children, over and above the general tendency for antisocial parents to have antisocial children. Nor is it clear how far this transmission is attributable to genetic as opposed to environmental factors; behaviour-genetic designs (e.g. twin or adoption studies) are needed to disentangle these factors. Chapter 4 by Terrie Moffitt and Avshalom Caspi discusses intergenerational continuity in more detail, with special reference to partner violence.

Risk and protective factors

Risk factors are prior factors that predict an increased probability of antisocial behaviour. Longitudinal data are required to establish the relative ordering of risk factors and antisocial outcomes. Few longitudinal studies have explicitly investigated risk factors for antisocial personality; the most relevant available information usually concerns risk factors for offending. Apart from the seminal work of Robins (1979), 'we have relatively few studies that have measured the effects of these [child and family] risks, prospectively measured, on adult personality disorder symptoms' (Cohen, 1996, p.126). However, in the Cambridge Study, risk factors for antisocial personality at age 32 (Farrington, 2000b) and for chronic offending (Farrington and West, 1993) were investigated.

Few studies have conducted research on risk factors for career features such as onset, persistence, escalation, and desistance as opposed to risk factors for antisocial behaviour in general. It is sometimes difficult to disentangle risk factors from antisocial outcomes. For example, impulsiveness may be regarded as a cause of antisocial behaviour or as an element of the antisocial personality syndrome. Because of the overall emphasis on prevention in this book, this chapter will concentrate on potentially changeable risk factors that could have causal effects on antisocial behaviour. It is important to study the independent, interactive, and sequential effects of risk factors on antisocial behaviour, but these factors will be briefly reviewed one by one in this chapter. Only a brief review of risk factors can be presented here; chapter 3 by Rolf Loeber, Stephanie Green and Ben Lahey provides a more extensive review of risk factors for antisocial personality.

Biological and individual risk factors

A number of biological risk factors for antisocial behaviour have been identified (Raine, 1993). How far these are changeable is not always clear. For example, there may be some genetic contribution. In the Minnesota study of identical twins brought up apart, the heritability of adult antisocial personality disorder was estimated to be 0.28 (Grove *et al.*, 1990). Neurochemical factors (e.g. testosterone), neurotransmitters (e.g. serotonin), psychophysiological factors (e.g. a low heart rate), and neuropsychological deficits (e.g. in executive functions) have all been linked to antisocial behaviour (Raine *et al.*, 1997). Other relevant factors include head injuries, pregnancy and birth complications, low birth weight of the child, and substance use in pregnancy by the mother (e.g. Kolvin *et al.*, 1990; Raine, Brennan and Mednick, 1994).

A major cluster of individual risk factors includes hyperactivity, impulsivity, attention problems, clumsiness, daring or risk-taking, and other elements of Attention Deficit Hyperactivity Disorder (ADHD). These factors are often closely linked to childhood conduct disorder, but hyperactivity-impulsivity-attention deficit and conduct problems at age 8–10 were independent predictors of later convictions in the Cambridge Study (Farrington, Loeber and van Kammen, 1990). Lynam (1996) argued that children who had both hyperactivity-impulsivity-attention deficit and conduct problems were especially at risk of becoming psychopaths. Also in the Cambridge Study, daring and poor concentration were among the best independent predictors of chronic offenders (Farrington and West, 1993).

The most extensive research on different measures of impulsiveness was carried out in another longitudinal study of males (the Pittsburgh Youth Study) by White *et al.* (1994). The measures that were most strongly related to self-reported delinquency at ages 10 and 13 were teacher-rated impulsiveness (e.g. 'acts without thinking'), self-reported impulsiveness, self-reported under-control (e.g. 'unable to delay gratification'), motor restlessness (from videotaped observations), and psychomotor impulsiveness (on the Trail Making Test). Generally, the verbal behaviour rating tests produced stronger relationships with offending than the psychomotor performance tests, suggesting that cognitive impulsiveness (based on thinking processes) was more relevant than behavioural impulsiveness (based on test performance).

Other important individual risk factors for antisocial behaviour include low intelligence, low attainment, low empathy, low guilt, unpopularity, and poor interpersonal skills (Blackburn, 1993). For example, in the Cambridge Study, low non-verbal IQ and low junior school attainment were strong childhood predictors of antisocial personality at age 32 (Farrington, 2000b). Similar results have been obtained in other projects (Lynam, Moffitt and Stouthamer-Loeber, 1993; Wilson and Herrnstein, 1985). Delinquents often do better on non-verbal performance tests, such as object assembly and block design, than on verbal tests (Walsh, Petee and Beyer, 1987), suggesting that they find it easier to deal with concrete objects than with abstract concepts.

Family interaction and socio-economic risk factors

Numerous family factors predict a child's later antisocial behaviour. Having criminal or antisocial parents has already been mentioned. Important family interaction factors include inconsistent, harsh or abusive parenting, cold or rejecting parental attitude, poor parental supervision or monitoring, low parental involvement with the child, separation/divorce and parental conflict (Farrington, 2002b; Smith and Stern, 1997). For example, in the Cambridge Study, poor parental supervision was an important childhood predictor of both chronic offending and antisocial personality at age 32. However, poor child-rearing (harsh or erratic attitude or discipline) predicted chronic offending but not antisocial personality, and separation from a parent (usually the father) predicted antisocial personality but not chronic offending (Farrington, 2000b; Farrington and West, 1993).

Numerous socio-economic factors predict a child's later antisocial behaviour, including low family income, large family size (which is also a family interaction factor), poor housing, a teenage mother, dependence on welfare benefits, and unemployed parents. For example, in the Cambridge Study, low family income, large family size (four or more biological siblings) and low socio-economic status (but not poor housing) were important childhood predictors of chronic offending and antisocial personality at age 32 (Farrington, 2000b; Farrington and West, 1993).

Peer, school and community risk factors

It is well established that having delinquent friends is an important correlate of offending; in the Cambridge Study, 75 per cent of chronic offenders had highly delinquent friends at age 14, compared with 33 per cent of non-chronic offenders and 16 per cent of non-offenders (Farrington and West, 1993). What is less clear is how far antisocial peers encourage and facilitate antisocial behaviour, or whether it is merely that "birds of a feather flock together". Delinquents may have delinquent friends because of co-offending, which is particularly common under age 21 (Reiss and Farrington, 1991). Interestingly, withdrawal from the delinquent peer group seemed to be an important influence on desistance in the Cambridge Study (West and Farrington, 1977).

It is also well established that delinquents disproportionately attend high delinquency rate schools, which have high levels of distrust between teachers and students, low commitment to the school by students, and unclear and inconsistently enforced rules (Graham, 1988). In the Cambridge Study, attending a high delinquency-rate school at age 11 significantly predicted both chronic offending and antisocial personality at age 32 (Farrington, 2000b; Farrington and West, 1993). However, what is less clear is how far the schools themselves influence antisocial behaviour by their organisation, climate and practices, and how far the concentration of offenders in certain schools is mainly a function of their intakes.

In the Cambridge Study, most of the variation between schools in their delinquency rates could be explained by differences in their intakes of troublesome boys at age 11 (Farrington, 1972).

Another well known result is that offenders disproportionately live in inner-city areas characterised by physical deterioration, neighbourhood disorganisation, and high residential mobility (Shaw and McKay, 1969). However, again, it is difficult to determine how far the areas themselves influence antisocial behaviour and how far it is merely the case that antisocial people tend to live in deprived areas (e.g. because of their poverty or council housing allocation policies). Interestingly, both neighbourhood researchers such as Gottfredson, McNeil and Gottfredson (1991) and longitudinal researchers such as Rutter (1981) have concluded that neighbourhoods have only indirect effects on antisocial behaviour via their effects on individuals and families.

Protective factors

There are several different definitions of protective factors. One suggests that protective factors are merely the opposite end of the scale from risk factors. For example, just as low intelligence is a risk factor, high intelligence may be a protective factor. Rae-Grant *et al.* (1989) used this definition in the Ontario Child Health Study and reported that the major protective factors for conduct disorder were getting along well with others, good academic performance and participation in organised activities.

On other definitions, protective factors are not just the opposite of risk factors. For example, a variable with a non-linear relationship to antisocial behaviour might be regarded as a protective factor but not a risk factor. This would be true if the risk of antisocial behaviour declined from medium to high levels of the factor but did not increase from medium to low levels. If high intelligence was linked to a low risk of antisocial behaviour, while medium and low intelligence were linked to a fairly constant average risk, intelligence could be regarded as a protective factor but not a risk factor. However, the reverse finding is more common (Farrington and Hawkins, 1991). In the Cambridge Study, the risk of conviction was high for males from large-sized families, but fairly constant over lower levels of family size. Therefore, large family size was a risk factor but small family size was not a protective factor in this sense.

Another possible definition of a protective factor is a variable that interacts with a risk factor to minimise the risk factor's effects (Rutter, 1985). If low intelligence was related to offending only for males from low income families, and not for males from higher income families, then higher income might be regarded as a protective factor against the effects of the risk factor of low intelligence. It is usual to investigate protective factors by identifying a subsample at risk (with some combination of risk factors) and then searching for factors that predict successful members of this subsample (those who do not have the antisocial outcome). For example, in Hawaii, Werner and Smith (1982) studied children who possessed four or more risk factors for delinquency before age 2 but who nevertheless did not develop behavioural difficulties during childhood or adolescence. They found that the major protective factors included being first-born, active and affectionate infants, small family size and receiving a large amount of attention from caretakers. More information about protective factors is provided in chapter 5 by Friedrich Lösel and Doris Bender.

Other issues

There is not space here to review many other issues. For example, it is important to study the effects of life events on the course of development of antisocial behaviour. In the Cambridge Study, getting married was followed by a decrease in offending compared with staying single, and separating from a wife was followed by an increase in offending compared with staying married (Farrington and West, 1995). Similarly, men committed more crimes during periods of unemployment than during periods of employment (Farrington *et al.*, 1986). Since crimes involving material gain (e.g. theft, burglary, robbery) increased during periods of unemployment, it seemed likely that financial need was an important link in the causal chain between unemployment and crime.

It is also desirable to investigate how accurately antisocial behaviour can be predicted, and what are the best risk assessment or screening devices (see Augimeri *et al.*, 2001). Ideally, onset, persistence, escalation and desistance should be predicted separately. There are many ways of measuring predictive accuracy other than focusing on false positives. For example, antisocial personality at age 8–10 predicted antisocial personality at age 32 in the Cambridge Study. While the false positive rate was high (63 per cent), the odds ratio for this comparison was 2.3, showing that the risk of adult antisocial personality was twice as great among antisocial boys (Farrington, 2000b).

Finally, it is important to formulate and test theories of the development of adult antisocial behaviour that can explain all the results reviewed so far in this chapter. Existing theories are too specific, in focusing only on a limited range of risk factors and on a limited number of outcomes (most commonly, offending). My own theory (Farrington, 2001, 2002a) attempts to integrate a number of earlier theories, but there is not space to outline it here.

Early prevention

In the remainder of this chapter, I will review some promising methods, applicable at an early age, of preventing adult antisocial behaviour. Unfortunately, much of the research on early prevention has not studied antisocial behaviour in general as an outcome, but more specific outcomes such as juvenile delinquency or adult crime (see Moran and Hagell, 2001). Also, most research has not assessed the effects of prevention programmes on the extreme (pathological) cases of antisocial behaviour, but rather on the full range of variation. Also, most research has focused on males, but chapter 9 by Deborah Gorman-Smith reviews prevention research with females.

Ideally, methods of preventing antisocial behaviour should be based on empirically validated theories about causes, but such theories are conspicuous by their absence. Consequently, the most useful prevention techniques are risk-focused ones that aim to tackle known risk factors (Farrington, 2000a). Because of limitations of space, I can only mention some of the more important programmes in this chapter; subsequent chapters (especially 6, 7 and 8) will provide more extensive reviews. Existing reviews of the literature on the prevention of antisocial behaviour (e.g. McCord and Tremblay, 1992; Tremblay and Craig, 1995) focus on antisocial behaviour in childhood and adolescence rather than in adulthood. I will focus on randomised experiments with reasonably large samples, since the effect of any intervention can be demonstrated most convincingly in such experiments (Farrington, 1983; Farrington, Ohlin and Wilson, 1986).

Pregnancy and infancy programmes

Problems in pregnancy and infancy can be alleviated by home visiting programmes designed to help mothers. For example, in New York State, Olds *et al.* (1986) randomly allocated 400 mothers either to receive home visits from nurses during pregnancy, or to receive visits both during pregnancy and during the first two years of life, or to a control group who received no visits. Each visit lasted about one and a quarter hours, and the mothers were visited on average every two weeks. The home visitors gave advice about prenatal and postnatal care of the child, about infant development, and about the importance of proper nutrition and the avoidance of smoking and drinking during pregnancy.

The results of this experiment showed that the postnatal home visits caused a decrease in recorded child physical abuse and neglect during the first two years of life, especially by poor unmarried teenage mothers; 4 per cent of visited versus 19 per cent of non-visited mothers of this type were guilty of child abuse or neglect. This last result is important because of the finding that children who are physically abused or neglected tend to become violent offenders later in life (Widom, 1989). In a fifteen-year follow-up, the main focus was on lower class unmarried mothers. Among these mothers, those who received prenatal and postnatal home visits had fewer arrests than those who received prenatal visits or no visits (Olds *et al.*, 1997). Also, children of these mothers who received prenatal and/or postnatal home visits had less than half as many arrests as children of mothers who received no visits (Olds *et al.*, 1998).

One of the very few prevention experiments beginning in pregnancy and collecting outcome data on delinquency was the Syracuse (New York) Family Development Research Programme (Lally, Mangione and Honig, 1988). The researchers began with a sample of pregnant women and gave them weekly help with child-rearing, health, nutrition and other problems. In addition, their children received free day care, designed to develop their intellectual abilities, up to age 5. This was not a randomised experiment, but a matched control group was chosen when the children were aged 3. The treated children had significantly higher intelligence than the controls at age 3 but were not different at age 5.

Ten years later, about 120 treated and control children were followed up to about age 15. Significantly fewer of the treated children (2 per cent as opposed to 17 per cent) had been referred to the juvenile court for delinquency offences, and the treated girls showed better school attendance and school performance. Hence, this prevention experiment agrees with others in showing that early home visits providing advice and support to mothers can have later beneficial outcomes, including the reduction of offending. Chapter 6 by Richard Tremblay and Christa Japel provides more details about these programmes.

Preschool programmes

One of the most successful prevention programmes has been the Perry Preschool Project carried out in Michigan by Schweinhart and Weikart (1980). This was essentially a 'Head Start' programme targeted on disadvantaged African-American children, who were allocated (approximately at random) to experimental and control groups. The experimental children attended a daily preschool programme, backed up by weekly home visits, usually lasting two years (covering ages 3–4). The aim of the 'plan-do-review' programme was to provide intellectual stimulation, to increase thinking and reasoning abilities, and to increase later school achievement.

About 120 children in the two groups were followed up to age 15, using teacher ratings, parent and youth interviews, and school records. As demonstrated in several other Head Start projects, the experimental group showed gains in intelligence that were rather short-lived. However, they were significantly better in elementary school motivation, school achievement at age 14, teacher ratings of classroom behaviour at 6 to 9, self-reports of classroom behaviour at 15 and self-reports of offending at 15. Furthermore, a later follow-up of this sample (Berrueta-Clement *et al.*, 1984) showed that, at age 19, the experimental group was more likely to be employed, more likely to have graduated from high school, more likely to have received college or vocational training, and less likely to have been arrested.

By age 27, the experimental group had accumulated only half as many arrests on average as the controls (Schweinhart, Barnes and Weikart, 1993). Also, they had significantly higher earnings and were more likely to be home-owners. More of the experimental women were married, and fewer of their children had been born out of wedlock. Hence, this preschool intellectual enrichment programme led to decreases in school failure, to decreases in offending, and to decreases in other undesirable outcomes.

The Perry Project is admittedly only one study based on relatively small numbers. However, its results become more compelling when viewed in the context of ten other similar American Head Start projects followed up by the Consortium for Longitudinal Studies (1983) and other preschool programmes such as the Carolina 'Abecedarian' Project, which began at age 3 months (Horacek *et al.*, 1987). With quite impressive consistency, all studies show that preschool intellectual enrichment programmes have long-term beneficial effects on school success, especially in increasing the rate of high school graduation and decreasing the rate of special education placements. The Perry Project was the only one to study offending, but the consistency of the school success results in all projects suggests that the effects on offending and antisocial behaviour might also be replicable. Chapter 6 by Richard Tremblay and Christa Japel provides more details about these programmes.

Parenting programmes

Many different types of parent training programmes have been used (Barlow, 1997; Kazdin, 1997), but the behavioural parent management training developed by Patterson (1982) in Oregon is one of the most promising approaches. His careful observations of parent–child interaction showed that parents of antisocial children were deficient in their methods of child rearing. These parents failed to tell their children how they were expected to behave, failed to monitor their behaviour to ensure that it was desirable, and failed to enforce rules promptly and unambiguously with appropriate rewards and penalties. The parents of antisocial children used more punishment (such as scolding, shouting, or threatening), but failed to make it contingent on the child's behaviour.

Patterson attempted to train these parents in effective child rearing methods, namely noticing what a child is doing, monitoring behaviour over long periods, clearly stating house rules, making rewards and punishments contingent on behaviour, and negotiating disagreements so that conflicts and crises did not escalate. His treatment was shown to be effective in reducing child stealing and antisocial behaviour over short periods in small-scale studies (Dishion, Patterson and Kavanagh, 1992; Patterson, Chamberlain and Reid, 1982; Patterson, Reid and Dishion, 1992). Chapter 7 by David Utting provides more details about these programmes.

Parent training was shown to reduce childhood antisocial behaviour in an experiment conducted by Scott *et al.* (2001) in London and Chichester. About 140 mainly poor, disadvantaged children aged 3–8 referred for aggressive and antisocial behaviour were allocated to experimental (parent training) or control (waiting list) groups. The parent training programme, based on videotapes, was given for two hours a week over thirteen–sixteen weeks, covering praise and rewards, setting limits, and handling misbehaviour. Follow-up parent interviews and observations showed that the antisocial behaviour of the experimental children decreased significantly compared to that of the controls. Furthermore, after the intervention, experimental parents gave their children far more praise to encourage desirable behaviour, and used more effective commands to obtain compliance.

Skills training

The most important prevention techniques that target the risk factors of impulsiveness and low empathy are cognitive-behavioural skills training programmes. For example, Ross and Ross (1995) devised a programme that aimed to teach people to stop and think before acting, to consider the consequences of their behaviour, to conceptualise alternative ways of solving interpersonal problems, and to consider the impact of their behaviour on other people, especially victims. It included social skills training, lateral thinking (to teach creative problem-solving), critical thinking (to teach logical reasoning), values education (to teach non-aggressive, socially appropriate ways to obtain desired outcomes), negotiation skills training, interpersonal cognitive problem-solving (to teach thinking skills for solving interpersonal problems), social perspective training (to teach how to recognise and understand other people's feelings), role-playing and modelling (demonstration and practice of effective and acceptable interpersonal behaviour).

Ross and Ross (1988) implemented this 'Reasoning and Rehabilitation' programme in Ottawa, and found (in a randomised experiment) that it led to a large decrease in reoffending for a small sample of adult offenders in a short nine-month follow-up period. Their training was carried out by probation officers, but they believed that it could be carried out by parents or teachers. This programme has been implemented widely in several different countries, and forms the basis of many accredited cognitive-behavioural programmes used in the UK prison and probation services, including the Pathfinder projects (McGuire, 2001).

Peer programmes

There are no outstanding examples of effective intervention programmes for antisocial behaviour on peer risk factors. The most hopeful programmes involve using high-status conventional peers to teach children ways of resisting peer pressure; this has been effective in reducing drug use (Tobler *et al.*, 1999). Also, in a randomised experiment in St Louis, Feldman, Caplinger and Wodarski (1983) showed that placing antisocial adolescents in activity groups dominated by prosocial adolescents led to a reduction in their antisocial behaviour (compared with antisocial adolescents placed in antisocial groups). This suggests that the influence of prosocial peers can be harnessed to reduce antisocial behaviour.

The most important intervention programme whose success seems to be based mainly on reducing peer risk factors is the Children at Risk programme (Harrell *et al.*, 1997), which targeted high risk youths (average age 12.4) in poor neighbourhoods of five cities across the United States. Eligible youths were identified in schools, and randomly assigned to experimental or control groups. The programme was a comprehensive community-based prevention strategy targeting risk factors for delinquency, including case management and family counselling, family skills training, tutoring, mentoring, after-school activities and community policing. The programme was different in each neighbourhood.

The initial results of the programme were disappointing, but a one-year follow-up showed that (according to self-reports) experimental youths were less likely to have committed violent crimes and used or sold drugs (Harrell, Cavanagh and Sridharan, 1999). The process evaluation showed that the greatest change was in peer risk factors. Experimental youths associated less often with delinquent peers, felt less peer pressure to engage in delinquency, and had more positive peer support. In contrast, there were few changes in individual, family or community risk factors, possibly linked to the low participation of parents in parent training and of youths in mentoring and tutoring (Harrell *et al.*, 1997, p.87). In other words, there were problems of implementation of the programme, linked to the serious and multiple needs and problems of the families.

School programmes

As important school-based prevention experiment was carried out by Kolvin *et al.* (1981) in Newcastle upon Tyne. They randomly allocated 270 junior school children (age 7–8) and 322 secondary school children (age 11–12) to experimental or control groups. All children had been identified as showing some kind of social or psychiatric disturbance or learning problems (according to teacher and peer ratings). There were three types of experimental programmes: (a) behaviour modification-reinforcement with the seniors, "nurture work" teaching healthy interactions with the juniors; (b) parent counselling-teacher consultations with both; and (c) group therapy with the seniors, play groups with the juniors.

The programmes were evaluated after eighteen months and after three years using clinical ratings of conduct disturbance. Generally, the experimental and control groups were not significantly different for the juniors, although there was some tendency for those in the nurture work and play group conditions to be better behaved than the controls at the three-year follow-up. For the seniors, those who received group therapy showed significantly less conduct disturbance at both follow-ups, and there was some tendency for the other two programmes also to be effective at the three-year follow-up. Other school-based prevention experiments have also been successful in reducing antisocial behaviour (Catalano *et al.*, 1998).

School bullying, of course, is a risk factor for offending (Farrington, 1993). Several school-based programmes have been effective in reducing bullying. The most famous of these was implemented by Olweus (1994) in Norway. It aimed to increase awareness and knowledge of teachers, parents and children about bullying and to dispel myths about it. A thirty-page booklet was distributed to all schools in Norway describing what was known about bullying and recommending what steps schools and teachers could take to reduce it. Also, a twenty-five-minute video about bullying was made available to schools. Simultaneously, the schools distributed to all parents a four-page folder containing information and advice about bullying. In addition, anonymous self-report questionnaires about bullying were completed by all children.

The programme was evaluated in Bergen. Each of the forty-two participating schools received feedback information from the questionnaire, about the prevalence of bullies and victims, in a specially arranged school conference day. Also, teachers were encouraged to develop explicit rules about bullying (e.g. do not bully, tell someone when bullying happens, bullying will not be tolerated, try to help victims, try to include children who are being left out) and to discuss bullying in class, using the video and role-playing exercises. Also, actions were taken to improve monitoring and supervision of children, especially in the playground. The programme was successful in reducing the prevalence of bullying by half.

A similar programme was implemented in twenty-three Sheffield schools by Smith and Sharp (1994). The core programme involved establishing a 'whole-school' anti-bullying policy, raising awareness of bullying and clearly defining roles and responsibilities of teachers and students, so that everyone knew what bullying was and what they should do about it. In addition, there were optional interventions tailored to particular schools: curriculum work (e.g. reading books, watching videos), direct work with students (e.g. assertiveness training for those who were bullied) and playground work (e.g. training lunch-time supervisors). This programme was successful in reducing bullying (by 15 per cent) in primary schools, but had a relatively small effect (a 5 per cent reduction) in secondary schools. The effects of these anti-bullying programmes on later antisocial behaviour need to be investigated. Chapter 8 by David Hawkins and Todd Herrenkohl provides more information about school-based prevention programmes.

Multiple component programmes

A combination of interventions may be more effective than a single method. For example, Tremblay *et al.* (1995) in Montreal identified about 250 disruptive (aggressive/hyperactive) boys at age 6 for a prevention experiment. Between ages 7 and 9, the experimental group received training to foster social skills and self-control. Coaching, peer modelling, role playing and reinforcement contingencies were used in small group sessions on such topics as 'how to help', 'what to do when you are angry' and 'how to react to teasing'. Also, their parents were trained using the parent management training techniques developed by Patterson (1982).

This prevention programme was quite successful. By age 12, the experimental boys committed less burglary and theft, were less likely to get drunk, and were less likely to be involved in fights than the controls. Also, the experimental boys had higher school achievement. At every age from 10 to 15, the experimental boys had lower self-reported delinquency scores than the control boys (Tremblay *et al.*, 1995). Interestingly, the differences in antisocial behaviour between experimental and control boys increased as the follow-up progressed.

One of the most important multiple component school-based prevention experiments was carried out in Seattle by Hawkins, von Cleve and Catalano (1991). This combined parent training, teacher training and child skills training. About 500 first grade children (aged 6) in 21 classes in 8 schools were randomly assigned to be in experimental or control classes. The children in the experimental classes received special treatment at home and school which was designed to increase their attachment to their parents and their bonding to the school. Also, they were trained in interpersonal cognitive problem-solving. Their parents were trained to notice and reinforce socially desirable behaviour in a programme called 'Catch them being good'. Their teachers were trained in classroom management, for example to provide clear instructions and expectations to children, to reward children for participation in desired behaviour, and to teach children prosocial (socially desirable) methods of solving problems.

This programme had long-term benefits. O'Donnell *et al.* (1995) focused on children in low income families and reported that, in the sixth grade (age 12), experimental boys were less likely to have initiated delinquency, while experimental girls were less likely to have initiated drug use. In the latest follow-up, Hawkins *et al.* (1999) found that, at age 18, the full intervention group (receiving the intervention from grades 1–6) admitted less violence, less alcohol abuse and fewer sexual partners than the late intervention group (grades 5–6 only) or the controls. It is generally true that a combination of interventions is more effective than a single technique (Wasserman and Miller, 1998), although combining interventions makes it harder to identify which was the 'active ingredient'.

Community programmes

One of the best ways of achieving risk-focused prevention is through multiple component community-based programmes including several of the successful interventions listed above, and *Communities that Care* (CTC) has many attractions (Farrington, 2002a). Perhaps more than any other programme, it is evidence-based and systematic: the choice of interventions depends on empirical evidence about what are the important risk and protective factors in a particular community and on empirical evidence about 'What works'. It is currently being implemented in twenty sites in England, Scotland and Wales, and also in the Netherlands and Australia (Communities that Care, 1997; France and Crow, 2001; Utting, 1999). While the effectiveness of the overall CTC strategy has not yet been demonstrated, the effectiveness of its individual components is clear (as reviewed above). If its small-scale implementation in Great Britain proves to be successful, there would be a strong argument for implementing CTC on a much larger scale.

CTC was developed as a risk-focused prevention strategy by Hawkins and Catalano (1992), and it is a core component of the US Office of Juvenile Justice and Delinquency Prevention's (OJJDP's) Comprehensive Strategy for Serious, Violent and Chronic Juvenile Offenders (Wilson and Howell, 1993). CTC is based on a theory (the social development model) that organises risk and protective factors. The intervention techniques are tailored to the needs of each particular community. The 'community' could be a city, a county, a small town, or even a neighbourhood or a housing estate. This programme aims to reduce delinquency and drug use by implementing particular prevention strategies that have demonstrated effectiveness in reducing risk factors or enhancing protective factors. It is modelled on large-scale community-wide public health programmes designed to reduce illnesses such as coronary heart disease by tackling key risk factors (Farquhar, 1985; Perry, Klepp and Sillers, 1989). There is great emphasis in CTC on enhancing protective factors and building on strengths, partly because this is more attractive to communities than tackling risk factors. However, it is generally true that health promotion is more effective than disease prevention (Kaplan, 2000).

CTC programmes begin with community mobilisation. Key community leaders (e.g. elected representatives, education officials, police chiefs, business leaders) are brought together, with the aim of getting them to agree on the goals of the prevention programme and to implement CTC. The key leaders then set up a Community Board that is accountable to them, consisting of neighbourhood residents and representatives from various agencies (e.g. school, police, social services, probation, health, parents, youth groups, business, church, media). The Community Board takes charge of prevention on behalf of the community.

The Community Board then carries out a risk and protective factor assessment, identifying key risk factors in that particular community that need to be tackled and key protective factors that need enhancing. This risk assessment might involve the use of police, school, social or census records or local neighbourhood or school surveys. After identifying key risk and protective factors, the Community Board assesses existing resources and develops a plan of intervention strategies. With specialist technical assistance and guidance, they choose programmes from a menu of strategies that have been shown to be effective in well-designed evaluation research.

The menu of strategies listed by Hawkins and Catalano (1992) includes prenatal/postnatal home visiting programmes, preschool intellectual enrichment programmes, parent training, school organisation and curriculum development, teacher training and media campaigns. Other strategies include child skills training, anti-bullying programmes in schools, situational prevention, and policing strategies. The choice of prevention strategies is based on empirical evidence about effective methods of tackling each particular risk factor, but it also depends on what are identified as the particular problems and strengths of the community.

Monetary costs and benefits

An important development in the 1990s was the increasing use of cost-benefit analysis in evaluating crime prevention programmes. The conclusion from the Perry Project that, for every dollar spent on the programme, seven dollars were saved in the long term (Schweinhart *et al.*, 1993, p.xviii) proved particularly convincing to policy makers. The monetary costs of crime are enormous. For example, Brand and Price (2000) estimated that they totalled £60 billion in England and Wales in 1999. There are tangible costs to victims, such as replacing stolen goods and repairing damage, and intangible costs that are harder to quantify, such as pain, suffering and a reduced quality of life. There are costs to the government or taxpayer for police, courts, prisons, crime prevention activities, and so on. There are also costs to offenders – for example, those associated with being in prison or losing a job.

To the extent that prevention programmes are successful in reducing crime, they will have benefits. These benefits can be quantified in monetary terms according to the reduction in the monetary costs of crime. Other benefits may accrue from reducing the costs of associated types of antisocial behaviour such as unemployment, divorce, education failure, drug addiction, welfare dependency, and so on. The fact that offending is part of a larger syndrome of antisocial behaviour (West and Farrington, 1977) is good news, because the benefits of a prevention programme can be many and varied. The monetary benefits of a programme can be compared with its monetary costs to determine the benefit:cost ratio. The adequacy of an economic analysis of the monetary benefits and costs of a prevention programme depends crucially on the methodological adequacy of the underlying evaluation design.

Surprisingly few cost-benefit analyses of crime prevention programmes have ever been carried out (Welsh and Farrington, 2000; Welsh, Farrington and Sherman, 2001). Existing analyses are difficult to compare, because researchers have taken account of different types of programme costs and programme effects, and have used different methods for calculating monetary costs and benefits. For example, Painter and Farrington (2001) used Home Office estimates of the monetary cost of each type of crime in calculating the benefit:cost ratio of improved street lighting as a crime prevention measure. There is a great need for a standard how-to-do-it manual to be developed and followed, that specifies a list of costs and benefits to be measured in all studies and their monetary values. Chapter 10 by Brandon Welsh reviews economic costs and benefits of primary prevention programmes.

Ethical, legal and practical issues

The ideas of early intervention and preventive treatment raise numerous theoretical, practical, ethical and legal issues. For example, should prevention techniques be targeted narrowly on children identified as potentially antisocial or more widely on all children living in a certain high-risk area (e.g. a deprived housing estate)? It is unclear how efficient primary prevention is with a rare outcome such as antisocial personality disorder (see chapter 2 by Jeremy Coid). Also, some treatments may be ineffective if they are targeted widely, if they depend on raising the level of those at the bottom of the heap relative to everyone else. It would be most efficient to target the children who are most in need of the treatment but it might be argued that early identification could have undesirable labelling or stigmatising effects. The degree of stigmatisation, if any, is likely to depend on the nature of the treatment. In order to gain political acceptance, it may be best to target deprived areas for prevention programmes rather than individuals.

The ethical issues raised by early prevention depend on the level of predictive accuracy and might perhaps be resolved by weighing the social costs against the social benefits. In the Cambridge Study, Farrington *et al.* (1988a, 1988b) found that three-quarters of vulnerable boys identified at age 10 were convicted. It might be argued that, if preventive treatment had been applied to these boys, the one-quarter who were 'false positives' would have been treated unnecessarily. However, if the treatment consisted of extra welfare benefits to families, and if it was effective in reducing the offending of the other three-quarters, the benefits might outweigh the costs and early identification might be justifiable. Also, the vulnerable boys who were not convicted had other types of social problems, including having few or no friends at age 8 and living alone in poor home conditions at age 32. Therefore, even the unconvicted males in the survey might have needed and benefited from some kind of preventive treatment designed to alleviate their problems.

The intervention methods reviewed here often provide promising rather than solid evidence of substantial reductions in antisocial behaviour. This may be because, as Kazdin (1987) argued, serious antisocial behaviour might be viewed as a chronic, long-lasting disease that requires continuous monitoring and intervention over the life course. It might be desirable to distinguish chronic from less seriously antisocial teenagers, and to apply different types of interventions to the two categories (LeBlanc and Frechette, 1989). If the chronics are the worst 5 per cent, interventions applied to the next 10 per cent may be more successful. However, success may depend on the extent to which risk factors specific to the next 10 per cent can be identified.

Conclusions

This chapter has attempted to set the scene for the more detailed chapters that follow, by reviewing knowledge about epidemiology, risk and protective factors, and early prevention programmes for adult antisocial behaviour. Unfortunately, few researchers on risk and protective factors or on prevention programmes have specifically addressed adult antisocial behaviour, and fewer still have studied antisocial personality disorder or psychopathy. Most research has been on delinquent or criminal behaviour. Hence, an obvious recommendation is that more research is needed on the definition, measurement, epidemiology, causes and prevention of adult antisocial behaviour, and especially antisocial personality disorder and psychopathy. However, all conclusions about what we know, what we need to know, and how we can find out will now be deferred until chapter 11 by David Farrington and Jeremy Coid, which sets out a detailed research agenda.

NOTE

I am very grateful to Maureen Brown for her speedy and efficient word processing.

REFERENCES

American Psychiatric Association (1994) *Diagnostic and Statistical Manual of Mental Disorders* (4th ed.). Washington, DC: American Psychiatric Association.

Augimeri, L. K., Koegl, C. J., Webster, C. D. and Levene, K. S. (2001) *Early Assessment Risk List for Boys (EARL-20B) Version 2*. Toronto: Earlscourt Child and Family Centre.

Barlow, J. (1997) *Systematic Review of the Effectiveness of Parent-Training Programmes in Improving Behaviour Problems in Children aged 3–10 Years*. Oxford: Health Services Research Unit.

Bebbington, P., Hurry, J., Tennant, C., Sturt, E. and Wing, J. K. (1981) Epidemiology of mental disorders in Camberwell. *Psychological Medicine, 11*, 561–79.

Berrueta-Clement, J. R., Schweinhart, L. J., Barnett, W. S., Epstein, A. S. and Weikart, D. P. (1984) *Changed Lives*. Ypsilanti, MI: High/Scope.

Blackburn, R. (1975) An empirical classification of psychopathic personality. *British Journal of Psychiatry, 127*, 456–60.

(1988) On moral judgements and personality disorders: The myth of psychopathic personality revisited. *British Journal of Psychiatry, 153*, 505–12.

(1993) *The Psychology of Criminal Conduct*. Chichester: Wiley.

Bland, R. C., Orn, H. and Newman, S. C. (1988) Life-time prevalence of psychiatric disorders in Edmonton. *Acta Psychiatrica Scandinavica 77* (Suppl. 338), 24–32.

Brand, S. and Price, R. (2000) *The Economic and Social Costs of Crime*. London: Home Office.

Catalano, R. F., Arthur, M. W., Hawkins, J. D., Berglund, L. and Olson, J. J. (1998) Comprehensive community and school based interventions to prevent antisocial behaviour. In R. Loeber & D. P. Farrington (eds.) *Serious and Violent Juvenile Offenders: Risk Factors and Successful Interventions* (pp. 248–83). Thousand Oaks, CA: Sage.

Clark, L. A., Livesley, W. J. and Morey, L. (1997) Personality disorder assessment: The challenge of construct validity. *Journal of Personality Disorders, 11*, 205–31.

Cohen, P. (1996) Childhood risks for young adult symptoms of personality disorder. *Multivariate Behavioural Research, 31*, 121–48.

Communities that Care (1997) *Communities that Care (UK): A New Kind of Prevention Programme*. London: Communities that Care.

Consortium for Longitudinal Studies (1983) *As the Twig is Bent . . . Lasting Effects of Preschool Programmes*. Hillsdale, NJ: Erlbaum.

Dishion, T. J., Patterson, G. R. and Kavanagh, K. A. (1992) An experimental test of the coercion model: Linking theory, measurement and intervention. In J. McCord and R. Tremblay (eds.) *Preventing Antisocial Behaviour* (pp. 253–82). New York: Guilford.

Farquhar, J. W. (1985) The Stanford five-city project: Design and methods. *American Journal of Epidemiology, 122*, 323–34.

Farrington, D. P. (1972) Delinquency begins at home. *New Society, 21*, 495–7.

(1983) Randomized experiments on crime and justice. In M. Tonry and N. Morris (eds.) *Crime and Justice*, vol.4 (pp. 257–308). University of Chicago Press.

(1990) Age, period, cohort, and offending. In D. M. Gottfredson and R. V. Clarke (eds.) *Policy and Theory in Criminal Justice: Contributions in Honour of Leslie T. Wilkins* (pp. 51–75). Aldershot: Avebury.

(1991) Antisocial personality from childhood to adulthood. *The Psychologist, 4*, 389–94.

(1993) Understanding and preventing bullying. In M. Tonry and N. Morris (eds.) *Crime and Justice*, vol. 17 (pp. 381–458). University of Chicago Press.

(1995) The development of offending and antisocial behaviour from childhood: Key findings from the Cambridge Study in Delinquent Development. *Journal of Child Psychology and Psychiatry, 36*, 929–64.

(1999) Conduct disorder and delinquency. In H-C. Steinhausen and F. C. Verhulst (eds.) *Risks and Outcomes in Developmental Psychopathology* (pp. 165–92). Oxford University Press.

(2000a) Explaining and preventing crime: The globalization of knowledge. *Criminology, 38*, 1–24.

(2000b) Psychosocial predictors of adult antisocial personality and adult convictions. *Behavioural Sciences and the Law, 18*, 605–22.

(2001) The causes and prevention of violence. In J. Shepherd (ed.) *Violence in Health Care,* 2nd ed. (pp. 1–27). Oxford University Press.

(2002a) Developmental criminology and risk-focussed prevention. In M. Maguire, R. Morgan and R. Reiner (eds.) *The Oxford Handbook of Criminology*, 3rd ed. (pp. 657–701). Oxford: Clarendon Press.

(2002b) Families and crime. In J. Q. Wilson and J. Petersilia (eds.) *Crime: Public Policies for Crime Control*, 2nd ed. (pp. 129–48). Oakland, CA: Institute for Contemporary Studies Press.

(2002c) Key results from the first 40 years of the Cambridge Study in Delinquent Development. In T. P. Thornberry and M. D. Krohn (eds.) *Taking Stock of Delinquency: An Overview of Findings from Contemporary Longitudinal Studies* (pp. 137–83). New York: Kluwer/Plenum.

Farrington, D. P., Barnes, G. and Lambert, S. (1996) The concentration of offending in families. *Legal and Criminological Psychology, 1*, 47–63.

Farrington, D. P., Gallagher, B., Morley, L., St Ledger, R. J. and West, D. J. (1986) Unemployment, school leaving, and crime. *British Journal of Criminology, 26*, 335–56.

(1988a) A 24-year follow-up of men from vulnerable backgrounds. In R. L. Jenkins and W. K. Brown (eds.) *The Abandonment of Delinquent Behaviour* (pp.155–73). New York: Praeger.

(1988b) Are there any successful men from criminogenic backgrounds? *Psychiatry, 51*, 116–30.

Farrington, D. P. and Hawkins, J. D. (1991) Predicting participation, early onset, and later persistence in officially recorded offending. *Criminal Behaviour and Mental Health, 1*, 1–33.

Farrington, D. P., Lambert, S. and West, D. J. (1998) Criminal careers of two generations of family members in the Cambridge Study in Delinquent Development. *Studies on Crime and Crime Prevention, 7*, 85–106.

Farrington, D. P., Loeber, R., Elliott, D. S., Hawkins, J. D., Kandel, D. B., Klein, M. W., McCord, J., Rowe, D. C. and Tremblay, R. E. (1990a) Advancing knowledge about the onset of delinquency and crime. In B. B. Lahey and A. E. Kazdin (eds.) *Advances in Clinical Child Psychology*, vol.13 (pp. 283–342). New York: Plenum.

Farrington, D. P., Loeber, R. and van Kammen, W. B. (1990) Long-term criminal outcomes of hyperactivity-impulsivity-attention deficit and conduct problems in childhood. In L. N. Robins and M. Rutter (eds.) *Straight and Devious Pathways from Childhood to Adulthood* (pp. 62–81). Cambridge University Press.

Farrington, D. P., Ohlin, L. E. and Wilson, J. Q. (1986) *Understanding and Controlling Crime: Toward a New Research Strategy*. New York: Springer-Verlag.

Farrington, D. P. and West, D. J. (1993) Criminal, penal and life histories of chronic offenders: Risk and protective factors and early identification. *Criminal Behaviour and Mental Health*, *3*, 492–523.

(1995) Effects of marriage, separation and children on offending by adult males. In J. Hagan (ed.) *Current Perspectives on Aging and the Life Cycle. Vol. 4: Delinquency and Disrepute in the Life Course* (pp. 249–81). Greenwich, CT: JAI Press.

Feldman, R. A., Caplinger, T. E. and Wodarski, J. S. (1983) *The St. Louis Conundrum*. Englewood Cliffs, NJ: Prentice-Hall.

France, A. and Crow, I. (2001) *CTC – The Story So Far*. York: Joseph Rowntree Foundation.

Gottfredson, D. C., McNeil, R. J. and Gottfredson, G. D. (1991) Social area influences on delinquency: A multi-level analysis. *Journal of Research on Crime and Delinquency*, *28*, 197–226.

Graham, J. (1988) *Schools, Disruptive Behaviour and Delinquency*. London: Her Majesty's Stationery Office.

Grove, W. M., Eckert, E. D., Heston, L., Bouchard, T. J., Segal, N. and Lykken, D. T. (1990) Heritability of substance use and antisocial behaviour: A study of monozygotic twins reared apart. *Biological Psychiatry*, *27*, 1293–304.

Hare, R. D. (1985) Comparison of procedures for the assessment of psychopathy. *Journal of Consulting and Clinical Psychology*, *53*, 7–16.

(1991) *The Hare Psychopathy Checklist-Revised*. Toronto: Multi-Health Systems.

Hare, R. D., Hart, S. D. and Harpur, T. J. (1991) Psychopathy and the DSM-IV criteria for antisocial personality disorder. *Journal of Abnormal Psychology*, *100*, 391–8.

Harrell, A. V., Cavanagh, S. E., Harmon, M. A., Koper, C. S. and Sridharan, S. (1997) *Impact of the Children at Risk Programme: Comprehensive Final Report*, vol. 2. Washington, DC: The Urban Institute.

Harrell, A. V., Cavanagh, S. E. and Sridharan, S. (1999) *Evaluation of the Children at Risk Programme: Results One Year After the Programme*. Washington, DC: National Institute of Justice.

Hawkins, J. D. and Catalano, R. F. (1992) *Communities that Care*. San Francisco: Jossey-Bass.

Hawkins, J. D., Catalano, R. F., Kosterman, R., Abbott, R. and Hill, K. G. (1999) Preventing adolescent health-risk behaviours by strengthening protection during childhood. *Archives of Paediatrics and Adolescent Medicine*, *153*, 226–34.

Hawkins, J. D., von Cleve, E. and Catalano, R. F. (1991) Reducing early childhood aggression: Results of a primary prevention programme. *Journal of the American Academy of Child and Adolescent Psychiatry*, *30*, 208–17.

Horacek, H. J., Ramey, C. T., Campbell, F. A., Hoffmann, K. P. and Fletcher, R. H. (1987) Predicting school failure and assessing early intervention with high-risk children. *Journal of the American Academy of Child and Adolescent Psychiatry*, *26*, 758–63.

Kaplan, R. M. (2000) Two pathways to prevention. *American Psychologist*, *55*, 382–96.

Kazdin, A. E. (1987) Treatment of antisocial behaviour in children: Current status and future directions. *Psychological Bulletin*, *102*, 187–203.

(1997) Parent management training: Evidence, outcomes and issues. *Journal of the American Academy of Child and Adolescent Psychiatry*, *36*, 1349–56.

Kolvin, I., Garside, R. F., Nicol, A. R., MacMillan, A., Wolstenholme, F. and Leitch, I. M. (1981) *Help Starts Here: The Maladjusted Child in the Ordinary School*. London: Tavistock.

Kolvin, I., Miller, F. J. W., Scott, D. M., Gatzanis, S. R. M. and Fleeting, M. (1990) *Continuities of Deprivation?* Aldershot: Avebury.

Lally, J. R., Mangione, P. L. and Honig, A. S. (1988) Long-range impact of an early intervention with low-income children and their families. In D. R. Powell (ed.) *Parent Education as Early Childhood Intervention* (pp. 79–104). Norwood, NJ: Ablex.

LeBlanc, M. and Frechette, M. (1989) *Male Criminal Activity from Childhood through Youth*. New York: Springer-Verlag.

Loeber, R. and LeBlanc, M. (1990) Toward a developmental criminology. In M. Tonry and N. Morris (eds.) *Crime and Justice*, vol. 12 (pp. 375–473). University of Chicago Press.

Lynam, D. (1996) Early identification of chronic offenders: Who is the fledgling psychopath? *Psychological Bulletin*, *120*, 209–34.

Lynam, D., Moffitt, T. E. and Stouthamer-Loeber, M. (1993) Explaining the relation between IQ and delinquency: Class, race, test motivation, school failure or self-control? *Journal of Abnormal Psychology*, *102*, 187–96.

Malgady, R. G., Rogler, L. H. and Tryon, W. W. (1992) Issues of validity in the Diagnostic Interview Schedule. *Journal of Psychiatric Research*, *26*, 59–67.

McCord, J. and Tremblay, R. E. (1992, eds.) *Preventing Antisocial Behaviour*. New York: Guilford.

McGuire, J. (2001) What works in correctional intervention? Evidence and practical implications. In G. A. Bernfeld, D. P. Farrington and A. W. Leschied (eds.) *Offender Rehabilitation in Practice: Implementing and Evaluating Effective Programmes* (pp. 25–43). Chichester: Wiley.

Moffitt, T. E. (1993) Adolescence-limited and life-course-persistent antisocial behaviour: A developmental taxonomy. *Psychological Review*, *100*, 674–701.

Moran, P. (1999) *Antisocial Personality Disorder: An Epidemiological Perspective*. London: Gaskell.

Moran, P. and Hagell, A. (2001) *Intervening to Prevent Antisocial Personality Disorder: A Scoping Review*. London: Home Office.

O'Donnell, J., Hawkins, J. D., Catalano, R. F., Abbott, R. D. and Day, L. E. (1995) Preventing school failure, drug use, and delinquency among low-income children: Long-term intervention in elementary schools. *American Journal of Orthopsychiatry*, *65*, 87–100.

Offord, D. R. and Bennett, K. T. (1994) Conduct disorder: Long-term outcomes and intervention effectiveness. *Journal of the American Academy of Child and Adolescent Psychiatry*, *33*, 1069–78.

Olds, D. L., Eckenrode, J., Henderson, C. R., Kitzman, H., Powers, J., Cole, R., Sidora, K., Morris, P., Pettitt, L. M. and Luckey, D. (1997) Long-term effects of home visitation on maternal life course and child abuse and neglect: Fifteen-year follow-up of a randomized trial. *Journal of the American Medical Association, 278*, 637–43.

Olds, D. L., Henderson, C. R., Chamberlain, R. and Tatelbaum, R. (1986) Preventing child abuse and neglect: A randomized trial of nurse home visitation. *Pediatrics, 78*, 65–78.

Olds, D. L., Henderson, C. R., Cole, R., Eckenrode, J., Kitzman, H., Luckey, D., Pettitt, L., Sidora, K., Morris, P. and Powers, J. (1998) Long-term effects of nurse home visitation on children's criminal and antisocial behaviour: 15-year follow-up of a randomized controlled trial. *Journal of the American Medical Association, 280*, 1238–44.

Olweus, D. (1994). Bullying at school: Basic facts and effects of a school based intervention programme. *Journal of Child Psychology and Psychiatry, 35*, 1171–90.

Painter, K. A. and Farrington, D. P. (2001) The financial benefits of improved street lighting, based on crime reduction. *Lighting Research and Technology, 33*, 3–12.

Patterson, G. R. (1982) *Coercive Family Process*. Eugene, OR: Castalia.

Patterson, G. R., Chamberlain, P. and Reid, J. B. (1982) A comparative evaluation of a parent training programme. *Behaviour Therapy, 13*, 638–50.

Patterson, G. R., Reid, J. B. and Dishion, T. J. (1992) *Antisocial Boys*. Eugene, OR: Castalia.

Perry, C. L., Klepp, K.-I. and Sillers, C. (1989) Community-wide strategies for cardiovascular health: The Minnesota Heart Health Programme youth programme. *Health Education and Research, 4*, 87–101.

Pilgrim, J. and Mann, A. (1990) Use of the ICD-10 version of the Standardized Assessment of Personality to determine the prevalence of personality disorder in psychiatric in-patients. *Psychological Medicine, 20*, 985–92.

Rae-Grant, N., Thomas, B. H., Offord, D. R. and Boyle, M. H. (1989) Risk, protective factors, and the prevalence of behavioural and emotional disorders in children and adolescents. *Journal of the American Academy of Child and Adolescent Psychiatry, 28*, 262–8.

Raine, A. (1993) *The Psychopathology of Crime: Criminal Behaviour as a Clinical Disorder*. San Diego: Academic Press.

Raine, A., Brennan, P. A. and Mednick, S. A. (1994) Birth complications combined with early maternal rejection at age 1 year predispose to violent crime at age 18 years. *Archives of General Psychiatry, 51*, 984–8.

Raine, A., Brennan, P. A., Farrington, D. P. and Mednick, S. A. (1997, eds.) *Biosocial Bases of Violence*. New York: Plenum.

Reiss, A. J. and Farrington, D. P. (1991) Advancing knowledge about co-offending: Results from a prospective longitudinal survey of London males. *Journal of Criminal Law and Criminology, 82*, 360–95.

Rey, J. M., Morris-Yates, A., Singh, M., Andrews, G. and Stewart, G. W. (1995) Continuities between psychiatric disorders in adolescents and personality disorders in young adults. *American Journal of Psychiatry, 152*, 895–900.

Robins, L. N. (1978) Aetiological implications in studies of childhood histories relating to antisocial personality. In R. D. Hare and D. Schalling (eds.) *Psychopathic Behaviour: Approaches to Research* (pp. 255–71). Chichester: Wiley.

Sturdy childhood predictors of adult outcomes: Replications from longitudinal studies. In J. E. Barrett, R. M. Rose and G. L. Klerman (eds.) *Stress and Mental Disorder* (pp. 219–35). New York: Raven Press.

Robins, L. N. and Price, R. K. (1991) Adult disorders predicted by childhood conduct problems: Results from the NIMH Epidemiological Catchment Area project. *Psychiatry*, *54*, 116–32.

Robins, L. N. and Regier, D. (1991, eds.) *Psychiatric Disorders in America*. New York: Macmillan/Free Press.

Robins, L. N., Tipp, J. and Przybeck, T. (1991) Antisocial personality. In L. N. Robins and D. Regier (eds.) *Psychiatric Disorders in America* (pp. 258–90). New York: Macmillan/Free Press.

Ross, R. R. and Ross, B. D. (1988) Delinquency prevention through cognitive training. *New Education*, *10*, 70–5.

Ross, R. R. and Ross, R. D. (1995, eds.) *Thinking Straight: The Reasoning and Rehabilitation Programme for Delinquency Prevention and Offender Rehabilitation*. Ottawa: Air Training and Publications.

Rutter, M. (1981) The city and the child. *American Journal of Orthopsychiatry*, *51*, 610–25.

Resilience in the face of adversity: Protective factors and resistance to psychiatric disorder. *British Journal of Psychiatry*, *147*, 598–611.

Rutter, M., Giller, H. and Hagell, A. (1998) *Antisocial Behaviour by Young People*. Cambridge University Press.

Rutter, M., Harrington, R., Quinton, D. and Pickles, A. (1994) Adult outcome of conduct disorder in childhood: Implications for concepts and definitions of patterns of psychopathology. In R. D. Ketterlinus and M. E. Lamb (eds.) *Adolescent Problem Behaviours* (pp. 57–80). Hillsdale, NJ: Erlbaum.

Schweinhart, L. J., Barnes, H. V. and Weikart, D. P. (1993) *Significant Benefits*. Ypsilanti, MI: High/Scope.

Schweinhart, L. J. and Weikart, D. P. (1980) *Young Children Grow Up*. Ypsilanti, MI: High/Scope.

Scott, S., Spender, Q., Doolan, M., Jacobs, B. and Aspland, H. (2001) Multicentre controlled trial of parenting groups for child antisocial behaviour in clinical practice. *British Medical Journal*, *323*, 194–6.

Shaw, C. R. and McKay, H. D. (1969) *Juvenile Delinquency and Urban Areas* (rev. ed.). University of Chicago Press.

Singleton, N., Bumpstead, R., O'Brien, M., Lee, A. and Meltzer, H. (2002) *Psychiatric Morbidity among Adults Living in Private Households, 2000: Summary Report*. London: Office for National Statistics.

Smith, C. A. and Stern, S. B. (1997) Delinquency and antisocial behaviour: A review of family processes and intervention research. *Social Service Review*, *71*, 382–420.

Smith, P. K. and Sharp, S. (1994) *School Bullying*. London: Routledge.

Storm-Mathisen, A. and Vaglum, P. (1994) Conduct disorder patients 20 years later: A personal follow-up study. *Acta Psychiatrica Scandinavica*, *89*, 416–20.

Tobler, N. S., Lessard, T., Marshall, D., Ochshorn, P. and Roona, M. (1999) Effectiveness of school-based drug prevention programmes for marijuana use. *School Psychology International*, *20*, 105–37.

Tonry, M. and Farrington, D. P. (1995) Strategic approaches to crime prevention. In M. Tonry and D. P. Farrington (eds.) *Building a Safer Society: Strategic Approaches to Crime Prevention* (pp. 1–20). University of Chicago Press.

Tremblay, R. E. and Craig, W. M. (1995) Developmental crime prevention. In M. Tonry and D. P. Farrington (eds.) *Building a Safer Society: Strategic Approaches to Crime Prevention* (pp. 151–236). University of Chicago Press.

Tremblay, R. E., Pagani-Kurtz, L., Vitaro, F., Masse, L. C. and Pihl, R. D. (1995) A bimodal preventive intervention for disruptive kindergarten boys: Its impact through mid-adolescence. *Journal of Consulting and Clinical Psychology*, *63*, 560–8.

Utting, D. (1999, ed.) *A Guide to Promising Approaches*. London: Communities that Care.

Walsh, A., Petee, T. A. and Beyer, J. A. (1987) Intellectual imbalance and delinquency: Comparing high verbal and high performance IQ delinquents. *Criminal Justice and Behaviour*, *14*, 370–9.

Wasserman, G. A. and Miller, L. S. (1998) The prevention of serious and violent juvenile offending. In R. Loeber and D. P. Farrington (eds.) *Serious and Violent Juvenile Offenders: Risk Factors and Successful Interventions* (pp. 197–247). Thousand Oaks, CA: Sage.

Welsh, B. C. and Farrington, D. P. (2000) Monetary costs and benefits of crime prevention programmes. In M. Tonry (ed.) *Crime and Justice*, vol. 27 (pp. 305–61). University of Chicago Press.

Welsh, B. C., Farrington, D. P. and Sherman, L. W. (2001, eds.) *Costs and Benefits of Preventing Crime*. Boulder, CO: Westview Press.

Werner, E. E. and Smith, R. S. (1982) *Vulnerable but Invincible: A Longitudinal Study of Resilient Children and Youth*. New York: McGraw-Hill.

West, D. J. and Farrington, D. P. (1977) *The Delinquent Way of Life*. London: Heinemann.

White, J. L., Moffitt, T. E., Caspi, A., Bartusch, D. J., Needles, D. J. and Stouthamer-Loeber, M. (1994) Measuring impulsivity and examining its relationship to delinquency. *Journal of Abnormal Psychology*, *103*, 192–205.

Widom, C. S. (1989) The cycle of violence. *Science*, *244*, 160–6.

Wikström, P.-O. H. (1991) *Urban Crime, Criminals and Victims: The Swedish Experience in an Anglo-American Comparative Perspective*. New York: Springer-Verlag.

Wilson, J. J. and Howell, J. C. (1993) *A Comprehensive Strategy for Serious, Violent and Chronic Juvenile Offenders*. Washington, DC: US Office of Juvenile Justice and Delinquency Prevention.

Wilson, J. Q. and Herrnstein, R. J. (1985) *Crime and Human Nature*. New York: Simon and Schuster.

World Health Organization (1992) *The ICD-10 Classification of Mental and Behavioural Disorders*. Geneva, Switzerland: World Health Organization.

Zoccolillo, M., Pickles, A., Quinton, D. and Rutter, M. (1992) The outcome of childhood conduct disorder: Implications for defining adult personality disorder and conduct disorder. *Psychological Medicine*, *22*, 971–86.

2 Formulating strategies for the primary prevention of adult antisocial behaviour: 'high risk' or 'population' strategies?

Jeremy W. Coid

Recognition that primary prevention is a key issue in criminology has been a relatively new development in the United Kingdom. There have been few large scale intervention strategies with children specifically aimed at preventing the early manifestation of delinquent behaviour, the transition between different phases of criminality over the lifespan, or the development of adult antisocial syndromes. Higher priority has been accorded in other countries, particularly in North America. However, the various approaches that have been taken elsewhere do not always fit within an overall theoretical approach or coherent strategy. This does not mean that researchers should be obliged to rigidly conform to a single approach, but it would be more helpful if those who intend to develop the area were able to plan their work within the context of some pre-existing theory, or series of theories, of prevention.

Preventive medicine has much to contribute to this research agenda through its theoretical approach to the prevention of disease. This comes about first through its foundations within the academic discipline of epidemiology, and second through the clinical involvement of the professional subdiscipline of Public Health which has traditionally been responsible for the prevention of outbreaks of disease. Theoretical approaches to Preventive Medicine are heavily influenced by the work of the late Geoffrey Rose, former Professor of Epidemiology at the London School of Hygiene and Tropical Medicine. In his book *The Strategy of Preventive Medicine*, Rose (1992) argued that when identifying risk factors and extrapolating these to the prevention of disease, many of the activities of physicians have been targeted at a vulnerable minority of individuals. Although this strategy may be entirely appropriate, it cannot solve the problems of mass diseases. Such a strategy is therefore symptomatic rather than radical.

But can the same notions be applied to crime? Although criminal behaviour is ultimately defined according to the law, it is associated with a wide range of additional social problems. Ultimately, the level and range of these social problems are determined by the mass characteristics of a population. These will have a direct effect on the development of its individual members. A deviant minority can therefore only be understood when seen within the wider societal context. Effective prevention would therefore ultimately require changes that involve the population as a whole, according to Rose's viewpoint.

This chapter will explore Rose's broad division of preventive measures into 'high risk' and 'population' strategies and the inevitable question of whether such strategies should be targeted at preventing the majority of young individuals from later manifesting antisocial behaviour. This implies a different approach from narrowly focusing on strategies which target high-risk children for the later development of adult antisocial syndromes or adult criminal recidivism. The population strategy is usually neglected however, often on the grounds that it is unrealistic, overly expensive, or even that it is utopian. However, Rose has presented strong mathematical arguments as to why such an approach should not be neglected. This chapter will attempt to translate his arguments and paradigms for future research from the disease to the crime field. Finally, it will conclude with a warning of what can happen if the population strategy is ignored.

Epidemiology, prevention, and crime

Criminal behaviour is clearly not inevitable. Crime is common in one place but uncommon in another and individuals who commit crimes at one stage of their lifespan will cease to commit crimes at another. Similarly, 'epidemics' of criminal behaviour can appear and disappear. In a single population, one type of crime that is highly prevalent can give way to another type. These changes in patterns of crime, as with diseases, reflect the way people live and their social, economic, and environmental circumstances – all of which can change very quickly. In theory then, criminal behaviour like disease should be highly preventable. But this poses certain major questions. For example, can the social, economic, and environmental factors that lead to crime be controlled or must researchers in the field spend their time merely observing and analysing them? Furthermore, when taking this approach to crime, it must be remembered that epidemiology has been refined within the medical model, usually with the aim of developing lifestyles which will minimise the development of disease. But to what extent can research be applied which will impact upon the lifestyles of individuals to prevent them either presenting at some stage over their lifespan with criminal behaviour or developing into an adult antisocial syndrome?

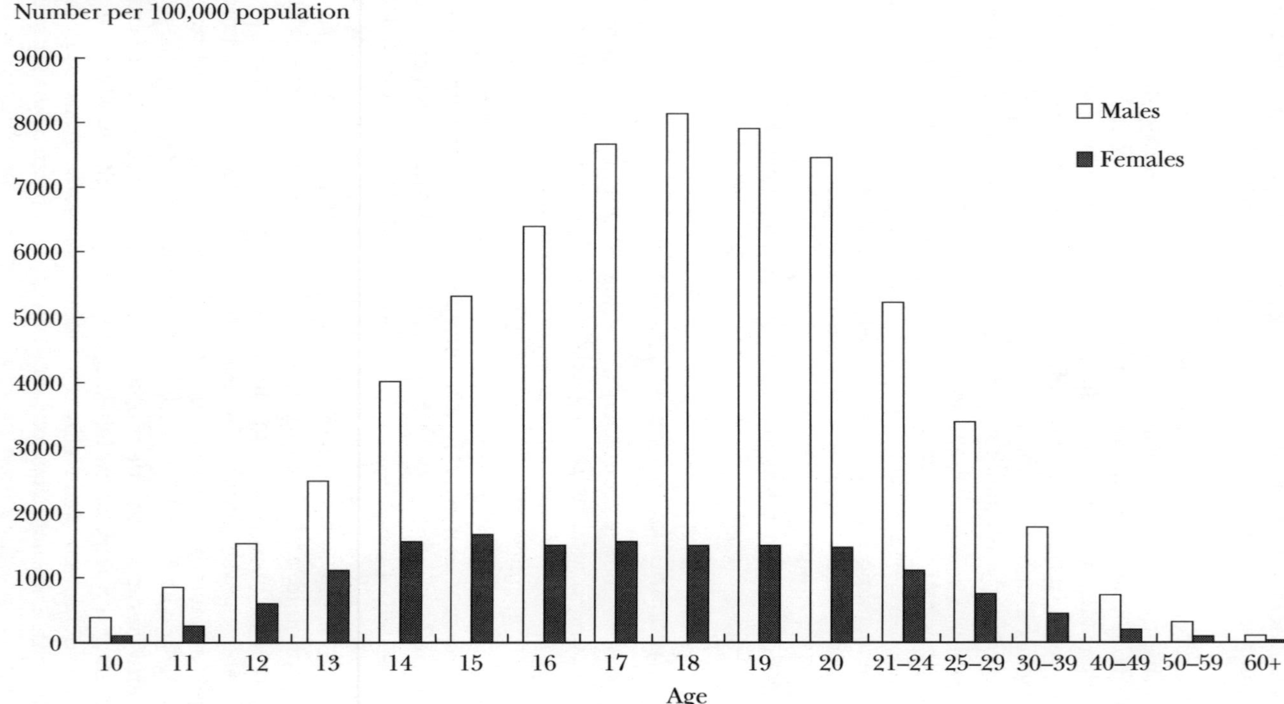

Figure 2.1. Persons found guilty of, or cautioned for, indictable offences per 100,000 population by age group, 1999 (From: Criminal Statistics, England and Wales 1999 CM.5001. Published by The Stationery Office)

Taking a deliberately simplistic view, Rose (1992) argued that the world could be divided into two classes: (shifting the emphasis to criminology in the context of this chapter) those who are criminal, conduct disordered, attention deficit disordered, or antisocial personality disordered; and those who are not. The question then arises over whether an intervention should be applied only to those who are defined according to these categories, or identified at high risk of developing one of these syndromes, and ignore the rest of the population. Alternatively, the entire population might be viewed as demonstrating a spectrum of criminality, or that many fulfil one or more criteria for these syndromes. For example, most westernised countries have reported an increase in crime in recent years and a substantial minority of males can expect to receive a conviction at some time in their life. However, convictions are predominantly recorded in the early and mid-teenage years. Figure 2.1 shows the distribution of criminal convictions according to age bands by sex in the UK population from national criminal statistics. This indicates that the most frequent age of conviction is 18 years in the case of males and 15 years in the case of females. Taking the population as a whole, the figure indicates that, with age, the number of persons who are convicted declines and is almost negligible in the older age groups. Clearly, if there was to be a prevention strategy on a population basis, it would be aimed at somehow diminishing the number of young males being convicted in their late teens and early 20s. Nevertheless, most offenders will desist from crime in late teenage and early adult years. But persistence is observed in a subgroup, which is associated with a range of other indicators of poor adult adjustment. In psychiatric classifications, these same associated factors have been adopted, together with criminal and violent behaviour, as the criteria for certain diagnostic categories, most notably Antisocial Personality Disorder (American Psychiatric Association, 1994), and as a continuous measure of Psychopathy (Hare, 1991). Both demonstrate that there is considerable overlap between criminological and psychiatric constructs.

Criminal careers and career criminals

Research has shown that a large proportion of serious crime is committed by a small segment of the criminal population (Wolfgang *et al.*, 1972; Petersilia *et al.*, 1978; Peterson and Braiker, 1980; Blumstein and Cohen, 1979) with 5–6 per cent of offenders accounting for 50–60 per cent of crimes (Farrington *et al.*, 1986; Wolfgang *et al.*, 1972). In addition, when examining these individuals more carefully, studies have confirmed strong associations between the persisting, or high-crime, subgroup, and factors such as having family members who also have criminal histories, drug abuse, social disruption, such as abandonment of families and illegitimate children, together with unemployment in the context of work being readily available (Langan and Greenfeld, 1983). These high-rate offenders begin their criminal careers earlier and continue them for more years. The financial costs to society as a result of police and Court involvement, failed rehabilitation, and the direct consequences of their offending are considerable, as are the emotional and interpersonal costs that these individuals exact from those around them. Lynam (1996) has argued that, by focusing interventions on those likely to become high-rate offenders, the greatest possible reduction in the total incidence of crime would be achieved, thereby promoting a high-risk approach to the problem. However, to achieve this aim would require greater accuracy in identification of those most likely to become high-rate offenders than is currently possible.

Delinquent careers can develop along several trajectories (Smith *et al.*, 1984). Compelling evidence suggests that the correlates, and probably the aetiology of criminality differs among subgroups of delinquents identified using age-related patterns of offending (Loeber, 1988; Patterson *et al.*, 1991; Moffitt, 1993, 1994). Studies in several different countries have identified four distinct groups of offenders (Farrington, 1983; Dilalla and Gottesman, 1989; Stattin and Magnusson, 1991; Nagin and Land, 1993; Kratzer and Hodgins, 1999). These include: (i) those displaying a stable pattern of anti-social behaviour from early childhood through adulthood (stable early-starters); (ii) those who commit crimes only as adolescents (adolescence-limited); (iii) those who commit crimes irregularly at different times in their lives (discontinuous offenders); and (iv) those who begin offending as adults (adult-starters). Age cut-offs for defining the groups are later for females than males and this typology is better at describing male than female offenders.

Most investigations have estimated that approximately 5–7 per cent of boys and between 0–2 per cent of girls can be classified as early-starters. However, there is less consistency in the prevalence of other categories between studies. Furthermore, early-starters are not a homogeneous group (Lynam, 1996; Rutter, 1996; Christian *et al.*, 1997; Hodgins *et al.*, 1998) and further research is needed to identify subgroups among these life course persistent offenders. Kratzer and Hodgins (1999) have argued that the historic failure to develop interventions which effectively modify the behaviour of early-start antisocial children may be largely due to the failure to match appropriate treatments to clients' needs.

For career criminals who fit the pattern of the stable early-starter, persistence through four successive stages can be observed (Figure 2.2): (a) pre-criminal (10–18 years), (b) early criminal (18-mid/late 20s),

1. **Pre-Criminal (10–18 years)**

Mostly nuisance and misdemeanours. Rarely specialised.
Larceny, burglary, car theft.
Usually with other adolescents. Thrill-seeking.
Majority desist from crime.

2. **Early Criminal (18–mid/late 20s)**

Progressive decline in proportion who offend.
Sub-group move towards career criminality.
Crimes: decrease in number but increase in seriousness.
Appearance of violent offences.
Money for drugs, material goods.
Criminal associations, incarceration, status in criminal world.

3. **Advanced (late 20s–early 40s**

Lowest proportion of dropouts during phase.
Criminal lifestyle shows escalation.

4. **Criminal burnout/maturity (early 40s onwards)**

Further proportion dropout from crime.
Changes in values, motivations.
Many still on fringes of crime and irresponsible.
Maturity or burnout?

Figure 2.2. Four stages of criminal careers

(c) advanced (late 20s to early 40s), (d) criminal burnout/maturity stage (early 40s onwards) (Walters, 1990). In the pre-criminal stage, the majority of arrests for all adolescents and children are for nuisances and misdemeanours (Petersilia *et al.*, 1978). Criminal behaviour is rarely specialised (Hindelang, 1971; Wolfgang *et al.*, 1972) but larceny, burglary, and car theft are the most common offences (LeBlanc and Frechette, 1989). These offences are frequently committed in the company of other adolescents and thrill-seeking is an important motive. This stage appears to hold the greatest prospect for change and a significant proportion of juveniles do not carry their criminality on to adulthood, as demonstrated in Figure 2.1. During the second, early criminal stages, the overall number of individuals committing offences progressively declines (Blumstein and Cohen, 1987). However, a subgroup begin to move towards career criminality as they find themselves in contact with new criminal associates, often met during incarceration, learn new criminal techniques, and acquire status in the criminal world (Gibbs and Shelley, 1982). Their overall number of crimes may decrease but their seriousness increases, both in the value of the property stolen (Langan and Farrington, 1983) and the appearance of violent offences (West and Farrington, 1977; Petersilia *et al.*, 1978). Motives also change from thrill-seeking and obtaining peer status to the desire to obtain money for drugs and non-essential material goods.

Voluntary dropping out of crime appears lowest during the advanced criminal stage. Walters (1990) describes these individuals as having now committed themselves to a criminal lifestyle and with an associated cognitive style. Their antisocial behaviour appears driven and out of control and they compensate by becoming increasingly concerned with gaining a sense of power and control over others. In the early 40s, a further stage is reached, corresponding with the mid-life transition when there is a further high rate of termination from a criminal lifestyle (Hirschi and Gottfredson, 1983). At this stage, some individuals begin to exhibit greater maturity associated with a change in their thinking, values, and motivations, accompanying their declining physical and mental energy. However, Walters has pointed out that maturity is not necessarily part of the process of desisting from criminal behaviour. Many individuals may remain on the fringes of crime, behaving in an irresponsible and self-indulgent manner, but no longer as intrusive in their criminal behaviour.

The targeted preventive approach would clearly aim at the prevention of a progression from the first to the second stage, and onwards. A second targeted approach might be to hasten the rate of drop-out of individuals from each stage. But longitudinal research has demonstrated that interventions are less likely to be effective for those who persist in their criminality from early adulthood onwards towards middle age. It might be preferable to somehow prevent individuals entering stage one in the first place. This strategy might include a targeted approach, concentrating on children identified as being at high risk. But it might also involve a preventive strategy applied to the entire population. Either way, the aim would be to formulate strategies to prevent the longitudinal development of a criminal lifestyle or the adult syndrome of Antisocial Personality Disorder (ASPD).

Antisocial personality disorder and the development of adult antisocial syndromes

The concept of a psychiatric 'syndrome' of persistent antisocial behaviour in adulthood is embodied in the diagnostic construct of 'antisocial personality disorder' (ASPD). This is currently included in the DSM-IV classificatory system (American Psychiatric Association, 1994) and is

A. Pervasive pattern of disregard for and violation of rights of others from 15 years. Indicated by 3 (or more) of:

1) Failure to conform to lawful social norms (indicated by repetitive criminal activity)

2) Deceitfulness (repeated lying, using aliases, conning others)

3) Impulsivity or failure to plan ahead

4) Irritability and aggressiveness (repeated physical fights or assaults)

5) Reckless disregard for safety of self or others

6) Consistent irresponsibility (repeated failure to sustain employment, pay debts)

7) Lack of remorse (indifferent to or rationalises mistreating other or stealing.

B. Individual is at least 18 years old.

C Evidence of Conduct Disorder before 15 years
Requires three (or more) criteria (see Figure 2.4)

D. Antisocial behaviour is not exclusively during schizophrenic or manic episode

Figure 2.3. Diagnostic criteria for DSM-IV, Axis II. 301.7 Antisocial Personality Disorder

defined by a series of behaviours which must be present before the age of 15 and in adulthood (see Figures 2.3 and 2.4). It has been identified by Farrington (1995) as equivalent to delinquency which persists into adulthood and the associated features demonstrated by individuals with this pattern of criminal development over their lifespan. The key feature of this diagnostic construct is the presence of a syndrome of conduct disordered behaviour in childhood which persists into adulthood. However, the diagnostic construct also embodies the notion that it is not just criminal behaviours that should be included as criteria, but a wide range of additional behavioural disorders.

ASPD is one of the most reliable diagnostic categories in psychiatry and is empirically derived from longitudinal study of delinquency and problem social behaviour. Robins (1966) followed up a series of 406 children who were referred to a child guidance clinic for their antisocial behaviour, 118 referred for other reasons (primarily with neurotic symptoms), and 100 controls from local schools in the neighbourhood of the clinic. Subjects were traced thirty years later. The original sample of conduct disordered children had parents of low occupational status and only a third were with both parents at the time of referral. A

A repetitive and persistent pattern of behaviour in which the basic rights of others or major age-appropriate social norms or rules are violated, as manifested by the presence of three (or more) of the following criteria:

Aggression to people and animals

1. often bullied, threatened, or intimidated others
2. often initiated physical fights
3. used a weapon that could cause serious physical harm
4. was physically cruel to people
5. was physically cruel to animals
6. stole whilst confronting a victim (e.g. mugging, purse snatching, extortion, armed robbery)
7. forced someone into sexual activity

Destruction of property

8. deliberately engaged in firesetting with intention of causing serious damage
9. deliberately destroyed others' property (other than firesetting)

Deceitfulness or theft

10. broke into someone else's house, building, or car
11. often lied to obtain goods, favours or to avoid obligations (i.e. conned others)
12. stole items of non-trivial value without confronting victim (e.g. shoplifting, forgery)

Serious violation of rules

13. often stayed out at night despite parental prohibitions, (beginning before 13 years)
14. ran away from home overnight at least twice while living in parental or parental surrogate home (or once without returning for a lengthy period)
15. was often truant from school, beginning before age 13 years

Figure 2.4. Diagnostic criteria for DSM-IV 312.8 Conduct Disorder component of Antisocial Personality Disorder

third had spent at least six months in an institutional foster home. Many fathers had deserted their families and/or drank heavily, many of the mothers failed to keep house or supervise the children. A substantial proportion of the children had siblings with behavioural disorders. Most were behind at school when referred and 52 per cent of boys and 35 per cent of girls were officially classified as juvenile delinquents. The median age of referral was 13 years and none of the children were above the age of 18 years. Girls were found to have had more disruptive lives than boys.

At thirty-year follow-up, the antisocial children were more likely to have left their area of origin, 75 per cent of men and 40 per cent of women had been arrested for non-traffic offences, and almost half the males had been arrested for at least one major crime. Arrests for serious offences such as rape and murder in adulthood were found only for the conduct disordered children. Prostitution was found only in the histories of conduct disordered females. Of the women referred for antisocial behaviour, 70 per cent were currently divorced, 23 per cent had been divorced more than once, and a third had married before the age of 17. Robins observed that these women tended to choose husbands who were unfaithful, or deserted, or failed to support them. There was a high rate of childlessness in this group, but those who did have children were more likely to have demonstrated behavioural problems than children of women in the two control groups. More than 20 per cent of mothers with antisocial behaviour in childhood had a child who had been arrested. Occupational history in adulthood was characterised by lower social status and more frequent unemployment.

Girls resembled the boys in their adult pattern but showed more frequent sexual misbehaviour. Unlike the conduct disordered children (who had a 1 in 5 chance of demonstrating a sociopathic personality in adulthood), children referred with other psychiatric disturbances (e.g. fearfulness, withdrawal, tics, speech defects, etc.) were no more likely to have psychiatric disorders as adults than the controls from the local schools.

Antisocial behaviour in the father was a good predictor for similar behaviour in adulthood for subjects of both sexes. Robins considered that lack of adequate discipline in the family home and the experience of living with a father who drank heavily, was chronically unemployed, arrested, or deserted the family, played an important part. However, early separation from the father did not appear to prevent the child developing later sociopathic behaviour and Robins concluded that taking children from parents was unlikely to help.

Remission and improvement in adulthood could be assessed in the majority of sociopaths. Robins judged that 12 per cent were in remission thirty years later (subjects were then in their 4th or 5th decade), 27 per cent showed a greatly reduced range in severity of antisocial behaviour, but 60 per cent still showed little improvement. The improvement observed in the first two subgroups happened progressively in each decade, most often within the 30–40 age range. It was thought that special life circumstances, sometimes the threat of further punishments following arrest, were a decisive factor. However, Robins believed that neither hospitalisation nor the experience of psychotherapy during the lives of her sociopathic subjects had any positive association with improvement.

From these findings, Robins devised the criteria for the construct 'sociopathic personality disorder', from which the diagnostic category 'antisocial personality disorder' in DSM-IV was ultimately derived. Robins

(1978) later replicated her original study with additional cohorts growing up in different eras and living in different parts of the USA. Her original study had included only white subjects. One further cohort consisted of young black males; a third cohort included Vietnam veterans, along with matched non-veterans. Despite considerable differences between the samples, and in sources of information, there were striking replications of her original study with respect to the childhood predictors of antisocial behaviour. She concluded that all types of antisocial behaviour in childhood could predict a high level of antisocial behaviour in adulthood, and that each kind of adult antisocial behaviour was predicted by the overall number of factors of antisocial behaviour. She argued that her findings indicated that adult and childhood antisocial behaviour formed both syndromes and that the two syndromes were closely connected. She also concluded that adult antisocial behaviour as a pervasive syndrome required a preceding pattern of childhood antisocial behaviour. However, the majority of conduct disordered children would not go on to become adults with sociopathy or antisocial personality disorder. It appeared that the variety of antisocial behaviour in childhood was in itself a better predictor of adult antisocial behaviour than any particular individual form of behaviour. Furthermore, the behaviour in childhood was a better predictor for the future than family background or social class.

Community surveys of Antisocial Personality Disorder

Since the publication of the DSM-III classification (American Psychiatric Association, 1980), there have been several community surveys that provide data on the prevalence of personality disorder. More information is available on ASPD than other categories of personality disorder because it has been included as a single personality disorder diagnosis in a number of epidemiological studies of major mental disorder. The most useful data on the prevalence of ASPD have been provided by large scale studies, representative of the populations surveyed, using the Diagnostic Interview Schedule (DIS) (Robins *et al.*, 1981) and more recently the Composite International Diagnostic Interview (CIDI) (Wittchen *et al.*, 1991). Figure 2.5 shows the prevalence of ASPD in a series of different populations, indicating that in westernised societies, the lifetime prevalence is approximately 2–3 per cent.

The epidemiological catchment area (ECA) study in three US sites surveyed the largest general population samples and showed one month, six month, and life-time prevalence rates for ASPD of 0.5 per cent,

AUTHORS	LOCATION	SAMPLE	METHOD	RATE/100
Robins and Regier (1991)	New Haven	5,034	DIS	2.0
	Baltimore	3,481	DIS	2.3
	St Louis	3,004	DIS	3.2
	Durham	3,921	DIS	1.5
	Los Angeles	3,125	DIS	2.9
	All five sites, USA	18,565	DIS	2.4
Bland *et al.* (1988 a,b)	Edmonton, Canada	3,258	DIS	3.7
Hwu *et al.* (1989)	Taiwan: Metro Taipei	5,005	DIS	0.14
	Small towns	3,004	DIS	0.07
	Rural villages	2,995	DIS	0.03
Wells *et al.* (1989)	New Zealand	1,498	DIS	3.1
Lee *et al.* (1990)	Korea: urban	3,134	DIS	2.1
	rural	1,966	DIS	0.9
Chen *et al.* (1993)	Hong Kong	7,229	DIS	2.8(m), 0.5(f)
Weissman and Myers (1980)	New Haven, USA	511	SADS-L	0.2*
Baron *et al.* (1985)	USA	376	SIB, SADS	0.5
Reich *et al.* (1989)	Iowa, USA	235	PDQ	0.4
Zimmerman and Coryell (1990)	Relatives - Iowa	697	PDQ SIDP	3.0
Maier *et al.* (1992)	Relatives - Mainz, Germany	447	SCID-II	0.2
Levav *et al.* (1993)	Israel	2,741	SADS-I	0.7
Kessler *et al.* (1994)	USA	8,098	CIDI	3.5
Samuels *et al.* (1994)	USA	810	DSM-III rating scale	1.5

* Current, not lifetime, rate

Figure 2.5. Life-time rates/100 of Antisocial Personality Disorder (DSM-III, DSM-III-R) based on community surveys or surveys of relatives

1.2 per cent, and 2.6 per cent respectively, the life-time prevalence rate varying between each site from 2.1–3.4 (Robins *et al.*, 1984; Robins and Regier, 1991). Life-time prevalence for males was significantly higher (4.5 per cent) than for females (0.8 per cent), highest in the 25–44 age groups, no higher in blacks than whites, commonest in those who had dropped out of high school, and most commonly found in inner city populations. A more recent US study from six sites also found a one month prevalence of 0.5 per cent, but confirmed a 2.5 per cent life-time diagnosis (Regier *et al.*, 1988).

The Christchurch, New Zealand, Psychiatric Epidemiological Study employed similar methods and revealed six month and life-time ASPD prevalence rates of 0.9 per cent and 3.1 per cent respectively (Wells *et al.*, 1989). Life-time rates for males were 4.2 per cent compared with 0.5 per cent for females, but differences were not statistically significant, probably because of the smaller sample size. This study included an examination of the one year recovery rate which showed a surprisingly high level of 51.6 per cent for ASPD. However, this may have reflected a distortion of state effects from substance abuse on the ASPD diagnosis. A subgroup of drug abusers no longer appeared personality disordered following abstinence.

A life-time prevalence rate of 3.7 per cent (6.5 per cent males, 0.8 per cent females) was found for ASPD in Edmonton, Canada, and was highest in the 18–34 age group and those who were widowed, separated, and divorced (Bland *et al.*, 1988a&b). Rates were considerably lower in Taiwan, ranging from 0.03 per cent in rural settings to 0.14 per cent in Metropolitan Taipei (Hwu *et al.*, 1989). But these figures generally correlated with overall lower rates of most DSM-III mental disorders which were measured in Taiwan. Compton *et al.*, (1991) have looked specifically at cross-cultural differences in the rates of antisocial personality disorder by comparing ECA data with those from the Taiwan Psychiatric Epidemiological Project. They concluded that while the considerably lower rate of disorder in Taiwan might be partially attributable to response bias, this was unlikely to explain the whole magnitude of difference. Furthermore, the low prevalence in Taiwan does not translate to other East Asian countries. Rates in Hong Kong (Chen *et al.*, 1993) and South Korea (Lee *et al.*, 1990) are comparable with the US. However, these countries have higher rates of alcoholism which has an association with ASPD (Ross, 1995; Tomasson and Vaglum, 1995).

Reich *et al.* (1989) and Zimmerman and Coryell (1990) also showed considerably lower rates, of 0.4 per cent and 0.9 per cent respectively, in two US studies, but used different instruments from the other researchers who had employed the Diagnostic Interview Schedule which had been specifically developed for epidemiological study (Robins *et al.*, 1981). Zimmerman and Coryell (1990) also demonstrated that the rates increased from 0.9 per cent to 3 per cent when interviewers were used, suggesting that self-report instruments may well underestimate ASPD and may not be suitable for epidemiological study. Similarly, problems with a high threshold when using the SADS-L may explain the low rates in Israel (Levav *et al.*, 1993) and two US sites (Baron *et al.*, 1985; Weissman and Myers, 1980).

Epidemiological studies have also revealed important characteristics of ASPD individuals. Males and females appear to have differing ages of onset, with males tending to present with conduct disorder at an earlier age than females who present around puberty (Robins, 1986). There are also sex differences in presenting symptoms, with men having more traffic offences and arrests, and exhibiting more promiscuity and illegal occupation, whereas women more often desert or hit their spouses or fail to work steadily. Men appear to have a special vulnerability to ASPD. Childhood environments of ASPD females are more disturbed, suggesting that more predisposing factors are required for the disorder to appear in women (Robins, 1985). Similarly, in a child guidance sample, records showed that women later diagnosed as sociopathic had lower IQs, had more frequently been in correctional institutions, more often had parents on welfare or who were chronically unemployed, and more often had alcoholic or sociopathic fathers than did male sociopaths (Robins, 1966).

ASPD appears to be associated with poverty and other indices of social failure. Koegel *et al.* (1988) found five times more ASPD among the homeless in Los Angeles than in the general population. Poor school success and poor work history predisposed to low status jobs and unemployment. However, Robins (1966) demonstrated that despite originating from families of low socio-economic status, the adult status of sociopaths still tended to fall below that of their parents during a study period which coincided with general economic and social improvement in the USA.

The important finding of an association between ASPD and inner city residence corresponds to the criminological tradition of linking urbanisation with increasing rates of crime (Shaw and McKay, 1942; Baldwin and Bottoms, 1976; Herbert, 1979; Bottoms and Wiles, 1997). However, it is not established whether high rates of crime in inner city areas are contributed to in any significant way by an excess of ASPD residents. Explanations such as a 'drift' of these individuals to inner city areas requires further examination, as do the observations that unstable and disadvantaged individuals tend to be placed in high crime and socially deprived areas as a result of housing policy in the UK (Rex and Moore, 1967; Gill, 1967). Black people are disproportionately over-represented in the prison populations in both the USA and UK. Although they disproportionately reside in inner city areas of both countries, US studies still show that the inner city black population has higher arrests and conviction rates than the white population (Shannon, 1978). As the best predictor of antisocial personality is childhood conduct disorder (Robins, 1978), an association of conduct problems with race will tend to imply a higher rate of ASPD in black people. For example, Rutter *et al.* (1974) noted a higher rate of conduct problems in black children in an inner London area than white children. Similarly, the ECA study retrospectively examined conduct problems in childhood and showed that black children had higher rates than white children. However, it is of some considerable importance that the black children were found to be less likely to continue these types of behaviour into adult life, resulting in similar rates of ASPD in adulthood.

Antisocial personality disorder appears to predominate in young adulthood and studies have suggested that the symptoms begin to diminish in a proportion during middle age. However, the disorder also involves a higher risk of death during early adulthood. Unfortunately, at least 20 per cent still meet the criteria when aged 45 and it has been estimated that they constitute 0.5 per cent of the US population, indicating that those who do not remit still pose a serious problem for clinicians and for society. Robins (1986) has also made the alarming proposal that there may be a rising proportion of individuals with ASPD in successive US generations over time.

Prison surveys of Antisocial Personality Disorder

Studies in prisons demonstrate a high prevalence of ASPD (see Figure 2.6). However, prisons vary in their concentrations of hardened, career criminals which may partly account for the differences observed between surveys. For example, a study of male prisoners who had posed the most serious disciplinary problems in English prisons demonstrated that 84 per cent had a diagnosis of ASPD (Coid, 1998). However, this was unsurprising as the high level of psychopathic traits in these individuals had contributed to their placement in these special facilities. When examining these surveys, it must also be questioned in each case to what extent the institutional setting was representative of prisons in general. Methods used to diagnose ASPD clearly influence prevalences found and the surveys based on clinical interviews with males (Hare, 1983) and females (Robertson, 1987) do not appear to correspond with other surveys that used research diagnostic instruments. Hodgins and Cote (1990) refer to three surveys carried out using the DIS in US penitentiaries that found prevalences ranging from 28.9–50 per cent. They found that 61.7 per cent of prisoners had ASPD in their Quebec survey using the same instrument (Cote and Hodgins, 1990).

AUTHORS	LOCATION	SAMPLE	METHOD	RATE/100
Males				
Hare (1983)	British Columbia, Canada			
	Provincial:	75	Clinical	33.3
	Federal:	171	Clinical	41.5
Cote and Hodgins (1990)	Quebec penitentiaries, Canada	495	DIS	61.7
Hodgins and Cote (1990)	Three US penitentiaries (quoted in chapter)	?	DIS	28.9-50-1
Coid (1998)	Three Special Units, UK prisons	81	SCID-II	61.0
Singleton *et al.* (1998)	Prison survey England & Wales			
	Remanded:	1,250	SCID-II screen	61.0
	Sentenced:	1,120	SCID-II screen	57.0
	Remanded:	181	SCID-II	63.0
	Sentenced:	210	SCID-II	49.0

* Current, not lifetime, rate

AUTHORS	LOCATION	SAMPLE	METHOD	RATE/100
Females				
Robertson (1987)	Winnipeg, Canada			
	Remanded:	100	Clinical	60.0
Jordan *et al.* (1996)	Raleigh, USA			
	Correctional institution:	805	CIDI	11.9
Teplin *et al.* (1996)	Chicago, USA			
	Jail detainees:	1,272	DIS	13.8
Singleton *et al.* (1998)	Prison Survey England & Wales			
	Remanded:	187	SCID-II screen	48.0
	Sentenced:	584	SCID-II screen	39.0
	Remanded and sentenced:	105	SCID-II	31.0

Figure 2.6. Lifetime rates/100 of Antisocial Personality Disorder in prison surveys

Only the national survey of prisoners in England and Wales used a truly representative sample, interviewing a proportion of subjects from every penal institution. This survey administered the SCID-II screen questionnaire as a self-report instrument and a 1 in 6 sub-sample were later re-interviewed by trained clinicians who administered the SCID-II. The self-report SCID-II screening questionnaire demonstrated satisfactory correlation with results using the structured clinical interview administered by clinicians, with 61–63 per cent of remanded men and 49–57 per cent of sentenced men estimated to have ASPD (Singleton *et al.*, 1998). Overall, the studies of male prisoners in Figure 2.6 suggest that the overall prevalence of ASPD is between 30–60 per cent.

Figure 2.6 demonstrates that rates for female prisoners are lower and in two US surveys were 11.9 per cent (Jordan *et al.*, 1996) and 13.8 per cent (Teplin *et al.*, 1996) respectively. The prevalence was higher among women prisoners in England and Wales (31–48 per cent) and it is unclear whether these findings reflect differences as a result of using a different research diagnostic instrument (although these differences are less marked in surveys of men), or differences in pathways into correctional facilities for women in the two countries.

Although these surveys reflect the high probability that individuals with ASPD are likely to spend some time in correctional facilities at some time in their lives, it is also important to consider the limitations of imprisonment as a means of reducing the number of individuals with ASPD in the general population by removing them from the community. Although the prevalence of ASPD may be much higher in prisons than the general population, epidemiological studies in Figure 2.5 demonstrate that the overwhelming majority of individuals with ASPD at any one time are in the general population.

Conduct disorder

A review of the literature has confirmed the poor prognosis and lack of treatment response for ASPD (Dolan and Coid, 1993). Clearly, it would be preferable if a prevention strategy could prevent the condition from developing in the first place. It has been estimated that between 4–10 per cent of children in Britain and the USA meet the criteria for Conduct Disorder (CD) (Rutter *et al.*, 1975; Kazdin, 1987; Institute of Medicine, 1989) (See Figure 2.4). More recently, a survey of psychiatric morbidity in children and adolescents in Great Britain found the prevalence of CD in boys age 5–15 was 7.4 per cent and girls 3.2 per cent. CD was more prevalent in black children than white or South Asians, in lone parent or reconstituted families, where parents had no educational qualifications, neither parent worked, and lived in social sector housing (Meltzer *et al.*, 2000). Estimates have also indicated that CD presents in one third to half of all child and adolescent clinic referrals (Robins, 1981; Herbert, 1987) and is the commonest reason for referral (Audit Commission, 1999). The condition is characterised by a persistent pattern of behaviour in which the child violates the basic rights of others and the major age appropriate social norms. Unfortunately, it is very difficult to ensure a high level of compliance with treatment regimes. It has been reported that between 40–50 per cent of families who begin treatment drop out prematurely (Kazdin, 1996), and the majority of children who enter outpatient treatment attend only one or two sessions (Ambruster and Fallon, 1994).

Up to 40 per cent of children diagnosed with CD can be expected to have serious psychosocial disturbance of one form or another in adulthood (Robins, 1970; Rutter and Giller, 1983; Rutter *et al.*, 1998; Farrington, 1995) including criminal convictions, substance misuse, erratic employment in unskilled jobs, violent relationships with partners, and few friends. It has been argued, however, that the diagnosis of CD is too broad, that many subjects may have little in common, and their antisocial behaviour may have different causes and can vary qualitatively and quantitatively, presenting in one setting but not in others (Kazdin, 1987). However, until the concept is refined, researchers require some way to identify young persons whose primary problem is antisocial behaviour and the diagnosis will therefore retain some usefulness if these limitations are recognised (Shamsie and Hluchy, 1991).

From its appearance in early childhood, aggressiveness is the most stable personality characteristic of CD (Loeber, 1982), although the aggression will be expressed differently at different stages of development. For example, Aschenbach and Edelbrock (1981) found that mothers reported younger problem children to be argumentative, stubborn, and prone to tantrums, while older children had oppositional behaviours. At a later date, they present with firesetting and stealing, and finally truancy, vandalism, and substance abuse. Loeber (1982) determined four factors predictive of chronic delinquency following CD from a review of the literature: (a) frequency of antisocial behaviours, (b) their variety, (c) age of onset, and (d) the presence of antisocial behaviour in more than one setting. These factors not only predispose to adult ASPD (Robins and Regier, 1991), but also to substance abuse (Hesselbrock, 1986), major mental disorder in a subgroup (Robins and Price, 1991), and a higher rate of violent death (Rydelius, 1988).

Conduct disorder is one of three subclasses of disruptive behaviour disorder of children along with attention deficit hyperactivity disorder (ADHD) and oppositional defiant disorder. Clinical evidence suggests that these disorders may transform from one to the other, but usually in a particular order from ADHD to oppositional defiant disorder to conduct disorder and ultimately to ASPD in adulthood. Lahey *et al.* (1999) argue that ADHD may not be a developmental precursor to CD in boys, but acknowledge that it is associated with earlier onset and a wider range of antisocial behaviour. There is consistent observation of comorbidity between ADHD and CD in clinical and epidemiological studies (Biederman *et al.*, 1992) with some evidence that ADHD with antisocial features constitutes a distinct form of ADHD (Faraone *et al.*, 1991, 1998; Biederman *et al.*, 1992). It remains unclear whether each of these conditions should be considered entirely separate or whether CD might be conceptualised as the middle phase of a very chronic psychiatric disorder beginning in early life and continuing into adulthood, but which can still abort at any point along the way and show improvement (see Loeber *et al.*, 1991).

Lynam (1996) has argued that children who manifest symptoms of hyperactivity–impulsivity–attention problems as well as CD are a sub-group at risk for becoming chronic offenders. Researchers have identified a dimension of temperament in children characterised by callous–unemotional behaviour which is considered similar to adult psychopathy, characterised by lack of empathy, lack of guilt, and superficial display of emotions (Frick *et al.*, 1994; Christian *et al.*, 1997). The presence of callous–unemotional traits in conjunction with CD may designate a further sub-group who show a very diverse pattern of antisocial behaviour. Lahey *et al.* (1999) have argued that in the most extreme case, this dimension may include enjoyment of dominating, intimidating, embarrassing, and hurting others.

Stability in CD is strongly related to age of onset, with earlier onset predicting greater persistence of the disorder over time (Loeber, 1990; Tolan, 1987). Certain authors have theorised that CD beginning in early childhood is qualitatively distinct from CD emerging during adolescence (Brown *et al.*, 1996; Hinshaw *et al.*, 1993; Loeber, 1988; Moffitt, 1993; Patterson, 1986; Tolan, 1987). DSM-IV recognises this by having two subtitles based on age of onset – ‘childhood onset type’ where at least one criterion of CD begins prior to 10 years, and ‘adolescent onset type’ – where there is an absence of any characteristic criteria before 10 years. It has been argued that by identifying subtypes it may be possible to shed light on aetiological processes and assist those who would devise interventions so they could tailor their treatments to specific populations (Hinshaw *et al.*, 1993; Lahey *et al.*, 1998).

Moffitt (1993) proposed a theoretical framework that makes specific predictions about which risk and protective factors (see below) should be related to early onset CD. Life course persistent (or early onset) is proposed as having its earliest roots in both neurological deficits and exposure to environmental risk such as poor parenting and parental antisocial behaviour. Neurological deficits give rise to difficult temperament, leading to the child becoming vulnerable to poor parenting from caretakers. These early risk factors start the child on a trajectory of increasing acts and behaviours that escalate through adolescence and persist into adulthood. Moffitt theorised that individuals with adolescent-limited behaviour begin their antisocial behaviour during the adolescent period, and desist after reaching young adulthood. The increase of rates of antisocial behaviour observed in adolescence (see Figure 2.1) is partly caused by the long gap between biological maturity (occurring in early adolescence) and social maturity (i.e. adult status) that exist in industrialised societies with a long period of formal education and dependency. In these societies, adolescents without developmental problems still engage in antisocial activities to gain access to adult privileges and to imitate deviant peers. Cultures or sub-cultures with a larger gap in biological and social maturity will produce larger numbers of this group of offenders, whereas those with a shorter gap will produce fewer.

It has been suggested that young offenders from African-American populations are less likely to have emotional/psychological dysfunction and troubled family backgrounds than their Caucasian counterparts, but more likely to associate with deviant peers (Dinges *et al.*, 1997). The barriers to achieving financial self-sufficiency through legitimate means may thus increase the acceptability of engaging in criminal behaviour within ethnic minority groups during adolescence, particularly when coupled with exposure to neighbourhoods with high rates of gang activity (National Centre for Education Statistics, 1995; Yung and Hammond, 1997). McCabe *et al.* (2001) found evidence in support of Moffitt's hypothesis in a study of children with CD, suggesting that individual and familial factors are more strongly related to childhood onset CD, whereas ethnic minority status and exposure to deviant peers were more strongly related to adolescent onset CD. Similarly, Taylor *et al.* (2000) further supported the importance of individual factors in the early onset group, demonstrating through family history data and twin analysis a greater genetic influence on early onset than late onset delinquency.

As CD is a relatively common condition in childhood, and as the majority of children with CD will not progress onwards to manifest ASPD in adulthood, future research is required to improve accuracy in identifying those children who are at highest risk of developing ASPD. It may be possible in the future to identify additional sub-groups among the high-risk group who require specific, targeted interventions that are individually tailored to their needs.

From this overview of the literature on CD and ASPD, primary prevention aimed at preventing the progression of CD to ASPD in adulthood might take four possible approaches:

1. Preventative programmes could be devised to stop children developing the CD precursor of the adult antisocial syndrome in the first place. These would concentrate on infancy and early childhood phases. The targeted approach would identify children with conditions thought to be precursors of CD, such as oppositional defiant disorder. However, a population approach might also be possible, for example improving parenting skills in large scale programmes.
2. Programmes aimed at increasing the rate of 'drop-outs'. These would aim to increase the rate at which children who are identified with CD drop-out before progressing to the adult syndrome of ASPD. For example, if 60 per cent of children with CD do not go on to manifest serious psycho-social disturbance in adulthood, could this be raised to 70 or 80 per cent ?
3. A targeted approach would focus on the sub-group of CD children currently identified as being at highest risk of adult ASPD, with a commitment to continued therapeutic input during their adolescence and into early adulthood to manage risk and maximise potential for positive change.
4. Prevention of inter-generational transmission. For example, programmes could be devised to target children in high-risk families who demonstrate signs of CD, using a multi-disciplinary, multi-agency approach, supportive of families and parents.

'High risk' or 'population' strategies?

The establishment of an adult syndrome of antisocial behaviour which develops from a syndrome of childhood conduct disorder has many advantages in terms of case definition. In the field of medicine, successful clinical management requires a system of unambiguous labels. However, more careful examination of conduct disorder, ASPD, and the life course of these conditions also indicate that they represent the severe end of a continuum that is present within the general population. By drawing a line at a certain point and constructing a diagnostic category, and then carrying out research which identifies the risk and protective factors for these syndromes, would at first appear to lead inevitably to the 'high risk' strategy of prevention. The population can be screened for individuals who present with robust predictive factors, derived from empirical research, and the rest of the population are omitted from any prevention strategies that might be introduced. But if there is truly a continuum of severity, this will considerably widen the task of prevention. It is well known that there is a very large burden of undetected crime in all communities. Questions then arise as to whether the range of the prevention strategy should be extended to influence the 'dark figure' of crime. The preventive medicine approach would argue that prevention should be extended more widely to non-case defined individuals because all levels of severity are important and because 'mild' can often lead to 'severe' at a later stage.

'High risk' prevention strategies

There are both strengths and weaknesses of the 'high risk' prevention strategy. The targeting of criminal individuals is often preferred by politicians rather than a recognition that national and social policies, or the neglect of them, could influence the level of crime in society. The notion of a targeted prevention strategy is also more easily conceptualised by the public and media. An additional advantage of targeted prevention is that it is appropriate to the individual and avoids any interference with those not at risk. It tends to fit well with the ethos and organisation of services that are well established and with established professional disciplines. It also represents a cost-effective use of resources and by employing a process of selectivity will improve the benefit-to-risk ratio. However, associating an antisocial syndrome with a specific organisation or a profession may also risk stigmatising the individual. The 'high risk' prevention strategy may ultimately be only palliative and temporary, and can often be inadequate in the context of the larger population. In the case of conduct disorder, the 'high risk' strategy may be limited by relative poor ability to predict a child's future. The majority of conduct disordered children will not develop ASPD. It may also be highly expensive and ultimately unfeasible. The epidemiological approach would indicate that the ultimate contribution of the high risk strategy to overall crime rates may be exceedingly small.

Any 'high risk' strategy will ultimately depend on the success of its screening programme. If screening is sufficiently accurate, the strategy can be closely matched to the needs of the individual. However, as well as concerns for accuracy, there are ethical, organisational, and problems of costs associated with screening for high risk individuals. Rose argued that screening without adequate resources for advice and the long-term care of individuals who screen positive may be unethical. If high risk individuals are identified this may cause considerable distress and anxiety to them and their families. How will a family react when informed that their 10-year-old son has a 1 in 3 chance of becoming a psychopath in adulthood? Furthermore, withdrawal of the preventive measure at a later stage of intervention may ultimately lead to a return to the former lifestyle, leading to increased risk of an antisocial syndrome and ultimately wasted effort. Selective screening may be more effective than mass screening, but this may vary according to the population and the factor being screened. In some cases it may be necessary for two stages of screening to take place. Most importantly, Rose emphasised that the purpose of screening is to assess the reversible risk and not merely the risk factors themselves. The intention is not just to identify those who screen positive for the risk of future criminality or an adult antisocial syndrome, but to identify those who can either be helped or helped most by the preventive action.

Screening for Conduct Disorder

It has been argued that interventions should be developed for high risk children and delivered as early as possible. Claims have been made that even in non-clinic populations of children as young as 4 and 5 years of age, 50 per cent or more of those with troublesome externalising symptoms (e.g. aggression against others, destruction of property, temper tantrums, non-compliance, etc) will develop persistent psychological problems (Campbell, 1995; Coie, 1996; Reid, 1993; Reid and Patterson, 1995). However, Bennett *et al.* (1998) point out that little attention has been directed at the accuracy of such risk assessments, with little or no discussion of the implications of classification issues or the usefulness of high risk, targeted intervention strategies. It is assumed that a targeted strategy will have successfully identified high risk children, but this can only be achieved if an accurate risk assessment model is available to classify children into high and low risk groups (Coie, 1996; Institute of Medicine, 1994). If many children who need the intervention are missed (false negatives) the result is poor coverage and a reduction of the public health impact of the intervention. If many children receive the intervention who do not need it (false positives), children are mistakenly labelled as high risk and resources may be wasted. Following a review of previous studies, Bennett and colleagues argued that using early externalising behaviours (assessed by the currently available methods) in children aged 3–5 from normal populations and designating them in the high risk category will result in a substantial level of misclassification. At least half the children who go on to develop CD or antisocial behaviour at a later stage will be missed using these measures. Furthermore, 50 per cent or more would receive an intervention who did not need it.

Bennett and colleagues' critique illustrates the major dilemma in the formulation of targeted strategies for primary prevention. Developing better screening procedures is clearly an essential area for future research. One alternative approach might be to broaden the range of screening variables employed in the screening process. For example, Nagin and Tremblay (2001) demonstrated that kindergarten boys displaying high levels of opposition and hyperactivity are at high risk of persistent physical aggression from 6 to 15 years. However, among the subgroup of boys in the high risk level of aggression group were two subgroups, one whose physical aggression remained chronically high and another group who demonstrated a high level of physical aggression in kindergarten but whose aggression then declined. The former group were characterised by having mothers (but not fathers) with low educational level and a teenage onset of childbearing. Although it would be premature to use such findings to create a new screening instrument, these findings would suggest that it will be necessary to combine risk factors from different domains (for example factors relating to the child, the family, the environment, etc) and that their combination may have greater potential for more accurate risk prediction. This would involve a research programme including statistical methods similar to those used in predicting violent behaviour following discharge from hospital (see Monahan *et al.*, 2001).

'Population' prevention strategy

Rose argued that 'a large number of people exposed to a small risk may generate many more cases than a small number exposed to a high risk'. This means that a high risk prevention strategy deals only with the margin of the problem and can ultimately improve on its achievement only by extending its coverage. The aim of the population prevention strategy is to bring about overall population change. A shift in the distribution of population values implies an associated change in the occurrence of extreme values. The more uniform or across the board the shift, the closer must be the correlation between the population average and the prevalence of deviance. Moderate and achievable change by the population as a whole might greatly reduce the number of people with conspicuous problems.

Figure 2.7 is taken from Rose's work and illustrates the theoretical implications of shifting the whole risk distribution and offering a small benefit to many people. Consider the implications of exposure to some criminogenic factor for which there is a graded risk which rises progressively with increasing levels of exposure. The diagram shows the existing distribution of the population according to the exposure level. For example, consider the exposure of children of age 11–16 to the number of

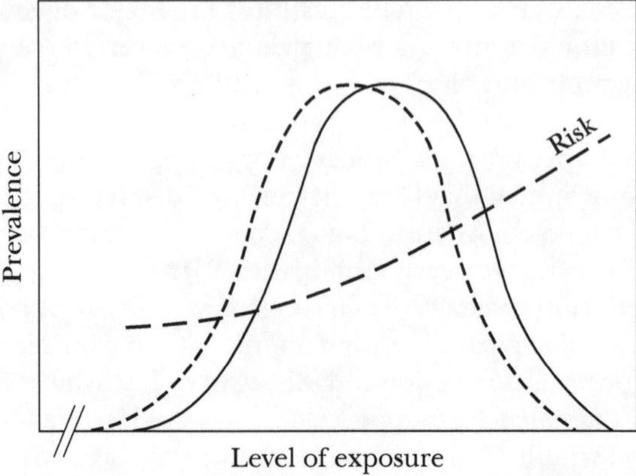

Figure 2.7. Schematic representation of the relation between risk of crime and the distribution of different levels of exposure to a cause. The broken curve shows the new (lower) distribution of exposure after a population-wide control measure.
Adapted from: Rose (1992) *The Strategy of Preventive Medicine. By permission of Oxford University Press*

delinquents amongst their peers in a school. A small number of children are exposed to a large excess risk but many are exposed to a small excess, which will depend on the nature of the school, many schools having a small number of delinquents in a child peer group. The number of cases attributable to each level of exposure can be calculated by multiplying the corresponding excess risk (the height of the risk curve above its baseline) by the number exposed at that level. In this example, most of the attributable cases will appear around the middle of the distribution because of the large numbers involved.

If the population control plan is successful, then the whole distribution of exposure levels will be lowered, as indicated by the new (broken) curve. All children now enjoy a slightly lower risk than before and by repeating the previous calculation the new total of attributable cases can be obtained.

Benefits from a generalised lowering of risk can come about by two processes. First by shifting high risk individuals out of the danger zone, and second because many people exposed to a small risk may generate more crime than a few exposed to a conspicuous risk, i.e. when many receive a little benefit the total benefit may be large. But to explore the potential of the population prevention strategy in a particular field, it is necessary to know the distribution of the risk factor in the local population, together with estimates of the relation between the exposure and outcome. It is then necessary to calculate the theoretic impact of some specified reduction in risk levels or the total burden of crime and assess how this overall benefit is shared among different levels of risk exposure.

When applying this model derived from epidemiology to criminology, it must be questioned what determines a population's mean level of crime and delinquency, violence, or tolerance of these factors. A second question must be what is the criminological counterpart of the identification and control of the equivalent of pollution. This was the achievement of Public Health Medicine which so impressively reduced the incidence of certain diseases at the end of the last century and was subsequently refined as a primary goal of preventive medicine.

There are both strengths and weaknesses of the population prevention strategy. The strategy implies the recognition that crime, which is common, reflects the behaviour and circumstances of society as a whole. If there are mass exposures to a range of different risk factors then mass remedies may be required. The high risk prevention strategy is appropriate if the problem is confined to an identifiable minority and if that problem can be successfully controlled in isolation. But it is an inadequate response to a common problem or a problem with a widespread cause. The population prevention strategy will be more appropriate for more individuals and the total benefit overall will ultimately be larger despite the individual benefits appearing small. A small shift in the distribution can result in a large number of individuals subsequently falling below the critical level. It can also operate at either a superficial or at a more basic level. An education approach which seeks simply to encourage or persuade people to behave differently would be a superficial approach. On the other hand, a radical approach might remove the adverse pressures to act in a criminal manner and by implication are likely to include social and political intervention.

The problem with this approach is that many interventions may be unacceptable and raise as many practical and ethical issues. But at the individual level, Rose (1981) has pointed out the problem of the 'prevention paradox': a preventive measure that brings large benefits to the community offers little to each participating individual.

Applying research into risk and protective factors

Research is progressively identifying the various risk and protective factors in childhood that lead to an adverse adult outcome and which might be usefully employed within a preventive strategy. In practice, most of these risk factors fit more readily into a 'high risk' strategy. But certain others might be employed within a 'population' prevention strategy, whereas some could be employed in either.

The Kauai Longitudinal Study

A series of studies by Werner and colleagues, involving a multiracial cohort of 698 children born on the Hawaiian island of Kauai, provides an important example of the potential of this research which has provided important data on longitudinal development and the interaction of social and biological factors on outcome in adulthood (Werner *et al.*, 1971; Werner and Smith, 1977, 1982; Werner, 1985). The main measures of adverse outcome included either a history of arrest or a psychiatric history by the age of 18. One of the primary achievements of this research is that it measures the interaction of different variables impinging on subjects over the lifespan. The original objectives were: to provide a longitudinal perspective on the children's' capacity to cope with perinatal stress, poverty, and serious disruptions of the family unit; to examine sex differences in vulnerability and resistance to biological and psychosocial stress; and to identify protective factors within the children and their care-giving environment that discriminate between resilient youngsters and peers who develop serious learning and/or behavioural problems in the first and second decades of life.

The study is remarkable in collecting its series during pregnancy. Thus, a small percentage of potential subjects were spontaneously aborted in the early stages. Data were collected on prenatal and perinatal adversity, and the presence of congenital defects at birth; at age 2 an assessment of physical development was made by a paediatrician. Later, intellectual development was measured, and at age 10 an assessment was made by an interdisciplinary panel to record any evidence of physical, learning, or behavioural problems, and to identify need for medical treatment, remedial education, or mental health care. Approximately 1 out of every 3 children in the birth cohort had some learning or behavioural problem during the first decade of life, and approximately 1 out of every 5 youths had records of serious delinquency or mental health problems in the second decade. Some were exposed to major perinatal insults that prevented normal development. Many more lived in chronic poverty or in a persistently disorganised family environment. Frequently, biological and psychosocial risk factors interacted and exposed these children to cumulative stresses too difficult to cope with unaided. Perinatal complications were consistently related to later impaired physical and psychological development only when they were combined with persistently poor environmental circumstances (e.g. chronic poverty, family instability, or maternal mental health problems). Children who were raised in more affluent homes, with an intact family and well educated mother, showed few, if any, negative effects from reproductive stress unless there was severe impairment of the central nervous

Major risk factors at birth:

Chronic poverty
Uneducated mother
Perinatal complications
Developmental delay
Genetic abnormality
Parental psychopathology

Major stress during childhood/adolescence:

Separation in first year
Repeated childhood illness
Parental illness/mental illness
Family discord
Father absence/divorce
Change of residence, school
Foster home
Teenage pregnancy

Figure 2.8. Vulnerability and stress factors relating to adverse adult outcome. Kauai Longitudinal Study.

system, thus confirming the importance of joint influences of reproductive risk and the quality of care-giving environment during the child's upbringing.

With respect to most of the problems identified in middle childhood, improvement had occurred spontaneously by the time the cohort reached 18 years, although positive changes in behaviour were noted more often for middle class than lower class children. Children with learning and/or behaviour problems that persisted into late adolescence had higher rates of moderate to severe perinatal stress, low birth weight, and 'chronic conditions leading to minimal brain dysfunctions' noted by paediatricians in infancy. At the same time, they tended to live more often in chronic poverty or with parental psychopathology than children whose problems were transient. It was an important finding that those with an adverse outcome had tended to elicit more negative responses from their caretakers, indicating a bi-directionality of the child–caretaker effect. Children with an adverse outcome had infantile temperamental traits which appeared distressing and non-rewarding to their caretakers and which may well have contributed to initial difficulties in attachment and bonding seen between parent and child. These disturbed child–caretaker transaction patterns had been observed in the postpartum period and during home visits in the early part of the study.

Figure 2.8 lists the variables which were considered the key predictors of serious coping problems in the Kauai Study. These can be divided

Within the child:

Intact CNS
Good natural disposition
Responsive, affectionate
Advanced self-help skills
Age-appropriate motor and language development
Positive self-concept
Focuses attention and controls impulses

Within care-giving environment:

Much attention in first year
Positive child–parent relationship
Additional caretakers besides mother
Structure and rules in household
Shared values - sense of coherence
Peer friends
Availability of counselling by teachers, ministers
Access to special services (health, education, social services)

Figure 2.9. Protective factors relating to positive outcome. Kauai Longitudinal Study.

into those which appear relevant at birth and later sources of stress. The presence of four or more of the predictors in the children's records by age 2 were strongly indicative of those who would go on to develop serious learning and/or behavioural problems at ages 10 and 18.

Having identified the major risk factors, Werner and colleagues went on to examine the characteristics of those children who were resistant to stress during their development.

Figure 2.9 lists the protective factors which could lead to a good outcome even in the presence of major risk factors in infancy and sources of stress during childhood and adolescence. These are divided into factors operating within the child and within the care-giving environment. Thus, despite an upbringing in poor conditions and a higher than average rate of perinatal stress, low birth weight, etc., certain children, who subsequently develop normally, appeared to be good natured and affectionate in the early years, were able to focus their attention and control their impulses, etc., and could thereby still develop into normal adults. Similarly, these same vulnerable children, but experiencing protective factors such as additional caretakers besides the mother, structure and rules within the household, and with ability to make good relations with other children, etc., could still derive considerable support from the care-giving environment. These appeared to outweigh the factors of vulnerability. Werner proposed a transactional model of development, noting that as disadvantage through an accumulative number of stressful life events increased, more protective factors in the children and their care-giving environment were needed to counterbalance these negative effects and to ensure a positive developmental outcome. Optimal adaptive development appeared to be characterised by a balance between the power of the person and the power of the social and physical environment.

Werner and colleagues proposed that future interventions on behalf of the children and youths might be conceptualised as an attempt to restore this balance, either by decreasing a young person's exposure to risk or stressful life events, or by increasing the number of protective factors (competencies, sources of support) that the individual can draw upon within him/herself or his/her care-giving environment. Werner made several important conclusions from her research which can be applied to the preventive approach:

a. There is a need to re-evaluate present efforts to deal with behavioural problems in the young. Professional and other resources need to be allocated according to the magnitude of needs and critical time periods at which an intervention appears to be most effective.
b. Development cannot be considered within the narrow context of the individual. The wider context of the family, neighbourhood, and community must also be considered.
c. The time which offers greatest promise of substantially reducing 'casualties' appears to be early in childhood, before the damage is done.
d. Many key predictors are recognisable in infancy. Every young child should have a thorough medical and developmental examination in early childhood. Children with major risk factors of a physical nature may require increased input in the form of special resources for their families.
e. Early programmes require co-operation and involvement of mothers. Some of the most effective interventions have focused on enhancing language development and intellectual skills, and on techniques which enhance a mother's sense of control over her life and that of her child.
f. Short term remedial work with identified school 'failures' appeared to be beneficial in middle childhood.
g. The importance of key 'other persons', such as peer counsellors, alternative care-givers, etc., were identified for vulnerable family units.

Werner and colleagues have clearly identified a series of strategies which fit both within the 'high risk' and 'population' strategies of prevention. The study indicates how screening might be applied to a population to identify high risk individuals and suggests the key risk factors, or combinations of individual risk factors, that are significant and therefore should be identified. By implication, the study would indicate a review of how professionals who are already employed should be reallocated to the screening and prevention strategies. For example, the use of paediatricians to carry out medical and developmental examinations, increasing the range of data collected by health visitors during the earliest years, etc. However, the wider influences of society clearly have a major effect, for example religious affiliations, patterns of childcare, etc. The context of the island of Kauai must also be placed in terms of its relationship to other populations in different geographical locations. High risk strategies are of increasingly little relevance in the context of populations which are demonstrating an overall change for the worse and where there are epidemics of crime, substance abuse, communicable disease, and a range of different forms of social disorder and indicators of societal breakdown. The most extreme degrees of breakdown have been observed during or after a state of war. But extreme degrees of social and environmental deterioration can also be observed in certain locations within some of the world's major cities. Lack of vigilance by epidemiologists, coupled with lack of political interest and public concern has lead, in certain urban locations, to epidemics of major social problems. In such settings, the high risk strategy is essentially redundant.

The price of ignoring the population strategy: lessons from the USA

The strongest arguments for the population strategy are contained in a body of epidemiological research carried out in urban environments in the USA during the 1980s and 1990s. During the 1970s and 1980s, delimited, yet still large areas of New York and certain other US urban centres came to resemble cities in Europe in the aftermath of World War II. Unvisited by tourists and by the majority population of the USA, few academics were aware of the large areas of crumbling, burned out, and abandoned buildings, and vacant lots where communities had once lived, or their significance for the epidemics of both health and social problems observed within these areas. Entire neighbourhoods, which had been home to generations of poor people in their transition from new immigrant life to employment and later economic security, had been consistently destroyed. It is ironic that studies in similar, and in some cases the same, areas gave rise to the ecological school of criminology (see Bottoms and Wiles, 1997). The further deterioration of these environments led to a rapid escalation of homelessness, including homeless mentally ill persons, epidemics of

AIDS, low birth weight babies (which local underfunded hospitals were unable to sustain), epidemics of substance abuse, and accompanying epidemics of crime and violence. Certain US epidemiologists have argued that these problems are closely interwoven, reflecting interlocked patterns of urban ecological collapse and deurbanisation which require major public health and political rethinking (Wallace, 1988; Wallace *et al.*, 1992; Wallace *et al.*, 1995). Within this context, the 'high risk' strategy is redundant and major 'population' approaches would have to be employed for the prevention of such a wide range of social and behavioural problems.

Public policy and deurbanisation

Wallace and colleagues (1992) observed an increasingly 'hollowed out' pattern seen in poor neighbourhoods in several US cities as a result of major loss of housing. For example, in the New York South Bronx, certain areas lost 55–81 per cent of their occupied housing units. An active process took place whereby an initial broad scattering of abandoned structures, characterised by the occurrence of many small groups of abandoned houses, was followed by a further intensification of this pattern over time, with later consolidation, but also with a clear element of contagion. These areas became a focus for vandalism and appeared to attract individuals inclined to arson. Research has demonstrated that the fire services had considerable difficulty in meeting the peaks of demand in these areas. This problem had been compounded by a progressive reduction of the fire services themselves as a result of municipal policy to reduce costs and in some cases to reduce taxation. In essence, there had been a 'planned' disbanding of the fire services in certain minority neighbourhoods, taking place in the context of a shrinkage of overall funding to a wide range of public services previously delivered to these areas. The resulting destruction of the environment subsequently lead to an increasing shift of population into adjacent neighbourhoods, which in return raised the population density and overcrowding in these new locations. Overuse and under-maintenance of housing in these new locations then lead to an increased risk of fire as the new overcrowded locations experienced the same factors that had lead to the phenomenon in the previous location, thereby further perpetuating the problem.

Within these deteriorating physical environments, a rapidly increasing range of social problems developed and which meanwhile continued unabated in the deteriorated environment that had been left behind. For example, it was observed by Wallace and colleagues that the age-adjusted mortality from all causes in Harlem by the late 1980s was double that of the rest of the USA and 50 per cent higher than US blacks in general. The highest ratios were for women in the 25–34 age band and men in the 35–44 year band. Chief causes in order included: cardiovascular disease, cirrhosis, homicide, neoplasms, and drug-related deaths. Black men in Harlem were less likely to reach 65 years than men in Bangladesh. Overall, the combination of homicide, cirrhosis, and drug deaths contributed to 40 per cent of Harlem's excess mortality. All of Harlem/East Harlem's five zip-codes were in the top ten (of 168 city-wide in New York) for admissions to city hospitals due to substance abuse, three of the top five for psychosis, and two of the five highest for HIV and cirrhosis admissions. Wallace and colleagues argued that contagious urban decay, rapid loss of housing, and population shift had had a dramatic effect increasing levels of substance abuse and risk of violent death. The social networks and social structure considered essential for the socialisation and control of deviant behaviour, and for the health maintenance of the population, had effectively been dismantled.

A body of literature has described how rapid in- and out-migration can weaken the bonds which tie individuals to society (Crutchfield *et al.*, 1982; South, 1987; Fullilove, 1996). The phenomena of fires and the abandonment of dwellings in inner cities during the 1970s and 1980s resulted in forced migration that caused collective stress to these populations and disrupted their social cohesion. Such extreme phenomena can have considerable effects on grief, anxiety, hostility, resentment, marital and family discord, increased substance abuse, and loss of interest in school by children. Combinations of such factors can lead to outbreaks of delinquency and homicidal violence which may feed back further into community decay. A series of studies have now pointed to a wide range of deviant behaviours and sexual practices that are associated with drug use in these communities, especially crack cocaine which had progressively supplemented or replaced heroin over this period (Donovan and Jessor, 1985; Osgood *et al.*, 1988; Fullilove and Fullilove, 1989; Fullilove *et al.*, 1990). The strongly addictive quality of crack abuse contributed to HIV transmission, early pregnancy, low birth weight infants, and a rapid increase in the numbers of children taken into care from these areas. It is of some interest that males in the 25–44 year age band in the South Bronx had attained a similar HIV prevalence level to parts of central Africa by the 1990s.

Criminal and violent activities, which were not previously tolerated, became more likely as the protective, stable, social, and family networks disintegrated, and economic activities disappeared from these areas. These factors then contributed further to community and physical deterioration. Loss of jobs, especially for men, lead to the growth of an underground economy and the participation in sales of drugs and other drug trade-related activity. Legitimate economic activities for women appeared a more complex area and some authors noted the ability of minority women to find work, in contrast to men (Bourgois, 1995). But at the same time, Wallace *et al.* (1992) observed that for a sub-group of women there were even fewer opportunities which did not even extend to the underground economy in which men could take part. For the most disadvantaged women, welfare and prostitution increased. At the same time, prostitution became associated with more high risk activities involving crack cocaine. These women prostitutes would carry out more dangerous and degrading sexual activities, often for less money or for small quantities of drugs, and thereby placed themselves at higher risk of sexually transmitted diseases (Inciardi, 1995). The outcome can be observed in studies of US female prisoners which have demonstrated escalating prevalence figures for HIV infection in the USA (Behrendt *et al.*, 1994; Brewer and Derrickson, 1992; Crawford, 1994; Dixon *et al.*, 1993).

These processes directly impacted on children who were forced to move more frequently, continuously needed to reform their friendship networks, experienced schools which failed and had repeated moves of school, and experienced violent episodes both within and between families as social networks failed. As Wallace and Wallace (1997) point out, 'youth behaviour such as doing well in school, getting a regular job, avoiding substance abuse, and maintaining stable relationships become more difficult as neighbourhood structures that value such attainments dissolve. Negative acts such as violent behaviour, multiple sexual conquests, and drug taking are messages that are more easily 'heard' in a dissolving community than positive acts. If such 'bad' behaviours damage a community's weak ties further – for example, by making street life more dangerous – the result may be a de-stabilising positive feedback between community disintegration and antisocial behaviour'.

With the breakdown of social cohesion within the parental generation (and for many young persons the absence of a parental generation), children in these areas were left unsupervised. This led to a range of problem behaviours such as delinquency, gang involvement, and recourse to the underground criminal economy. The risks of teenage pregnancy increased and, with use of drugs, particularly crack cocaine, the risk of sexually transmitted disease, including HIV infection. These risks were further increased in a sub-culture characterised by a 'macho' approach to sexual activity and which promoted the use of stimulant substances associated with enhanced sexual enjoyment (Fullilove *et al.*, 1990).

Integrated community treatment – population strategies

It is unsurprising that researchers who are proponents of the 'contagion' model of de-urbanisation have cited Rose's work and asserted that targeted attempts to 'treat' affected individuals and families in these social contexts will have little impact (Wallace *et al.*, 1992). They argued instead that 'reform' activities, aimed at stabilising the social and economic conditions of these communities, and additionally aimed at bringing about a reduction in the skewed population distributions of health and behavioural pathologies, were required. They proposed four main approaches:

i. Maintenance of an adequate infrastructure to maintain population density (specifically restoration of fire, sanitation, and housing-related services adequate to maintain urban population densities in these areas, and prevent further outbreaks of contagious urban decay).
ii. Intensive programmes of community organisation and empowerment to address the 'shredded' social networks of the poor in affected communities.
iii. Provision of adequate housing (specifically provision of many units of low income housing to relocate the displaced, the burned-out, and the 'doubled-up').
iv. Attention to economic restitution.

However, these proposals must also be viewed in the political context of North America and parts of western Europe during this period where economic policies, including controls on spending and limitations on or reductions in taxation, militated against successful implementation.

Income distribution or containment of the urban underclass?

Research has provided increasing evidence that distribution of income, in addition to the absolute standard of living enjoyed by the poor, are key determinants of a population's health (see Kawachi and Kennedy, 1997; Brunner, 1997; Roberts, 1997). A large gap between rich and poor is considered to lead to higher mortality through the breakdown of social cohesion. A recent surge in income inequality had been observed in many countries by the late 1990s and was accompanied by a marked increase in the residential concentration of both poverty and affluence. Residential segregation diminishes the opportunities for social cohesion. This leads to increased rates of crime and violence, and impedes productivity and economic growth. The extent of inequality in society is often the consequence of explicit political policy and public choice. Wallace and Wallace (1997) have argued that attempting to contain problems of disease and disorder to the inner city will fail. There is a false assumption implicit in the policies which created these conditions that such problems can be confined largely to the inner city communities, kept separate from the suburbs and areas where affluent people live, and where political power currently lies. In a review of population rates of AIDS, violent crime, and TB, they found that as the rates within the inner city epicentre of several US cities rose (exemplified par excellence by Manhattan), so did the rates in the regional localities. They argued that a cascading diffusion process of inner city problems of disease and disorder will move out from the large, marginalised, inner city communities within the largest municipalities, first along the national travel routes to smaller cities, and then from central cities into the surrounding, more affluent suburbs, following the pattern of daily journey to work. Public policies and economic practices which increase marginalisation ultimately act to damage 'weak ties' of the community and social networks which bind central city neighbourhoods into functioning units. The spread of disease and disorder can then be interpreted as the indices which can be used to measure the resulting social disintegration and which are driven by this policy.

Conclusion

High risk strategies of primary prevention are most effective when criminal behaviour and the occurrence of adult antisocial syndromes are effectively confined, either to isolated subgroups of the population, or in isolated populations. This chapter has demonstrated that crime is not isolated in such a manner. Although conditions such as Antisocial Personality Disorder do show some degree of geographical concentration, they are still relatively common and distributed widely. Similarly, official policies of neglect and the withdrawal of basic supports and services are based on the false premise that the ensuing widespread social problems of substance abuse, communicable diseases, crime, and other forms of accompanying social disorder can be successfully confined and contained within marginalised, minority subgroups living in inner urban areas. Both public health and public order arise from intact personal, community, and domestic social networks that are dependent upon stable socioeconomic and physical circumstances. The population approach to prevention must therefore involve measures that maintain and stabilise social and economic conditions within communities. Such interventions are clearly the responsibility of policy-makers rather than the academics or professionals who are likely to be involved in a targeted intervention strategy. Within this context, the role of the academic is limited to influencing the policy-makers' decisions.

Rose (1992) pointed out that both the public and politicians may be highly ambivalent towards 'experts' and advisors. Experts may be trusted because they know a lot and can speak with authority, but they can also be mistrusted because they may confuse their technical authority with a right to decide what is best. Rose cautioned against experts who bring their personal views to advice on public issues. He proposed a practical approach to advising policy-makers and helping them in their decision making. First, it is necessary to advise more narrowly on scientific issues and to identify to what extent the risk factor is a cause of the problem to be prevented. It is then necessary to advise on how reversible is the risk. Second, it is necessary to advise on operational issues, for example by how much can the risk distribution within the population actually be changed and, if the intention is to change the distribution, what are the resource needs and costs? Finally, it is necessary to advise how much of the total benefit is actually realisable. It may be necessary to construct a balance sheet setting out the best estimates of gains and losses, identifying and quantifying each item which needs to be taken into account, and assigning to each some measure of its uncertainty.

This chapter has highlighted the importance of both income inequality and the concentration of various forms of social deprivation in specific locations. When advising policy-makers, it is important to identify the negative costs of not intervening. As Kawachi and Kennedy (1997) have argued, income inequality induces 'spill-over' effects on quality of life, even for people who are not normally affected by material wants. Wide income disparities can result in frustration, stress, and family disruption, which then increase rates of crime and violence (Wilkinson, 1996). Those who can afford to will feel increasingly impelled to isolate themselves in secure environments away from the underclass. The resulting middle-class outward migration from poor neighbourhoods can result in progressive deterioration of the public education system and the erosion of support for local schools. Wide income disparities tend to co-exist with under-investment in human capital, measured in a variety of ways, including high rates of drop-out from school, reduced public spending on education, and lower literacy rates. With an increasing rise in the numbers of an underclass of poorly educated and under-skilled citizens, society must ultimately pay the cost through lower productivity and slow economic growth. In extreme cases, such as those documented in certain inner city areas, the breakdown of social cohesion brought about by income inequality can threaten the functioning of democracy. Low levels of democracy and low levels of civic trust spill over into lack of trust and confidence in government.

Direct intervention by redressing income inequality and features of social deprivation are by no means the only strategies that can be recommended to policy-makers. Rose drew attention to the importance of a range of other factors that can lead to population change. Equally, policy-makers will be quick to point out that not all countries, or urban locations, which have wide disparities in income automatically show an inclination towards crime and disorder. The importance of culture, religion, and the influence of leaders and opinion formers on young persons' behaviour may all have powerful effects. Thus, taking timely opportunity of certain fashions, or providing clear evidence of the negative influence of certain fashions on young persons' behaviour, may provide opportunities for policy-makers to intervene. But such interventions would need to be based on scientific evidence and may even then be politically unacceptable. For example, intervention by prominent persons who comment negatively on the positive portrayal of drug use by the fashion media, or the introduction of legislation to prevent sales of alcohol to persons below a certain age, are both examples which are relatively straightforward and simple in their cost-to-benefit ratio and where these benefits can potentially be observed by the majority. However, interventions in allowing the renting of violent videos to young persons may involve greater uncertainties within the available evidence, resulting in the arguments for and against the intervention becoming relatively more complex.

If population strategies are to be successfully introduced into the field of primary prevention of antisocial behaviour and adult antisocial syndromes there would need to be more effective systems of surveillance of the population than currently exist. The aim would be to monitor the shifts and trends that will ultimately lead to changes in the occurrence of both risk and protective factors that are in operation and which influence the immediate behaviour and longitudinal development of young persons. No professional discipline currently has this responsibility or can be compared with Public Health in its surveillance of communicable diseases and the noxious effects of environmental pollution. Organisational barriers can often prevent the effective service organisation that is needed. Some agencies are simply not aware that antisocial behaviour in childhood leads to high costs, as these fall on a wide range of agencies including health, education, social services, and voluntary agencies, as well as the criminal justice system, none of which are primarily responsible for antisocial behaviour.

At present, a range of different disciplines contribute to the development of prevention programmes. Most of these are high risk strategies targeted at subgroups of individuals identified through a screening process.

But questions remain over the accuracy of current screening methods. It is therefore important that future research developments do not neglect population strategies. Primary prevention could ultimately combine elements of both the high risk and the population strategy.

REFERENCES

Ambruster, P. and Fallon, T. (1994) Clinical, sociodemographic, and systems risk factors for attrition in a children's mental health clinic. *American Journal of Orthopsychiatry*, *64*, 577–85.

American Psychiatric Association (1980) *Diagnostic and Statistical Manual of Mental Disorders* (3rd ed.). Washington DC: APA.

(1994) *Diagnostic and Statistical Manual of Mental Disorders* (4th ed.). Washington DC: APA.

Aschenbach, T. M. and Edelbrock, C. S. (1981) Behavioural problems and competencies reported by parents of normal and disturbed children aged four through sixteen. *Monographs of the Society for Research in Child Development*, *46*, 1–82.

Audit Commission (1999) *Children in Mind*. London: Audit Commission.

Baldwin, J. and Bottoms, A. E. (1976) *The Urban Criminal*. Tavistock: London.

Baron, M., Gruen, R., Rainer, J. D. *et al*. (1985) A family study of schizophrenic and normal control probands: implication for the spectrum concept of schizophrenia. *American Journal of Psychiatry*, *142*, 447–55.

Bartley, M., Blane, D. and Montgomery, S. (1997) Socio-economic determinants of health: Health and the life course: Why safety nets matter. *British Medical Journal*, *314*, 1194–6.

Behrendt, C., Kendig, N., Dambita, C., Horman, J. *et al*. (1994) Voluntary testing for human immunodeficiency virus (HIV) in a prison population with a high prevalence of HIV. *American Journal of Epidemiology*, *139*, 918–26.

Bennett, K. J., Lipman, E. C., Racine, Y. and Offord, D. R. (1998) Annotation: do measures of externalising behaviour in normal populations predict later outcome? Implications for targeted interventions to prevent conduct disorder. *Journal of Child Psychology and Psychiatry*, *39*, 1059–70.

Biederman, J., Faraone, S., Keenan, K., Benjamin, J., Kritcher, B., Moore, C., Sprich, S., Ugaglia, K., Jellinck, M. S., Steingard, R., Spencer, T., Norman, D., Kiloday, R., Kraus, I., Perrin, J., Keller, M. B. and Tsuang, M. T. (1992) Further evidence for family-genetic risk factors in attention deficit hyperactivity disorder (ADHD): Patterns of comorbidity in probands and relatives in psychiatrically and pediatrically referred samples. *Archives of General Psychiatry*, *49*, 728–38.

Bland, R. C., Newman, S. C. and Orn, H. (1988a) Age of onset of psychiatric disorders. *Acta Psychiatrica Scandinavica*, *77* (suppl. 338), 43–9.

(1998b) Lifetime prevalence of psychiatric disorders in Edmonton. *Acta Psychiatrica Scandinavica*, *77* (suppl. 338), 24–32.

Blumstein, A. and Cohen, J. (1987) Characterising criminal careers. *Science*, *237*, 985–91.

Bottoms, A. E. and Wiles, P. (1997) Environmental criminology. In Maguire, M., Morgan, M. and Reiner, R. (eds.) *The Oxford Handbook of Criminology* (2nd ed.) Oxford: Clarendon Press.

Bourgois, P. (1995) *In Search of Respect: Selling Crack in El Barrio*. Cambridge: Cambridge University Press.

Brewer, T. F. and Derrickson, J. (1992) AIDS in prison: A review of epidemiology and preventive policy. *AIDS, 6*, 623–38.

Brown, S. A., Gleghorn, A., Schuckit, M. A., Myers, M. G. and Mott, M. A. (1996) Conduct disorder among adolescent alcohol and drug abusers. *Journal of Studies on Alcohol, 57*, 314–24.

Brunner, E. (1997) Socio-economic determinants of health: Stress and the biology of inequality. *British Medical Journal, 314*, 1472–6.

Campbell, S. B. (1995) Behaviour problems in preschool children: A review of recent research. *Journal of Child Psychology and Psychiatry, 36*, 113–49.

Chen, C., Wong, J., Lee, N. *et al.* (1993) The Shatin community mental health survey in Hong Kong II: Major findings. *Archives of General Psychiatry, 50*, 125–33.

Christian, R. E., Frick, P. J., Hill, N. L., Tyler, L. and Frazer, D. (1997) Psychopathy and conduct problems in children, II: Implications for subtyping children with conduct problems. *Journal of the American Academy of Child and Adolescent Psychiatry, 36*, 233–41.

Coid, J. W. (1996) Psychopathology in psychopaths: A study of diagnostic comorbidity and aetiology. MD thesis. University of London.

(1998) The management of dangerous psychopathy in prison. In Millon, T., Simonsen, E., Birket-Smith, M. and Davis, R. D. (eds.) *Psychopathy. Antisocial, Criminal, and Violent Behaviour*. New York: Guilford Press pp. 431–57.

Coie, J. (1996) Prevention of violence and antisocial behaviour. In R. Der Peters and R. J. McMahon (eds.) *Preventing Childhood Disorders, Substance Abuse and Delinquency*. New York: Sage, pp. 1–18.

Compton, W. M., Helzer, J. E., Hwu H.-G. *et al.* (1991) New methods in cross-cultural psychiatry: Psychiatric illness in Taiwan and the United States. *American Journal of Psychiatry, 148*, 1697–704.

Cote, G. and Hodgins, S. (1990) Co-occurring mental disorders among criminal offenders. *Bulletin of the American Academy of Psychiatry and the Law, 18*, 271–81.

Crawford, C. A. (1994, November) Health care needs in corrections: NIJ responds. *National Institute of Justice Journal*, 31–8.

Crutchfield, R. G., Geerken, M. and Gove, W. (1982) Crime rates and social integration: The impact of metropolitan mobility. *Criminology, 20*, 467–78.

DiLalla, L. F. and Gottesman, I. I. (1989) Heterogeneity of causes for delinquency and criminality: Lifespan perspectives. *Development and Psychopathology, 1*, 339–49.

Dinges, N., Atlis, M. M. and Vincent, G. M. (1997) Cross-cultural perspectives on antisocial behavior. In D. M. Stoff and J. Breiling (eds.) *Handbook of Antisocial Behavior*. New York: Wiley, pp. 474–95.

Dixon, P. S., Flanigan, T. O., DeBuono, B. A., Lavrie, J. J. *et al.* (1993) Infection with human immunodeficiency virus in prisoners: Meeting the health care challenge. *American Journal of Medicine, 95*, 629–35.

Dolan, B. and Coid, J. (1993) Psychopathic and antisocial personality disorders. *Treatment and Research Issues*. London: Gaskell.

Donovan, J. and Jessor, R. (1985) Structure of problem behaviour in adolescence and young adulthood. *Journal of Consulting and Clinical Psychology*, *53*, 890–904.

Faraone, S., Biederman, J., Keenan, K. and Tsuang, M. T. (1991) Separation of DSM-III attention deficit disorder and conduct disorder: Evidence from a family-genetic study of American child psychiatric patients. *Psychological Medicine*, *21*, 109–21.

Faraone, S. V., Biederman, J., Mennin, D., Russell, R. and Tsuang, M. T. (1998) Familial subtypes of Attention Deficit Hyperactivity Disorder: A 4-year follow-up study of children from Antisocial-ADHD families. *Journal of Child Psychology and Psychiatry*, *39*, 1045–53.

Farrington, D. P. (1983) Offending from 10 to 25 years of age. In Van Dusen, K. T. and Mednick, S. A. (eds.) *Prospective Studies of Crime and Delinquency*. The Hague: Kluwer-Nijhoff.

The development of offending and antisocial behaviour from childhood: key findings from the Cambridge Study in Delinquent Development. *Journal of Child Psychology and Psychiatry*, *360*, 929–64.

Farrington, D. P., Ohlin, C. E. and Wilson, J. Q. (1986) *Understanding and Controlling Crime: Toward a New Research Strategy*. New York: Springer-Verlag.

Frick, P., O'Brien, B., Woolton, J. and McBurnett, K. (1994) Psychopathy and conduct problems in children. *Journal of Abnormal Psychology*, *103*, 700–7.

Fullilove, M. T. (1996) Psychiatric implications of displacement: contributions from the psychology of place. *American Journal of Psychiatry*, *153*, 1516–23.

Fullilove, M. T. and Fullilove, R. E. (1989) Intersecting epidemics: Black teen crack use and sexually transmitted disease. *Journal of the American Medical Women's Association*, *44*, 146–56.

Fullilove, R. E., Fullilove, M. T., Bowser, B. P. and Gross, S. A. (1990) Risk of sexually transmitted disease among black adolescent crack users in Oakland and San Francisco. *Journal of the American Medical Association*, *263*, 851–5.

Gibbs, J. J. and Shelly, P. L. (1982) Life in the fast lane: A retrospective view of commercial thieves. *Journal of Research in Crime and Delinquency*, *19*, 299–330.

Gill, O. (1967) *Luke Street. Housing Policy, Conflicts and the Creation of the Delinquent Area*. London: Macmillan.

Hare, R. D. (1983) Diagnosis of antisocial personality disorder in two prison populations. *American Journal of Psychiatry*, *140*, 887–90.

(1991) *The Hare Psychopathy Checklist – Revised*. Toronto: Multi Health Systems.

Herbert, D. T. (1979) Urban crime: A geographical perspective. In *Social Problems and the City. Geographical Perspectives* (eds. D. T. Herbert and D. M. Smith). Oxford University Press.

Herbert, M. (1987) *Conduct Disorders of Childhood and Adolescence: A Social Learning Perspective* (2nd ed.). Chichester: John Wiley.

Hesselbrock, M. N. (1986) Childhood behaviour problems and adult antisocial personality disorder in alcoholism. In *Psychopathology and Addictive Disorders* (ed. R. E. Myer). New York: The Guilford Press.

Hindelang, M. J. (1971) The social versus solitary nature of delinquent involvements. *British Journal of Criminology, 11*, 167–75.

Hinshaw, S. P., Lahey, B. B. and Hart, E. L. (1993) Issues of taxonomy and comorbidity in the development of conduct disorder. *Development and Psychopathology, 5*, 31–50.

Hirschi, T. and Gottfredson, M. (1983) Age and the explanation of crime. *American Journal of Sociology, 89*, 552–84.

Hodgins, S. and Cote, G. (1990) Prevalence of mental disorders among penitentiary inmates in Quebec. *Canada*'s *Mental health.* 1–4.

Hodgins, S., Cote, G. and Toupin, J. (1998) Major mental disorders and crime: An aetiological hypothesis. In Cooke, D., Forth, A., Hare, R. D. (eds.) *Psychopathy: Theory, Research and Implications for Society*. Dordrecht, The Netherlands: Kluwer pp. 231–56.

Home Office (1996) *Criminal Statistics. England and Wales 1995*. London HMSO. Cm 3421.

Hwu, H. F., Yeh, E. K. and Chang, L. Y. (1989) Prevalence of psychiatric disorders in Taiwan defined by the Chinese Diagnostic Interview Schedule. *Acta Psychiatrica Scandinavia, 79*, 136–47.

Inciardi, J. A. (1995) Crack, crack house sex, and HIV risk. *Archives of Sexual Behaviour, 24*, 249–69.

Institute of Medicine (1989) *Research on Children and Adolescents with Mental, Behavioural and Development Disorders*. Washington, DC: National Academic Press.

(1994) *Reducing Risks for Mental Disorder: Frontiers for a Preventive Intervention Research*. Washington, DC: National Academy Press.

Jordan, B. K., Schlenger, W. E., Fairbank, J. A. and Caddell, J. M. (1996) Prevalence of psychiatric disorders among incarcerated women. II. Convicted Felons Entering Prison. *Archives of General Psychiatry, 53*, 513–19.

Kawachi, I. and Kennedy, B. P. (1997) Socio-economic determinants of health: Health and social cohesion: Why care about income inequality? *British Medical Journal, 314*, 1037–40.

Kazdin, A. E. (1987) Treatment of antisocial behaviour in children: Current status and future directions. *Psychological Bulletin, 102*, 187–203.

(1996) Dropping out of child psychotherapy: Issues for research and implications for practice. *Clinical Child Psychology and Psychiatry, 1*, 133–56.

Koegel, P., Burman, A. and Farr, R. K. (1988) The prevalence of specific psychiatric disorders among homeless individuals in the inner city of Los Angeles. *Archives of General Psychiatry, 45*, 1085–92.

Kratzer, L. and Hodgins, S. (1999) A typology of offenders: a test of Moffitt's theory among males and females from childhood to age 30. *Criminal Behaviour and Mental Health, 9*, 57–73.

Lahey, B. B., Loeber, R., Quay, H., Applegate, B., Shaffer, D., Waldman, I., Hart, E., McBurnett, K., Frick, P. J., Jensen, P. S., Dulcan, M. K., Canino, G. and Bird, H. R.(1998) Validity of DSM-IV subtypes of conduct disorder based on age of onset. *Journal of the American Academy of Child & Adolescent Psychiatry, 37*, 435–42.

Lahey, B. B., Waldman, I. D. and McBurnett, K. (1999) Annotation: The development of antisocial behaviour: an integrative causal model. *Journal of Child Psychology and Psychiatry, 40*, 669–82.

Langan, P. A. and Farrington, D. P. (1983) Two-track or one-track justice? Some evidence from an English longitudinal survey. *Journal of Criminal Law and Criminology, 74*, 519–46.

Langan, P. A. and Greenfeld, L. A. (1983) *Career Patterns in Crime. Bureau of Criminal Statistic Special Report NCJ-88672*. Washington, DC: Bureau of Justice Statistics.

LeBlanc, M. and Frechette, M. (1989) *Male Criminal Activity from Childhood through Youth. Multilevel and Developmental Perspectives*. New York: Springer-Verlag.

Lee, C. K., Kwak, Y. S., Yamamoto, J. *et al.* (1990) Psychiatric epidemiology in Korea Part I: Gender and age differences in Seoul. *Journal of Nervous and Mental Disease, 178*, 242–52.

Levar, I., Kohn, R., Dohrenwen, B. P. *et al.* (1993) An epidemiological study of mental disorders in a 10-year cohort of young adults in Israel. *Psychological Medicine, 23*, 691–707.

Loeber, R. (1982) The stability of antisocial and delinquent child behaviour: A review. *Child Development, 53*, 1431–46.

(1988) Natural histories of conduct problems, delinquency and associated substance use: Evidence for developmental progressions. In Lahey, B. B. and Kazdin, A. E. (eds.) *Advances in Clinical Child Psychology* Vol. 11. New York: Plenum Press.

(1990) Development and risk factors of juvenile antisocial behaviour and delinquency. *Clinical Psychology Review, 10*, 1–14.

Loeber, R., Lahey, B. B. and Thomas, C. (1991) Diagnostic conundrum of oppositional defiant disorder and conduct disorder. *Journal of Abnormal Psychology, 100*, 379–90.

Lynam, D. R. (1996) Early identification of chronic offenders: Who is the fledgling psychopath? *Psychological Bulletin, 120*, 209–34.

McCabe, K. M., Hough, R., Wood, P. A. and Yeh, M. (2001) Childhood and adolescent onset conduct disorder: a test of the developmental taxonomy. *Journal of Abnormal Child Psychology, 29*, 305–16.

Meltzer, H., Gatward, R., Goodman, R. and Ford, T. (2000) *Mental Health of Children and Adolescents in Great Britain*. London: The Stationery Office.

Moffitt, T. E. (1993) Adolescence – limited and life- course – persistent antisocial behaviour: A developmental taxonomy. *Psychological Review, 100*, 674–701.

(1994) Natural histories of delinquency. In Weitekamp, E. G. M. and Kerner, H.-J. (eds.) *Cross-national Longitudinal Research on Human Development and Criminal Behaviour*. The Netherlands: Kluwer Academic Publishers, pp. 3–61.

Monahan, J., Steadman, H. J., Silver, E., Appelbaum, P. S., Robbins, P. C., Mulvey, E. P., Roth, L. H., Grisso, T. and Banks, S. (2001) *Rethinking*

Risk Assessment. The Macarthur Study of Mental Disorder and Violence. Oxford University Press.

Nagin, D. S. and Land, K. C. (1993) Age, criminal careers, and population heterogeneity: Specification and estimation of a non-parametric, mixed poisson model. *Criminology*, *31*, 327–62.

Nagin, D. S. and Tremblay, R. E. (2001) Parental and early childhood predictors of persistent physical aggression in boys from kindergarten to high school. *Archives of General Psychiatry*, *58*, 389–94.

National Centre for Education Statistics (1995) The pocket edition of education 1995 (NCES 95–817). Washington, DC: US Department of Education.

Osgood, D., Johnston, L., O'Malley, P. and Bachman, J. (1988) The generality of deviance in late adolescence and early adulthood. *American Sociological Review*, *53*, 81.

Patterson, G. R. (1986) Performance models for antisocial boys. *American Psychologist*, *41*, 432–44.

Patterson, G. R., Capaldi, D. and Bank, C. (1991) An early starter model for predicting delinquency. In Pepler, D. J. and Rubin, K. H. (eds.) *The Development and Treatment of Childhood Aggression*. Hillsdale, NJ: Lawrence Erlbaum.

Petersilia, J., Greenwood, P. W. and Lavin, M. (1978) *Criminal Careers of Habitual Felons*. Washington, DC: US Government Printing Office.

Peterson, M. A. and Braiker, H. B. (1980) *Doing Crime: A Survey of California Prison Inmates*. Santa Monica, CA: RAND.

Regier, D. A., Boyd, J. H., Burke, J. D. *et al.* (1988) One-month prevalence of mental disorders in the United States. *Archives of General Psychiatry*, *45*, 977–86.

Reich, J., Boerstler, H., Yates, W. *et al.* (1989) Utilisation of medical resources in persons with DSM-III personality disorders in a community sample. *International Journal of Psychiatry in Medicine*, *19*, 1–9.

Reid, J. B. and Patterson, G. R. (1995) Early prevention and intervention with conduct problems: A social international model for the integration of research and practice. In G. Stoner, M. R. Shian and H. M. Walker. *Interventions for Achievement and Behaviour Problem*. Silver Spring, MD: The National Association of School Psychologists.

Reid, J. B. (1993) Prevention of conduct disorder before and after school entry: Relating interventions to developmental findings. *Development and Psychopathology*, *5*, 243–62.

Rex, J. and Moore, R. (1967) *Race, Community and Conflict: A Study of Sparkbrook*. London: Oxford University Press for the Institute of Race Relations.

Roberts, H. (1997) Socio-economic determinants of health: Children, inequalities, and health. *British Medical Journal*, *314*, 1122–5.

Robertson, R. G. (1987) The female offender: A Canadian study. *Canadian Journal of Psychiatry*, *32*, 749–55.

Robins, L. N. (1966) *Deviant Children Grown Up: A Sociological and Psychiatric Study of Sociopathic Personality*. Baltimore: Williams and Wilkins.

(1970) Follow-up studies of childhood conduct disorder. In E. H. Hare and J. K. Wing (eds.) *Psychiatric Epidemiology*. Baltimore: Williams and Wilkins.

(1978) Sturdy childhood predictors of adult antisocial behaviour: Replications from longitudinal studies. *Psychological Medicine*, *8*, 611–22.

(1981) Epidemiological approaches to natural history research: Antisocial disorders in children. *Journal of the American Academy of Child Psychiatry*, *20*, 556–80.

(1985) Epidemiology of antisocial personality. In *Psychiatry*. 3 (19) 1–14.

(1986) The consequences of conduct disorders in girls. In *Development of Antisocial and Prosocial Behaviour. Research, Theories and Issues*. (eds. D. Olweus, J. Block and M. Radke-Yarrow). Orlando: Academic Press.

Robins, L. N., Helzer, J. E., Croughan, J. *et al*. (1981) National Institute of Mental Health Diagnostic interview schedule: Its history, characteristics and validity. *Archives of General Psychiatry*, *39*, 381–9.

(1991) NIMH Diagnostic interview schedule. *Archives of General Psychiatry*, *38*, 381–9.

Robins, L. N., Helzer, J. E., Weissman, M. M. *et al*. (1984) Lifetime prevalence of specific psychiatric disorders in Three Sites. *Archives of General Psychiatry*, *41*, 949–58.

Robins, L. N. and McEvoy, L. T. (1990) Conduct problems as predictors of substance abuse. In *Straight and Devious Pathways to Adulthood* (eds. L. N. Robins and M. R. Rutter). Cambridge University Press.

Robins, L. N. and Price, R. K. (1991) Adult disorders predicted by childhood conduct problems: results from the NIMH Epidemiological Catchment Area Project. *Psychiatry*, *54*, 116–32.

Robins, L. N. and Regier, D. A. (1991) *Psychiatric Disorder in America. The ECA Study*. New York: Free Press.

Rose, G. (1981) Strategy of prevention: Lessons from cardiovascular disease. *British Medical Journal*, *282*, 1847–51.

(1992) *The Strategy of Preventive Medicine*. Oxford University Press.

Ross, H. E. (1995) DSM-II-R alcohol abuse and dependence and psychiatric comorbidity in Ontario: Results from the Mental Health Supplement to the Ontario Health Survey. *Drug and Alcohol Dependence*, *39*, 111–28.

Rutter, M. (1996) Concepts of antisocial behaviour, of cause, and of genetic influences. In Bock, G. R. and Goode, J. A. (eds.) *Genetics of Criminal and Antisocial Behaviour*. New York: Wiley, pp. 1–15.

Rutter, M., Cox, A., Tupling, C. *et al*. (1975) Attainment and adjustment in two geographical areas: I. The prevalence of psychiatric disorder. *British Journal of Psychiatry*, *126*, 493–509.

Rutter, M. and Giller, H. (1983) *Juvenile Delinquency: Trends and Perspectives*. Harmondsworth: Penguin.

Rutter, M., Giller, H. and Hagell, A. (1998) *Antisocial Behaviour by Young People*. Cambridge University Press.

Rutter, M., Yule, W., Berger, E. *et al*. (1974) Children of West Indian immigrants: I. Rates of behavioural deviance and of psychiatric disorder. *Journal of Child Psychology and Psychiatry*, *15*, 241–6.

Rydelius, P. A. (1988) The development of antisocial behavioural and sudden violent death. *Acta Psychiatrica Scandinavica*, *77*, 398–403.

Shamsie, J. and Hluchy, C. (1991) Youth with conduct disorder: a challenge to be met. *Canadian Journal of Psychiatry*, *36*, 405–14.

Shannon, L. W. (1978) A longitudinal study of delinquency and crime. In *Quantitative Studies in Criminology* (ed. C. Welford) Beverly Hills, CA: Sage Publications.

Shaw, C. R. and McKay, H. D. (1942) *Juvenile Delinquency and Urban Areas.* Chicago University Press.

Singleton, N., Meltzer, H., Gatward, R., Coid, J. and Deasy, D. (1998) *Psychiatric Morbidity among Prisoners in England and Wales.* London: The Stationery Office.

Smith, D. R., Smith, W. and Noma, E. (1984) Delinquent career-lines: A conceptual link between theory and juvenile offences. *Sociological Quarterly, 25,* 155–72.

South, S. (1987) Metropolitan migration and social problems. *Social Science Quarterly, 68,* 3–18.

Stattin, M. and Magnusson, D. (1991) Stability and change in criminal behaviour up to age 30. *British Journal of Criminology, 31,* 327–45.

Taylor, J., Iacono, W. G. and McGue, M. (2000) Evidence for a genetic etiology of early-onset delinquency. *Journal of Abnormal Psychology, 109,* 434–643.

Teplin, L. A., Abram, K. M. and McClelland, G. (1996) Prevalence of psychiatric disorders among incarcerated women. I. Practical jail detainees. *Archives of General Psychiatry, 53,* 505–12.

Tolan, P. H. (1987) Implications of age of onset for delinquency risk. *Journal of Abnormal Child Psychology, 15,* 47–65.

Tomasson, K. and Vaglum, P. (1995) A nationwide representative sample of treatment seeking alcoholics: A study of psychiatric morbidity. *Acta Psychiatrica Scandinavica, 92,* 378–85.

Wallace, R. (1988) A synergism of plagues: "Planned shrinkage", contagious housing destruction, and AIDS in the Bronx. *Environmental Research, 47,* 1–33.

Wallace, R., Fullilove, M. T. and Wallace, D. (1992) Family systems and deurbanization: implications for substance abuse. In *Substance Abuse. A Comprehensive Textbook.* Eds. J. Lowinson, R. Ruiz and R. Millman. Baltimore. Williams & Wilkins, pp. 944–55.

Wallace, R. and Wallace, D. (1997) Socio-economic determinants of health: Community marginalisation and the diffusion of disease and disorder in the United States. *British Medical Journal, 314,* 1341–5.

Wallace, R., Wallace, D., Andrews, H., Fullilove, R. and Fullilove, M. T. (1995) The spatiotemporal dynamics of AIDS and TB in the New York metropolitan region from a sociodemographic perspective: Understanding the linkages of central city and suburbs. *Environment and Planning, 27,* 1085–108.

Walters, G. D. (1990) *The Criminal Lifestyle. Patterns of Serious Criminal Conduct.* Newbury Park, CA: Sage Publications.

Weissman, M. M. and Myers, J. K. (1998) Psychiatric disorders in a US community. *Acta Psychiatrica Scandinavica, 62,* 99–111.

Wells, E. J. Bushnell, J. A., Hornblow, J. *et al.* (1989) Christchurch psychiatric epidemiology study, part I: Methodology and lifetime prevalence for specific psychiatric disorders. *Australian and New Zealand Journal of Psychiatry, 23,* 315–26.

Werner, E. E. (1982) *Vulnerable But Invincible: A Longitudinal Study of Resilient Children and Youth*. New York: McGraw Hill.

Werner, E. E. (1985) Stress and protective factors in childrens' lives. In *Longitudinal Studies in Child Psychology and Psychiatry* (ed. A. R. Nicol). Chichester: Wiley.

Werner, E. E., Bierman, J. M. and French, E. E. (1971) *The Children of Kauai: A Longitudinal Study from the Prenatal Period to Age Ten*. Honolulu: University of Hawaii Press.

Werner, E. E. and Smith, R. S. (1977) *Kauai's Children Come of Age*. Honolulu: University of Hawaii Press.

West, D. and Farrington, D. P. (1977) *The Delinquent Way of Life: Third Report of the Cambridge Study in Delinquent Development*. London: Heinemann.

Wilkinson, R. G. (1996) *Unhealthy Society. The Afflictions of Inequality*. London: Routledge.

Wittchen, H.-V., Robins, L. N., Cottler, L. B. *et al.* (1991) Participants in the multicentre WHO/ADAMHA field trials. Cross-cultural feasibility, reliability and sources of variance in the Composite International Diagnostic Interview (CIDI) *British Journal of Psychiatry*, *159*, 645–53.

Wolfgang, M., Figlio, R. F. and Sellin, T. (1972) *Delinquency in a Birth Cohort*. University of Chicago Press.

Yung, B. R. and Hammond, W. R. (1997) Antisocial behavior in minority groups: Epidemiological and cultural perspectives. In D. M. Stoff, J. Breiling (eds.) *Handbook of Antisocial Behavior*. New York: John Wiley, pp. 474–95.

Zimmermann, M. and Coryell, W. H. (1990) Diagnosing personality disorders in the community. *Archives of General Psychiatry*, *47*, 527–31.

3 Risk factors for adult antisocial personality

Rolf Loeber, Stephanie M. Green and Benjamin B. Lahey

Antisocial personality is a serious disorder of adulthood that is highly refractory to treatment. Indeed, its prognosis is so poor that the most viable strategy may be to focus on the eventual development of preventive interventions. Because antisocial personality clearly arises from childhood conduct problems (Robins, 1966), researchers have long sought to specify the characteristics of those children who will later develop antisocial personality. When this is accomplished, the etiology of antisocial personality can be studied at the time of its earliest emergence and preventive interventions can be developed. Currently however, there are serious gaps in our knowledge about the childhood origins of antisocial personality.

There are several diagnoses that have been implicated in the development of Antisocial Personality Disorder (APD) (or ASPD sometimes) (American Psychiatric Association, 1994), including Conduct Disorder (CD), Oppositional Defiant Disorder (ODD), and Attention Deficit-Hyperactivity Disorder (ADHD). The essential features of CD are a repetitive and persistent pattern of behaviour in which the basic rights of others and major age-appropriate societal norms or rules are violated. ODD is a recurrent pattern of negativistic, defiant, disobedient, and hostile behaviour toward authority figures, which leads to impairment. The most important features of ADHD are overactivity, impulsivity, and attention problems at levels atypical for a child's age.

Although most evidence suggests that CD always precedes Antisocial Personality Disorder (American Psychiatric Association, 1994), some evidence suggests that antisocial personality often arises in individuals with a history of Attention-Deficit Hyperactivity Disorder (ADHD) during childhood, instead of CD. We will address this important controversy by examining whether CD and/or ADHD is the necessary developmental precursor to antisocial personality.

Even if the hypothesis that CD is a necessary stage in the development of antisocial personality is accurate, however, much remains to be learned before one can predict accurately *which* children with CD will develop antisocial personality. Studies show that only about 30–40 per cent of children with CD develop antisocial personality (Robins, 1966, 1991; Robins, Tipp, and Przybeck, 1991), but the quality of current data about exactly which children with CD develop antisocial personality is not strong.

The following are some key issues to be considered in this context:

a. Is the age of onset of CD-symptoms earlier in those children who advance from CD to antisocial personality compared to those CD youth who do not progress to APD?
b. What are important interactive relationships among variables? For example, although we hypothesise that ADHD is not a precursor of antisocial personality by itself, we posit that ADHD increases the risk of antisocial personality when it co-occurs with CD.
c. Among boys who eventually qualify for antisocial personality, what is their family history of psychopathology and antisocial behaviour, and other distinctive risk factors such as family functioning, socioeconomic status, intelligence, peer relationships, and comorbid emotional disorders?
d. What are ways to distinguish these key variables from partially confounded variables that are false correlates of persistent CD? And what are ways to identify variables that serve as mediators or moderators of other variables for antisocial personality? For example, it may be that parental APD is a key predictor of persistent CD in children, and that harsh and inadequate parenting is the mechanism (i.e., mediator) through which parental APD increases the risk that childhood CD will persist into adult antisocial personality.
e. Are predictors of antisocial personality different from predictors of adult criminal behaviour in subjects who do not meet criteria for antisocial personality? For example, does either antisocial personality or serious adult criminal behaviour emerge often in individuals who did not previously exhibit CD (but exhibited ADHD, ODD, or other disorders instead)?

In addition, several other issues are important for our understanding of the course of antisocial personality: various definitions of the disorder, prevalence, the unfolding of symptoms over time, and models of the development of the disorder. We also need to know more about risk and protective factors for antisocial personality, comorbid conditions, and impairments in adulthood resulting from early disruptive behaviour. This chapter addresses these issues from a psychiatric point of view, and because of restrictions in the availability of studies, focuses on males only. Thus, although there are valuable papers on antisocial behaviour in adulthood (e.g., Farrington, chapter 1, this volume; Farrington, 1996; Robins and Ratcliff, 1979), we will concentrate on studies with antisocial personality as the outcome.

Definition

The characteristics of antisocial personality are well-known, but scholars have disagreed about essential features and subdimensions (Hare, Hart and Harpur, 1991; Widiger, 1992; Widiger and Corbitt, 1993), provoking the criticism that APD is 'the most controversial of all the personality disorders' (Frances, 1980, p.1053; see also Cooke, 1997). Criteria for APD according to DSM-III-R and DSM-IV, criteria for Psychopathic Personality Disorder (PPD), and criteria for Dissocial Personality Disorder according to the ICD-10 (World Health Organisation, 1992) have been summarised in Table 3.1. Briefly, DSM-III-R and DSM-IV criteria primarily capture a single factor of irresponsible and antisocial behaviour (Robins, 1966; Robins *et al.*, 1991). In contrast, Hare (Hare *et al.*, 1991), based on the criteria developed by Cleckley (1976), distinguished between two factors of Psychopathic Personality Disorder (PPD) (Hare *et al.*, 1990; Hare *et al.*, 1991; Harpur, Hare and Hakstian, 1989).

The first personality factor reflects egocentricity, callousness, and manipulativeness. The ICD-10 definition of Dissocial Personality Disorder shares many factors with APD and PPD. A second factor reflects behavioural characteristics, such as impulsivity, chronic instability, an irresponsible lifestyle, and antisocial behaviour. The two factor scores are correlated with the number of DSM-III-R CD symptoms in incarcerated juveniles (Harpur *et al.*, 1989). Although there are DSM-III-R and DSM-IV symptoms of APD in both of Hare's factors, the overlap of the second factor with the DSM definitions of APD is greater.

The definitions of APD and PPD emphasise different aspects of antisocial behaviour, with APD placing more emphasis on overt criminal acts, while the PPD definition emphasises more general personality traits. The search for the etiology of antisocial personality needs to take into account different definitions and dimensions of the construct. We will only occasionally refer further to distinctions between APD and PPD, and will mostly refer to antisocial personality to capture shared components of each.

The distinction between APD and delinquency is important. Delinquency refers to law breaking, whereas APD contains more subtle aspects of antisocial behaviour not captured in labels of delinquent activities. Further, it should be understood that only a proportion of known delinquents or CD boys progresses or eventually qualifies for APD. It is this subgroup of delinquents that is of greatest interest. The present chapter, however, concentrates on CD-symptoms (which are only partly akin to delinquent acts) as precursors to APD.

Table 3.1 *Definitions of Antisocial Personality Disorder, Psychopathic Personality Disorder, and Dissocial Personality Disorder*

Criteria for Antisocial Personality Disorder

DSM-III-R (American Psychiatric Association, 1987)	*DSM-IV* (American Psychiatric Association, 1994)
A. Current age at least 18	A. Current age at least 18
B. Evidence of conduct disorder before age 15	B. Evidence of conduct disorder onset before age 15
C. A pattern of irresponsible and antisocial behaviour since age 15, as indicated by at least four of the following:	C. A pervasive pattern of disregard for and violation of the rights of others as indicated by at least three of the following:
1. Unable to sustain consistent work behaviour	1. Failure to conform to social norms with respect to lawful behaviour
2. Fails to conform to social norms with respect to lawful behaviour	2. Deceitfulness
3. Is irritable and aggressive	3. Impulsivity or failure to plan ahead
4. Fails to honor financial obligations	4. Irritability and aggressiveness
5. Fails to plan ahead or is impulsive	5. Reckless disregard for safety of self or others
6. Has no regard for the truth	6. Consistent irresponsibility as indicated by repeated failure to sustain consistent work behaviour or honour financial obligations
7. Is reckless regarding his or her own or others' personal safety	7. Lacks of remorse
8. If parent, lacks ability to function as a responsible parent	
9. Has never sustained a totally monogamous relationship for more than one year	
10. Lacks remorse	

Criteria for Psychopathic Personality Disorder (Hare, Hart and Harpur, 1991)

Factor 1: callous, selfish, remorseless use of others	Factor 2: chronically unstable and antisocial lifestyle
1. Glib and superficial	6. Early behaviour problems
2. Inflated and arrogant self-appraisal	7. Adult antisocial behaviour
3. Lacks remorse	8. Impulsive
4. Lacks empathy	9. Poor behavioural controls
5. Deceitful and manipulative	10. Irresponsible

Criteria for Dissocial Personality Disorder according to ICD-10 (World Health Organisation, 1992)

Dissocial personality disorder is defined as 'usually coming to the attention of gross disparity between behaviour and the prevailing social norms'. It is characterised by:

1. Callous unconcern for the feelings of others
2. Gross and persistent attitude of irresponsibilty and disregard for social norms, rules and obligations
3. Incapacity to maintain enduring relationships, though having no difficulty establishing them
4. Very low tolerance to frustration and a low threshold for discharge of aggression, including violence
5. incapacity to experience guilt and to profit from experience, particularly punishment
6. Marked proneness to blame others, or to offer plausible rationalisations, for the behaviour that has brought the patient into conflict with society.

Conduct disorder during childhood and adolescence, though not invariably present, may further support the diagnosis.

Prevalence

According to the Epidemiologic Catchment Area study, the one-year prevalence of APD is 3.8 per cent for 18–29-year-old males (Robins *et al.*, 1991). A large survey in Edmonton, Canada, showed life-time prevalence rates of 6.5 per cent for males and 0.8 per cent for females (Swanson, Bland and Newman, 1994), which is close to 5.7 per cent and 0.6 per cent for males and females, respectively, reported in a New Zealand study (Newman *et al.*, 1996). Given these modest base rates, the etiology of antisocial personality can best be studied either in very large community samples or in samples of subjects who carry many of the risk factors for antisocial personality, as is the case for clinic-referred boys with disruptive behaviour disorders (see below).

The prevalence of APD is higher among known delinquents than among nondelinquents (e.g., Patrick, Zempolich and Levenston, 1997), which is partly due to overlapping criteria. However, only a modest proportion of known delinquents qualify for a diagnosis of APD. For example, Patrick *et al.* (1997) reported that only 15.3 per cent of adult incarcerated offenders scored high on the construct of psychopathy.

The unfolding of symptoms over time

We view the development of antisocial personality as the culmination of the gradual hierarchical unfolding of disruptive symptoms along a dimension of less to more serious behaviours. We hypothesise that the earliest manifestations of disruptive behaviour are ODD symptoms, followed by CD symptoms, with the onset of moderately serious CD symptoms (such as lying or truancy) occurring prior to the onset of advanced CD symptoms, including robbery, burglary, assault with a weapon, and rape (Lahey and Loeber, 1994; Loeber, Green *et al.*, 1992; Loeber, Keenan *et al.*, 1997; Loeber, DeLamatre *et al.*, 1998; Loeber, Wung *et al.*, 1993). Boys with advanced CD are very likely to have gone through earlier stages of less serious CD-symptoms (e.g., truancy, frequent lying) (Robins and Wish, 1977). Some symptoms of antisocial personality (such as 'impulsivity', 'shallow emotions', and 'lacks empathy') are thought to emerge in part during childhood, and continue to develop during adolescence (Frick, O'Brien, Wootton and McBurnett, 1994) and early adulthood. Some of the antisocial personality symptoms, unlike those of ODD or CD, only become developmentally relevant from adulthood onward ('unable to sustain consistent work behaviour,' and 'unable to sustain a monogamous relation for more than one year'). Typically, studies of ODD, CD and antisocial personality have not sufficiently employed a developmental model integrating these disorders.

The succession of symptoms described above tends to persist over time. For example, evidence has been mounting on the continuity of delinquent

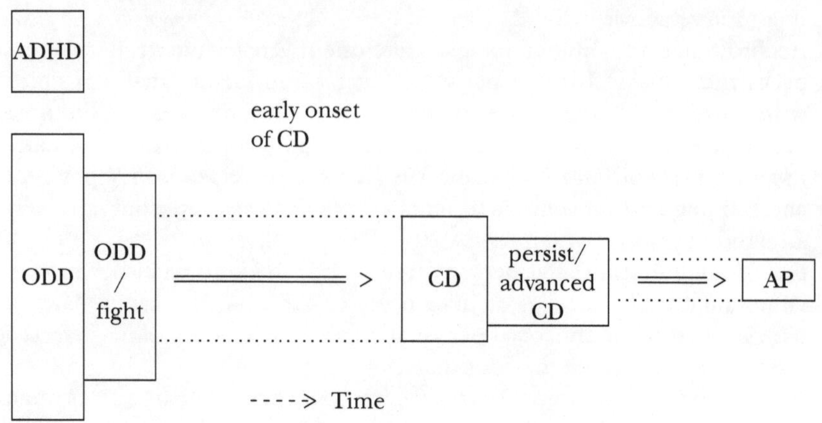

Note: The size of each bar indicates the relative prevalence of a disorder. ADHD = Attention Deficit-Hyperactivity Disorder; ODD = Oppositional Defiant Disorder; CD = Conduct Disorder; AP = Antisocial Personality.

Figure 3.1. A hierarchical developmental model of ADHD, ODD, CD, and AP

behaviours (Blumstein, Cohen, Roth and Visher, 1986; Loeber, 1982; Sampson and Laub, 1993) and aggression (Olweus, 1979). Moreover, Loeber (1988b) proposed that, instead of one disruptive symptom replacing another symptom, heterotypic continuity occurs primarily in that new problem symptoms are added to existing ones, gradually leading to a diversification of problem behaviour. What type of model can best fit both diversification and persistence of disruptive behaviours over time?

Developmental models of antisocial personality

There are several ways to conceptualise the development of antisocial personality. One model can be described as a *hierarchical developmental model* (Figure 3.1), in which a relatively large proportion of boys experience the onset of ODD earlier in life, but from this group only a proportion (particularly those who have ODD and who physically fight) escalate to conduct problems and eventually qualify for CD. Out of the latter group, only a subgroup of those with CD will progress further to antisocial personality. In this model, a distinction can be made between those subjects who experience the onset of a behaviour but after a relatively short interval desist, and those who continue after onset to display the problems. This feature of the model helps to account for the fact that many boys at one time or another display some conduct problems, but only a proportion eventually qualify for a diagnosis of CD *and* persist in the behaviours over time. ADHD also enters into this model, but is primarily associated with an early onset of ODD and CD. Therefore, onset and persistence are key parameters in the hierarchical model. Another crucial feature of the model is that a *dependent variable* in one stage of the model (e.g., CD) can become an *independent variable* to predict another outcome such as antisocial personality at another stage of the model.

The hierarchical model can be contrasted with a *de novo entry model* in which individuals become affected with antisocial personality over time without having experienced the earlier onset of ODD or CD. Of course, it is quite possible that a combination of the two models would best explain longitudinal data. One way to evaluate this is to examine conditional probabilities between successive disruptive disorders. The hierarchical model would best apply when most of those boys developing CD had manifested ODD earlier in life. In the Developmental Trends Study of a clinic-referred sample of 177 boys at two sites, we found that over 90 per cent of boys who met criteria for CD met criteria for ODD at an earlier age. A similar issue can be addressed by examining the proportion of adults with antisocial personality who qualified earlier in life for a diagnosis of CD. Judging from Robins' work (1966, 1986), almost all individuals with adult antisocial personality had qualified for a diagnosis of CD earlier in life.

A crucial question remains, however, regarding the proportion of boys with CD who develop antisocial personality. Robins (1978), summarising her studies, showed that only about a third of the youth with CD later developed APD. The percentage was somewhat higher (40 per cent) in an English sample of boys who had been reared away from home (Zoccolillo *et al.*, 1992).

We reviewed existing retrospective and prospective studies of the prediction of adult APD from childhood CD in males. We were able to calculate the relative risk of APD in males with and without childhood CD from five independent studies (Harrington, Fudge, Rutter, Pickles and Hill, 1991; Robins, 1966; Robins and Ratcliff, 1979; Robins *et al.*, 1991; Zoccolillo *et al.*, 1992). The relative risks ranged from 3.2 to 18.0, and when combined in meta-analytic fashion across differing definitions of disorder and design, but weighting for sample size, the overall estimate of relative risk was 16.8 for the prediction of CD from APD. Specifically, 1.7 per cent of individuals without a history of CD were given the diagnosis of APD in adulthood across studies compared to 28.5 per cent of individuals with a history of childhood CD. This very high relative risk for predicting APD from childhood CD is consistent with the DSM-IV view that few individuals will meet adult criteria for APD without exhibiting at least three symptoms of CD in childhood.

Against this background of findings on the continuity of disruptive behaviour over time, we should consider two other important aspects that remain to be investigated. Previous studies have rarely addressed the 'true' continuity between disruptive behaviours (Lahey *et al.*, 1995; Loeber, 1991). Continuity often occurs against the background of short-term fluctuations in the severity of the disorder. This is often lost in empirical studies limited to only two assessments. In our own work in the Developmental Trends Study (Lahey *et al.*, 1995), we found that in many boys the number of CD-symptoms fluctuated above and below the diagnostic threshold from year to year, but remained relatively high. Among boys with CD in Year 1 of the study, 88 per cent met criteria again for CD in one or more of the next three assessment years, and 54 per cent met criteria again for CD in two or more subsequent years. Thus, the continuity of CD can be seen to be substantially greater when more frequent assessments are conducted, because a substantial proportion of boys who did not qualify for CD at one follow-up assessment, do so in one or more subsequent assessments. We expect that this also would apply to the assessment of antisocial personality.

Finally, it should be kept in mind that antisocial personality may not be a homogeneous disorder, and its possible heterogeneity may require different predictive models.

Developmental conceptualisations

We propose that the most promising developmental model of antisocial personality is a hierarchical model of the heterotypic development of problem behaviour from early oppositional behaviour to antisocial personality in adulthood in which symptoms of antisocial personality and symptoms of CD develop concurrently and synergistically. A central concept in our model is the transition toward more serious behaviour over time, characterised by the onset of more or less distinct stages of deviant development. As part of our model, we postulate the following testable hypotheses:

a. ODD increases the probability of the onset of CD (especially when ODD is accompanied by physical fighting, see below), but ODD is only a precursor of antisocial personality if it first leads to CD.
b. ADHD is associated with an earlier age of onset of CD, but ADHD without comorbid ODD rarely leads to CD, and ADHD without CD is unlikely to lead to adult antisocial personality. However, it should be recognised that ADHD consists of quite varied sets of symptoms – hyperactivity, impulsivity, and attention problems. It is likely that some

of these symptoms, particularly impulsivity, contribute to later antisocial personality.

c. Boys with an early onset of CD, boys who have progressed to the most developmentally advanced level of CD (such as robbery, rape, assault with a weapon) during childhood, and boys who have more persistent CD during childhood and adolescence, are at markedly greater risk of developing antisocial personality than other boys with CD. A retrospective study on a prison population lends some support for this. Vitelli (1997) found that 94.7 per cent of the early starters (defined as a first arrest by age 14) qualified for a diagnosis of APD compared to 73.1 per cent for the late starters. There is an obvious need to replicate this finding with a prospective, normative sample.

Which early manifestations?

Which early manifestations of problem behaviours can help to identify boys who are most prone to make transitions to APD? We will consider ADHD, physical aggression, early symptoms of APD, and the number of CD-symptoms.

ADHD We conceptualise two important questions regarding the role of ADHD in the genesis of antisocial personality. First, does ADHD by itself (in the absence of comorbid CD in childhood) increase the risk of antisocial personality? Second, as Lynam (1996) has stressed, is childhood CD more likely to persist into antisocial personality if it is comorbid with ADHD?

A number of prospective longitudinal studies have shown that children with ADHD exhibit increased levels of antisocial behaviour during adolescence and adulthood (Hechtman, Weiss and Perlman, 1984b; af Klinteberg, 1997; Loney, Kramer and Milich, 1982; Satterfield, Hoppe and Schell, 1982). It is not possible to conclude that ADHD by itself is a precursor to later antisocial behaviour, however, as no attempt was made in these studies to exclude children with comorbid CD during childhood. It is possible that the elevated rates of antisocial behaviour in adulthood are due to comorbid CD during childhood rather than ADHD. More recent studies have directly investigated the possibility that childhood ADHD by itself may be a precursor to later antisocial behaviour, either by excluding children with CD or comparing the outcomes of children with ADHD who did or did not exhibit comorbid CD.

These studies have failed to provide a clear answer, however, due perhaps to a wide range of samples and definitions of disorders and outcomes. Indeed, few studies actually assessed antisocial personality in adulthood (as opposed to more broadly defined antisocial behaviour). Two prospective studies have found that youths with ADHD alone had no higher rates of antisocial behaviour in adolescence or adulthood than children with neither ADHD nor CD (Loeber, 1988a; Magnusson and Bergman, 1990). One study found increased levels of antisocial behaviour during adolescence, but not adulthood (Farrington, Loeber and van Kammen, 1990). Another study found increased rates of antisocial behaviour during adolescence (Lambert, 1988), and two studies found higher rates of antisocial behaviour in both adolescence and adulthood (Gittelman, Mannuzza, Shenker and Bonagura, 1985; Mannuzza, Klein, Bonagura, Malloy, Giampino and Addalli, 1991; Mannuzza, Klein, Bessler, Malloy and LaPadulla, 1993).

We estimated the relative risk of adult APD from childhood ADHD in three independent prospective studies (Loney, Whaley-Klahn, Kosier and Conboy, 1981; Mannuzza, Klein *et al.*, 1993; Weiss, Hechtman, Milroy and Perlman, 1985). The relative risk of adult APD in individuals given the diagnosis of ADHD in childhood versus controls ranged from 2.5 to 9.6, with a weighted average across studies of 7.5. This estimate of relative risk is lower than for CD (see above) and is consistent with our hypothesis that although many individuals with ADHD will develop adult APD, the risk is primarily due to individuals who develop CD at some time during childhood or adolescence.

However, an early age of onset is an important marker for the development of APD. Results of a large population study by Swanson *et al.* (1994) showed that in the majority of the APD cases (using DSM-III criteria) the onset of symptoms was under age 10, with half of those developing APD having their onset of symptoms by age 7 or 8, and 95 per cent having their onset by age 12 or 13.

Somewhat more consistent evidence exists to answer the second question regarding the effects of comorbid ADHD and CD in childhood. Four published prospective studies have reported that children with comorbid ADHD and CD exhibited markedly higher levels of antisocial behaviour during adolescence and adulthood than children with either CD or ADHD alone (Farrington *et al.*, 1990b; Loeber, 1988a; Magnusson and Bergman, 1990; Schachar, Rutter and Smith, 1981; see also review by Lynam, 1996). Only Lambert (1988) found that youths with ADHD or CD alone had adolescent outcomes that were as poor as youths with both ADHD and CD.

Unfortunately, none of these studies used definitions of CD and ADHD that were similar enough to DSM-III-R and DSM-IV conceptions to be certain that the findings are comparable, and none assessed APD *per se* as an adult outcome. If comorbid ADHD is found to be associated with an increased likelihood of antisocial personality among youths with CD in childhood as we predict, the impact of comorbid ADHD is probably linked in some way to an earlier age of onset of CD. The most consistent finding across studies is that youths with CD (or antisocial behaviour defined in other ways) and comorbid ADHD have a much earlier age of onset of disruptive behaviour than youths with CD alone (Moffitt, 1990; Offord, Sullivan, Allen and Abrams, 1979; Walker, Lahey, Hynd and Frame, 1987).

Our earlier work in the Developmental Trends Study (Loeber, Green, Keenan and Lahey, 1995), shows that once the presence of ODD is taken into account, ADHD by itself does not increase the likelihood that a child will meet criteria for CD. On the other hand, ADHD is associated with an *early onset* of CD. Therefore, we hypothesise that ADHD is not a precursor to antisocial personality by itself, but ADHD indirectly increases the likelihood of antisocial personality by influencing the age of onset, and probably the degree of aggression and the persistence of CD. Thus, in our developmental model of antisocial personality, only children with ADHD who also exhibited comorbid ODD will develop CD in childhood (Lahey *et al.*, 1992; Lahey and Loeber, 1994; Loeber, Green *et al.*, 1995), with a subset of the children with CD later developing antisocial personality. Thus, we hypothesise a heterotypic developmental continuity (changing manifestations of the same disorder) in ODD, CD, and AP, but we see a role for ADHD in influencing the developmental progression from less serious to more serious manifestations of CD.

Physical aggression It has long been known that most adult chronic offenders have been highly physically aggressive since childhood (Loeber, 1988b), and that antisocial adults often were highly aggressive when young (e.g., Lynam, 1996; Moffitt, 1993; Moffitt *et al.*, 1996). Along that line, Cadoret and Stewart (1991) found that a childhood history of ADHD was not directly related to APD, 'but indirectly through a set of aggressive behaviours' (p. 79). However, that retrospective study could not show the extent to which prior aggression influenced the onset of antisocial personality. It was also unclear to what extent aggression was truly independent from antisocial personality (because one of the symptoms of antisocial personality is aggressiveness).

Early antisocial symptoms In our discussion of the gradual unfolding of disruptive symptoms during childhood and adolescence, we emphasised that some of the symptoms of antisocial personality may already appear early in life. We explored this in the Developmental Trends Study. The boys were 7 to 12 years of age at the time of the first assessment, and have been reassessed for nine years (of which eight years are analysed in the present chapter). Ninety-six boys were recruited from the Western Psychiatric Outpatient Service at the University of Pittsburgh, and eighty-one from the Emory University Clinic in Atlanta and the Georgia Children's Center in Athens, Georgia. At each site, one group of subjects had been referred by parents, teachers or counsellors for disruptive behaviours, while a comparison group consisted of boys referred for internalising problems.

Subject selection and measures have been described in detail by Lahey *et al.* (1995) and are only summarised here. Parents, teachers, and boys were interviewed at yearly intervals[1] over a nine-year period. Participation rates have remained exceptionally high, averaging 96.3 per cent (range 93 to 100 per cent). Parents and children were interviewed in person, and teachers were interviewed over the phone and completed questionnaires through the past. Nearly all interviewers were newly hired each year and were blind to the subjects' diagnostic status in preceding years.

The sample was composed of Caucasian (70 per cent) and African-American boys (30 per cent), with families ranging across all five levels of the four factor index of socio-economic status (Hollingshead, 1975). For more details on the subjects, the reader is referred to Loeber, Green, Lahey and Stouthamer-Loeber (1989). Currently and over the next few years (Years 10 to 13) assessments of antisocial personality are being made on the participants in this sample. However, the study sheds light on precursors to antisocial personality, including its early manifestations and the development of CD with or without ADHD.

We examined to what extent boys with CD already had early symptoms of antisocial personality in Year 1 of the study. For that purpose, we selected items corresponding to criteria for APD or PPD from the Child Behaviour Checklist (CBCL; Achenbach and Edelbrock, 1983; Edelbrock and Achenbach, 1984) and the Covert Antisocial Checklist (Loeber and Bowers, 1985) in Year 1. Six items were found on the CBCL or the Covert Antisocial Checklist that corresponded to DSM-IV symptoms of APD: 'gets arrested' (parent reported only), 'acts sneakily', 'impulsive', 'behaves explosively', 'daring', and 'doesn't feel guilty after misbehaving'.

Subjects who displayed three or more of these symptoms according to their parent or teacher were provisionally labelled 'APD' (in accord with the DSM-IV criterion of three symptoms). Six items were also found on the CBCL or the Covert Antisocial Checklist that corresponded with PPD symptoms: 'smooth talker', 'brags or boasts', 'doesn't feel guilty after misbehaving', 'manipulates people or acts sneakily,' 'impulsive', and 'behaves irresponsibly'. The cut-off for the PPD score was four or more items, based on the scoring requirements of the Psychopathy

Checklist (Hare *et al.*, 1991). The results show that the percentage of subjects diagnosed with CD in Year 1 who had three or more APD symptoms was significantly higher (69.1 per cent compared to 38.5 per cent) than the percentage of non-CD subjects ($X^2(1) = 15.7$, $p < 001$). Similarly, subjects diagnosed with CD also had more PPD symptoms. 67.6 per cent of the CD subjects had a high number of PPD symptoms, compared to 38.5 per cent of the non-CD subjects ($X^2(1) = 14.2$, $p < .001$). Thus, subjects in this sample with CD already display a high number of symptoms of antisocial personality long before the age of 18 when they first can qualify for a diagnosis of APD.

We consider the above results only a first step towards a specification of what are behavioural antecedents to antisocial personality. Some of these behavioural antecedents imply and/or represent deficits in affective and cognitive components as well, such as callousness, lack of guilt feelings, remorse, and empathy. In the Pittsburgh Youth Study we found that parents' and teachers' reports of boys' lack of guilt was one of the strongest factors associated with serious delinquency in three samples of boys (Loeber, Farrington, Stouthamer-Loeber and Van Kammen, 1998).

Number of CD-symptoms One of the premises of the diagnosis of APD is the presence of CD before age 18. Robins and Ratcliff (1979) found that the higher the number of childhood antisocial behaviours before age 15, the higher the number of adult antisocial behaviours. Does this mean that the higher the number of CD-symptoms before adulthood, the higher the stability of APD? Dinwiddle and Daw (1998) addressed this issue in a sample of 407 adults, who were initially part of a family study on alcoholism and sociopathy. The authors found that the higher the number of retrospectively reported CD-symptoms the higher the persistence of APD over an eight-year period. Similar findings for Hare's psychopathy construct have been reported by Rogers, Johansen, Chang and Salekin (1997) in a sample of adolescent offenders. However, the results in both studies need to be validated with prospective information about the CD-symptoms before adulthood.

The prediction of conduct disorder

Since we see CD as an intermediate step in the prediction of antisocial personality, we are interested in the predictors of the *onset* of CD. In an earlier paper, using Year 1 to Year 6 data from the Developmental Trends Study (Loeber, Green, Keenan and Lahey, 1995), we found that among all symptoms of CD, physical fighting predicted the onset of CD. Stepwise logistic regression of eight independent variables revealed ODD, SES, and parental substance abuse to be the best predictors of the onset of new cases of CD in Years 2–6 of the study. Thus, although many factors are associated with CD, the logistic regression showed that the combination of the child's oppositional behaviour and the liabilities associated with lower SES and parental substance abuse are the factors most strongly associated with the onset of CD in Years 2–6. Specific parenting deficits, and lower intelligence, while significant in bivariate analyses. were probably not significant in the logistic regression because they are correlated with substance abuse and SES.

We further systematically tested whether, aside from physical aggression, any other CD symptom, when co-occurring with ODD, improved the prediction of the onset of CD. *Of all the CD symptoms, only the symptom of physical fighting improved this prediction*: 37.1 per cent of the new CD cases had prior ODD and had physically fought, compared to 14.3 per cent of those boys who did not make the transition to CD ($X^2(1) = 6.7$, $p < .01$). This finding agrees with other studies indicating that physical fighting is implicated in the developmental course toward chronic offending (summarised in Loeber, 1988b). We also found that of those boys who fought at Year 1, 86.4 per cent were rated high on this behaviour in subsequent years.

Since many children fight at one time or another, we need to address the question whether recurrent or persistent physical fighting predicts CD better than occasional fighting. We addressed this in a separate set of analyses (Loeber, Green and Lahey, 1997). Logistic regressions showed that CD in Year 7 (irrespective of age of onset) was best predicted by ODD in Year 1 and *stable* fighting over more than one year (Odds Ratios 4.2 and 3.4, respectively). When the number of diagnoses at Year 7 was the outcome, stable fighting was the only significant predictor (Odds Ratio = 2.6).

These results are provocative, but should be seen as only preliminary in identifying optimal predictors of antisocial personality.

Risk and protective factors

We will now examine the risk and protective factors for APD, and whether such factors are identical to the risk and protective factors for CD.

Risk factors

Risk factors are defined here as events or conditions associated with an increased likelihood of deviance. Risk factors for disruptive behaviour may lie in the child's own behaviour, in his/her social and physical environment, or in disruptors of caretakers' child rearing practices (Werner, 1986a). *The importance of risk factors lies in their potential to serve as 'red flags' signalling increased likelihood of deviant development*. In that role, they can fulfill an important function in theory and preventive practice. In past decades, an impressive body of empirical findings has accumulated about risk factors for disruptive child behaviours and delinquency (Loeber and Farrington, 1998; Loeber and Stouthamer-Loeber, 1987; Robins, 1991; Rutter and Giller, 1983; Wilson and Herrnstein, 1985), of which we present some highlights and critical issues.

Although earlier research emphasised how risk factors can affect different forms of psychopathology in the same way (Rutter, 1988), there is increasing evidence that certain risk factors play a role in the development of specific forms of psychopathology (such as those applicable to attention deficits/hyperactivity as compared to conduct problems, see e.g., Loeber, Brinthaupt and Green, 1990). Second, more needs to be learned about risk factors which are uniquely associated with *onset* or *initiation* compared to *escalation*, or *de-escalation* and *desistance* of disruptive behaviours. Third, findings on differences among risk factors associated with early versus late onset will be particularly important because of the chronic outcome often associated with early onset (Loeber, 1982). Although Hirschi and Gottfredson (1983) discounted the possibility that risk factors for offending and conduct problems varied with age, this does not agree with available evidence (Loeber and Le Blanc, 1990). Only a few studies have examined the *duration* of risk factors, indicating that the longer youngsters are exposed to risk factors, the more dramatic the effect on their behaviour (Cohen and Brook, 1987).

There are several known risk factors for antisocial personality. It is likely that no single risk factor can explain APD; instead, the accumulation of risk factors in such areas as childhood experiences and family functioning appears important in determining who will qualify eventually for APD.

Childhood factors For example, childhood victimisation in males is a significant predictor of APD, even when demographic characteristics and criminal history were controlled for (Luntz and Widom, 1994). Race did not predict APD status in that study. Even though there are racial differences in the prevalence of serious forms of delinquency (Loeber and Farrington, 1998), Robins *et al.* (1991) found similar rates of APD among whites, Hispanics, and African Americans. Further, these authors found that childhood behaviour problems were about equally prognostic of APD for African Americans and white.

The relationship between educational performance and APD is different from that and delinquency. Whereas poor educational performance predicts the prevalence and severity of delinquency (Maguin and Loeber,

1996), Robins *et al.* (1991) reported that the highest rate of APD did not occur among those individuals with the least education, but among those who entered high school but did not complete it. However, low intelligence is known to explain the relationship between poor educational performance and delinquency (Maguin and Loeber, 1996). Robins *et al.* (1991) found that individuals who had one or more indicators of intellectual retardation had an increased risk of APD, but only in whites and not in Hispanics or African Americans. The difference in findings, however, should be studied in the context of other risk factors to which minorities are often exposed.

Family factors Several studies have focused on parental characteristics and behaviour as predictors of APD in their offspring. Two studies demonstrated that youths with CD whose parents exhibited higher levels of antisocial behaviour were more likely to meet criteria for APD in adulthood (Robins, 1966; Robins and Ratcliff, 1979), while parental substance abuse has been linked to conduct problems (Tarter, Blackson, Martin, Loeber and Moss, 1993; Werner, 1986b).

Previous studies have found that factors such as parental education and occupation (the bases of the Hollingshead index of SES) are related to the persistence of antisocial behaviour from childhood to adulthood (Robins and Ratcliff, 1979). SES usually added little or nothing, however, to the prediction of later antisocial behaviour among children with high numbers of antisocial behaviours (Robins, 1966; Robins and Ratcliff, 1979).

Urban residence It is well known that serious forms of delinquency are more common in urban compared to rural settings (Loeber and Farrington, 1998). Robins *et al.* (1991) found that the life-time APD in white males and females was higher in urban compared to rural St Louis (5.5 per cent and 1.2 per cent in urban settings, respectively, versus 3.7 per cent and 0.5 per cent in rural settings). For example, these differences were not apparent for African Americans.

There is a scarcity of prospective longitudinal studies in which a wide range of predictors of antisocial personality were measured, allowing regression analyses to determine which factors were most predictive when controlling for other factors. However, Farrington (1996), using an antisocial behaviour construct at age 32, found that the best predictors were convicted parent by age 10, early school leaving by age 14, hospitalisation for illness by age 18, and an unskilled manual job at age 18 (only one interaction was significant: early school leaving and an unskilled manual job). Thus, risk factors from several domains (child, parent, school) all contributed to the risk of antisocial behaviour in adulthood.

In summary, several factors in the individual, the family, and setting appear associated with APD. These risk factors are largely the same as those known for CD (Lahey *et al.*, 1994; Robins *et al.*, 1991; Robins and Ratcliff, 1979), suggesting a continuum of influences that may take place over decades. However, firmer conclusions about patterns of risk factors leading to later APD are severely restricted by the lack of predictive studies covering a wider gamut of potential risk factors. To encourage further study, we postulate several hypotheses concerning risk factors for CD and APD:

a. Because virtually all subjects with antisocial personality at ages 18–19 will have met criteria for CD during childhood or adolescence, all risk factors for ever meeting criteria for CD (regardless of the age, severity, or persistence of CD) are likely to be risk factors for antisocial personality.
b. However, factors associated with the early onset, developmental advancement, and especially the persistence of CD will be the risk factors that account for the greatest amount of variance in the prediction of adult antisocial personality.

Protective factors

Protective factors are defined as factors associated with a low likelihood of an occurrence of a deviant outcome, or a high likelihood of a desirable outcome taking place. For example, family stability is known as a protective factor for boys' adaptation success (Richters and Martinez, 1993), and as a protective factor for CD (Quinton, Pickles, Maughan and Rutter, 1993).

There are several important issues in the study of protective factors. It has been argued that most known protective factors are the inverse of risk factors (Stouthamer-Loeber, Loeber *et al.*, 1993). Using data from three epidemiological samples in Pittsburgh, the authors showed that most risk factors also functioned as protective factors, but some risk factors, such as ADHD and ODD were risk factors only and did not have a protective effect.

There are several ways in which risk and protective effects can be distinguished (Stouthamer-Loeber *et al.*, 1993). For example, the *shape of the function relating the predictor to the outcome* can be used to distinguish between risk and protective factors. If the function is linear, the predictor variable can be said to have both positive and negative effects depending on the value of the variable; such a variable would have both risk and protective effects. On the other hand, if the function is flat at either higher or lower values it can be said to be primarily a risk or protective factor, respectively.

Another issue is to improve our understanding of the interplay between risk and protective factors in determining long-term outcomes such as antisocial personality. The crucial question here is to what extent can the presence of protective factors 'buffer' the impact of risk factors? For example, Jenkins and Smith (1990) found that a child having a good relationship with an adult outside the family buffered the negative effect of poor marital relationships between the parents of the child. Likewise, Robins (1966) reported that the protective effect of a child's exposure to strict or adequate discipline was found even among those with antisocial fathers.

The significance of comorbid conditions

The importance of studying target disorders in the context of comorbid disorders has been highlighted in several reviews (Caron and Rutter, 1991; Loeber and Keenan, 1994; Nottelman and Jensen, 1995). There is ample evidence that APD in adulthood often co-occurs with other disorders (Newman *et al.*, 1996), such as depression (Harrington *et al.*, 1991), alcoholism (e.g., Lewis and Bucholz, 1991; Shubert *et al.*, 1988), and drug abuse (Brooner *et al.*, 1993; Robins and Przybeck, 1984; Shubert *et al.*, 1988). We briefly review the state of knowledge of comorbidities of CD and discuss their relevance for antisocial personality.

Anxiety There is a growing literature that suggests that the interplay of CD and anxiety disorders is important and complex. On the one hand, several epidemiologic studies indicate that prepubertal children with anxiety disorders who do not have CD are at a *reduced* risk for later conduct problems in adolescence (Graham and Rutter, 1973; Rutter, Tizard and Whitmore, 1970). On the other hand, a substantial body of evidence suggests that CD and anxiety disorders are comorbid at *substantially higher than chance rates* during childhood and adolescence (Loeber and Keenan, 1994; Zoccolillo, 1992). Similarly, adult males in the Epidemiologic Catchment Area study with APD were 2.0–5.3 times more likely to exhibit anxiety disorders, especially at higher levels of severity of antisocial behaviour (Robins *et al.*, 1991). Paradoxically, then, childhood anxiety disorders seem to protect against future antisocial behaviour when they occur alone, but youth who do develop CD (and adults with antisocial personality) are at an increased risk for comorbid anxiety disorder.

It has been well established that psychopaths have lower levels of anxiety than nonpsychopaths (e.g., Lykken, 1957; Fowles, 1980; Hare, 1970). Examination of the startle reflex, which is an indicator of anxiety, shows that psychopaths do not show the expected potentiation of the startle reflex that normally occurs during the process of aversive clues such as unpleasant photographs or punishment clues (Patrick, 1994). How early in life this aspect of the startle response can be reliably measured as a predictor of adult APD remains to be established.

Depression Recent investigations of the relationship between CD and depressive symptomatology show that the two often co-occur; studies of their temporal relationship, however, have produced more controversial results (Capaldi, 1992; Holmes and Robins, 1987; Kovacs, Paulauskas, Gatsonis and Richards, 1988). There are at least four reasons why the interplay of these disorders should be a focus of a longitudinal study of CD and antisocial personality. First, it is possible that CD is a precursor to depression in some children (Capaldi, 1992; Holmes and Robins, 1987; Lahey, 1994). Second, the course of both CD and depression may be different when they co-occur; indeed, a diagnostic category of 'depressive conduct disorder' has been proposed (Puig-Antich *et al.*, 1989). Third, it has been suggested that some proportion of late-onset nonaggressive CD is actually secondary to depression and distinct from other CD (Masten, 1988; Puig-Antich, 1982). Fourth, both CD and depression have been linked to substance abuse (Buydens-Branchey *et al.*, 1989) and suicide (Shaffer, 1974; Shaffi, Carrigan, Whittinghill and Derrick, 1985), particularly when they co-occur. We expect that in clinic-referred populations, depression will become increasingly comorbid with CD over time and we predict that boys with CD and comorbid depression will be more at risk for using psychoactive substances, suicidal behaviour, and antisocial behaviour than boys with CD alone.

Substance use Concurrent studies have shown that the more serious the substance use the higher the likelihood that individuals engage in serious forms of delinquency (Bukstein, Brent and Kraminer, 1989; Loeber, 1988b). Concurrent studies, however, do not indicate the direction of effect, nor whether a decrease in substance use is followed by a decrease in conduct problems or delinquent activities. Studies of the direction of effect have shown that increased substance use may be associated with an increase in delinquency, but the reverse may also apply. For example, longitudinal analyses reported by Van Kammen and Loeber (1994) showed that the onset of illegal drug use and drug dealing in adolescent males was associated with an increase in person-related offences and carrying a concealed weapon. In addition, drug dealing was associated with an increase in car- and fraud-related crimes. It can be argued, however, that delinquency may also activate substance use. Van Kammen and Loeber (1994) found that this was the case with previous involvement in property offences increasing the risk of the onset of illegal drug use. Also, previous involvement in both property and person-related offences increased the risk of the onset of drug dealing.

If drug involvement and delinquency are intertwined, does this also mean that a decrease in drug use is followed by a decrease in delinquent activities? There is evidence for this in interview studies of narcotic addicts. When individuals began using hard drugs less frequently, their criminal involvement also decreased (Ball, Shaffer and Nurco, 1983; Nurco, Shaffer, Ball and Kinlock, 1985). This is not surprising in light of the decreased need to obtain funds to purchase the drugs. Longitudinal analyses on juveniles (Van Kammen and Loeber, 1994) also showed that discontinuation of illegal drug use (or drug selling) was associated with a decrease in delinquent activities. The extent to which a decrease in delinquency is associated with a subsequent decrease in drug involvement is not clear from the available studies. Thus, substance use probably is an important comorbid condition of conduct problems and delinquent acts, influencing their course over time. In clinic-referred samples, however, we expect that deceleration or desistance in substance use will be uncommon during adolescence or early adulthood. Rather, we hypothesise that in such samples, boys with CD will begin using psychoactive substances at an earlier age, and their use of illegal substances will increase the risk for antisocial personality after controlling for early CD.

Conclusions about comorbidities

In clinical samples, depression and substance use appear to emerge concurrently with CD. Particularly, we need to investigate the extent that comorbid conditions affect the onset and course of CD and the onset of antisocial personality.

Other impairments

Robins (1966) was one of the first authors to demonstrate the wide variety of functional deficits shown by individuals with antisocial personality in adulthood. She showed that, among antisocial adults with a CD diagnosis in childhood, 94 per cent experienced employment troubles, 72 per cent had multiple vehicular moving violations, and 67 per cent had severe marital difficulties in adulthood. Barkley *et al.* (1993), who followed ADHD adolescents into adulthood, also reported that ADHD youth with comorbid ODD and CD were at highest risk for traffic citations and negative driving-related outcomes. Research by Cadoret and Stewart (1991) showed that ADHD is associated with accident-proneness and accidental self-poisoning; however, the extent that these or other medical problems are associated with antisocial personality is less clear.

The mental and physical health of those individuals with CD *who do not* develop antisocial personality can also be of great concern. Robins showed that 69 per cent of the former CD cases who did not develop APD, suffered from a wide range of social dysfunction in adulthood. Also, Zoccolillo *et al.* (1992), who traced the development of children raised in group homes, showed that only 13 per cent of children with CD went on to develop adequate social functioning in adult life. Likewise, Farrington, Gallagher, Morley, St Ledger and West (1988) demonstrated that non-convicted vulnerable youth (i.e., scoring high on risk factors) differed from unconvicted non-vulnerable individuals, by living in more dirty housing conditions, having lower status jobs, a lower income, living by themselves, getting along badly with their mother, and being heavy smokers. Thus, high risk environments, even when not leading to chronic offending (and presumably antisocial personality), still are associated with a wide range of long-term impairments.

Several conclusions can be drawn from these findings: (a) diverse forms of impairment are associated with antisocial personality; (b) a high proportion of those individuals who exhibit early CD or serious delinquent behaviour in adolescence, but cease their problem behaviour in adulthood, still show substantial social dysfunction; (c) it is unclear what protective factors shield individuals from these impairments.

Methodological shortcomings of previous research

Several studies on antisocial personality have increased our knowledge about the disorder. However, studies have generally been cross-sectional in nature (e.g., Widiger and Corbitt, 1993; Robins *et al.*, 1991), had adults rather than younger individuals as subjects (Robins *et al.*, 1991), and often were restricted to incarcerated populations (e.g, Guze, 1976). Longitudinal studies, although pioneering, were either (a) studies of adults who had formerly been seen in child guidance clinics and for whom past clinical records were scored to quantify childhood conduct problems (e.g., Robins, 1966), or (b) retrospective studies in which adults were interviewed about both their current symptoms of antisocial personality and their childhood symptoms of CD (Robins *et al.*, 1991; Robins and Ratcliff, 1979; Zoccolillo *et al.*, 1992).

Most importantly, we identified few published prospective longitudinal studies with antisocial personality as an outcome (af Klinteberg, 1997;

Loney *et al.*, 1981; Mannuzza *et al.*, 1993; Weiss *et al.*, 1985). Most of these studied focused on childhood hyperactivity rather than ODD or CD or *excluded* children with CD (Mannuzza *et al.*, 1993). Thus, there is a great scarcity of prospective studies in which relevant etiological factors, including ODD and CD, are measured *prior* to the development of antisocial personality. Also, subjects were only contacted once or twice and, as a consequence, these studies had long gaps of years without intermediate assessments to track the course of disruptive disorders.

Research to identify critical etiological factors in antisocial personality is hampered by practical constraints such as the relatively low prevalence of the disorder in general populations (Robins *et al.*, 1991). We propose that a more fruitful search for etiological factors would be based on the prospective follow-up of a population of youth at risk for antisocial personality. There are several options for the identification of high risk samples, including off-spring of known antisocial personality adults, youth from high crime areas, and large epidemiological surveys of representative samples. Cost and yield are some of the principal criteria for the evaluation of these options. We maintain that among these choices, a final selection should (a) optimise yield by using an existing high risk sample, particularly a sample with known ODD and CD, thereby reducing the length of time it takes to produce information relevant to antisocial personality; (b) use an existing sample which has been followed up rigorously with reliable measures and with a low attrition rate; (c) use a sample whose measurement allows an examination of the influence of comorbid conditions.

Postscript

Since writing this chapter, participants have been followed up over more waves, and have been assessed for Antisocial Personality Disorder (APD) at ages 18 and 19. Several of our hypotheses mentioned in this chapter were confirmed in analyses prospectively predicting APD. For the results of these analyses, see: R. Loeber, J. D. Burke, and B. B. Lahey (2002). What are adolescent antecedents to Antisocial Personality Disorder? *Criminal Behaviour and Mental Health*, 12, 24–36.

ACKNOWLEDGEMENTS

The study was supported by grants from the National Institute of Drug Abuse (DA411018), the National Institute of Mental Health (MH50778), and the Office of Juvenile Justice and Delinquency Prevention (96-MU-FX-0012). Points of view or opinions in this document are those of the authors and do not necessarily represent the official position of OJJDP, the Department of Justice, NIMH, or NIDA.

NOTE

1 Year 5 did not consist of a full assessment because of limited funding.

REFERENCES

Achenbach, T. M. and Edelbrock, C. S. (1983) *Manual for the Child Behaviour Checklist and Revised Child Behavior Profile*. Burlington, VT.

American Psychiatric Association (1987) *Diagnostic and Statistical Manual of Mental Disorders* (3rd ed., revised). Washington, DC: US Government Printing Office.

(1994) *Diagnostic and Statistical Manual of Mental Disorders* (4th ed.). Washington, DC: US Government Printing Office.

Ball, J. C., Shaffer, J. W. and Nurco, D. (1983) Day to day criminality of heroin addicts in Baltimore – A study in the continuity of offense rates. *Drug and Alcohol Dependence, 12*, 119–42.

Barkley, R. A., Guevremont, D. C., Anastopoulos, A. D., DuPaul, G. J. and Shelton, T. L. (1993) Driving-related risks and outcomes of Attention Deficit Hyperactivity disorder in adolescents and young adults: A 3 to 5 year follow up survey. *Pediatrics, 92*, 212–18.

Blumstein, A., Cohen, J., Roth, J. A. and Visher, C. A. (eds.) (1986) *Criminal Careers and 'Career Criminals'*. Washington, DC: National Academy of Sciences.

Brooner, R. K., Herbst, J. H., Schmidt, C. W., Bigelow, G. E. and Costa, P. T. (1993) Antisocial Personality Disorder among drug abusers – Relations to other personality diagnoses and the 5-factor model of personality. *Journal of Nervous and Mental Disease, 181*, 313–24.

Bukstein, O. G., Brent, D. A. and Kraminer, Y. (1989) Comorbidity of substance abuse and other psychiatric disorders in adolescents. *American Journal of Psychiatry, 146*, 1131–41.

Buydens-Branchey, L., Branchey, M. H. and Noumair, D. (1989) Age of alcoholism onset. I. Relationship to psychopathology. *Archives of General Psychiatry, 46*, 225–30.

Capaldi, D. M. (1992) The co-occurrence of conduct problems and depressive symptoms in early adolescent boys: II. A 2-year follow-up at Grade 8. *Development and Psychopathology, 4*, 125–44.

Cadoret, R. J. and Stewart, M. A. (1991) An adoption study of attention deficit/aggression and their relationship to adult antisocial personality. *Comprehensive Psychiatry, 32*, 73–82.

Caron, C. and Rutter, M. (1991) Comorbidity in child psychopathology: Concepts, issues and research strategies. *Journal of Child Psychology and Psychiatry, 32*, 1063–80.

Cleckley, H. (1976) *The Mask of Sanity* (5th ed.) St Louis, MO: Mosby.

Cohen, P. and Brook, J. (1987) Family factors related to the persistence of psychopathology in childhood and adolescence. *Psychiatry, 50*, 332–40.

Cooke, D. J. (1997) Psychopaths: oversexed, overplayed but not over here? *Criminal Behaviour and Mental Health, 7*, 3–11.

Dinwiddle, S. H. and Daw, E. W. (1998) Temporal stability of antisocial personality disorder: Blind follow-up study at 8 years. *Comprehensive Psychiatry, 39*, 28–34.

Edelbrock, C. and Achenbach, T. (1984). The teacher version of the Child Behavior Profile: I. Boys aged six through eleven. *Journal of Consulting and Clinical Psychology*, *52*, 207–17.

Farrington, D. P. (1996) Psychosocial influences on the development of antisocial personality. In A. Dawes et al. (eds.), *Psychology, Law and Criminal Justice* (pp. 424–44). Berlin: De Gruyter.

Farrington, D. P., Gallagher, B., Morley, L., St Ledger, R. J. and West, D. J. (1988) A 24-year follow-up of men from vulnerable backgrounds. In R. L. Jenkins (ed.), *The Abandonment of Delinquent Behavior: The Turnaround* (pp. 155–73). New York: Praeger.

Farrington, D. P., Loeber, R. and van Kammen, W. B. (1990a) Long term criminal outcomes of hyperactivity-impulsivity-attention deficit and conduct problems in childhood. In L. N. Robins and M. R. Rutter (eds.), *Straight and Devious Pathways to Adulthood* (pp. 62–81). New York: Cambridge University Press.

Farrington, D. P., Loeber, R., Elliott, D. S., Hawkins, J. D., Kandel, D. B., Klein, M. W., McCord, J., Rowe, D. C. and Tremblay, R. E. (1990b) Advancing knowledge about the onset of delinquency and crime. In B. B. Lahey and A. E. Kazdin (eds.), *Advances in Clinical Child Psychology* (vol. 13, pp. 283–342). New York: Plenum.

Fowles, D. C. (1980) The three arousal model: Implications of Gray's two-factor learning theory for heart rate, electrodermal activity, and psychopathy. *Psychophysiology*, *17*, 87–104.

Frances, A. J. (1980) The DSM-III personality section: A commentary. *American Journal of Psychiatry*, *137*, 1050–4.

Frick, P. J., O'Brien, B. S., Wootton, J. M. and McBurnett, K. (1994) Psychopathy and conduct problems in children. *Journal of Abnormal Psychology*, *103*, 700–7.

Gittelman, R., Mannuzza, S., Shenker, R. and Bonagura, N. (1985) Hyperactive boys almost grown up. *Archives of General Psychiatry*, *42*, 937–47.

Graham, P. and Rutter, M. (1973) Psychiatric disorders in the young adolescent: A follow-up study. *Proceedings of the Royal Society of Medicine*, *66*, 1226–9.

Guze, S. B. (1976) Criminality and Psychiatric Disorders. New York: Oxford University Press.

Hare, R. D. (1970) *Psychopathy: Theory and Research*. New York: Wiley.

Hare, R. D., Hart, S. D. and Harpur, T. J. (1991) Psychopathy and the DSM-IV Criteria for Antisocial Personality Disorder. *Journal of Abnormal Psychology*, *100*, 391–8.

Hare, R. D., Harpur, T. J., Hakstian, A. R., Forth, A. E., Hart, S. D. and Newman, J. P. (1990) The revised Psychopathy Checklist: Reliability and factor structure. *Psychological Assessment: A Journal of Consulting and Clinical Psychology*, *2*, 338–41.

Harpur, T. J., Hare, R. D. and Hakstian, A. R. (1989) Two-factor conceptualization of psychopathy: Construct validity and assessment implications. *Psychological Assessment: A Journal of Consulting and Clinical Psychology*, *1*, 6–17.

Harrington, R., Fudge, H., Rutter, M., Pickles, A. and Hill, J. (1991) Adult outcomes of childhood and adolescent depression: II. Links with antisocial disorders. *Journal of the American Academy of Child and Adolescent Psychiatry*, *30*, 434–9.

Hechtman, L., Weiss, G. and Perlman, T. (1984) Hyperactives as young adults: Past and current substance abuse and antisocial behavior. *American Journal of Orthopsychiatry*, *54*, 415–25.

Hirschi, T. and Gottfredson, M. (1983) Age and the explanation of crime. *American Journal of Sociology*, *89*, 552–84.

Hollingshead, A. B. (1975) *Four Factor Index of Social Status*. New Haven, CT: Yale University.

Holmes, S. J. and Robins, L. N. (1987) The influence of childhood disciplinary experience on the development of alcoholism and depression. *Journal of Child Psychology and Psychiatry*, *28*, 399–415.

Jenkins, J. M. and Smith, M. A. (1990) Factors protecting children living in disharmonious homes: Maternal reports. *Journal of the American Academy of Child and Adolescent Psychiatry*, *29*, 60–9.

Klinteberg, B. af (1997) Hyperactive behaviour and aggressiveness as early risk indicators for violence: Variable and person approaches. *Studies on Crime and Crime Prevention*, *6*, 21–34.

Kovacs, M., Paulauskas, S., Gatsonis, C. and Richards, C. (1988) Depressive disorders in childhood. *Journal of Affective Disorders*, *15*, 205–17.

Lahey, B. B. (1994) *An Interactive Developmental Model of Conduct Disorder and Depression*. Presentation to the Annual Meeting of the Society for Research in Child and Adolescent Psychopathology, London, England, June 1994.

Lahey, B. B., Hart, E. L., Pliszka, S., Applegate, B. and McBurnett, K. (1993) Neurophysiological correlates of Conduct Disorder: A rationale and review of research. *Journal of Clinical Child Psychology*, *22*, 141–53.

Lahey, B. B. and Loeber, R. (1994) Framework for a developmental model of Oppositional Defiant Disorder and Conduct Disorder. In D. K. Routh, (ed.), *Disruptive Behavior Disorders in Childhood: Essays Honoring Herbert C. Quay* (pp. 139–80). New York: Plenum.

Lahey, B. B., Loeber, R., Hart, E. L., Frick, P. J., Applegate, B., Zhang, Q., Green, S. M. and Russo, M. F. (1995) Four-year longitudinal study of conduct disorder in boys: Patterns and predictors of persistence. *Journal of Abnormal Psychology*, *104*, 83–93.

Lahey, B. B., Loeber, R., Quay, H. C., Frick, P. J. and Grimm, J. (1992) Oppositional Defiant and Conduct Disorders: Issues to be resolved for DSM-IV. *Journal of the American Academy of Child and Adolescent Psychiatry*, *31*, 539–46.

Lambert, N. M. (1988) Adolescent outcomes for hyperactive children: Perspectives on general and specific patterns of childhood risk for adolescent educational, social, and mental health problems. *American Psychologist*, *43*, 786–99.

Lewis, C. E. and Bucholz, K. K. (1991) Alcoholism, antisocial behavior and family history. *British Journal of Addiction*, *86*, 177–94.

Loeber, R. (1982) The stability of antisocial and delinquent child behavior: A review. *Child Development*, *53*, 1431–46.

(1988a) Behavioral precursors and accelerators of delinquency. In W. Buikhuisen and S. A. Mednick (eds.), *Explaining Criminal Behavior*. Leiden: Brill, 51–67.

(1988b) The natural histories of juvenile conduct problems, substance use and delinquency: Evidence for developmental progressions. In B. B. Lahey and A. E. Kazdin (eds.) *Advances in Clinical Psychology* (vol. 11). New York: Plenum.

(1991) Antisocial behavior: More enduring than changeable? *Journal of the Academy of Child and Adolescent Psychiatry, 30*, 393–7.

Loeber, R. and Bowers, B. (1985) *A Five Year Follow-up Evaluation of the Multiple Gating Procedure*. Unpublished manuscript, Western Psychiatric Institute and Clinic, University of Pittsburgh, PA.

Loeber, R., Brinthaupt, V. P. and Green, S. M. (1990) Attention deficits, impulsivity, and hyperactivity with or without conduct problems: Relationship to delinquency and unique contextual factors. In R. J. McMahon and R. D. Peters (eds.), *Behavior Disorders of Adolescence: Research, Intervention, and Policy in Clinical and School Settings*. New York: Plenum.

Loeber, R., DeLamatre, M., Keenan, K. and Zhang, Q. (1998) A prospective replication of developmental pathways in disruptive and delinquent behavior. In R. Cairns, L. Bergman and J. Kagan (eds.), *Methods and Models for Studying the Individual* (pp. 185–215). Thousand Oaks, CA: Sage.

Loeber, R. and Farrington, D. P. (eds.) (1998) *Serious and Violent Juvenile Offenders: Risk Factors and Successful Interventions*. Thousand Oaks, CA: Sage.

Loeber, R., Farrington, D. P., Stouthamer-Loeber, M. and Van Kammen, W. B. (1998) *Antisocial Behavior and Mental Health Problems: Explanatory Factors in Childhood and Adolescence*. Mawhaw, NJ: Lawrence Erlbaum.

Loeber, R., Green, S. M., Keenan, K. and Lahey, B. B. (1995) Which boys will fare worse? Early predictors of the onset of conduct disorder in a six-year longitudinal study. *Journal of the American Academy of Child and Adolescent Psychiatry, 34*, 499–509.

Loeber, R., Green, S. M. and Lahey, B. B. (1997) *Physical Fighting as a Mental Health Risk*. Unpublished manuscript. Western Psychiatric Institute and Clinic, University of Pittsburgh, PA.

Loeber, R., Green, S. M., Lahey, B. B., Christ, M. A. G. and Frick, P. J. (1992) Developmental sequences in the age of onset of disruptive child behaviors. *Journal of Child and Family Studies, 1*, 21–41.

Loeber, R., Green, S. M., Lahey, B. B. and Stouthamer-Loeber, M. (1989) Optimal informants on childhood disruptive behaviors. *Development and Psychopathology, 1*, 317–37.

Loeber, R. and Keenan, K. (1994) The interaction between conduct disorder and its comorbid conditions: Effects of age and gender. *Clinical Psychology Review, 14*, 497–523.

Loeber, R., Keenan, K. and Zhang, Q. (1997) Boys' experimentation and persistence in developmental pathways toward serious delinquency. *Journal of Child and Family Studies, 6*, 321–57.

Loeber, R. and Le Blanc, M. (1990) Toward a developmental criminology. In M. Tonry and N. Morris (eds.) *Crime and Justice*. University of Chicago Press.

Loeber, R. and Stouthamer-Loeber, M. (1987) Prediction. In H. C. Quay (ed.), *Handbook of Juvenile Delinquency*, New York: Wiley.

Loeber, R., Wung, P., Keenan, K., Giroux, B., Stouthamer-Loeber, M., Van Kammen, W. B. and Maughan, B. (1993) Developmental pathways in disruptive child behavior. *Development and Psychopathology*, *5*: 101–32.

Loney, J., Kramer J. and Milich, R. J. (1982). The hyperactive child grows up: Predictors of symptoms, delinquency and achievement at followup. In K. D. Gadow and J. Loney, (eds.), *Psychosocial Aspects of Drug Treatment for Hyperactivity*. Boulder, CO: Westview Press, 351–415.

Loney, J., Whaley-Klahn, M. A., Kosier, T. and Conboy, J. (1981) Hyperactive boys and their brothers at 21: Predictors of aggressive and antisocial outcomes. In K. T. Van Dusen and S. A. Mednick, (eds.), *Prospective Studies of Crime and Delinquency* (pp. 181–208). Boston: Kluwer-Nijhoff.

Luntz, B. K. and Widom, C. S. (1994) Antisocial personality disorder in abused and neglected children grown up. *American Journal of Psychiatry*, *151*, 670–4.

Lykken, D. T. (1957) A study of anxiety in the sociopathic personality. *Journal of Abnormal and Clinical Psychology*, *55*, 6–10.

Lynam, D. R. (1996) Early identification of chronic offenders: Who is the fledgling psychopath? *Psychological Bulletin*, *20*, 209–34.

Magnusson, D. and Bergman, L. R. (1990) A pattern approach to the study of pathways from childhood to adulthood. In L. Robins and M. Rutter (eds.), *Straight and Devious Pathways from Childhood to Adulthood* (pp. 101–15).

Maguin, E. and Loeber, R. (1996) Academic performance and delinquency. In M. Tonry (ed.) *Crime and Justice* (vol. 20, pp. 145–264). University of Chicago Press.

Mannuzza, S., Klein, R. G., Bessler, A., Malloy, P. and LaPadula, M. (1993) Adult outcome of hyperactive boys: I. Educational achievement, occupational rank, and psychiatric status. *Archives of General Psychiatry*, *50*, 565–76.

Mannuzza, S., Klein, R. G., Bonagura, N., Malloy, P., Giampino, T. L. and Addalli, K. A. (1991) Hyperactive boys almost grown up: Replication of psychiatric status. *Archives of General Psychiatry*, *48*, 77–83.

Masten, A. S. (1988) Toward a developmental psychopathology of early adolescence. In M. D. Levine and E. R. McArney (eds.), *Early Adolescent Transitions* (pp. 261–78). Lexington, MA: Heath.

Moffitt, T. E. (1990) Juvenile delinquency and Attention Deficit Disorder: Boys' developmental trajectories from age 3 to age 15. *Child Developmental*, *61*, 893–910.

(1993) Adolescence-limited and life-course-persistent antisocial behavior: A developmental taxonomy. *Psychological Review*, *100*, 674–701.

Moffitt, T. E., Caspi, A., Dickson, N., Silva, P. and Stanton, W. (1996) Childhood-onset versus adolescent-onset antisocial conduct problems in males: Natural history from ages 3 to 18 years. *Development and Psychopathology*, *8*, 399–424.

Newman, D. L., Moffitt, T. E., Caspi, A., Magdolm L., Silva, P. A. and Stanton, W. R. (1996) Psychiatric disorder in a birth cohort of young adults: Prevalence, comorbidity, clinical significance, and new case incidence from ages 11 to 21. *Journal of Consulting and Clinical Psychology*, *64*, 552–62.

Nottelman, E. D. and Jensen, P. (1995) Comorbidity of disorders in children and adolescents: Developmental perspectives. In T. H. Ollendick and R. J.

Prinz (eds.), *Advances in Clinical Child Psychology* (pp. 109–55). New York: Plenum.

Nurco, D. N., Shaffer, J. W., Ball, J. C. and Kinlock, T. W. (1985) Trends in the commission of crime among narcotic addicts over successive periods of addiction and nonaddiction. *American Journal of Drug and Alcohol Abuse, 10*, 481–90.

Offord, D. R., Sullivan, K., Allen, N. and Abrams, N. (1979) Delinquency and hyperactivity. *Journal of Nervous and Mental Disease, 167*, 734–41.

Olweus, D. (1979) Stability of aggressive reaction patterns in males: A review. *Psychological Bulletin, 86*, 852–7.

Patrick, C. J. (1994) Emotion and psychopathy: Startling new insights. *Psychophysiology, 31*, 319–30.

Patrick, C. J., Zempolich, K. A. and Levenston, G. K. (1997) Emotionality and violent behavior in psychopaths. In A. Raine, P. A. Brennan, D. P. Farrington and S. A. Mednick (eds.), *Biosocial Bases of Violence* (pp. 145–62). New York: Plenum.

Puig-Antich, J. (1982) Major depression and conduct disorder in prepuberty. *Journal of the American Academy of Child Psychiatry, 21*, 118–28.

Puig-Antich, J., Goetz, D., Davies, M., Kaplan, T., Davies, S., Ostow, L., Asnis, L., Twomey, J., Iyengae, S. and Ryan, N. (1989) A controlled family history study of prepubertal major depressive disorder. *Archives of General Psychiatry, 46*, 406–18.

Quinton, D., Pickles, A., Maughan, B. and Rutter, M. (1993) Partners, peers, and pathways: Assortative pairing and continuities in conduct disorder. *Development and Psychopathology, 5*, 763–83.

Richters, J. E. and Martinez, P. E. (1993) Violent communities, family choices, and children's chances: An algorithm for improving the odds. *Development and Psychopathology, 5*, 609–27.

Robins, L. N. (1966) *Deviant Children Grown Up: A Sociological and Psychiatric Study of Sociopathic Personality*. Baltimore: Williams & Wilkins.

(1978) Sturdy childhood predictors of adult antisocial behavior: Replication from longitudinal studies. *Psychological Medicine, 8*, 611–22.

(1986) Changes in Conduct Disorder over time. In D. C. Farren and J. D. McKinney (eds.), *Risk in Intellectual and Psychosocial Development*. New York: Academic Press, pp. 227–59.

(1991) Conduct Disorder. *Journal of Child Psychology and Psychiatry, 32*, 193–212.

Robins, L. N. and Przybeck, T. R. (1984) Age of onset of drug use as a factor in drug and other disorders. In C. Jones and R. Battjes (eds.), *Etiology of Drug Abuse: Implications for Prevention.* NIDA Research Monograph *56*.

Robins, L. N. and Ratcliff, K. S. (1979) Risk factors in the continuation of childhood antisocial behavior into adulthood. *International Journal of Mental Health, 7*, 96–116.

Robins, L. N., Tipp, J. and Przybeck, T. (1991) Antisocial personality. In L. N. Robins and D. A. Regier, (eds.), *Psychiatric Disorders in America* (pp. 224–71). New York: Free Press.

Robins, L. N. and Wish, E. (1977) Childhood deviance as a developmental process: A study of 223 urban black men from birth to 18. *Social Forces, 56*, 448–73.

Rogers, R., Johansen, J. Chang, J. J. and Salekin, R. T. (1997) Predictors of adolescent psychopathy: Oppositional and conduct-disordered symptoms. *Journal of the American Academy of Psychiatry and Law*, *25*, 281–71.

Rutter, M. (ed.) (1988) *Studies of Psychosocial Risk. The Power of Longitudinal Data*. Cambridge University Press.

Rutter, M. and Giller, H. (1983) *Juvenile Delinquency: Trends and Perspectives*. Middlesex: Penguin.

Rutter, M., Tizard, J. and Whitmore, K. (1970) *Education, Health and Behavior*. New York: Wiley.

Sampson, R. J. and Laub, J. H. (1993) *Crime in the Making*. Cambridge, MA: Harvard University Press.

Satterfield, J. H., Hoppe, C. M. and Schell, A. M. (1982) A prospective study of delinquency in 110 adolescent boys with attention deficit disorder and 88 normal adolescent boys. *American Journal of Psychiatry*, *139*, 795–8.

Schachar, R., Rutter, M. and Smith, A. (1981) The characteristics of situationally and pervasively hyperactive children: Implications for syndrome definition. *Journal of Child Psychology and Psychiatry*, *22*, 375–92.

Shaffer, D. (1974) Suicide in childhood and early adolescence. *Journal of Child Psychology and Psychiatry*, *15*, 275–91.

Shaffi, N., Carrigan, S., Whittinghill, J. R. and Derrick, A. (1985) Psychological autopsy of completed suicide of children and adolescents. *American Journal of Psychiatry*, *142*, 1061–4.

Shubert, D. S. P., Wolf, A. W., Patterson, M. B., Grande, T. P. and Pendleton, L. (1988) A statistical evaluation of the literature regarding the associations among alcoholism, drug abuse, and antisocial personality disorder. *International Journal of the Addictions*, *23*, 797–808.

Stouthamer-Loeber, M., Loeber, R., Farrington, D. P., Zhang, Q., Van Kammen, W. B. and Maguin, E. (1993) The double edge of protective and risk factors for delinquency: Interrelations and developmental patterns. *Development and Psychopathology*, *5*, 683–701.

Swanson, M. C., Bland, R. C. and Newman, S. C. (1994) Antisocial personality disorders. *Acta Psychiatrica Scandinavica*, *89*, 63–70.

Tarter, R., Blackson, T., Martin, C., Loeber, R. and Moss, H. B. (1993) Characteristics and correlates of child discipline practices in substance abuse and normal families. *American Journal on Addictions*, *2*, 18–25.

Van Kammen, W. B. and Loeber, R. (1994) Are fluctuations in delinquent activities related to the onset and offset in juvenile illegal drug use and drug dealing? *Journal of Drug Issues*, *24*, 9–24.

Vitelli, R. (1997) Comparison of early and late start models of delinquency in adult offenders. *International Journal of Offender Therapy and Comparative Criminology*, *41*, 351–7.

Walker, J. L., Lahey, B. B., Hynd, G. W. and Frame, C. L. (1987) Comparison of specific patterns of antisocial behavior in children with conduct disorder with or without coexisting hyperactivity. *Journal of Consulting and Clinical Psychology*, *55*, 910–13.

Weiss, G., Hechtman, L., Milroy, T. and Perlman, T. (1985) Psychiatric status of hyperactives as adults: A controlled prospective 15-year follow-up of 63 hyperactive children. *Journal of the American Academy of Child Psychiatry*, *24*, 211–20.

Werner, E. E. (1986a) The concept of risk from a developmental perspective. In B. K. Keogh (ed.) *Advances in Special Education* (vol. 5). Greenwich, CT: JAI Press.

(1986b) Resilient offspring of alcoholics: A longitudinal study from birth to age 18. *Journal of Studies on Alcohol*, *47*, 34–40.

Widiger, T. A. (1992) DSM-IV in progress: Antisocial Personality Disorder. *Hospital and Community Psychiatry*, *43*, 6–8.

Widiger, T. A. and Corbitt, E. M. (1993) Antisocial personality disorder: Proposals for DSM-IV. *Journal of Personality Disorders*, *7*, 63–77.

Wilson, J. Q. and Herrnstein, R. J. (1985) *Crime and Human Nature*. New York: Simon & Schuster.

World Health Organization, *The ICD-10 Classification of Mental and Behavioural Disorders*. Geneva: World Health Organization, 1992.

Zoccolillo, M. (1992) Co-occurrence of conduct disorder and its adult outcomes with depressive and anxiety disorders: A review. *Journal of the American Academy of Child and Adolescent Psychiatry*, *31*, 547–56.

Zoccolillo, M., Pickles, A., Quinton, D. and Rutter, M. (1992) The outcome of conduct disorder: Implications for defining adult personality disorder and conduct disorder. *Psychological Medicine*, *22*, 1–16.

4 Preventing the inter-generational continuity of antisocial behaviour: implications of partner violence

Terrie E. Moffitt and Avshalom Caspi

Antisocial behaviour is highly stable across the life course of individuals (Farrington, 1995; Loeber, 1982), and it runs strongly from generation to generation within families (Huesmann *et al.*, 1984; Rowe and Farrington, 1997). Indeed, the correlation between measures of fathers' and sons' antisocial behaviour appears to be about as high as the correlation between measures of antisocial behaviour taken at two points in the life course of the same individual. Behavioural genetic studies reveal that less than half of this inter-generational continuity can be ascribed to heritable factors (Carey, 1994; Miles and Carey, 1997). Moreover, behavioural genetic studies estimate that environmental factors shared by family members must account for as much as one-third of the population variance in children's antisocial behaviour (averaged across six large-scale twin studies available when this chapter was written: Edelbrock *et al.*, 1995; Eley, Lichtenstein and Stevenson, 1999; Gjone *et al.*, 1996; Schmitz *et al.*, 1995; Silberg *et al.*, 1994; Thapar, 1995). The antisocial behaviour of almost all seriously antisocial adults first emerged during early childhood in the context of the family home (Moffitt, 1993; Moffitt, Caspi, Dickson, Silva and Stanton, 1996; Robins, 1978). When official crime records are searched for all of the mothers, fathers, sisters, and brothers in a large sample of families, over 50 per cent of the offences are concentrated in only 5 per cent of the families (Farrington, Barnes and Lambert, 1996). In combination, these facts make it critical for preventionists to examine closely the *social* processes by which antisocial behaviour is transmitted to children in the context of the family.

The purpose of this essay is to direct attention to one factor that evidence suggests plays a central role in the social transmission of antisocial behaviour to children: parental partner violence. Other chapters in this volume will examine other family risk factors, such as inconsistent parenting, harsh discipline, unstable family structure, and poverty. We limit our focus to partner violence for three reasons. First, people mate assortatively on antisocial behaviour; that is, 'birds of a feather mate together' (note that we say 'mate' not 'marry') (Krueger, Moffitt, Caspi, Bleske and Silva, 1998; Rowe and Farrington, 1997). Second, young couples who mate assortatively on antisocial behaviour tend to begin child-bearing early (Krueger *et al.*, 1997). Third, couples who share similar antisocial behaviours are more likely to have offspring who become delinquent (Rowe and Farrington, 1997). These findings imply risk converging from two quarters: children who inherit some vulnerability to antisocial behaviour are also selectively more likely than other children to be exposed to aggressive antisocial behaviours when their parents experience conflict at home. Whilst it is both unfeasible and unthinkable to interfere with human inheritance, it is both feasible and desirable to intervene in partner conflict and domestic violence. Thus, a close examination of partner violence may offer a handle on an important risk factor that is amenable to change for disrupting the inter-generational transmission of antisocial behaviour within the family.

Violence between adult intimate partners has increasingly attracted the concern of the general public (Hunt and Kitzinger, 1996) and medical professionals (Skolnick, 1995), as well as mental health practitioners who treat adults (Danielson, Moffitt, Caspi and Silva, 1998). Yet, much of the literature on the treatment of partner violence emphasises the benefits of treatment for adult victims, with relatively less emphasis on the preventive benefits for children. Moreover, criminologists have barely begun to attend to parental partner violence as a factor in the origins and continuity of criminal offending. We prepared this chapter because research suggests that adult partner violence has some important consequences for the emergence of children's antisocial conduct as well as its subsequent continuity into adult life. We present four reasons why professionals who strive to prevent adult antisocial behaviour by intervening in the lives of children and adolescents should be knowledgeable about partner violence:

(I) Young children's conduct problems are promoted by witnessing violence between the adults in their homes.
(II) Adult partners who are violent toward each other are also at increased risk of abusing their children.
(III) Childhood conduct problems are the strongest developmental risk factors for adult partner violence.
(IV) Partner violence is not confined to adults; it is a feature of adolescents' earliest intimate experiences.

We review research evidence to support each of these assertions, and discuss implications of each for preventive intervention. We organise this chapter in chronological order, beginning with implications of partner violence during childhood and infancy, followed by implications for middle childhood and ending with implications in adolescence, coming full circle to the birth of the next generation.

Infancy and early childhood: Young children's conduct problems are promoted by witnessing violence between the adults in their homes

The demographics of partner violence reveal that a large number of young children live in homes where they encounter opportunities to witness violence between adult partners. Four observations lead to this inference. First, the 1993 National Crime Victimisation Survey of 100,000 American households showed that women aged 19 to 29 have rates of violent victimisation by a partner that are twice the rate for any other age group (Bureau of Justice Statistics, 1995). Second, this peak victimisation age coincides with the peak age of child-bearing, which is ages 17 to 30 for women (Rindfuss, 1991). Third, the peak victimisation age also coincides with the peak age for non-marital cohabitation, which is pertinent because unmarried couples who live together have the highest rates of partner violence compared to couples of the same age who date or marry (Magdol, Moffitt, Caspi and Silva, 1998; Stets and Straus, 1990).

Fourth, partner abuse is most common among the young parents of small children. This was revealed in our own study of a birth cohort of 1000 New Zealanders. Before their twenty-first birthday, 10 per cent of the young women had one or more children, and 53 per cent of those young mothers were involved in a violent relationship, as compared to 26 per cent of the non-mothers (Moffitt, Caspi, Rutter and Silva, 2001). It remains unclear whether parenthood coincides with partner violence because child rearing stresses parents, because violence is provoked by conflict over the children (Jaffe, Wolf and Wilson, 1990), or merely because young people who habitually display aggression are selectively likely to leave home early, cohabit early, cohabit with an abusive partner, and bear children early (Bardone, Moffitt, Caspi, Dickson and Silva, 1996). Whatever the reason, these demographic statistics suggest that young children and partner violence are concentrated together in the same segment of the population, with the result that many children witness adults' partner violence.

There is currently great concern about children who are exposed to violence in their neighbourhood streets and schools (Reiss, Richters, Radke-Yarrow and Scharff, 1993). However, there is reason to believe that more detrimental consequences may follow from exposure to parental violence at home. This is because partner violence is concentrated in homes, where children spend time, whereas street violence is concentrated at locations (e.g., bars) and times (e.g., late at night) less often frequented by small children (Sherman, Garten and Buerger, 1989). Moreover, parental partner violence exposes children to repeated incidents of violence between actors with whom the child has a personal relationship, whereas street violence is more likely to expose children to isolated incidents involving unknown actors. For these reasons, numerous studies have examined the effects on children of exposure to parental conflict and violence. Most of these studies have been described in an exhaustive review by Grych and Fincham (1990), and subsequent to that review other studies have been reported (e.g., Fantuzzo, DePaola, Lambert, Martino, Anderson and Sutton, 1991; McCloskey, Figueredo and Koss, 1995).

Grych and Fincham (1990) reviewed studies of marital conflict; studies of parental physical violence are a subset of that literature. Those authors highlighted four issues on which the research tends to agree. Greater *frequency* of parent conflict is consistently associated with worse behaviour problem outcomes for children. Likewise, greater *intensity* of conflict is consistently associated with worse behaviour problem outcomes for children, with physical violence between adults being more detrimental than verbal conflict. The *child's gender* does not appear consistently to influence his or her reaction to parental partner violence, over and above the customary sex-typed pattern in which problem boys show more symptoms of externalising disorders while problem girls show more symptoms of internalising disorders. Finally, the *child's age* does not appear consistently to influence outcome; Grych and Fincham (1990) speculate that older children are more aware than younger children of the implications of parental conflict, but this awareness may be offset by the older child's more mature coping repertoire.

Many studies document that children who are exposed to partner violence experience behaviour problems, but few studies illuminate why and how partner conflict affects children (Fincham, 1994). One hypothesis is that partner violence disrupts the quality of parenting, and thus poor parenting mediates the link between partner violence and children's behaviour problems. This hypothesis receives support from Holden and Ritchie (1991), who found that measures of parenting stress and inconsistent parenting accounted for variation in the behaviour problems of a small sample of children of battered women. A second hypothesis is that partner violence generates intense emotional stress when children believe their security is threatened by parental conflict, or when children believe they are responsible for parental conflict. In this view, stress mediates the link between partner violence and children's behaviour problems (Davies and Cummings, 1994). This hypothesis receives support from a series of experiments showing that children who are exposed to adults' anger respond with both verbal and physiological expressions of distress (El-Sheikh, Cummings and Goetsch, 1989), and that such stress responses are strongest among children whose parents have a history of conflict (Cummings, Pelligrini, Notarius and Cummings, 1989).

A third hypothesis is that children who witness adults' partner violence imitate it. This hypothesis receives support from a series of studies showing that children imitate aggressive behaviours modelled by adults, and that they are more likely to imitate their parents than other adults because parents are models with authority and affectional ties (Bandura, 1973, 1977). Contemporary reformulations of Bandura's original social learning hypothesis add that children do not merely imitate parents' violence, they also learn social cognitions from it that subsequently encourage them to generalise violent tactics to other relationships inside and outside the family (Dodge, 1986). In particular, children learn that violence is a normative part of family relationships, that violence is an effective way to control others, and that perpetrators of intimate violence usually go unpunished (Osofsky, 1995).

A fourth hypothesis requires mention because it has challenged the implicit assumption of the above-mentioned three hypotheses that exposure to partner violence *causes* children's conduct problems. Note that all studies showing a link between partner violence and child behaviour have been correlational, so there is yet no empirical evidence that parents' violence actually causes children's maladjustment (Fincham, Grych and Osborne, 1994). Behavioural genetic studies of adoptees and twins have found evidence that aggressive behaviours span generations within a family because there is some heritable liability toward aggression (Carey, 1994; Mednick, Gabrielli and Hutchings, 1984; Ciba Foundation, 1996). Therefore, it is possible that the children of abusive parents would develop conduct problems, *whether or not* they ever witnessed adults' violence (DiLalla and Gottesman, 1991). This is unlikely to be the complete story, however, because, as we mentioned in the introduction to this chapter, behavioural genetic studies (by controlling for heritability) have uniquely been able to show that antisocial behaviour must be influenced by the environmental aspects of family life (Hetherington, Reiss and Plomin, 1994).

One possibility is that children's conduct problems arise from an interaction between genes and environment, wherein a heritable liability toward violence develops into violent behaviour when children witness parental violence. Consistent with this possibility, a study of 197 adoptees found that the biological parents' antisocial personality most strongly predicted their adopted-away children's aggressiveness and conduct disorder when the child was reared by adoptive parents who had marital conflict

(Cadoret, Yates, Troughton, Woodworth and Stewart, 1995). More studies of this gene-environment interaction hypothesis are needed to inform prevention, as such interactions can identify protective factors that may be intentionally harnessed to reduce the inter-generational transmission of violence to those most at risk (Rutter, 1994). One option for research is to measure directly parental partner violence in the context of a twin design to ascertain interactions between heritable risk and social risk (Moffitt, Caspi and Rutter, 1998). Another option is to conduct an intervention experiment to compare the response of children who do versus do not carry heritable vulnerability to antisocial behaviour (from parental antisocial personality disorder) to successful treatment of their parents' partner violence.

The adverse effect on children of witnessing parental partner violence has implications for preventive practice. Family and child practitioners may need to assess whether child patients are being exposed to violence, particularly if the patient is the child of young, unmarried parents. If a child who presents with behaviour disorders has been exposed to parental partner violence, therapy may need to address the child's cognitions that violence is normal, is effective, and usually goes unpunished. Additional clinical issues and strategies for working with children who have witnessed violence have been outlined by others (Black and Kaplan, 1988; Jaffe, Wolfe and Wilson, 1990; Wolfe and Korsch, 1994; Zuckerman, Augustyn, Groves and Parker, 1995). For clinicians who prevent children's problem behaviour by involving their parents in parenting education programmes, it may be helpful to incorporate instruction about conflict between adult partners: *Not in front of the children, please.* It is worth noting that whereas researchers tend to focus on children seeing parental violence, similar consequences could arise from overhearing parental violence or from detecting a parent's injuries.

Infancy and early childhood: Adult partners who are violent toward each other are also at increased risk of abusing their children

An apparent link between wife abuse and child abuse has long been part of the clinical experience of family violence practitioners. In their account of the battered women's movement in Britain, Dobash and Dobash (1992) quote a memorandum from a parliamentary report: 'A woman entering a refuge . . . has come to realize that the level of violence used against her is intolerable . . . [but] she leaves [home] because she thinks the children are in danger' (p.118). Such personal observations born of cumulative experiences in refuges and courts are persuasive. Nonetheless, it remained possible that the presumed link between wife abuse and child abuse was more apparent than real, because personal observations can be unduly influenced by a few salient, horrific cases. Recently, however, personal observations have been confirmed by systematic research. The research suggests that pre-pubertal children whose parents engage in partner violence are at increased risk for physical abuse.

Two epidemiological studies provide the most reliable information about the link between partner abuse and child abuse, the 1975 American National Family Violence Survey and the Christchurch Child Development Study of New Zealand. Additional research on this link is reviewed by Bowker, Arbitell, and McFerron (1988). The 1975 National Family Violence Survey of more than 2000 American families (Straus, 1990) was notable for demonstrating that more than 90 per cent of respondents used some physical means of punishing their children. However, to differentiate 'serious child abuse' from normative physical punishment, Straus defined serious abuse as having used physical acts that are likely to injure (e.g., strangle, kick, hit, beat up) three or more times in the past year. 'Serious spouse abuse' was defined in the same way. Among parents with no inter-spouse abuse, fewer than 10 per cent reported that they engaged in child abuse. In contrast, among parents who engaged in serious spouse abuse, half of the fathers and one-quarter of the mothers said they had also engaged in serious child abuse. Moreover, the link was not restricted to 'serious spouse abuse' cases; even parents who engaged in only 'ordinary' partner abuse (e.g., pushing, slapping, shoving, and throwing things) were at more than double the risk for abusing their child.

The 1975 American survey provided important first data, but it was limited because it surveyed only families with intact marriages, who under-represent families at risk for domestic violence. Complementary data come from the Christchurch Child Development Study, which began with a 1977 birth cohort of 1265 children, and then repeatedly assessed mothers' reports of assault by their male partners over the years as the children grew from age 2 to 15 (Fergusson, Horwood, Kershaw and Shannon, 1986). When the children themselves were 18 years old, they were asked to report their memories of their parents' punishment practices. As in the American survey, approximately 90 per cent had experienced some means of physical punishment. However, the Christchurch researchers differentiated 'serious child abuse' by defining it as 'at least one parent used physical punishment too often and too severely,' or 'at least one parent treated me in an abusive way.' Among the 18-year-olds who did not recall any child abuse by a parent, fewer than 10 per cent had mothers who had earlier reported inter-partner abuse. In contrast, among the 18-year-olds who did recall that they had been physically abused by a parent, one half had a mother who had reported partner violence between adults in the home earlier in the course of the longitudinal study (Lynskey and Fergusson, personal communication, November 1996). The convergence of reports from mother and adult child, taken years apart, makes this study's findings compelling. Recent reports from the Christchurch Study add to the story by showing that the adult children's memories of maltreatment and memories of their parents' domestic violence are both significant correlates of their own conduct disorder and criminal offending, even after controlling for a host of other family risk factors (Fergusson and Horwood, 1998; Fergusson and Lynskey, 1997).

Taken together, statistics from these and other studies are suggesting that the risk of child abuse is elevated between three and nine times in homes where adult partners hit each other. This link between partner abuse and child abuse has implications for preventive assessment. Practitioners should be aware that knowledge about adult partner violence may signal the potential for child abuse in a family. When battery between adults brings a couple into treatment, the needs of their children warrant assessment too. Alternately, when child abuse is suspected, the clinical interview might begin with a focus on conflict between adults in the family. Both partner abuse and child abuse are undeniably difficult to assess (Gelles, 1982). However, beginning with questions about conflict between adults may be more acceptable and less threatening as a way to broach the topic of family violence than beginning with direct questions about hurting the children. Successful assessment and treatment of abused children is important for preserving the life and health of individual children, but it is also one key for breaking the 'cycle of violence,' wherein abused children return abuse to others later in life. This cycle of violence was once assumed, then later challenged (Kaufman and Zigler, 1987; Widom, 1989a), but has now been documented with well-designed prospective studies (Dodge, Bates and Pettit, 1990; Maxfield and Widom, 1996; Widom, 1989b). Although the early claim that abused children inevitably become antisocial adults has proven to be an exaggeration (Zingraff, Leiter, Myers and Johnsen, 1993), it is generally agreed that the cycle of violence does happen, and does warrant assiduous prevention efforts.

Middle childhood: Childhood conduct problems are strong developmental risk factors for adult partner violence

Partner violence appears to be one manifestation of a more longstanding aggressive approach to the world. In fact, one study shows that a developmental history of conduct problems is the *strongest* predictor of adult partner violence among numerous risk factors, which include poor family socioeconomic resources, conflicted early family relations, and weak childhood cognitive functioning and educational difficulties. We recently completed this study, one of only two prospective child-to-adult longitudinal examinations of risk markers for partner abuse (Magdol, Moffitt, Caspi and Silva, 1998). This research is part of the Dunedin Multidisciplinary Health and Development Study, the aforementioned longitudinal study of a representative 1972 birth cohort of 1000 individuals in Dunedin, New Zealand. The Dunedin sample has been assessed at ages 3, 5, 7, 9, 11, 13, 15, 18, and 21. Thus, we began the prospective study with persons in their childhood family context and followed them until they formed adulthood partner relationships, when we measured partner violence. Using prospective data gathered from birth to age 15, we examined the contributions to adult partner violence of family socioeconomic resources (six measures, including social class and family structure), early family relations (seven measures, including family conflict and harsh discipline), cognitive and educational attainments (five measures, including IQ, reading, and early school leaving), and antisocial problem behaviours (six measures, including the symptoms of conduct disorder, aggressive delinquency, and police contacts). Multivariate analyses showed that the most consistent independent predictor of partner violence was a history of antisocial problem behaviours, assessed as early as age 7. This finding held for both men and women, even after controlling for all of the other risk factors (including social class, conflict between family members, and harsh physical discipline).

The outcome measure of adult partner violence perpetration in the Dunedin study was a self-report measure of thirteen physically violent acts, ranging in severity from slapping the partner to using a weapon on the partner. We had reason to believe that the Dunedin study members at age 21 would provide frank reports of their partner violence perpetration because they have revealed sensitive problem behaviours to us over the many years of the study yet their confidentiality has never been violated. To strengthen our confidence, we also interviewed the study members' partners, who provided corroborative information about their experiences of victimisation at the hands of Dunedin study members (Moffitt, Caspi, Krueger, Magdol, Margolin, Silva and Sydney, 1997). A repeat of the prediction analyses substituting partners' reports of study members' violence for the earlier-analysed self-reports produced a replication of the finding. Study members with a history of conduct disorder were three times more likely than their peers to perpetrate severe physical violence against a partner when they reached adulthood (e.g., strangle, kick, beat up, use a knife or gun).

The importance of this link between childhood conduct problems and adult partner violence was all but unmentioned in the literature on family violence until recently. However, a diligent search of the literature reveals four additional studies that report the link. Farrington (1994) reported from the Farrington and West (1990) longitudinal study of 411 London boys that measures of the boys' antisocial behaviour were the strongest predictors of hitting a spouse at age 32 among 50 measures of the boys and their families from age 8 to 14, with the additional finding that the best independent predictor in that study was having a convicted parent (Farrington, 1994). Adolescent antisocial conduct was the best predictor of dating violence among individual and family predictors recently examined in the Iowa longitudinal study (Simons, Lin and Gordon, 1998) and in the Oregon Social Learning Study (Capaldi and Clark, 1998). In another longitudinal study, Huesmann, Eron, Lefkowitz and Walder (1984) reported a significant correlation between aggressiveness in late childhood, as measured by peer nominations in schools, and spouse abuse twenty-two years later, as measured by spouses' reports.

If the continuity from childhood conduct problems to adult partner violence is robust over many years of development, why has conduct disorder been virtually ignored as a risk factor by family violence research? We can think of two reasons: one is methodological and one is theoretical. With respect to methodology, previous studies have tried to identify childhood antecedents of partner abuse by conducting retrospective assessments, in which identified batterers are asked to recall experiences that took place many years ago. But such retrospective measures suffer from forgetting and from systematic biases in which batterers may recall their childhoods in ways that serve to justify their current predicament (Henry, Moffitt, Caspi, Langley and Silva, 1994; Rutter, Maughan, Pickles and Simonoff, 1998). Specifically, batterers are more likely to blame their behaviour on their circumstances ('I learned it from my bad parents') than on themselves ('Since childhood I have always hit people to get my way').

With respect to theory, for many years family researchers, women's rights advocates, and feminist scholars asserted that the causes of partner violence were uniquely different from causes of other forms of antisocial behaviour. This led many partner violence researchers to focus their etiological inquiries on a limited set of variables, such as witnessing parental conflict, to the virtual neglect of other risk factors, including childhood conduct problems (Reiss and Roth, 1993). For example, a review of fifty-two retrospective studies of partner violence risk factors revealed that only three studies had inquired about childhood aggression, and those studies focused on a single symptom of conduct disorder, hitting other children (Hotaling and Sugarman, 1986).

Our finding that young people who have a history of antisocial conduct problems are likely to employ similar aggressive tactics later in their primary adult relationships suggests the hypothesis that the causes of conduct disorder are also the root causes of partner violence. This raises the related question of whether partner violence is a situational problem arising from the special dynamics of an intimate relationship between two adults, *or* is part of a perpetrator's pattern of repeated aggression toward others persisting over the life course, with a series of victims from siblings to schoolmates to dating partners to strangers to a spouse (Fagan, Stewart and Hansen, 1983; Hotaling, Straus and Lincoln, 1989; Moffitt, Krueger, Caspi and Fagan, 2000; Simons, Wu, Johnson and Conger, 1995). We do not think that the link between conduct disorder and partner violence implies that the study of partner violence should be abandoned on the grounds that 'we already know all there is to know'. Little is known about what factors account for the link between childhood conduct disorder and partner violence. It is likely that some factors that mediate the link may be unique to partner violence, such as heightened sensitivity to rejection and jealousy (Downey and Feldman, 1996), increased opportunity for violence afforded by the privacy of cohabiting in a home (Magdol, Moffitt, Caspi and Silva, 1998), or tolerance of family violence within some cultural groups (Archer, 2000; Torres, 1991). Uncovering the mechanisms that mediate continuity from childhood to adulthood, and across generations, is critical in order to identify which factors may be most amenable to therapeutic intervention and change.

Our finding that young persons who have conduct problems are at risk for future violent intimate relationships has implications for prevention practice. Interventions conceptualised as treatments for conduct problems gain even more urgency if they are re-conceptualised as primary prevention for future domestic violence and the transmission of violence to the next generation. Furthermore, it is known that conduct disorder is an urgent matter for treatment because it predicts not only partner violence, but also a host of other undesirable outcomes (Moffitt, Caspi, Rutter and Silva, 2001; Robins, 1966), including initiation of coitus, cohabitation, and childbearing at a young age (Bardone *et al.*, 1996). This observation that childhood conduct problems may lead to the co-occurrence of partner violence with teen intimacy and sexuality brings us to the next section of this essay.

Adolescence: Partner violence is not confined to adults; it is a feature of adolescents' earliest intimate experiences

The term 'domestic violence' implies that the involved individuals share a domicile, while terms such as 'wife beating', 'spouse abuse', and 'marital violence' echo the belief that 'the marriage licence is a hitting license' (Straus, 1980). In this chapter we have deliberately used the term 'partner violence' because, according to research, many young couples are hitting without a marriage licence, including couples of secondary school age. In addition, for this article we have generally used the phrase 'experienced partner violence' rather than specifying roles as perpetrator or victim because research has shown that most partner violence is characterised by mutual exchanges of violence rather than by gender-typed roles of male perpetrator and female victim. This finding is now well-accepted, because females have reported as much perpetration as males on every partner-violence measure in every epidemiological survey, and because males report high rates of victimisation by females (for reviews see Archer, 2000; Magdol, Moffitt, Caspi, Newman, Fagan and Silva, 1997). Moreover, a study of 360 young couples showed that womens' reports of perpetration are corroborated by their male victims, and vice versa (Moffitt *et al.*, 1997). Additional research shows that females' alleged perpetration is not merely in self-defence; respondents report that females hit first half the time and males hit first half the time (Stets and Straus, 1990). Also arguing against a strict self-defence explanation, the childhood risk factors and adolescent personality traits that prospectively predict who will abuse their partners are the same for women abusers as for men abusers (Moffitt, Caspi, Rutter and Silva, 2001). Although males are less often injured during partner abuse, when a lethal weapon or other means is used to equalise the disparity between the sexes in physical strength, historical domestic homicide rates confirm that women can perpetrate almost as often as men (Mann, 1988; Wilson and Daly, 1992).

Initial reports of abusive behaviours among unmarried dating couples described the self-reported experiences of university students (Archer and Ray, 1989; Pirog-Good and Stets, 1989). Those studies revealed high rates of partner violence, which were unexpected because the university respondents represented an unusually advantaged segment of the population. There are fewer surveys of adolescents in secondary schools, but these studies too reveal non-trivial rates of dating violence. Estimates of the prevalence rate of dating violence among secondary school students range widely, from 9 per cent to 42 per cent (Bergman, 1992; Ferraro and Johnson, 1984; Henton, Cate, Koval, Lloyd and Christopher, 1983;

Jezl, Molidor and Wright, 1996; O'Keefe, Brockopp and Chew, 1986; Roscoe and Callahan, 1985). These six studies surveyed sample sizes ranging from 200 to 700 students, and generally estimated prevalence as the portion of respondents who experienced at least one or more of the violent acts on the Conflict Tactics Scale (CTS) in the past year. The CTS inquires about these acts: push/grab/shove, throw object, slap, kick/bite, hit, beat up, choke/strangle, threaten with knife or gun, and use knife or gun (Straus, 1987).

The differences in prevalence estimates across studies partially reflect differences in measurement and reporting period. Some of the highest rates emerge from studies that added items assessing sexual coercion to the standard CTS. As a general rule, the longer the reporting period and the more questions about violence a study asked, the higher the resulting prevalence estimate. The lowest estimate of the prevalence of dating violence comes from the 1992 Youth Risk Behaviour Survey of a representative sample of 10,645 Americans aged 12 to 21 years, which asked respondents a single question about being in a physical fight in the past year, instead of administering the full CTS. Results for respondents between 12 and 17 years old showed that 2 per cent said they had been in a fight with a boyfriend, girlfriend, or a date (Centers for Disease Control, 1994). Of those who reported being in such a fight in the prior year, more than half said it had happened more than once.

The true rate at which adolescents experience serious physical dating violence undoubtedly lies somewhere between the reported rates of 2 per cent and 42 per cent, but even the more modest prevalence rates reported may be sufficient to warrant attention from researchers and clinicians who work with adolescents to prevent violence. Few victims of adolescent dating violence are getting such attention. Bergman (1992) asked 631 secondary school students who they had told about their experience with violence. Among those who said they had 'been hurt physically' or had 'been forced to do something sexual' while they were out on a date, fewer than 5 per cent said they had told any adult. In a similar survey of more than 1200 university students, fewer than 3 per cent of victims had told their parents and fewer than 1 per cent had told a counsellor, physician, or justice authority (Pirog-Good and Stets, 1989). These statistics suggest that clinicians should ask adolescent patients about dating violence rather than depend on adolescents to disclose it.

Adolescents are less willing than younger children to confide in adults about many issues. However, research on the context surrounding dating violence suggests three reasons why adolescents do not tell adults about dating violence in particular. First, adolescents may conceal partner violence because they fear that adults will force them to break off their relationship. A nationally representative survey of 18–21-year-old daters found that violence was most common in relationships of longer duration and relationships that were rated by respondents as more serious and committed (Stets, 1992). Moreover, more than 70 per cent of secondary school couples who experienced violence said they had continued their relationship despite the violence (Bergman, 1992). Second, adolescents may conceal partner violence because they do not want to attract adult reprimands about their use of alcohol. The aforementioned nationally representative survey of daters found that both victims and perpetrators were likely to say they had been drinking alcohol before the incident erupted into violence (Stets and Henderson, 1991). Third, adolescent girls may conceal partner violence because they believe that they share the blame for it. Virtually all of the studies we reviewed for this article report that adolescent girls say they perpetrate violence as often as they are victimised (Archer and Ray, 1989; Centers for Disease Control, 1994; Henton *et al.*, 1983; Jezl *et al.*, 1996; O'Keefe *et al.*, 1986; Stets and Henderson, 1991). And, as in studies of adults, girls' alleged perpetration is not merely in self-defence; teens report that girls hit first half the time (Henton *et al.*, 1983). Although girls are at greater risk for injury than boys, perceptions of equal blame may stop them from seeking help.

Taken together, these findings suggest that teenagers do not invite adults to intervene when violence breaks out in a relationship because girls may feel that they are as much to blame as their dates, teens may not want to attract chastisement for drinking alcohol, and they may not want their relationship forcibly ended. The prevalence of dating violence makes it apparent that early interventions are needed to help teenagers prevent and respond to partner violence (LaVoie, Vezina, Piche and Boivin, 1995), but practitioners may also need to address the unique concerns of adolescents when broaching the possibility of intervention. In any case, one overarching implication from research findings about dating violence is that secondary school is not too early to teach healthy ways to handle conflicts with intimate partners. Recall that in the aforementioned Dunedin longitudinal study, half of the girls with conduct disorder before their fifteenth birthday later became involved in a violent intimate relationship, and 30 per cent of the former conduct-disordered girls became teen mothers, compared to only 8 per cent of non-disordered girls (Bardone *et al.*, 1996). This pattern calls for integrating violence education with sex education for minimising the transmission of antisocial behaviour to the next generation.

Conclusions

Research on partner violence has struggled to gain scientific legitimacy. In the past, it was difficult to draw responsible implications from the partner violence literature because much of the early research used small clinical samples and was politically motivated, and because disagreements between researchers within the field about basic findings sometimes reached vitriolic proportions (Gelles and Loseke, 1993). In our estimation, the state of the literature has improved enough to support our contention that partner violence harms the health and well-being of children. The myth that 'all married couples are at equal risk for violence' has been replaced by data showing that partner violence is concentrated among unmarried young men and women who cohabit and bear children at a young age, especially young men and women who have a developmental history of conduct problems. We have reviewed evidence that violence between parents is linked to their children's maltreatment. Research also shows that maltreatment and witnessing parental aggression during early childhood predict that children will develop conduct problems. Conduct problems, in turn, predict later partner violence, which first emerges in adolescents' dating experiences. Rates of partner violence double among young couples who move from dating into cohabiting, and who bear children at a young age. And so, aggressive behaviour becomes highly stable across the life course of individuals, and is transmitted from generation to generation within families. If research continues to support this cyclic view of family violence, then violence between intimate partners should become a primary target among the interventions designed to prevent antisocial behaviour in subsequent generations.

REFERENCES

Archer, J. (2000) Sex differences in aggression between heterosexual partners: A meta-analytic review. *Psychological Bulletin*.

Archer, J. and Ray, N. (1989) Dating violence in the United Kingdom: A preliminary study. *Aggressive Behavior*, *15*, 337–43.

Bandura, A. (1973) *Aggression: A Social Learning Analysis*. Englewood Cliffs, NJ: Prentice-Hall.

(1977) *Social Learning Theory*. Englewood Cliffs, NJ: Prentice-Hall.

Bardone, A. M., Moffitt, T. E., Caspi, A., Dickson, N. and Silva, P. A. (1996) Adult mental health and social outcomes of adolescent girls with depression and conduct disorder. *Development and Psychopathology*, *8*, 811–29.

Bergman, L. (1992) Dating violence among high school students. *Social Work*, *37*, 21–6.

Black, D. and Kaplan, T. (1988) Father kills mother: Issues and problems encountered by a child psychiatric team. *British Journal of Psychiatry, 153*, 624–30.

Bowker, L. H., Arbitell, M. and McFerron, J. R. (1988) On the relationship between wife beating and child abuse. In K. Yllo and M. Bograd (eds.). *Feminist Perspectives on Wife Abuse* (pp. 158–74). Newbury Park, CA: Sage.

Bureau of Justice Statistics, (1995) *Violence Against Women: Estimates From the Redesigned Survey*. Washington, DC: U.S. Dept. of Justice, Office of Justice Programs.

Cadoret, R. J., Yates, W. R., Troughton, E., Woodworth, G. and Stewart, M. A. (1995) Genetic-environmental interaction in the genesis of aggressivity and conduct disorders. *Archives of General Psychiatry, 52*, 916–24.

Capaldi, D. M. and Clark, S. (1998) Prospective family predictors of aggression toward female partners for young at-risk males. *Developmental Psychology, 34*, 1175–88.

Carey, G. (1994) Genetics and violence. In A. J. Reiss, Jr., K. A. Miczek and J. A. Roth (eds.) *Understanding and Preventing Violence: vol. 2, Biobehavioral Influences* (pp. 21–58). Washington, DC: National Academy Press.

Caspi, A. and Moffitt, T. E. (1995) The continuity of maladaptive behavior: From description to explanation in the study of antisocial behavior. In D. Cicchetti and D. Cohen (eds.), *Developmental Psychopathology, (vol. 2)*, (pp. 472–511). New York: Wiley.

Centers for Disease Control (1994) Health-risk behaviors among persons aged 12–21 years – United States, 1992. *Mortality and Morbidity Weekly Report, 43*, 231–5.

Ciba Foundation (1996) *Genetics of Criminal and Antisocial Behaviour*. Chichester: Wiley.

Cummings, J. S., Pellegrini, D. S., Notarius, C. I. and Cummings, E. M. (1989) Children's responses to angry adult behavior as a function of marital distress and history of interparent hostility. *Child Development, 60*, 1035–43.

Danielson, K., Moffitt, T. E., Caspi, A. and Silva, P. A. (1998) Co-morbidity between abuse of an adult and DSM-IIIR mental disorders. *American Journal of Psychiatry, 155*, 131–3.

Davies, P. T. and Cummings, E. M. (1994) Marital conflict and child adjustment: An emotional security hypothesis. *Psychological Bulletin, 116*, 387–411.

DiLalla, L. F. and Gottesman, I. I. (1991) Biological and genetic contributions to violence – Widom's untold tale. *Psychological Bulletin, 109*, 125–9.

Dobash, R. E. and Dobash, R. P. (1992) *Women, Violence and Social Change*. London: Routledge.

Dodge, K. A. (1986) A social-information-processing model of social competence in children. In M. Perlmutter (ed.), *Minnesota Symposia on Child Psychology* 18th ed. (pp. 77–125). Hillsdale, NJ: Erlbaum.

Dodge, K. A., Bates, J. E. and Pettit, G. S. (1990) Mechanisms in the cycle of violence. *Science, 250*, 1678–83.

Downey, G. and Feldman, S. (1996) Implications of rejection sensitivity for intimate relationships. *Journal of Personality and Social Psychology, 70*, 1327–43.

Edelbrock, C., Rende, R., Plomin, R. and Thompson, L. A. (1995) A twin study of competence and problem behavior in childhood and early adolescence. *Journal of Child Psychology and Psychiatry*, *36*, 775–85.

Eley, T. C., Lichtenstein, P. and Stevenson, J. (1999) Sex differences in the aetiology of aggressive and non-aggressive antisocial behavior: Results from two twin studies. *Child Development*, *70*, 155–68.

El-Sheikh, M., Cummings, E. M. and Goetsch, V. L. (1989) Coping with adults' angry behavior: Behavioral, physiological, and verbal responses in preschoolers. *Developmental Psychology*, *25*, 490–8.

Fagan, J. A., Stewart, D. K. and Hansen, K. V. (1983) Violent men or violent husbands? Background factors and situational correlates. In D. Finkelhor, R. J. Gelles, G. T. Hotaling and M. A. Straus (eds.). *The Dark Side of Families: Current Family Violence Research* (pp. 49–67). Beverly Hills, CA: Sage.

Fantuzzo, J. W., DePaola, L. M., Lambert, L., Martino, T., Anderson, G. and Sutton, S. (1991) Effects of interparental violence on the psychological adjustment and competencies of young children. *Journal of Consulting and Clinical Psychology*, *59*, 258–65.

Farrington, D. P. (1994) Childhood, adolescent and adult features of violent males. In L. R. Huesmann (ed.), *Aggressive Behavior: Current Perspectives*. (pp. 215–40). New York: Plenum.

(1995) The development of offending and antisocial behavior from childhood. *Journal of Child Psychology and Psychiatry*, *36*, 929–64.

Farrington, D. P., Barnes, G. C. and Lambert, S. (1996) The concentration of offending in families. *Legal and Criminological Psychology*, *1*, 47–63.

Farrington, D. P. and West, D. J. (1990) The Cambridge study in delinquent development: A long-term follow-up of 411 London males. In H. J. Kerner and G. Kaiser (eds.). *Kriminalitat* (pp. 117–38). New York, NY: Springer-Verlag.

Fergusson, D. M. and Horwood, L. J. (1998) Exposure to interparental violence in childhood and psychosocial adjustment in young adulthood. *Child Abuse & Neglect*, *2*, 339–57.

Fergusson, D. M., Horwood, L. J., Kershaw, K. L. and Shannon, F. T. (1986) Factors associated with reports of wife assault in New Zealand. *Journal of Marriage and the Family*, *48*, 407–12.

Ferraro, K. J. and Johnson, J. M. (1984, August) *The Meanings of Courtship Violence*. Paper presented at the Second National Family Violence Research Conference, University of New Hampshire, Durham, NH.

Fergusson, D. M. and Lynskey, M. T. (1997) Physical punishment/maltreatment during childhood and adjustment in young adulthood. *Child Abuse and Neglect*, *1*, 617–30.

Fincham, F. D. (1994) Understanding the association between marital conflict and child adjustment: Overview. *Journal of Family Psychology*, *8*, 123–7.

Fincham, F. D., Grych, J. H. and Osbourne, L. N. (1994) Does marital conflict cause child maladjustment? Directions and challenges for longitudinal research. *Journal of Family Psychology*, *8*, 128–40.

Gelles, R. J. (1982) Applying research on family violence to clinical practice. *Journal of Marriage and the Family*, *44*, 9–20.

Gelles. R. J. and Loseke, D. R. (eds.) (1993) *Current Controversies on Family Violence*. Newbury Park, CA: Sage.

Gjone, J., Stevenson, J., Sundet, J. M. and Eilertsen, D. E. (1966) Changes in heritability across increasing levels of behavior problems in young twins. *Behavior Genetics, 26*, 419–26.

Grych, J. H. and Fincham, F. D. (1990) Marital conflict and children's adjustment: A cognitive-context framework. *Psychological Bulletin, 108*, 267–90.

Henry, B., Moffitt, T. E., Caspi, A., Langley, J. and Silva, P. A. (1994) On the "remembrance of things past": A longitudinal evaluation of the retrospective method. *Psychological Assessment, 6*, 92–101.

Henton, J., Cate, R., Koval, J., Lloyd, S. and Christopher, S. (1993) Romance and violence in dating relationships. *Journal of Family Issues, 4*, 467–82.

Hetherington, E. M., Reiss, D. and Plomin, R. (eds.) (1994) *Separate Social Worlds of Siblings: The Impact of Nonshared Environment on Development*. Hillsdale, NJ: Erlbaum.

Holden, G. W. and Ritchie, K. L. (1991) Linking extreme marital discord, child rearing, and child behavior problems: Evidence from battered women. *Child Development, 62*, 311–27.

Hotaling, G. T., Straus, M. A. and Lincoln, A. J. (1989) Intrafamily violence, and crime and violence outside the family. In L. Ohlin and M. Tonry (eds.). *Family Violence* (pp. 315–75). University of Chicago Press.

Hotaling, G. T. and Sugarman, D. B. (1986) An analysis of risk markers in husband to wife violence: The current state of knowledge. *Violence and Victims, 1*, 101–24.

Huesmann, L. R., Eron, L. D., Lefkowitz, M. M. and Walder, L. O. (1984) Stability of aggression over time and generations. *Developmental Psychology, 20*, 1120–34.

Hunt, K. and Kitzinger, J. (1996) Public place, private issue? The public's reaction to the Zero Tolerance campaign against violence against women. In H. Bradby (ed.), *Defining Violence* (pp. 45–58). Aldershot: Avebury.

Jaffe, P. G., Wolfe, D. A. and Wilson, S. K. (1990) *Children of Battered Women*. Newbury Park, CA: Sage Publications.

Jezl, D. R., Molidor, C. E. and Wright, T. L. (1996) Physical, sexual and psychological abuse in high school dating relationships: Prevalence rates and self-esteem issues. *Child and Adolescent Social Work Journal, 13*, 69–87.

Kaufman, J. and Zigler, E. (1987) Do abused children become abusive parents? *American Journal of Orthopsychiatry, 57*, 186–92.

Krueger, R. F., Moffitt, T. E., Caspi, A., Bleske, A. and Silva, P. A. (1998) Assortative mating for antisocial behavior: Developmental and methodological implications. *Behavior Genetics, 28*, 173–86.

LaVoie, F., Vezina, L., Piche, C. and Boivin, M. (1995) Evaluation of a prevention program for violence in teen dating relationships. *Journal of Interpersonal Violence, 10*, 516–24.

Loeber, R. (1982) The stability of antisocial and delinquent child behavior: A review. *Child Development, 53*, 1431–46.

Lynskey, M. and Fergusson, D. Personal communication, November 1996.

Magdol, L., Moffitt, T. E., Caspi, A., Newman, D. L., Fagan, J. and Silva, P. A. (1997) Gender differences in partner violence in a birth-cohort of 21-year-olds: Bridging the gap between clinical and epidemiological approaches. *Journal of Consulting and Clinical Psychology*, *65*, 68–78.

Magdol, L., Moffitt, T. E., Caspi, A. and Silva, P. A. (1998a) Developmental antecedents of partner abuse: A prospective-longitudinal study. *Journal of Abnormal Psychology*, *107*, 375–89.

(1998b) Hitting without a license: Testing explanations for differences in partner abuse between young adult daters and cohabitors. *Journal of Marriage and the Family*, *60*, 41–55.

Mann, C. R. (1988) Getting even? Women who kill in domestic encounters. *Justice Quarterly*, *5*, 33–51.

Maxfield, M. G. and Widom, C. S. (1996) The cycle of violence revisited 6 years later. *Archives of Pediatric and Adolescent Medicine*, *150*, 390–5.

McCloskey, L. A., Figueredo, A. J. and Koss, M. P. (1995) The effects of systemic family violence on children's mental health. *Child Development*, *66*, 1239–61.

Mednick, S. A., Gabrielli, W. F. and Hutchings, B. (1984) Genetic factors in criminal behavior: Evidence from an adoption cohort. *Science*, *224*, 891–3.

Miles, D. R. and Carey, G. (1997) Genetic and environmental architecture of human aggression. *Journal of Personality and Social Psychology*, *72*, 207–17.

Moffitt, T. E. (1993) "Life-course-persistent" and "adolescence-limited" antisocial behavior: A developmental taxonomy. *Psychological Review*, *100*, 674–701.

Moffitt, T. E. and Caspi, A. (1998) *Findings about Partner Violence from the Dunedin Multidisciplinary Health and Development Study*. Research in Brief Monograph. Washington, DC: National Institute of Justice.

Moffitt, T. E., Caspi, A., Dickson, N., Silva, P. A. and Stanton, W. (1996) Childhood-onset versus adolescent-onset antisocial conduct in males: Natural history from age 3 to 18. *Development & Psychopathology*, *8*, 399–424.

Moffitt, T. E., Caspi, A., Krueger, R. and Fagan, J. (2000) Partner abuse and general crime: how are they the same? How are they different? *Criminology*, *38*, 199–232.

Moffitt, T. E., Caspi, A., Krueger, R. F., Magdol, L., Margolin, G., Silva, P. A. and Sydney, R. (1997) Do partners agree about abuse in their relationship? A psychometric evaluation of interpartner agreement. *Psychological Assessment*, *9*, 47–56.

Moffitt, T. E., Caspi, A. and Rutter, M. (1998) Environmental risk in the origins of disruptive behavior. Unpublished manuscript.

Moffitt, T. E., Caspi, A., Rutter, M. and Silva, P. A. (2001) *Sex Differences in Antisocial Behaviour: Conduct Disorder, Delinquency, and Violence in the Dunedin Longitudinal Study*. Cambridge University Press.

O'Keefe, N., Brockipp, K. and Chew, E. (1986) Teen dating violence. *Social Work*, *31*, 465–8.

Osofsky, J. D. (1995) Children who witness domestic violence: The invisible victims. *SRCD Social Policy Report*, *9(3)*, 1–16.

Pirog-Good, M. A. and Stets, J. E. (1989) The help-seeking behavior of physically and sexually abused college students. In M. A. Pirog-Good and J. E. Stets (eds.). *Violence in Dating Relationships* (pp. 108–25). New York: Praeger.

Reiss, A. J. and Roth, J. A. (eds.) (1993) *Understanding and Preventing Violence*. Washington, DC: National Academy Press.

Reiss, D., Richters, J. E., Radke-Yarrow, M. and Scharff, D. (eds.) (1993) *Children and Violence*. New York: Guilford Press.

Rindfuss, R. R. (1991) The young adult years: Diversity, structural change, and fertility. *Demography*, *28*, 493–512.

Robins, L. N. (1966) *Deviant Children Grown Up*. Baltimore, MD: Williams and Wilkins.

(1978) Sturdy childhood predictors of adult antisocial behavior: Replications from longitudinal studies. *Psychological Medicine*, *8*, 611–22.

Roscoe, B. and Callahan, J. E. (1985) Adolescents' self-report of violence in families and dating relations. *Adolescence*, *20*, 545–53.

Rowe, D. C. and Farrington, D. P. (1997) The familial transmission of criminal convictions. *Criminology*, *35*, 177–201.

Rutter, M. (1994) Family discord and conduct disorder: Cause, consequence, or correlate? *Journal of Family Psychology*, *8*, 170–86.

Rutter, M., Maughan, B., Pickles, A. and Simonoff, E. (1998) Retrospective recall recalled. In R. B. Cairns, J. Kagan and L. Bergman (eds.). *The Individual in Developmental Research: Essays in Honor of Marian Radke-Yarrow*. Newbury Park, CA: Sage.

Schmitz, S., Fulker, D. W. and Mrazek, D. A. (1995) Problem behavior in early and middle childhood: An initial behavior genetic analysis. *Journal of Child Psychology and Psychiatry*, *36*, 1443–58.

Sherman, L. W., Gartin, P. R. and Buerger, M. E. (1989) Hot spots of predatory crime: Routine activities and the criminology of place. *Criminology*, *27*, 27–55.

Silberg, J. L., Erickson, M. T., Meyer, J. M., Eaves, L. J., Rutter, M. and Hewitt, J. K. (1994) The application of structural equation modeling to maternal ratings of twins' behavioral and emotional problems. *Journal of Consulting and Clinical Psychology*, *62*, 510–21.

Simons, R., Wu, C. I., Johnson, C. and Conger, R. D. (1995) A test of various perspectives on the intergenerational transmission of domestic violence. *Criminology*, *33*, 141–71.

Simons, R., Lin, K. and Gordon, L. C. (1998) Socialization in the family of origin and male dating violence: A prospective study. *Journal of Marriage and the Family*, *60*, 467–78.

Skolnick, A. A. (1995) Physician, heal thyself – then aid abused women. *Journal of the American Medical Association*, *273*, 1744–5.

Stets, J. (1992) Interactive processes in dating aggression: A national study. *Journal of Marriage and the Family*, *54*, 165–77.

Stets, J., and Henderson, D. A. (1991) Contextual factors surrounding conflict resolution while dating: Results from a national study. *Family Relations*, *40*, 29–36.

Stets, J. E. and Straus, M. A. (1990) The marriage license as a hitting license: A comparison of assault in dating, cohabiting, and married couples. In M. A.

Straus and R. J. Gelles (eds.). *Physical Violence in American Families: Risk Factors and Adaptions to Violence in 8,145 Families* (pp. 227–44). New Brunswick, NJ: Transaction.

Straus, M. A. (1979) Measuring intrafamily conflict and violence: The Conflict Tactics (CT) Scales. *Journal of Marriage and the Family*, *41*, 75–88.

(1980) The marriage license as a hitting license: Evidence from popular culture, law and social science. In M. A. Straus and G. T. Hotaling (eds.), *The Social Causes of Husband-Wife Violence*. Minneapolis: University of Minnesota Press.

(1990) Ordinary violence, child abuse, and wife beating: What do they have in common? In M. A. Straus and R. J. Gelles (eds.). *Physical Violence in American Families: Risk Factors and Adaptions to Violence in 8,145 Families* (pp. 403–24). New Brunswick, NJ: Transaction.

Thapar, A. (1995) *A Twin Study of Psychiatric Symptoms in Childhood*. Unpublished doctoral dissertation, University of Wales, Cardiff.

Torres, S. (1991) A comparison of wife abuse between two cultures: Perceptions, attitudes, nature, and extent. *Issues in Mental Health Nursing*, *12*, 113–31.

Widom, C. S. (1989a) The cycle of violence. *Science*, *244*, 160–6.

(1989b) Does violence beget violence? A critical examination of the literature. *Psychological Bulletin*, *106*, 3–28.

Wilson, M. and Daly, M. (1992) Who kills whom in spouse killings? On the exceptional sex ratio of spousal homicides in the United States. *Criminology*, *30*, 189–216.

Wolfe, D. A. and Korsch, B. (1994) Witnessing domestic violence during childhood and adolescence: Implication for pediatric practice. *Pediatrics*, *94*, 594–9.

Zingraff, M. T., Leiter, J., Myers, K. A. and Johnsen, M. C. (1993) Child maltreatment and youthful problem behavior. *Criminology*, *31*, 173–202.

Zuckerman, B., Augustyn, M., Groves, B. M. and Parker, S. (1995) Silent victims revisited: The special case of domestic violence. *Pediatrics*, *96*, 511–13.

5 Protective factors and resilience

Friedrich Lösel and Doris Bender

Introduction

The majority of studies on antisocial behaviour have focused on causes and risk factors. Thanks particularly to prospective longitudinal studies, we now have a pretty good understanding of the characteristics of youngsters who are at risk of becoming serious offenders (e.g., Loeber and Farrington, 1998). Developmental models such as Moffitt's (1993a) taxonomy of adolescence-limited and life course-persistent antisociality, the distinction between early and late starters (Patterson *et al.*, 1991), or the three pathways model of overt, covert, and authority conflict from Loeber and Hay (1994) offer explanations for the onset, persistence, and aggravation of various forms of antisocial behaviour. Although researchers do not agree about the number and structure of different pathways to serious delinquency (Loeber and Stouthamer-Loeber, 1998; Nagin and Tremblay, 1999), children who show both overt and covert antisocial behaviour and early official delinquency seem to be particularly at risk for chronic offending (Farrington and Loeber, 2001; Patterson *et al.*, 1998).

However, most research on persistent antisociality focuses on risks, deficits, and negative behavioural trends. Much less attention is paid to processes of abstaining or desistance (Farrington, 1994; Loeber and Stouthamer-Loeber, 1998; Nagin and Tremblay, 1999). Such processes are no rarity: for example, in the Kauai Study (Werner and Smith, 1992; see below), one out of three high-risk children grew into a competent, confident, and caring young adult. Robins (1978) and Moffitt *et al.* (1996) have shown that about one half of children with conduct disorders or extreme antisociality did not go on to serious criminal outcomes. According to Haapasalo and Tremblay (1994), 8 per cent of boys were stable frequent fighters from kindergarten age to ages 10–12, whereas 12 per cent had desisted by this time. In a study of physical aggression from age 6 to age 15, the group of desisters was even much larger than the group of boys who remained chronically aggressive (4 per cent versus 28 per cent; Nagin and Tremblay, 1999). Although Patterson *et al.* (1998)

found a clearly persistent pathway, approximately 50 per cent of children who were high in antisocial behaviour at age 9–10 did not move through the progression to early arrest and chronic offences by age 18. Asking why a substantial proportion of children do not set out on a deviant pathway despite exposure to serious risks or why they leave it again leads us to the issue of protective factors and mechanisms.

At first glance, processes of abstaining and desistance seem to contradict the research on prediction of antisocial behaviour: as numerous studies have shown, antisocial behaviour and particularly aggressivity is relatively stable. Depending on the time interval, stability coefficients may reach 0.70 (Olweus, 1979; Zumkley, 1994). Up to 80 per cent of serious and violent offenders at age 18 can be classified correctly on the basis of prior antisociality and other individual and social predictors at age 10 (Hawkins *et al.*, 1998; Lipsey and Derzon, 1998; Lösel, 2002). However, when the base rates are taken into account, the percentage of false positives may become similarly large (Lipsey and Derzon, 1998). Even high correlations between Time 1 and Time 2 indicate only a relative stability in rank ordering that may still be accompanied by substantial changes in absolute prevalence, frequency, and seriousness of antisocial behaviour (Farrington, 1990; Loeber and Stouthamer-Loeber, 1998; Tremblay, 2000). Success rates also tend to be lower when predictions are replicated or go beyond one point of outcome measurement. For these and other reasons, errors in the prediction of antisociality in childhood and adolescence should not just be viewed as a technical deficit. They are also indicators of general phenomena of multifinality and equifinality in development (Cicchetti and Rogosch, 1996). When we want to improve explanation, prediction, and prevention, we must learn from the protective mechanisms that contribute to nondeviance or desistance in the natural environment. The same applies to successful cases or 'spontaneous' remissions from the untreated control groups in prevention and intervention studies. On the one hand, these phenomena contribute to a weaker programme effect (Lösel, 1995). But, on the other hand, they indicate important processes of developmental flexibility in the natural history of antisocial behaviour.

It is only recently that researchers have started to investigate protective factors against antisociality. The increased interest is related to the upswing of resilience research in developmental psychopathology (Cicchetti and Garmezy, 1993; Luthar, 1993; Luthar *et al.*, 2000a; Rutter, 1985). This investigates why some persons remain healthy or recover relatively easily from disorders despite marked stressors and risks, whereas, under comparable conditions, others are particularly vulnerable. Resilience is viewed here as the opposite pole of vulnerability (Basic Behavioral

Science Task Force, 1996). The concept is used to describe not only the process of biopsychosocial adaptation but also its outcome (see Lösel *et al.*, 1989; Masten and Garmezy, 1985). Whereas the initial discussion focused on more or less idealised cases of 'invulnerable' children (Anthony, 1974), the current concern is with a *relative* power of resistance to pathological circumstances and events that may vary across time and situations (Rutter, 1985). According to Masten *et al.* (1990), the phenomena of elastic adaptation include: (a) healthy development despite high-risk status (e.g., growing up in a multiproblem milieu), (b) maintaining competence under specific stressors (e.g., coping with parental divorce), or (c) recuperating from severe trauma (e.g., child abuse). It is noteworthy that these adaptations correspond to elementary biological mechanisms such as (a) protection (e.g., through immune defence), (b) regeneration (e.g., during sleep), and (c) repair (e.g., in wound healing).

This chapter will sketch findings from resilience research with particular emphasis on protection against antisocial behaviour. The first section will discuss basic concepts, research examples, and problems. The second part will consider a selection of protective factors and underlying processes in more detail. Finally, conclusions and perspectives for future research will be sketched.

Basic concepts, research examples, and problems

At first glance, the concept of protective factors seems very plausible: when risk factors increase the probability of the onset, persistence, or aggravation of problem behaviour, protective factors may compensate for their effects and reduce the probability of negative outcomes. However, protective effects are often less obvious than risks, and they can be detected only when research is designed sensitively to detect them. With emphasis on processes, Rutter (1987) has discriminated between risk, vulnerability, and protective mechanisms. Risk mechanisms lead directly to disorder. In a vulnerability process, such a risk function is strengthened, and a previously adaptive trajectory is turned into a negative one. In a protective process, a risk trajectory is weakened and changed to one with a greater likelihood of a positive outcome. In principle, these two latter processes can be based on analogue factors and mechanisms.

The various hypothetical models of such processes (e.g., Garmezy *et al.*, 1984; Gest *et al.*, 1993; Luthar *et al.*, 2000a) and related research designs or data analyses (e.g., von Eye and Schuster, 2000) cannot be addressed here. We shall also not discuss the problems of the resilience concept from a general perspective (e.g, Gordon and Wang, 1994; Kaplan, 1999; Lösel and Bliesener, 1990; Luthar *et al.*, 2000a; Tarter and

Vanyukow, 1999; Tolan, 1996). These problems include, for example, the ambiguity in definitions and central terminology; the heterogeneity in risks experienced and competence achieved by 'resilient' individuals; the instability of the phenomena of resilience; and the usefulness of the construct for developmental theory and prevention (Luthar *et al.*, 2000a). As our focus is primarily on antisocial behaviour, we shall give some research examples from this area and use them to illustrate basic theoretical and methodological problems. These are associated with the main concepts: (1) protective factors, (2) risk factors, and (3) behavioural outcome.

Protective factors

Variables may function simultaneously as both risk and protective factors. This places us in a terminological dilemma (Rutter, 1985; Seifer and Sameroff, 1987). For example, whereas the presence of a stable emotional bond to a caregiver is regarded as a protective factor against psychological disorders (Tress *et al.*, 1989), its absence is viewed as an important risk factor (Bowlby, 1982). It is confusing when two constructs are used to describe different manifestations of one and the same variable. This is not just a problem in dichotomous variables, but also in quantitative ones, particularly when there is a linear relation to psychosocial adaptation (Hawkins *et al.*, 1992). For example, whereas high intelligence proves to be a protective factor against antisocial behaviour (Kandel *et al.*, 1988), low intelligence is a well-replicated risk factor (Moffitt, 1993b).

To gain a differentiated view of the 'other side of the coin', one can test the specific effect of both poles of one variable. Such research designs have been developed by Stouthamer-Loeber *et al.* (1993) and Farrington (1994). Stouthamer-Loeber *et al.* (1993) examined three cohorts each containing about 500 boys in the 1st, 4th, and 7th grades of Pittsburgh public schools. In a cross-sectional analysis of their longitudinal study, the authors split each sample approximately according to the 25th and 75th percentile of its score distribution on potential risk and/or protective factors. This trichotomisation resulted in a best quarter, a middle half, and a worst quarter. The degree of delinquency was also trichotomised. A protective effect was indicated when the best quarter of scores in a variable promoted nondelinquency or suppressed serious delinquency in comparison with the middle half. A risk effect was present when the worst quarter promoted serious delinquency or suppressed nondelinquency. An odds ratio of 2.0 or more in comparison with the middle half was viewed as an indicator. The authors found that some variables exhibited only risk effects (e.g., attention deficit/hyperactivity, oppositional defiant behaviour, attitude toward antisocial behaviour, age of mother at birth of child, education of caretaker, neighbourhood crime, caretaker stress). Others functioned as both risk and protective factors (e.g., children's accountability, trustworthiness, ability to feel guilt, school motivation, mathematical achievement test score, peer delinquency, bad friends, parental supervision, communication, relationship with parents). However, no variables were found to have exclusively protective effects.

Farrington (1994) used a similar but prospective-longitudinal design to test protective effects in his Cambridge Study in Delinquent Development. This examined 411 males from a working-class area of London from childhood to adulthood. It assessed how far predictors recorded at ages 8–10, 12–14, and 16–18 exhibited risk and/or protective effects on delinquency when the sample were adolescents (age 10–16 years), 'teenagers' (age 17–20 years), and adults (21–32 years). A broad variety of individual and social factors was included. Some variables could only be dichotomised. Convictions as well as self-report data were used to measure delinquency outcomes. With odds ratios of 2.0 or more for both outcome criteria, the major protective factors for adolescent offending proved to be low troublesomeness at the age of 10 years, high parental interest in education at age 8, low dishonesty at age 10, being in a high school track at age 10, and high verbal IQ at age 10. The most important protective factors against 'teenage' offending were parents' expectation that their 14-year-old son would stay on at school until he was at least 17 years old, being rated as highly energetic by his teacher at age 12–14, having few or no friends at age 8, high verbal IQ at age 8–10, and a high vocabulary at age 14. The major protective factors against adult offending were low self-reported delinquency at age 18, mainly solitary activities at age 16, nondelinquent friends at age 14, high introversion at age 16, and most of one's friends still attending school at age 16.

Compared with the large number of variables assessed, only a small proportion had clear and consistent protective effects. Moreover, variables such as earlier problem behaviour can be viewed only as statistical mediators and not as true protective factors. The theoretically most plausible and most consistent protective effects were found in the areas of school achievement and social isolation. This was also confirmed in an interesting analysis of the various offending trajectories. A participant's status as an offender (O) or nonoffender (NO) when an adolescent, teenager, or adult resulted in eight possible trajectories: (1) NO-NO-NO, (2) NO-NO-O, (3) NO-O-NO, (4) NO-O-O, (5) O-NO-NO, (6) O-NO-O, (7) O-O-NO, and (8) O-O-O. By comparing the various trajectories, it was possible to ascertain protective factors for stable nonoffending as well as for desistance at various ages. These proved to be mostly variables of school career, intelligence, peer contacts, and low aggression or impulsivity.

In Farrington's (1994) study, some variables had a clear protective effect at one pole but a weak or no risk effect at the other (e.g., various school-related measures). It is only when this sort of finding is obtained that we may talk about an isolated protective factor. In this case, we are dealing with nonlinear relations to the outcome of problem behaviour. Whereas the positive pole of a variable is related to a low risk of delinquency, risk is average for *both* medium and more negative scores. In this sense, Rae-Grant *et al.* (1989) reported that good academic performance and getting along well with others prove to be protective factors against conduct disorder. Overall, however, 'pure' protective factors seem to be rare.

Therefore, we should not talk about protective factors in general, but only about the protective functions of certain levels of variables. However, this also raises problems: with dichotomous variables or dichotomised, continuous variables, we cannot carry out independent tests. Furthermore, the risk level of variables is relatively infrequent in the population as a whole and thus the effect of the positive side is more or less 'normal'. As Osborn (1990) has suggested, in that case, we should not talk about a protective effect. Another problem with the research approach sketched above is that each risk or protective factor is examined in isolation from others. However, within a variable-oriented research strategy, the concept of protection refers not just to main effects but also to interactions. In an individual-oriented approach, configurations or patterns of variables should be considered (Magnusson and Bergman, 1988). Bergman and Magnusson (1997), for example, found that aggression and motor restlessness at age 13 were related to criminality and alcohol abuse at age 18–23. A closer inspection of subgroups or clusters of persons revealed, however, that this general correlation was only due to youngsters with a severe multiproblem syndrome (approximately 10 per cent of the whole sample). The clusters of boys with weak restlessness or weak aggression at age 13 had no enhanced risk to be in clusters of criminality or both criminality and alcohol abuse at age 18–23. However, youngsters with a syndrome of both aggression and hyperactivity or with a multiproblem syndrome were overrepresented in these two clusters of adult problem behaviour.

Differentiated relations between risks and outcomes are addressed in the *moderator concept* of protective factors (Rutter, 1985). This concept labels a variable as protective only when it reduces or buffers the pathogenic effects of specific risks; in other words, when the variable moderates the relation between risk factors and problem behaviour. In one research design, the effect of a risk factor is tested in the presence of a protective factor. For example, Neighbors *et al.* (1993) have shown that children who have a good relationship with their mother (protective factor) are better able to cope with severe conflicts between their parents and divorce than other children. Another example is the personality characteristic of ego resiliency (Block and Block, 1980) that may help to prevent life stressors from becoming a risk for behavioural or emotional problems (see the section on temperament and personality). In the most frequent research design, risk factors are present, and the aim is to test which protective factors minimise their effects. A typical study would investigate two groups with equivalent risk of which one group exhibits healthy development whereas the other is or becomes deviant. An example is the above-mentioned study of Kandel *et al.* (1988) on the protective function of intelligence. The risk factor was a criminal father. Those persons who did not get into trouble with the law despite this risk proved to be more intelligent than those who had gone to prison like their fathers.

The most well-known study on the moderator concept of protective factors is that carried out by Werner and Smith (1982, 1992) on the Hawaiian island of Kauai. They applied a prospective longitudinal study of the entire 1955 birth cohort from the first year of life up to adulthood. Some children did not develop any serious behavioural problems despite the presence of at least three risk factors (e.g., poverty, psychotic parent, birth complications). The protective effects of personal and social resources at various ages were examined by comparing these resilient individuals with those exposed to similar risk who had developed behavioural problems. Only a few of the numerous findings can be mentioned here: resilient children were more active, sociable, easy tempered, independent, and self-confident. They were also more communicative, learned better at school, and exhibited specific interests or hobbies. At the end of high school, they had developed a reliable bond to a reference person inside or outside the family. They received social support from adults or other social networks, had positive role models, and at least one close friend. They were also higher in self-esteem and internal locus of control. As young adults, most of them had continued education beyond high school. They were achievement-oriented and had a stable employment history. They experienced their life as meaningful and satisfying. Most of the females were married and had children in whom they tried to promote resiliency as well. Werner and Smith (1982, 1992) found various differences in protective mechanisms for males and females. Moreover, they did not just study protective factors in persistently resilient persons, but also factors that led to desistance in youngsters who had become delinquent. Three-quarters of the males and nine-tenths of the females with a record of juvenile offending avoided arrest upon reaching adulthood. A more intact family, external support, a favourable heterosexual partnership, military service, or adult education programmes contributed to such turning points and positive development (see, also, Elder, 1986).

In contrast, Farrington's (1994) interaction analysis has shown no clear protective factors that explained the turning points in offending. Obviously, the extent to which protective mechanisms can be confirmed may depend on the research design used. In Farrington's study, the less typical trajectories were relatively infrequent. Thus, when testing for interaction effects, the low number of cases in individual categories impeded statistical significance. Interaction effects are also less robust in replications. We should also bear in mind that not all interaction effects are equally relevant for resilience (Luthar *et al.*, 2000b). Moreover, when there are large time intervals between measurements and only variables close to these time points are assessed, it is mainly distal protective factors that will be investigated. Potentially more influential proximal factors may be tapped in repeated measurements with shorter intervals or in detailed retrospective longitudinal data covering the whole time period (which should, however, avoid post-hoc interpretation biases).

Increasing or lowering a risk does not just depend on the direct positive or negative impact of a variable. Protective factors that enhance resilience in high-risk children may operate through both *direct* and *indirect* effects in the form of chain reactions (Rutter, 1990). Unpleasant and potentially dangerous events may even harden individuals if they cope with them successfully (Anthony, 1987; Rutter and Rutter, 1993). One example of this is the way that moderate amounts of stress produce neurochemical changes in the brain that increase resistance to later stressors (see Meaney *et al.*, 1991). Finally, it should be noted that earlier offending is a relatively strong predictor of later criminality (Loeber and Dishion, 1983; Lipsey and Derzon, 1998). Desistance trajectories thus may not be buffered by a single protective factor but only by more complex, multivariate protective influences.

Risk factors

Although risk factors are predictors of a particular disorder, the statistical risk concept does not inform us about the underlying causal mechanisms. Baldwin *et al.* (1990) have discriminated between distal and proximal risk factors as the two poles of one continuum. The effects of distal factors such as poverty or a broken home are often not direct but mediated by proximal factors such as parental disharmony or childrearing deficits. If no proximal risk factors are present as mediators, there may well be no significant relation between distal variables and the child's adaptation, as found, for example, in poor families with a climate of parental harmony and favourable parental care. With regard to the general risk of poverty, such children would be assessed as resilient. However, a closer inspection would reveal that, actually, they had been exposed to a lower risk (Richters and Martinez, 1993; Rutter, 1996).

In predictions of antisociality or other behavioural problems, most single risks have only low correlations with the outcome (Compas and Phares, 1991; Lipsey and Derzon, 1998; Lösel, 1991). What is more significant is their cumulation. The probability of developing serious antisociality or other disorders increases strongly as a function of the growing number of risks (e.g., Coyne and Downey, 1991; Farrington, 1997a; Hawkins *et al.*, 1998; Rutter, 1990). In such cases, effects may be not only additive but also multiplicative or exponential (e.g., Garmezy, 1985; Masten *et al.*, 1990).

The degree or dosage of risk is a central criterion for proving a protective effect. Studies vary widely in degree of risk. The more potential risks entered as predictors in a multiple regression, the less variance should be left over for protective effects of positive poles of variables. Whereas, for example, Kandel *et al.* (1988) have defined risk through one factor, or Werner and Smith (1992) through at least four factors, we addressed adolescents in youth welfare institutions who were exposed to a multiple level of risk (Bender *et al.*, 1996; Lösel, 1994; Lösel and Bliesener, 1994). Case conferences, a seventy-item risk index, educator ratings, and self-reported problem behaviour were used for group formation. We selected sixty-six relatively well-adapted adolescents (resilients) and eighty with serious externalising and other problems (deviants). Both groups had a similarly high risk load. Because other studies have shown that the youngsters' own perceptions of stress are particularly relevant risks (e.g., Compas, 1987; Rende and Plomin, 1992), we also included factors such as perceived conflict, neglect, alcohol, or financial problems in the family.

Overall, an index of these subjective factors correlated more strongly with self-reported behavioural problems than an index of objective features such as divorce or low SES. However, the correlation was high in the deviant group, moderate in a normal group, and small in the resilient group. This is a clear indication of buffering effects in the latter. The resilient and deviant youngsters were assessed at age 15–16 and also two years later. As our study investigated particularly high-risk cases, it was relatively hard to confirm protective effects. Nonetheless, there were consistent differences between the resilient and deviant groups: stable resilients were more flexible but less impulsive in temperament, more realistic in their plans for the future, more active and less avoiding in their coping behaviour, less helpless and more self-confident, and more achievement-oriented and successful at school. They more often had a reference person outside the core family, were more satisfied with received social support, had a better relationship to school, and experienced a more positive social-emotional as well as norm-oriented educational climate in their residential homes. The latter educational factors were also particularly relevant for behavioural changes from early to late adolescence.

As the dosage of risks is an important aspect of the research design, Rutter (1985) and Stattin and Magnusson (1996) have suggested that a factor should be labelled protective only if a variable reduces the problem behaviour when risk is high but has no impact when risk is low. Stattin *et al.* (1997) have followed up 7,577 Swedish conscripts in official registers from the age of 18 through to 36 years. They recorded five risk variables in their home background: chronic illness, divorce, mental disorders, financial problems, and father's alcohol drinking. The authors also assessed seven behavioural risk factors: contact with the police or youth authorities, truancy, attendance at special education classes, lower school grades due to poor conduct, running away from home, drug abuse, and alcohol abuse. Five personal resources were included as protective factors: physical health, intellectual capacity, emotional control, social maturity, and mental energy.

Approximately one third of the sample received criminal convictions during the follow-up period. It was found that the behavioural risks and most of the home-background risks correlated clearly with convictions after the age of 18 years. Both behavioural risks and home-background risks had slight to moderate negative correlations with personal resources. However, among subjects with a high behavioural risk, those with no pronounced personal resources were convicted considerably more often in later life than their peers with many resources. This applied equally to subjects with few and many home-background risks. Hardly any differences in conviction rates were found between low-risk individuals with some versus many documented resources. Analyses of home-background risks had similar findings.

This study shows the importance of cumulation not only in risk factors but also in protective factors. Stronger effects are to be anticipated from such cumulations than from individual factors. Figure 5.1 contains a simple compensatory model of potential relations between accumulated risk factors and protective factors. It also includes results of our abovementioned study on adolescents from multiproblem milieus (Lösel *et al.*, 1992).

Overall, the data seem to fit our predictions rather well, in particular to the expectation of nonlinear cumulative effects. However, as the right

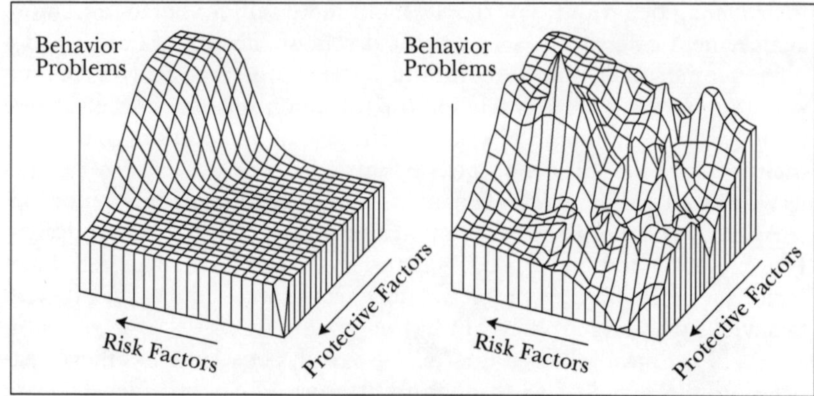

Figure 5.1. Hypothetical model (left) and empirical results (right) on the relationship between accumulated risk factors, accumulated protective factors, and the intensity of problem behaviour
(From Lösel *et al.*, 1992)

edge of the figure shows, protective factors already had a buffering function at relatively low levels of risk. This difference compared with the results from Stattin *et al.* (1997) may be due to the multiproblem background of all our youngsters. Thus, even a relatively low level of risk was above the average level in a normative sample.

Although cumulations of risk and protective factors may enhance statistical relations, we should not overlook the problems involved with this strategy: the respective constructs become heterogeneous and make causal analyses more difficult than when dealing with single variables or homogeneous constructs.

Behavioural outcome

The criteria for positive behavioural outcomes or for resilience are a further source of variance in findings. From a pathogenetic perspective, these criteria are defined as the absence of certain diseases, disorders, or behavioural problems despite the presence of risks (e.g., Luthar and Zigler, 1991; Luthar *et al.*, 2000a; Rutter and Quinton, 1984). Most studies on factors that protect against antisocial behaviour follow this approach. Risk factors and their attendant protective factors may differ depending on the respective outcome problem. This means that we always have to ask 'risk for what?'and 'protection against what?' If, for example, a young male is rated 'resilient' because he exhibits no serious aggression or delinquency, he may well have less obvious internalising symptoms such as anxiety, depression, social withdrawal, or psychosomatic complaints.

Luthar (1991) and Parker *et al.* (1990) have found that the depression and anxiety scores of children who lived in very stressful conditions, but were nonetheless socially competent, were almost as high as those in a comparison group of less competent children. At the same time, these scores were markedly higher than those of competent children from a less stressful milieu. Farber and Egeland (1987) have observed that although abused and neglected children possessed coping strategies that they could use to adapt socially, they still had major emotional problems. Similarly, Farrington (1987) has reported that boys who exhibited no delinquent behaviour even though they came from a criminogenic milieu showed symptoms of nervousness and social withdrawal. In the Kauai Study, stress-related health problems were frequent among both resilient males and females in adulthood (Werner and Smith, 1992). Resilient males also often lived without a partner. This may have been the price they had to pay for mastering the adversities in their lives.

Such findings suggest that the impact of protective factors should not be restricted to very narrow criteria. This is also supported by results on comorbidities of antisocial disorders (Dolan and Coid, 1993; Loeber *et al.*, 1998). For example, various studies point to a broad problem behaviour syndrome that includes, among others, violence, theft, lying, substance abuse, risky or drunk driving, accidents, sexual promiscuity, heavy gambling, and unstable working patterns (Elliott *et al.*, 1989; Jessor *et al.*, 1991; Junger *et al.*, 1995; Lösel and Bliesener, 1998). Other studies suggest that such problems frequently may accompany internalising problems (Caron and Rutter, 1991; Loeber *et al.*, 1998). Moreover, early antisocial behaviour seems to be a marker for a broad range of later psychiatric disorders (Robins and Price, 1991) and there is also some overlap in the explanatory factors for both antisociality and internalising problems (e.g., McCord and Ensminger, 1997; Loeber *et al.*, 1998).

Nonetheless, comorbidity may reflect quite different causal mechanisms as well as sources of artifact (Rutter, 1997). For example, although attention deficit/hyperactivity is among the precursors of conduct problems, explanatory factors are not the same for the two disorders (Farrington *et al.*, 1990; Loeber *et al.*, 1998). Similarly, although the manifestations, causes, and correlates of drug use and aggression overlap, there are also differences between them, as well as distinct subgroups exhibiting problems in only one area (Brook *et al.*, 1995; Loeber *et al.*, 1998; Lösel and Bliesener, 1998). These and other results suggest that research on protective factors should neither focus on a too narrow definition of a 'positive outcome' nor on a too broad problem behaviour syndrome. Luthar *et al.* (2000b) suggest that it would be unrealistic to expect uniformity in positive or negative outcomes across theoretically unrelated domains. However, comorbidities can lead to complex interactions in protective mechanisms. For example, although it has been shown that shyness may be a protective factor against juvenile delinquency, the risk of delinquency is particularly high when children are shy *and* aggressive (Ensminger *et al.*, 1983; Farrington *et al.*, 1988). Furthermore, a 'protective' factor such as social isolation may impede delinquency, but it may also contribute to depression and suicide.

How far a positive outcome is ascertained depends not only on the breadth or narrowness of the disorder concept but also on the methods of assessment, the time window, and gender.

With respect to *assessment*, for example, Farrington's (1994) study has shown that there were sometimes considerable differences in the protective effects depending on whether the outcome criterion was self-reports or convictions. Lösel and Bliesener (1990) found differences in protective factors when comparing self-report and educator ratings as measures of resilience. Such inconsistencies are not infrequent. Different informants from different contexts show only moderate levels of agreement in their ratings of problem behaviour (Achenbach *et al.*, 1987). A multivariable, multisetting, and multi-informant approach would be desirable (Achenbach *et al.*, 1987; LeBlanc, 1998). Although this is often hard to achieve, one should at least trace back how far protective factors depend on the same data source as the behavioural outcomes. Particularly in cross-sectional designs, this may well indicate confounds with the symptomatology.

The *time period* is important, because factors that protect against antisocial behaviour may be different at various ages. They may also not be the same as those leading to persistent nondeviance. Although individuals who develop antisocial personalities often exhibit early onset and long-term persistence (Robins, 1978; Hodgins *et al.*, 1998; Loeber, 1990), there are also groups of severely criminal persons whose deviance surfaces only in adulthood or who desist from offending in adolescence only to start again later (Farrington, 1994; Loeber *et al.*, 1997; Robins and Ratcliff, 1980; Stattin and Magnusson, 1996; Windle and Windle, 1995). Such 'negative' discontinuity probably relates to serious life stress, critical life events, mental health problems, and the breakdown of previous protective mechanisms (Hodgins *et al.*, 1998; Mawson, 1987; Stattin and Magnusson, 1996). There are indications that late starters were not truly problem-free in earlier life but exhibited internalising and other problems (e.g., Windle and Windle, 1995). In some cases, this may point to overcontrolled aggressors (Blackburn, 1993; Megargee, 1966). These would be individuals who become aggressive only when their anger arousal is intense enough to overcome their strong inhibitions.

Gender can also play a role in confirming protective effects. Antisocial behaviours of males and females differ in terms of behavioural patterns, onset, and development over time (Loeber and Stouthamer-Loeber, 1998). From elementary school age onward, girls not only show less but also more indirect, relational, and nonphysical forms of aggression (Crick and Grotpeter, 1995; Loeber and Hay, 1997; Lösel and Bliesener, 1999a). Males seem to be more likely to be exposed to multiple risks than females (e.g., McCord and Ensminger, 1997). In line with their earlier maturation, females outgrow antisocial behaviour somewhat earlier than males (e.g., Elliott, 1994). Additionally, the two sexes also seem to react in some ways differently to adversities. For example, females more frequently have relatively stable problems in the less 'visible' internalising domain (Costello and Angold, 1995; McCord and Ensminger, 1997). Gender differences observed in resilience research (e.g., Werner, 1993) may relate to such differences in the development of problem behaviour. If studies refer to only one type of outcome, one or the other sex may more often be rated incorrectly as resilient.

Such problems have led some authors to define resilience not only through the absence of specific disorders but also through positive criteria of social competence or achievement (e.g., Garmezy *et al.*, 1984; Luthar, 1991; Radke-Yarrow and Sherman, 1990). This approach requires the completion of certain developmental tasks as a precondition, and thus introduces a higher threshold of resilience. However, there are no clear developmental norms available for such operationalisations (Masten *et al.*, 1990; Masten and Coatsworth, 1995). As Kaufman *et al.* (1994) have shown, results may differ according to whether social competence, academic achievement, or clinical symptomatology are used to define resilience. These authors conclude that the most appropriate definition depends on the aims of the study. Resilience cannot generally be conceptualised as absence of disorder or high competence but must refer to an *unexpected* positive adaptation (Luthar *et al.*, 2000b). Therefore, in the following we shall refer primarily to protective effects in the sense of avoidance or reduction of antisociality despite risk. Nonetheless, as we have shown, it is sometimes meaningful to extend the focus beyond antisocial behaviour and also keep an eye on mental health and competence in general.

Selected protective factors and processes

Direct indications about protective factors against antisocial behaviour are to be found in studies of specific risks for delinquency. Indirect indications can also be gained from studies of resilient children and adolescents

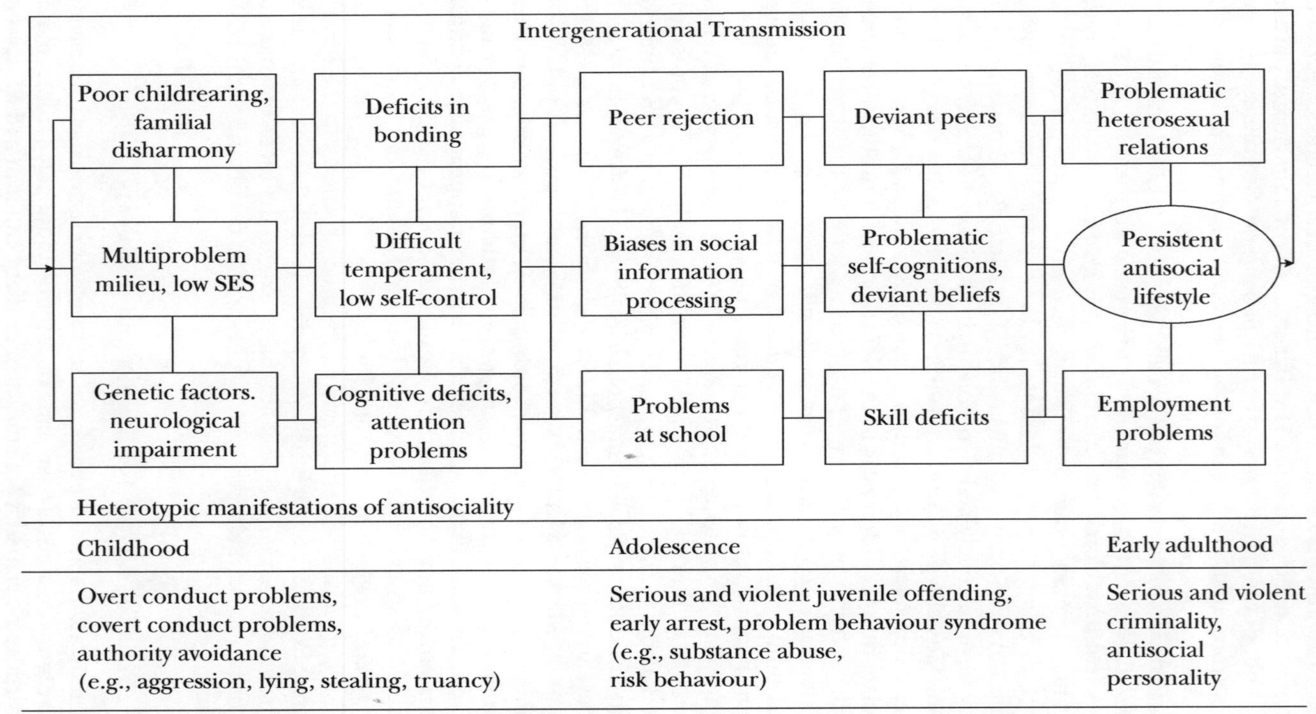

Figure 5.2. A model of cumulating risks in the development of persistent antisocial behaviour

growing up under a variety of adversities that may lead not only to antisocial behaviour but also to various mental health problems. Such examples are: parental divorce; families exposed to multiple stress; living in disorganised or dangerous neighbourhoods; families that have experienced poverty or severe economic reversals; families with a history of child abuse and neglect; families with mentally disordered parents; and growing up in care institutions.

However, although these studies vary greatly in terms of type of sample, social contexts, methods, age periods, risk factors, and outcome measures, literature reviews demonstrate a number of relatively consistent findings (e.g., Bender and Lösel, 1998; Garmezy, 1985; Luthar and Ziegler, 1991; Rutter, 1990). This led early resilience researchers to emphasise protective factors that exert a broad impact (e.g., Werner, 1989). These particularly include: (a) individual dispositions like temperament, cognitive competencies, and self-confidence; (b) a good emotional climate and bond to a reference person within the family; and (c) social support from outside the family. As the discussion above has shown, it is also necessary to examine specific protective mechanisms under specific constellations of risk and with respect to specific outcomes.

In the following, we shall discuss various factors and mechanisms that are particularly relevant for protecting against persistent antisocial behaviour. The development of chronic antisociality is seen as a chain reaction in which different risks are accumulating and reinforcing each other over time (e.g., Loeber, 1990; Moffitt, 1993a; Patterson *et al.*, 1998; Tremblay and Craig, 1995; Yoshikawa, 1994). Figure 5.2 illustrates such a prototypical chain reaction. It goes without saying that the sequence cannot be interpreted as a strict causal order. None of the factors is a precondition for the development of persistent antisociality. However, progressive accumulation of conditions and consequences of an antisocial lifestyle can restrict access to nondeviant opportunities in life (Caspi and Moffitt, 1995).

Protective mechanisms can interrupt such chain reactions in various areas and at different stages. This will be sketched in the following. For reasons of space, we shall restrict our overview to factors that may have a causal function and are supported by relatively consistent findings. The following personal and social resources will be discussed: (1) biological and psychophysiological factors; (2) temperament and other personality characteristics; (3) cognitive competencies; (4) attachment to significant others; (5) childrearing in the family and other contexts; (6) school achievement, school bonding, and employment; (7) social networks and peer groups; (8) self-related cognitions, social cognitions, and beliefs; and (9) neighbourhood and community factors. We have not included potential protective factors such as no substance abuse. Although recoveries from alcohol dependency, for example, may also have a protective function against antisociality, these kinds of problem behaviours are so closely connected that desistance in both areas often goes hand in hand (Kerner *et al.*, 1997).

Biological and psychophysiological factors

Biological factors may contribute in numerous ways to the development of antisocial behaviour (Raine, 1993; Raine *et al.*, 1997a). This is demonstrated, for example, by research on behaviour genetics (Ciba Foundation, 1996), autonomic arousal (Raine, 1997), hormonal influences (Brain and Susman, 1997), neurotransmitter processes (Berman *et al.*, 1997), perinatal complications (Brennan *et al.*, 1997), maternal smoking during pregnancy (Fergusson *et al.*, 1998; Räsänen *et al.*, 1999), or fetal alcohol syndrome (Steinhausen *et al.*, 1993). Biological risks of antisociality may have not only main effects but interact with social factors. For example, pregnancy and birth complications are risks for central nervous system damage resulting in neurological and neuropsychological deficits that can lead to persistent and violent offending (Moffitt, 1993b). These complications are not directly related to violence (e.g., Denno, 1990), but are related primarily when combined with social risks such as maternal rejection, low SES, or family instability (Brennan *et al.*, 1997). Similarly, blood serotonin level seems to be linked to violence primarily among men who have grown up in families with little cohesion and much conflict (Moffitt *et al.*, 1997). However, unstable social environments could produce both behaviour and neurotransmitter changes that may be statistically associated but not causally related (Berman *et al.*, 1997).

There is also evidence for genetic components in variables that appear to be purely social factors (Plomin, 1994; Rowe, 1994). These include, for example, the experience of critical life events, parental warmth, child-rearing practices, and social support. Ge *et al.* (1996) found a genotype-environment association for parental discipline that was less clear in previous research. Genetic components of social family factors can operate in various ways (Pike *et al.*, 1996): (1) children may inherit environments along with genes from their parents (passive), (2) parents or other caregivers may react to genetically influenced child characteristics (reactive), or (3) children may seek out their own environmental niche suited to their genotype (active). Whereas Pathways 1 and 2 are most plausible in young children, active selection should play a more important role in later ages and outside the family, for example, in peer selection or assortive marriage (Caspi and Herbener, 1990; Quinton *et al.*, 1993).

From an evolutionary perspective, Belsky *et al.* (1998) have hypothesised that there may be inherited child differences in susceptibility to rearing influences that optimise reproductive fitness in the face of environmental uncertainty. Although we cannot discuss such questions here, we must be aware of the role of genetic components in social risks and protective factors. These components should not be misinterpreted as determining phenotypic social behaviour; they 'only' set the limits of the reaction range. The relative amounts of population variance explained depend on the respective measures and heterogeneity of individuals and environments. However, when referring to social protective factors, we should bear in mind that there are multiple causal pathways that also include genetic components of resilience.

Relatively few studies of biological variables have directly addressed potential protective mechanisms against antisociality. One exception is the field of autonomic arousal. A number of studies have shown a reduced arousal level in antisocial youngsters (Raine, 1993; Raine *et al.*, 1997b). Various explanations address imbalances between the behaviour activation system (BAS) and the behaviour inhibition system (BIS; Gray, 1987; Quay, 1993). Raine (1997) has integrated findings on low resting heart rate level (HRL), slow EEGs, and reduced skin conductance (SC) into a prefrontal dysfunction hypothesis: this pattern results in deficits in arousal, orienting, and anticipatory fear (in addition to personality and cognitive deficits) that predispose toward antisocial behaviour. Although measurement problems, body mass, alcohol consumption, smoking and other alternative explanations must be taken into account, the relationship between resting HRL and antisocial behaviour in young people has proved to be robust and substantial (Raine, 1997; Raine *et al.*, 1996). Low HRL is also a long-term predictor of adult crime and violence (Farrington, 1987, 1997b; Raine *et al.*, 1990; Wadsworth, 1976). These psychophysiological differences seem to be particularly crucial in samples that are not exposed to social risks like low SES or adverse family conditions (Raine and Venables, 1981).

By inverting the risk hypothesis, various authors have assumed a buffering or compensatory effect of elevated autonomic arousal. For example, Brennan *et al.* (1997) allocated ninety-four adult males from a Copenhagen hospital to four groups: (a) criminal with criminal father, (b) noncriminal with criminal father, (c) criminal with noncriminal father, and (d) noncriminal with noncriminal father. SC and HRL were measured within an orienting experiment. Both variables showed significantly higher scores in the second group (noncriminal, criminal father) compared with the other three groups. This protected group exhibited not only 'normal' autonomic functioning but also higher responsiveness compared with the noncriminal controls in the fourth group. Similarly, Raine and Venables (1981) have reported that prosocial boys from low SES backgrounds exhibited markedly lower SC conditioning than either low SES boys who became antisocial or high SES boys who developed prosocially.

Prospective longitudinal data are also consistent with these cross-sectional results: in his Cambridge Study, Farrington (1994, 1997b) found that although a low HRL led to more violence among young persons from large families with a poor parent–child relationship and other social risks, high HRL had a protective effect in low SES families and also tended to protect against a poor parent–child relationship. Raine *et al.* (1995, 1996) have investigated autonomic and CNS measures of arousal, orienting, and classical conditioning in unselected 15-year-old boys. In this sample, antisocial adolescents who desisted from crime when adult were matched in terms of adolescent antisocial behaviour and demographic variables with a group of antisocial adolescents who had become criminal by age 29 and also with a group of nonantisocial/later noncriminal controls. In comparison with persistent criminals, desistors had significantly higher HRL, higher SC arousal, higher SC orienting, better SC conditioning, and faster half-recovery times for the SC response. The respective mean scores of the desistors were also above those of controls.

Kindlon *et al.* (1995) have found not only a risk effect of low HRL but also a protective effect of high HRL in 11-year-old boys within a low SES and a disruptive sample. Our own study of adolescents from multiproblem backgrounds revealed a protective effect of high resting HRL against externalising problem behaviour (Lösel and Bender, 1997). However, there was no symmetric risk effect of low HRL, but more of a curvilinear relationship. The latter has also been reported by Farrington (1994). When evaluating such findings, it has to be noted that samples are often small, and there may well be interactions with moderator variables as well as different mediating mechanisms. For example, Raine *et al.* (1997b) reported a buffering effect against the risk of low HRL at age 3. In boys, those who had not become antisocial at age 11 showed good school performance. In girls, abstainers with low HRL were less depressive, withdrawn, or schizotypical.

While such findings point to gender differences in protective biological mechanisms, they also suggest that other behavioural or emotional problems need to be taken into account. For example, although enhanced HRL has a protective function against the development or persistence of antisocial behaviour, it is also a risk factor for shy, anxious, and withdrawn behaviour in children (Kagan, 1994). Internalising problems may sometimes be the 'costs' for protection against antisociality. Findings reported by Lösel *et al.* (1998) point in the same direction: they examined HRL in a resting condition and during experimental conflict interactions in adolescents who had been classified as bullies, victims, or normal students about two years before. Bullies had the lowest HRL. Victims had the highest HRL and also enhanced scores on anxiety, depression, and social withdrawal scales. The HRL differences were particularly clear in subgroups with a low-stress family background. Perhaps, this is where biological personality differences have their strongest impact (Raine, 1997). However, low arousal can also be a marker for social influences: for example, a low HRL correlated with parental divorce during early childhood (Wadsworth, 1976) and with the experience of parental violence (Gottman and Katz, 1989).

Other physiological protective mechanisms are probably to be found in hormones. It has been shown repeatedly that high salivary, serum, and CFS testosterone levels in adolescent or adult males relate to chronic aggressiveness, violent crime, and other forms of problem behaviour (e.g., Dabbs *et al.*, 1991; Scerbo and Kolko, 1994; Virkkunen *et al.*, 1994). However, the causal direction is not yet clear, and high testosterone level (TL) may be more of a consequence of dominance than a cause of aggression (Archer, 1991). According to Brain and Susman (1997) it seems unlikely that androgens have a simple causal effect on aggression, but patterns of steroids do appear to alter aggressive feelings, self image and social perceptions that predispose to carry out such actions. As a result, we cannot necessarily assume that a low testosterone level will have a protective effect.

Although there is some evidence that treatment with antiandrogen hormones can be successful in the specific group of sexual offenders (Hall, 1995), potential natural protective effects on antisociality may interact with social factors. For example, Kemper (1990) has hypothesised that the relation of TL with dominance and aggression depends on the subcultural behaviour patterns of low SES people. Tremblay *et al.* (1997) have found different correlations between TL and aggression at different ages. At age 16, aggressive boys had a higher mean TL than nonaggressive boys; at age 13, however, the relation was reversed. At age 12, the aggressive boys were rated much less popular by their peers than the nonaggressive boys. This social constellation and further problems at school may have led to less dominance and more stress that, in turn, could have had a moderating influence on TL. Indeed, Tremblay *et al.* (1997) found that more aggressive boys had already left school at age 16. However, there was no significant effect of later school dropout on the age x group interaction of TL.

Whether the stress hormone cortisol inhibits TL and thus moderates its relationship to antisocial behaviour has not been confirmed clearly (Scerbo and Kolko, 1994; Tremblay *et al.*, 1997). The same applies to the direct relation between antisociality and cortisol. Both positive and negative relations have been found, with negative relations seeming to be particularly evident for the overt aggressive form of antisociality (e.g., McBurnett *et al.*, 1996). Enhanced salivary cortisol accompanies shyness, anxiety, depression, and arousal in some studies (Dabbs and Hopper, 1990; Kagan *et al.*, 1988; Scerbo and Kolko, 1994), so that this may represent a buffering mechanism. However, preadolescent boys who were both anxious and conduct-disordered have exhibited higher levels of salivary cortisol than other groups (McBurnett *et al.*, 1991). Present day experiences and changes in the physiological context (i.e., pregnancy) also may alter the links between cortisol and emotions or antisociality (Susman and Ponirakis, 1997). Furthermore, stress reactions probably play a stronger role in transient rather than persistent forms of antisociality (Mawson, 1987).

In sum, there are complex bidirectional and interactional effects between hormones, antisocial behaviour, and context (Brooks-Gunn *et al.*, 1994; Susman and Ponirakis, 1997). More longitudinal and experimental studies with multivariate biological parameters and precisely defined subtypes of antisociality are needed to clarify potential protective mechanisms.

Temperament characteristics/personality

Biological dispositions in interaction with the environment contribute to a psychological profile that is described as temperament (e.g., Schwartz *et al.*, 1996). Although these temperament traits cannot be distinguished very clearly from other personality variables, Cloninger *et al.* (1993) have suggested important differences between *temperament* and *character*: temperament traits are moderately heritable, consolidated early, relatively stable throughout life, and related to associative learning and conditioning. Character traits are weakly heritable, moderately influenced by social experiences, mature in a stagelike manner, and related to conceptual learning and insight. Temperament traits refer to individual differences in basic emotional responses such as anger, fear, and disgust; character traits to individual differences in goals, values, and self-conscious emotions (shame, guilt, and empathy).

Although there are differences between various concepts of temperament in childhood and adulthood (e.g. Bates, 1989; Buss and Plomin, 1975; Cloninger *et al.*, 1997; Eysenck, 1977; Zuckerman, 1994), numerous studies have shown that characteristics such as impulsivity, hyperactivity, negative emotionality, sensation seeking, and risk taking are predictors of antisocial behaviour and particularly violence (e.g, Cloninger *et al.*, 1997; Hawkins *et al.*, 1998; Zuckerman, 1994). In research on protective factors, the temperament concept of Thomas and Chess (1977) has gained much influence: these authors distinguish between nine temperament dimensions and three types. The latter are the *easy* child, the *slow-to-warm-up* child, and the *difficult* child. Various studies have shown that resilient children and adolescents often have an easy temperament (e.g., Cowen *et al.*, 1990; Elder *et al.*, 1986; Garmezy, 1985; Lösel and Bliesener, 1994; Werner and Smith, 1982). Such advantageous dispositions are, for example, regularity of biological functions (e.g., sleep-wake rhythm), low irritability, sociability, a tendency not to avoid new situations, an ability to adapt flexibly, and an even, predominantly positive mood (Chess and Thomas, 1985; Schwartz *et al.*, 1996; Zentner, 1993).

Moffitt *et al.* (1996) compared the following five groups of boys from their prospective longitudinal study in Dunedin (New Zealand) from age 3 to 18 years: (1) boys who met criteria for extreme antisocial behaviour across both childhood and adolescence (life-course-persistent, LCP path; 7.0 per cent of the sample of 457 youngsters); (2) boys who met criteria for extreme antisocial behaviour in adolescence but not in childhood (adolescence-limited, AL path; 23.6 per cent); (3) boys who had been extremely antisocial as children but did not meet the antisociality criterion in adolescence (recoveries; 5.9 per cent); (4) boys who had been rated less antisocial than was normative for their age at every assessment age and across data sources (abstainers; 5.5 per cent); and (5) boys not meeting criteria for any of the four comparison groups (unclassified boys; 58.0 per cent). The authors compared the groups in terms of temperament and various other factors.

At age 3 and 5 years, an independent observer rated the boys' behaviour on a scale of difficult temperament (e.g., emotional lability, restlessness, short attention span, negativism, roughness). At both times, the abstainers exhibited the least difficult temperament. The AL path group and the unclassified boys ranked about average. The LCP path boys and the recoveries were rated as most difficult. On the one hand, this is a sign of early temperament differences between the LCP and AL path and a potential protective function of an easy temperament in the abstaining group. On the other hand, it has to be noted that about one-half of the antisocial children recovered, and these boys showed a similarly difficult temperament to the LCP path (at age 3 years, they even had the highest scores). In contrast to the LCP path boys, however, the temperament scores of the recoveries improved not only in childhood but also later.

In a personality test at age 18 years, the LCP path youngsters showed the highest scores in impulsivity, aggressiveness, and nervousness, and the lowest scores in harm avoidance and sociability. The scores of the AL group were in the same direction as those of the LCP group, but were less deviant. Abstainers were most controlled as well as least aggressive, stressed, and harm avoidant. Unclassified boys had approximately medium scores on most scales, and recoveries came relatively close to them (but were highest in self-reported well-being). Although temperament traits are relatively stable over time, this obviously does not exclude substantial changes in phenotype. The difficult temperament of the recoveries was in accordance with their antisociality in childhood, and both problems may have been related to temporal stress reactions.

The latter hypothesis would fit with findings that differences in childhood temperament can be due partially to variance in perceived family stress (e.g., Rende and Plomin, 1992). Protective functions of temperament may reflect not only inherited dispositions of behaviour regulation but also influences from the environment. An easy temperament makes interaction with caregivers smooth, and is also reinforced (Kagan, 1994). In contrast, children with a difficult temperament are more frequently targets of parental criticism, irritability, and hostility (Rutter, 1990). This makes it more likely that they will develop problem behaviour. A difficult temperament has also been found more frequently in children who have been victims of parental neglect and physical abuse (e.g., Masten *et al.*, 1990a). This, in turn, increases the risk of later aggressiveness (Emery and Laumann-Billings, 1998; Lynch and Cicchetti, 1998).

That parental behaviour may not only be a cause but also a consequence of child behaviour is suggested by behaviour genetics (e.g., Pike *et al.*, 1996). However, this relationship may vary according to age. Very early temperament differences in the child do not seem to be a main source of negative parental behaviour but rearing experience in the first year may affect infant negativity (e.g., Belsky *et al.*, 1991; Engfer, 1991). A difficult temperament becomes particularly risky when parents are under stress, have problems themselves, and the family has deficits in social resources and competencies (Loeber *et al.*, 1998; Moffitt, 1993a). If difficult temperaments and family conflicts cumulate during preschool age, this increases the frequency of externalising disorders as well as internalising ones (e.g., Tschann *et al.*, 1996). An easy temperament in the child, in contrast, can serve as a protective factor that reduces risky parental behaviour.

The temperament characteristics of the easy child are related to Block's (1971) concept of ego resiliency. This typology of personality functioning integrates hypotheses from psychoanalysis and Lewinian field theory on the dynamics of emotional and motivational states. It differentiates two basic constructs: ego control and ego resiliency. Ego control refers to the tendency to contain versus express emotional and motivational impulses. On one end of the dimension, we find rigid ego overcontrol (impulse containment, delay of gratification, inhibition of action, etc.); the other end represents rigid ego undercontrol (impulsivity, inability to delay gratification, immediate affect expression, etc.). In contrast to such states of overcontrol and undercontrol, ego resiliency refers to the dynamic capacity of the individual to modify his or her level of ego control in either direction. This change in ego boundaries relates functionally to the demands of the environment.

Various studies have demonstrated the validity of Block's typological approach. Robins *et al.* (1996), for example, found that a sample of 300 twelve-year-old boys from the Pittsburgh Youth Study could be clustered reliably into resilients, overcontrollers, and undercontrollers. According to caregiver and teacher reports, about three quarters of the resilients showed no signs of psychopathology. In contrast, the overcontrollers exhibited far more internalising problems. The undercontrollers had the highest rate of externalising problems and nearly 50 per cent of them were rated as being deviant in both syndromes. Undercontrollers also showed more difficulties in school behaviour and more delinquency than the other two groups.

Whereas Robins *et al.* (1996) did not control for risk in other areas, Cicchetti *et al.* (1993) found that maltreated children who were more ego-resilient or more overcontrolled adapted better than others. Such a reserved, controlled, and rational way of interacting may have protected them from being targets of continued abuse. Cicchetti and Rogosch (1997) studied socioeconomically disadvantaged, maltreated, and non-maltreated children from 6 to 11 years of age over a period of three years. Specifically for maltreated children, ego resiliency and ego overcontrol predicted adaptive functioning better than relationship variables. Features of overcontrol such as low impulsivity or low activity level were also found to protect juveniles against aggression and delinquency (e.g., Farrington, 1994; Bender and Lösel, 1998b).

Although the personality types of ego control are expected to show themselves during adolescence (Block, 1971), childhood temperament seems to be an important precursor (e.g. Caspi and Silva, 1995). For example, children who had been inhibited (shy, cautious, withdrawn) at age 3 had significantly fewer externalising problems at age 13 than uninhibited children (Schwartz *et al.*, 1996). This is in accordance with the findings on protective effects of high HRL mentioned above. However, relations to research on attention-deficit hyperactivity disorder (ADHD) or hyperactivity-impulsivity-attention disorder (HIA) are a little puzzling: ADHD in children is related closely to conduct disorders (CD), and is, on the one hand, a predictor of long-term antisociality (Loeber, 1990). On the other hand, it has been shown that, to some extent, the two disorders have differential determining constellations: CD relates more closely to socialisation variables and parental problems (Loeber *et al.*, 1990; Loeber *et al.*, 1998), whereas ADHD is tied more closely to internalising problems such as depressive mood, anxiety and shyness/withdrawal and may be more dependent on constitutional and psychological factors (Biederman *et al.*, 1991; Loeber *et al.*, 1994). Furthermore, internalising problems correlate with measures of antisocial behaviour (e.g., Loeber *et al.*, 1998) but are not long-term predictors of its serious forms (e.g., Hawkins *et al.*, 1998).

These results seem to contradict the above-mentioned protective effect of an inhibited temperament against antisociality. Different ages, measures, subgroups, degrees, or subdimensions of temperament and problem behaviour may be responsible for these patterns. For example, ADHD contains primarily impulsive as well as primarily inattentive cases. However, only impulsivity seems to be a core mediator of later persistent antisociality and psychopathy (see Klinteberg, 1996). Pliszka (1989) found that children with coexistent ADHD and anxiety show reduced impulsivity relative to those with ADHD alone. Inhibited children also change more easily over time than uninhibited ones (Kagan, 1994), and internalising child problems seem to be less stable than externalising problems (Robins, 1966). Thus, in the study of Schwartz *et al.* (1996), an inhibited temperament predicted low externalising problems at age 13 but not high internalising problems (except when paired with low externalising scores).

At a similar age (in the oldest cohort), Loeber at al. (1998) found that the correlations of shyness and depressed mood with antisocial behaviour were lower or even reversed their direction. How far characteristics of an inhibited temperament possess a protective function probably relates to the specific form or intensity of problem behaviour concerned (e.g., LCP antisociality and under-controlled aggression). As Henry *et al.* (1996) have shown in another analysis of the boys from the Dunedin Study, lack of control in temperament at ages 3 and 5 was associated with violent convictions at age 18 but not with nonviolent delinquency. In our study of high-risk juveniles, there were not only main effects but also interactions between temperament and previous problem behaviour. High flexibility was a protective factor for the less deviant youngsters and a risk for those who had already been more antisocial (Bender and Lösel,

1998b). In combination with high activity, the latter result points toward some kind of undercontrolled superficial 'adaption' that is found in later psychopathy (e.g., Lynam, 1996).

Cognitive competencies

In general, intelligence relates negatively to antisocial behaviour. Both cross-sectional and prospective longitudinal studies have shown lower IQs and, particularly, lower verbal scores in official or self-reported delinquents compared with other groups (e.g., Hirschi and Hindelang, 1977; Moffitt, 1993b; Rutter *et al.*, 1998; Ward and Tittle, 1994; West and Farrington, 1973). This link seems to be direct and robust after race, SES, and test motivation have been controlled (Lynam *et al.*, 1993). Likewise, above-average or high intelligence has been found to be a protective factor against antisocial behaviour (e.g., Egeland *et al.*, 1993; Farrington, 1994; Felsman and Vaillant, 1987; Kandel *et al.*, 1988; Kolvin *et al.*, 1988; Lösel and Bliesener, 1994; McCord and Ensminger, 1997; Stouthamer-Loeber *et al.*, 1993; Masten *et al.*, 1988; Radke-Yarrow and Brown, 1993; Werner and Smith, 1982; White *et al.*, 1989). This is not just a main effect; good intelligence also buffers against individual risks such as a criminal father (Kandel *et al.*, 1988), a high-risk milieu (Lösel and Bliesener, 1994; Werner and Smith, 1982), and earlier antisociality (Stattin *et al.*, 1997; White *et al.*, 1989).

Causal mechanisms relate to executive neuropsychological functioning. Intelligent children may be more capable of planning their behaviour, anticipating negative outcomes, settling conflicts verbally, developing alternatives to aggressive reactions, and making better decisions. Research on neuropsychological functioning (Moffitt, 1993b; Raine, 1993), on social information processing (Crick and Dodge, 1994; Huesmann, 1997), and on self-control (Gottfredson and Hirschi, 1990; Lösel, 1975) clearly reveals deficits in these and other competencies among antisocial individuals. The discussion about whether or not impulsivity is involved in the IQ-antisociality relation (Block, 1995; Lynam and Moffitt, 1995), seems to be too highly polarised. Probably, both primarily cognitive and more temperamental aspects of self-control are involved, and various subdimensions of impulsivity need to be differentiated (Beelmann *et al.*, 2000; Lösel, 1975; White *et al.*, 1994).

Resilient youngsters with high intelligence may also experience more positive reactions at school and in the family. As we shall discuss below, these can enhance their chances of breaking chain reactions in other areas. If intelligent children learn nonaggressive problem-solving skills and coping strategies early enough, this may promote behavioural plasticity and enable them to 'construct' a more favourable environment (McCall, 1981). In the opposite direction, antisocial behaviour may also disrupt academic potential and thereby impair intellectual development (Huesmann *et al.*, 1987).

Nonetheless, some studies reveal only partial confirmation of the protective function of intelligence: for example, only for males (Elder *et al.*, 1986; McCord and Ensminger, 1997), for various subfactors of intelligence (Farrington, 1994; Stouthamer-Loeber *et al.*, 1993), or for specific operationalisations of antisociality (Lösel and Bliesener, 1990). In the current state of research, there are still not enough replications of such differential findings. In older cohorts, a stronger effect in males may depend on the lesser importance of academic or occupational careers for females in the past. When the protective effect is reflected more strongly in teacher ratings than in self-reports, halo effects may play a role. Furthermore, scales such as the Youth Self-Report from Achenbach and Edelbrock (1987) contain items tapping conflict behaviour and difficulties with authorities for which we have to assume a degree of verbal intelligence (Bender and Lösel, 1996). The protective effect of intelligence should also not be generalised to psychopaths who do not exhibit below-average levels of intelligence (Hare, 1995).

Some studies of children from stressful milieus have found positive correlations between intelligence and depression or other disorders in the internalising domain (e.g., Luthar, 1991; Masten *et al.*, 1988; for females only: McCord and Ensminger, 1997). One explanation for this could be that intelligent persons are more discriminating in their perceptions of the environment and therefore respond to stress more sensitively. Thus, their greater cognitive competence may lead to more internalised problem processing (Masten *et al.*, 1988; Zigler and Farber, 1985). Positive correlations between intelligence and competence, in contrast, were found only at a low level of stress (Luthar *et al.*, 1992).

Other protective competencies address communication skills (Luthar and Zigler, 1991; Masten, 1989). Resilient children exhibit, for example, more empathy and more effective problem-solving abilities (Block and Block, 1980; Parker *et al.*, 1990; Werner, 1990). Luthar (1991) has reported that resilient adolescents had a stronger ability to express themselves socially. Resilient children have also been described as being particularly charming and as the favourite children in the family (Hetherington, 1989; Radke-Yarrow and Brown, 1993; Werner and Smith, 1982). Rutter and Quinton (1984) found that young women who had developed positively despite long periods of residential care planned their life more carefully. They also had better school experiences and chose better husbands. As various sophisticated data analyses have shown, their planning ability was a key factor across these later turning points in life (Pickles and Rutter, 1991). Similarly, the resilient adolescents in residential care in our study had a more realistic appraisal of personal goals than those who had become antisocial (Bender *et al.*, 1996). Competent children from families with a mentally ill parent had a more realistic appraisal of social contexts and interpersonal relations (Garmezy, 1987). Among resilient adults, Werner and Smith (1992) found tendencies of realistic distancing from the domestic problems of their parents. Such cognitive processes tie in with opportunities to prevent antisociality for the next generation. This may be the case when high-risk females who exhibit more planning and critical reflection about their situation select more caring partners and thus provide better family conditions for their own offspring (Quinton and Rutter, 1988).

Attachment to reference persons

Developmental psychopathology emphasises the lack of secure bonds as an important risk factor (e.g., Ainsworth, 1991; Bowlby, 1982). For example, neglected and abused children more frequently have insecure attachments to parents than comparable controls (Schneider-Rosen and Cicchetti, 1984). While having insecure bonds is not a disturbance in itself, it may increase the probability of child disorder. Particularly in high-risk samples, insecure attachment (e.g., avoidant, coercive, disorganised) is a predictor of externalising and other problem behaviour (Fagot and Pears, 1996; Greenberg *et al.*, 1993). Equally, a secure bond between child and caregivers can be a protective factor against other risks (Egeland *et al.*, 1993; Tress *et al.*, 1989). This has been demonstrated in, for example, coping with family conflicts and distress (Jenkins and Smith, 1990; Newcomb, 1997; Rutter, 1979), child abuse (Farber and Egeland, 1987; Hunter and Kilstrom, 1979), multiple life burdens (Wyman *et al.*, 1991), and having a mentally ill parent (Fisher *et al.*, 1987; Radke-Yarrow and Sherman, 1990).

A good relationship with parents also promotes nondelinquency and suppresses serious delinquency in youngsters (Stouthamer-Loeber *et al.*, 1993). In the Newcastle Study, it was particularly the mother-child involvement and daily stimulation by the mother that reduced hyperactivity and conduct disorders in elementary school children from deprived family backgrounds (Kolvin *et al.*, 1988, 1990a, b). Having a good relationship to their mothers enabled youngsters to cope with divorce following a period of extreme conflict between parents (Neighbors *et al.*, 1993). Moreover, it was also the positive emotional relationship to their mothers that protected children from the punishing and rejecting behaviour of fathers during periods of economic decline (Elder *et al.*, 1984). Emotionally attentive, supportive, and interested parents prove to be a major factor in the acquisition of social competence among children from deprived lower-class milieus (Osborn, 1990) and in the social advancement of Afro-American lower-class children (Williams and Kornblum, 1985). Competent boys in families with cumulated life stress were found to have an emotionally responsive and supportive mother (Pianta *et al.*, 1990). Attachment to a competent caregiver promotes experiences of emotional security even within otherwise stressful contexts (Cummings and Davies, 1996). This may result in a structured, predictable, regulated enviroment that contributes to a healthy social and cognitive development. In contrast, maternal deprivation in early childhood may disrupt basic aspects of brain development and neuronal functioning that are relevant for the regulation of aggressive behaviour (e.g., Kraemer, 1997).

Although the first years of life are most important for brain development, later contextual inputs should not be underestimated (e.g., Boyce *et al.*, 1998). Because delinquent individuals frequently come from a particularly adverse family milieu, it is noteworthy that positive functions of attachment do not seem to be restricted to parents (e.g., Lösel, 1994; Rutter, 1985; Werner and Smith, 1982). To some degree, they may also be exercised by grandparents, an older sibling, educators, teachers, members of church groups, or other persons outside the family. Such positive relationships give young people not only emotional support but also the feeling of being important for the other person (Freedman, 1993; Werner and Smith, 1992).

Later bonding with a life partner can also exercise such a protective function. For example, Sampson and Laub (1993) have shown that a strong marital attachment contributed to desistance in young men with a history of delinquency. Those who had developed favourably had not only close, warm feelings toward their wives but also more responsibilities. A good relationship to a spouse or partner also had a stabilising function for youngsters with a very problematic past, as shown in the Kauai Study (Werner, 1993). This was somewhat more true for women compared with men. As mentioned above, for girls who had grown up in residential care, selecting a supportive partner in young adulthood impacted favourably on their further development (Quinton *et al.*, 1984; Rutter and Quinton, 1984). Similar results were found for males who had been in care institutions or had exhibited conduct problems (Quinton *et al.*, 1993). This study suggests gender differences in the protective functions of supportive spouses that may be partially due to the lower rate of deviant women. A caring and emotionally responsive relationship was also important in explaining why some mothers were able to break an intergenerational cycle of abuse (e.g., Egeland *et al.*, 1988). Positive effects of reliable partner relations or marital support have been reported in various other areas of mental health (e.g., Brown and Harris, 1978).

It should be emphasised that it is not the relationship itself but its quality that is crucial for a protective function. If the partner is antisocial or unreliable, the relationship may well have a risk function (e.g., Sampson and Laub, 1993). An example is the delinquency-promoting influence of heterosexual friendships on girls with early puberty (Caspi *et al.*, 1993; Silbereisen and Kracke, 1993). However, this seems to be primarily an acceleration effect that disappears in late adolescence (Stattin and Magnusson, 1996). Nonetheless, if it leads to adolescent pregnancy, it may result in a crime risk for the offspring (Nagin *et al.*, 1997).

Although bonding theory assumes a stable representation (internal working model) that is already acquired in early childhood, attachment should not be seen as too static (e.g., Ainsworth, 1991; Waters *et al.*, 2000). The above-mentioned and other findings suggest some flexibility in attachment. Due to the child's development of competencies and the mother's behaviour, changes in attachment categories may already occur at preschool age (Crittenden, 1992; Fagot and Pears, 1996). Age-appropriate moves toward separation are also inherent to the protective function of an emotionally secure bond (Grossmann and Grossmann, 1991). Otherwise, there is a risk of overprotection and dependency. Furthermore, it is questionable how far representations of the early attachment figure generalise to other relationships. On the one hand, there even seems to be a relation between child-parent attachment and representations of peer relations (e.g., Cassidy *et al.*, 1996). On the other hand, emotional bonds to later reference persons do not necessarily require a secure parental bond in infancy (Asendorpf *et al.*, 1997). Nonetheless, high-risk young mothers seem to stabilise more easily when they have already had experiences of secure bonding in the past (Werner, 1989).

Childrearing and educational climate

Emotional bonds to parents or other caregivers are closely related to childrearing. Rejecting, aggressive, inconsistent, or lax parental behaviour are important risk factors for persistent antisociality (Loeber and Stouthamer-Loeber, 1986; Patterson *et al.*, 1991). Equally, it has been shown that positive levels of parenting may serve as protective factors. For example, Stouthamer-Loeber *et al.* (1993) reported that good communication and supervision have a protective effect against delinquency. In the Kauai Study, resilient youngsters had received more affection and positive identification models from their parents or other caregivers (Werner and Smith, 1992). Alongside emotionally positive features of parenting, fixed rules and being assigned household duties contributed to a sense of responsibility and autonomy in adolescence. Kolvin *et al.* (1990a) observed an improvement in conduct problems and hyperactivity among high-risk elementary school children when parents, or particularly mothers were involved, stimulating, firmly controlling, and reasoning with their children. These characteristics were less relevant for changes in neurotic behaviour.

Osborn (1990) studied a sample of resilient children from the 1970 British birth cohort. He traced approximately 15,000 children through ages 5 to 10 years. A vulnerable group was selected from the lowest decile of a composite social index based on indicators of low SES such as parental occupation or accommodation. This index correlated negatively with an index of child competence that included mother and teacher ratings of conduct disorder and hyperactivity as well as reading, mathematics, and general ability test scores. Two resilient groups were analysed: those children who, at age 10, were behaviourally nondeviant and at least average on all three tests (competent group) and those who were nondeviant and above average in abilities (exceptional group). Of all factors investigated, parental attitudes and behaviour made the strongest contribution to the probability of a socially disadvantaged child acquiring competence. Nonauthoritarian attitudes, child-centered parenting, and strong positive attitudes toward the child's education outweighed negative contextual effects.

Similarly, competent boys from otherwise multiply stressed lower-class families had a more stimulating, emotionally warmer, and better organised upbringing (Pianta *et al.*, 1990). According to Garmezy (1985, 1987), multiply stressed families that produce competent children engage more frequently in joint activities, have a more warm-hearted emotional climate, but also have fixed behavioural rules. Likewise, favourable effects of support and structuring have been found in children of divorce (Hetherington, 1989). Not only emotional acceptance of the child but also supervision, control, and clear behavioural rules seem to be even more important for a healthy development when the social environment is difficult and threatening (Baldwin *et al.*, 1990; Wyman *et al.*, 1991).

However, some studies confirm the protective function of parental attitudes and behaviours only in part. For example, in Farrington (1994), although parental interest in education proved to be protective, measures of parenting and family harmony showed risk effects only at their negative poles. One aspect to be considered here is that family climate variables are sometimes linked so closely to other factors that they become hard to isolate as independent protective factors. In other studies, parenting factors are included only as risks for antisociality in order to test the protective function of further variables (e.g., Hoge *et al.*, 1996).

The potential buffering function of a positive educational climate and behaviour against a variety of developmental risks is also demonstrated outside the family context (Garmezy, 1991; Rutter *et al.*, 1979). Studies at schools in high delinquency risk areas have shown relations between fewer behavioural problems, good school achievement, and positive self-esteem among students and the following features: a prosocial atmosphere and attitude toward achievement, structured teaching, the provision of incentives, adequate control and supervision, as well as the delegation of responsibilities to students (Olweus, 1993; Mortimore, 1995; Rutter *et al.*, 1979). A positive social-emotional as well as norm-oriented educational climate in residential care institutions was most important for resilience in juveniles from multiproblem milieus (Bender *et al.*, 1996; Lösel, 1994). In male risk groups, military service can also exercise a stabilising function. This is attributable to their experiencing a structured and regulated daily life, as well as the opportunities it provides to make up for deficits in academic and vocational training (Elder, 1986; Werner, 1993).

An emotionally positive, attentive, and accepting as well as norm-oriented, adequately demanding, and controlling upbringing has a fundamental function for healthy mental development in children (Baumrind, 1989). Such an 'authoritative' educational climate requires a clear exercise of the parental role. This is supported by Garmezy and Nuechterlein's (1972) findings in a study of Afro-American children from disadvantaged families. Mothers of less competent children behaved more frequently as if they were pseudo-sisters or girlfriends. In contrast, mature and resilient mothers are able to buffer negative influences of disadvantage on their children (Kolvin *et al.*, 1990a; Werner and Smith, 1992).

However, as mentioned above, childrearing is not a one-sided influence but a reciprocal process depending also on the youngster's own behaviours and dispositions (Boyce *et al.*, 1998; Hinde, 1992). Resilient mothers may be responsible for a partial transfer of resilience to their offspring through shared genetic information. Genetic factors explain substantial variance in both parental and child behaviour, and the latter also has an influence on parenting (Plomin, 1994). In siblings, nonshared environmental variance is relatively large (Rowe, 1994). The same childrearing practices may have different results in children with different temperament. In a longitudinal study of children during their first three years, Belsky *et al.* (1998) found that infants high in negativity were most susceptible to parenting influences. There were also differences in impact between parents. Mothering was a stronger predictor of externalising problems and fathering was more related to inhibition.

Differences in reactivity to educational practices may also moderate effects outside the family. For example, Hoge *et al.* (1996) found a protective effect against reoffending among those juvenile delinquents who reacted positively to authority (e.g., to probation officers). With respect to the educator's side, Aber *et al.* (1998) reported different reactions of teachers who received a training and coaching programme for violence prevention. Overall, the children's aggressive fantasies, hostile attributional biases, and aggressive negotiation strategies increased during the school year. However, in those children who received a relatively high number of programme lessons the negative development could be reduced. This was due to teachers who received at least a moderate amount of training and coaching and taught many lessons in the classroom. Children whose teachers had received a high level of training but taught only few lessons showed faster growth in aggressive cognitions and behaviours.

School achievement, school bonding, and employment

Negative school experiences are predictors of serious delinquency (e.g., Hawkins *et al.*, 1998). Similarly, one can expect a protective function of positive school experiences (e.g., Gottfredson, 2001; Mortimore, 1995). Two main features of this are academic achievement and school bonding. As mentioned above, Farrington (1994) has shown that parental interest in a school career, attending schools providing more than a basic education, achievement orientation, and success at school protect youngsters from delinquency. Stouthamer-Loeber *et al.* (1993) reported that strong school motivation protects against the aggravation of delinquency. High achievement motivation and an education beyond high school typified resilient individuals in the Kauai Study (Werner and Smith, 1992). Likewise, in the Seattle Social Development Study, school bonding was related to reduced violence, although more strongly in African-American students and boys compared with European-American students and girls (Williams, 1994). In the Dunedin Study, the percentage of boys leaving high school before age 16 years was lowest in the group of abstainers and in the group of recoveries from childhood antisociality (11 per cent and 24 per cent). In contrast, 72 per cent of the youngsters from the LCP path and 45 per cent from the AL path had left school at this age (Moffitt *et al.*, 1996). As McCord and Ensminger (1997) have shown, low school attendance in first grade was associated with adult violence of males and females but not with depression and alcohol problems.

Good school achievement was a protective factor in a study of young offenders in Canada (Hoge *et al.*, 1996). Some of the risk factors these authors investigated were family relationship problems (e.g., poor parent–child relations or low cohesion) and family structuring problems (e.g., lack of or inconsistent discipline). Outcome measures were indices of reoffending and compliance during a 12- to 18-month probation period. Among older participants (15- to 17-year-olds) with family relationship problems, good school achievement had a strong protective effect on compliance and a weaker effect on reoffending. Effects on participants with family structuring problems showed a similar trend. The protective function existed at all levels of the risk variables and no interactions were found.

Good school achievement and school bonding still seem to exercise a protective function against antisocial behaviour when they are not accompanied by above-average intelligence (e.g., Baldwin *et al.*, 1990; Conrad and Hammen, 1993; Elder *et al.*, 1986; Felsman and Vaillant, 1987; Hetherington, 1989; Radke-Yarrow and Brown, 1993; Spencer *et al.*, 1993; Werner and Smith, 1982). Among the risk children in the Kauai Study, good school achievement and reading skills were more relevant than intelligence for successful psychosocial adjustment in adulthood (Werner, 1993). Raine (1993) has shown that preschool boys who exhibited a low HRL did not become antisocial up to age 11 if they exhibited good school achievement, even if they did not differ in IQ. Our own study of high-risk adolescents in residential care revealed that school success and a good relationship to both teachers and friends at school (but not in the residential care center) had stronger protective effects than intelligence (Bender *et al.*, 1996). Werner and Smith (1992) have reported similar findings. Positive experiences at school were also tied to more successful marriages and careers in young women who had grown up in residential care (Rutter and Quinton, 1984).

One explanation for such protective effects is that school success is a source of self-affirmation that helps to compensate for negative experiences in the family (Rutter, 1990; Werner and Smith, 1982). Moreover, a positive school career is also an indicator of bonds to society (Hirschi, 1969) and holds a door open for nondeviant opportunities in life (Caspi and Moffitt, 1995). A similar effect is found for positive work behaviour and job stability that may lead to turning points in the development of early delinquents when they enter young adulthood (Sampson and Laub, 1993). In this re-analysis of the data from Glueck and Glueck (1950), young men who desisted from juvenile delinquency had a strong desire for better academic, vocational, or professional schooling and were eager to improve themselves and their families. In the Cambridge Study, those men who desisted from offending in adulthood had a better employment history than the persisters (Farrington, 1989). In the Dunedin Study, abstainers and recoveries showed similarly low unemployment rates at age 18 years to the unclassified (normal) boys, whereas both the LCP and the AL path showed higher rates (Moffitt *et al.*, 1996).

In sum, school bonding and achievement as well as occupational stability can be important protective factors against antisociality (Catalano and Hawkins, 1996). However, we should not overestimate their impact on negative chain reactions: these variables are not necessarily causal factors in the development of antisocial behaviour. Tremblay *et al.* (1992), for example, have shown that the best path model for boys was a direct causal link between Grade 1 disruptive behaviour and delinquent behaviour at age 14. Poor school achievement in Grades 1 and 4 was not a causal mediator. Similar results have been obtained with older boys (Huesmann *et al.*, 1987). As Hämäläinen and Pulkkinen (1996) have shown in an analysis of various developmental patterns, the impaired school success pathway was not the most relevant one for adult criminality. Criminal offences in adulthood were best predicted by an accumulation of various behavioural problems over the entire school period. Similarly, Bergman and Magnusson (1997) found that the cluster of youngsters with low school achievement at age 13 had no enhanced risk for criminality at age 18–23. The subgroup with a low school-motivation syndrome, however, had a significant risk to become both criminal and alcohol abusing adults. Other studies have found either no or no long-term relationship between school bonding and juvenile violence (Elliott, 1994; Maguin *et al.*, 1995). It should also not be forgotten that extreme school-related motivations may sometimes have unfavourable effects in other domains, for example, when an excessive focus on achievement in students or parents contributes to fears of failure and psychosomatic disturbances (Holler-Nowitzki, 1994).

Social networks and peer groups

The availability and use of social support from family members, relatives, teachers, educators, ministers of religion, and friends also contributes to resilience. This has been confirmed in, for example, children from multiply stressed families (Werner, 1993), in adolescent mothers (Cutrona, 1989), in children of divorce (Hetherington, 1989), and in families with mentally ill parents (Garmezy, 1985). Extrafamilial support is probably particularly important for youngsters from disadvantaged families, because it provides them with a relationship that compensates for their social background (Comer, 1988). Support outside the family not only helps children directly, but can also promote healthy development indirectly by reducing the stress on the parents (Wertlieb *et al.*, 1989; Wyman *et al.*, 1991).

Supportive persons do not just help to solve immediate problems; at the same time, they provide models of active and constructive coping behaviour (Hetherington, 1989; Murphy and Moriarty, 1976; Werner and Smith, 1982). For example, in the Kauai Study, the achievement-oriented behaviour of resilient girls was related to the model of educated and professionally committed mothers. High-risk children who reduced their antisocial behaviour more often had 'resilient' mothers with good self-esteem, low helplessness, and active coping behaviour (Kolvin *et al.*, 1990a). Similarly, competent girls from divorced families had working mothers who promoted autonomy and self-reliance when rearing their children (Hetherington, 1989).

Whereas, generally, social support from prosocial adults has a positive function, the influence of the peer group has to be viewed in a more differentiated manner. This is particularly the case with regard to the development of antisocial behaviour. Numerous studies have shown that juvenile delinquency is often a group phenomenon (Elliott *et al.*, 1985, 1989; Reiss and Farrington, 1991; Patterson *et al.*, 1992). Reiss and Farrington (1991), for example, found that 60 per cent of offenders and co-offenders lived within a one mile distance from each other, and one-half of their offences were committed within the same distance from their homes. Deviant peers model and reinforce antisocial behaviour, drug use, and other forms of problem behaviour. Peer delinquency is one of the strongest predictors of serious and violent juvenile offending (Hawkins *et al.*, 1998; Thornberry and Krohn, 1997). This is particularly the case for membership in youth gangs that seems to give juvenile antisociality a different 'quality' (Thornberry, 1998). Even when the impact of delinquent peers is controlled, gang membership facilitates all kinds of offending and drug use (e.g., Battin *et al.*, 1998).

However, differentiation between delinquent peer groups and gangs is not always clear, and, particularly outside North America, only a small portion of young offenders belong to stable gang-like networks (e.g., Reiss, 1995). Peers may also be a protective factor, when they have an emotionally supportive and development-promoting function (Bender and Lösel, 1997; Jessor *et al.*, 1991; Moffitt, 1993a). In Werner and Smith (1992), for example, resilient boys and girls had at least one close friend, and girls often had several. In Farrington (1994), high popularity proved on the one hand to be a protective factor in boys. On the other hand, having few or no friends and preferring solitary activities also had a protective function. Whether the peer network has a risk or protective effect depends essentially on whether these peers are antisocial or not.

Stouthamer-Loeber *et al.* (1993) have reported a protective effect when friends were nondelinquent. Bad friends were, however, a risk factor. Likewise, Farrington (1994) found that it was nondelinquent peers or friends from school who protected against the persistence or onset of criminality. Among the youthful offenders investigated by Hoge *et al.* (1996), those who had positive peer relations and a more effective use of leisure time were more frequently desistors. Moffitt *et al.* (1996) found that both the abstainers and recoveries named fewer delinquent friends than the antisocial boys from the LCP and AL paths.

From a causal perspective, it must be asked whether association with deviant friends is a precursor of delinquency (e.g., Keenan *et al.*, 1995), or whether antisocial behaviour leads to delinquent friends (e.g., Tremblay *et al.*, 1995). There are probably different influences of the social network on different pathways of antisocial behaviour. Children with early onset, undersocialised-aggressive, and life-course-persistent antisociality seem to be vulnerable to rejection by others, leading them to join deviant groups that reinforce their antisocial behaviour (Cairns and Cairns, 1991; Patterson *et al.*, 1992; Price and Dodge, 1989). Various studies have demonstrated the impact of peer rejection and lack of social support on subsequent maladjustment (e.g., Parker *et al.*, 1995). Peer rejection also leads to internalising problems (Hoza *et al.*, 1995; Rubin *et al.*, 1995), and a combination of aggressive behaviour and rejection is a particularly good predictor of later aggression and delinquency (Bierman and Wargo, 1995; Coie *et al.*, 1995).

Youngsters should not just be viewed as passive objects of social influences, because individuals actively construct the contexts that then proceed to exert an influence on them. According to the confluence hypothesis (Cohen, 1977; Dishion *et al.*, 1994), youngsters join peer groups on the basis of similar interests and attitudes, and then reinforce each other's behaviour. However, when selection is limited, deviant peers may have a negative impact. Kellam *et al.* (1998), for example, found strong interactive effects on the risk of being highly aggressive in middle school between the boys' own level of aggressive behaviour in first grade and the overall level of aggressive behaviour in the first grade classrooms. Aggressive first grade boys in aggressive classes had the highest risk of being aggressive five years later. Probably, selection and facilitation processes are similarly important for the effects of antisocial peers. For youth gangs, however, facilitation may have the larger impact (Thornberry, 1998).

In contrast to persistent antisociality, late onset and adolescence-limited forms depend on more normative peer relationships (Hinshaw *et al.*, 1993; Stattin and Magnusson, 1996). During adolescence, antisocial peers seem to become more attractive for nondeviant individuals (Moffitt, 1993a). Persistent bullies, for example, are well-accepted in the class (Lösel and Bliesener, 1999a; Olweus, 1993). Although delinquency, substance use, and aggressive behaviour are part of the peer group's activities, in a milder form such peer relations provide support, reinforcement, and role models that may help in mastering transitions to adulthood (Caspi and Moffitt, 1995; Jessor *et al.*, 1991; Silbereisen and Noack, 1990). How far the peer group exerts a long-term positive or negative influence depends not least on the quality of relationships with parents and school. When, for example, parents accept and supervise the child, there is a stronger probability that youngsters will not turn to a deviant peer group (Dishion *et al.*, 1995; Kandel, 1996; Quinton *et al.*, 1993). School bonding and attachment to teachers may have a similar protective effect (Thornberry, 1998). If the relationship with peers is perceived as being satisfactory, behaviour patterns shared with the peer group will stabilise (Bender and Lösel, 1997; Tremblay *et al.*, 1995). In our study, satisfied youngsters with a history of good adaptation continued to develop positively, whereas deviants continued their problem behaviour. When, in contrast, juveniles were not embedded in a social network, this had a protective effect in those with a history of deviance, but a risk effect in those who were formerly nondeviant.

The influence of the social network on antisocial behaviour also differs somewhat according to gender. Aggressive girls, for example, affiliate with aggressive friends at an older age than boys do (Cairns *et al.*, 1988). Girls are also more dependent on intimate relationships, and are particularly at risk for antisocial behaviour if they enter puberty at an early age and have older friends (Caspi *et al.*, 1993; Stattin and Magnusson, 1990; Silbereisen and Kracke, 1993). Similarly, Farrington (1994) has found that not having a girlfriend has a protective effect in boys. Early heterosexual relationships can be viewed as indicators of separation from the family and transition to a partly deviant lifestyle. However, in some studies, the enhanced risk in early-maturing girls was found only in coeducational schools (Caspi *et al.*, 1993), while in others, it did not persist into young adulthood (Stattin and Magnusson, 1996). In later adolescence or young adulthood, positive heterosexual relationships may have a protective effect for both sexes (Bender and Lösel, 1997; Sampson and Laub, 1993).

The subdimensions, dosages, and objective versus subjective features of the social network require a differentiated analysis. Furthermore, it should be pointed out that the dimensions and operationalisations of the various constructs vary greatly (e.g., Parker *et al.*, 1995; Robinson and Garber, 1995). With the exception of serious delinquent peers and youth gangs, it may be difficult to disentangle protective and risky network effects. Too much support can lead to dependency and reduce a person's own coping efforts (e.g., Cauce *et al.*, 1982; Holler-Nowitzki, 1994). The overall low protective effects of social support in meta-analyses

(Schwarzer and Leppin, 1991) probably have something to do with such partially negative aspects.

Self-related cognitions, social cognitions and beliefs

The idea that self-related cognitions protect against aggression and delinquency is suggested by social-cognitive learning theories (e.g., Bandura, 1986, 1997). Neutralisation of moral standards, lack of self-critique, and deficits in feelings of guilt are cognitive mechanisms enabling individuals to act antisocially and to persist with such behaviour. In line with this, Stouthamer-Loeber *et al.* (1993) have shown that the ability to feel guilt has a protective effect that promotes nondelinquency and suppresses serious delinquency. The ability to learn effectively from both positive and negative experiences is linked to internal causal attributions. Thus, resilient children, adolescents, and young adults exhibit stronger internal control beliefs (Luthar, 1991; Murphy and Moriarty, 1976; O'Grady and Metz, 1987; Parker *et al.*, 1990; Werner, 1989). However, these are not extreme beliefs but ones that indicate a positive basic trend of realistic control (Cowen *et al.*, 1997). A rigid internal locus of control would probably increase vulnerability for emotional problems when faced with uncontrollable events (see Cowen *et al.*, 1990; Masten *et al.*, 1990).

Clear indications about the importance of cognitive factors are also revealed by studies on social information processing in aggressive children and adolescents (Coie and Dodge, 1998; Crick and Dodge, 1994; Huesmann, 1997). An impressive body of research suggests that aggressive and nonaggressive youngsters differ in the phases of (a) encoding of cues, (b) interpretation of cues, (c) clarification of goals, (d) response access or construction, (e) response evaluation and decision, and (f) behavioural enactment (Crick and Dodge, 1994). For example, antisocial individuals tend to overperceive aggression-relevant stimuli (e.g., Lochman and Dodge, 1998), attribute more hostile intentions to others (e.g., Guerra and Slaby, 1990), are more egocentric and antisocial in their goal setting (e.g., Rubin *et al.*, 1991), generate more aggressive-impulsive alternatives of reacting (e.g., Lösel and Bliesener, 1999b), expect relatively positive consequences of aggressive behaviour (e.g., Perry *et al.*, 1986), and show less social skills for nonaggressive interactions (e.g., Dodge *et al.*, 1986). Although this research focuses on the risk pole of variables, the observed differences between aggressive and nonaggressive youngsters also point to protective functions of more adequate cognitive schemata (Lösel and Bliesener, in press). For example, abstainers and recoveries perceive the risk of detection for a crime as substantially higher than the boys from the AL and LCP paths of antisociality (Moffitt *et al.*,

1996). The relative success of cognitive-behavioural programmes for antisocial youngsters (Lipsey and Wilson, 1998; Lösel, 1996) also suggest that cognitive schemata and beliefs have protective functions.

Aggression-prone modes of social information processing correlate not only with antisocial behaviour but also with experiences of aggression and conflict in social contexts such as the family, school, peer group, and mass media (Coie and Dodge, 1998; Lösel *et al.*, in press). Thus, concepts of social information processing are important mediators between social influences, individual dispositions, and situational risks of antisocial behaviour. As mentioned above, representations of relationships with parents may generalise to relations with peers. The child's peer-related representations influence his or her behaviour to peers. A person's own positive behaviour contributes to being well-liked and this, in turn, increases the likelihood of receiving positive behaviour that, in turn, reinforces positive representations of others (e.g., Cassidy *et al.*, 1996).

Social cognitions are related to young persons' more general self-images that seem to exert protective effects in various domains (see Basic Behavioural Science Task Force, 1996). Studies have reported that resilient youngsters possess self-confidence, positive self-esteem, and beliefs in self-efficacy alongside a low feeling of helplessness (e.g., Cicchetti and Rogosch, 1997; Cowen *et al.*, 1990, 1997; Garmezy, 1985; Hetherington, 1989; Lösel and Bliesener, 1994; Parker *et al.*, 1990; Werner, 1990; Wyman *et al.*, 1993). Personal judgements on how well one can execute the courses of action required to deal with prospective situations have proved to be important for numerous positive outcomes in clinical or educational settings (Bandura, 1997). Believing that one is not helpless may cause stressors to be evaluated as being more challenging and thus result in more active and fewer avoidant coping strategies (e.g., Compas, 1987; Lösel and Bliesener, 1994). Positive future expectations and cognitions of self-worth predict resilient functioning in children from highly-stressed urban backgrounds (Cowen *et al.*, 1997; Wyman *et al.*, 1993). Cognitions of self-worth may derive from positive experiences in the family and at school and may, in turn, have feedback effects on bonding to these social contexts. Even when social protective factors are weak, cognitions of self-esteem and self-reliance seem to be central organisers of resilience in highly stressed youngsters (Cicchetti and Rogosch, 1997; Cowen *et al.*, 1997).

However, we should not overestimate the protective functions of a positive self-image. It may also have a risk effect, in particular when it is so extreme that it leads to egocentric and unrealistic behaviour. Whereas Farrington (1994), Werner and Smith (1992), and others have found that high self-esteem can protect against delinquency, a review from Baumeister *et al.* (1996) suggests that self-esteem plays an ambiguous etiological role in the development of aggression: violent persons often have an inflated self-esteem. Hughes *et al.* (1997) found that already at age 7, aggressive children had more idealised and inflated ratings of competence and relationship quality than nonaggressive children. This may be a defensive posture of aggressive youngsters. In consequence, an individual with a very favourable but fragile self-image may more easily show aggression in response to perceived disrespect or otherwise negative feedback from others (Bushman and Baumeister, 1998). Such individuals also do not realise the influences of their own cognitive schema, modes of information processing, and behaviour in negative interactions. For example, in psychopaths, a grandiose sense of self-worth and other egocentric cognitions contribute to manipulative, aggressive, and unsympathetic behaviour and impede any motivation to change (Dolan and Coid, 1993; Hare, 1995; Lösel, 1998).

Likewise, Antonovsky (1987) discusses the problems of a too positive self-image in terms of a dysfunctionally rigid sense of coherence (SOC). The normally protective function of SOC is mainly studied in adults and less in resilient youngsters (Köferl, 1988). However, the subdimensions of comprehensibility, manageability, and meaningfulness come close to the above-mentioned characteristics of self-efficacy and self-worth in resilient children. Beardslee (1989) has worked out similar dimensions of self-understanding: (a) adequate cognitive appraisal, (b) realistic appraisal of the capacities for and consequences of action, (c) action orientation, (d) developmental perspective, and (e) experience of understanding as a protective factor.

Protective processes of meaning and structure are related to functions of attachment and childrearing. They also may be promoted by bonding to other prosocial institutions (Anthony, 1987; Elliott *et al.*, 1985; Jessor *et al.*, 1991). For example, religious and ethical values in youngsters and their perceived emphasis in social contexts can protect against antisociality and other problem behaviour (see Baldwin *et al.*, 1990; Comer, 1988; Jessor *et al.*, 1991; Lösel, 1994; Werner and Smith, 1992). Similarly buffering strengths may be derived from specific hobbies, long-term interests, commitment to nontrivial leisure-time activities, or the exercise of special talents (Garmezy, 1987; Hetherington, 1989; Hoge *et al.*, 1996; Werner and Smith, 1992). As mentioned above, more distanced and realistic evaluations of the adversities in one's own family are frequent when resilients become more mature (Garmezy, 1987; Werner and Smith, 1992). Such tendencies of an open, subjectively meaningful restructuring of the past are similar to the process that may occur in successful psychotherapy (Orlinsky *et al.*, 1994). In line with the assumption of differentiated and flexible self-related cognitions, a certain sense of humour also seems to be protective (Masten, 1986).

Under extremely stressful circumstances, psychological adaptation can be attained by subscribing to rigid political, ultrareligious, or other ideologies (Bettelheim, 1943). This seems to happen with children in dangerous neighbourhoods or war zones (Garbarino, 1990). Whereas this probably reduces problems within the in-group, hostility toward the enemy group will be maintained or even increased through stereotyped attributions and schemata. Bonding to shared ideologies does not just involve meaning-making processes. The active participation in groups that provide social support and structure also has an influence (Anthony, 1987; Werner, 1993). As with other factors, protective or risk functions depend on the specific content and degree of such influences. For example, in some religious sects, group processes may form psychopathological processes that give rise to violence or suicide. Similarly, whereas shared subcultural beliefs and lifestyles in mildly delinquent peer groups may help to cope successfully with social transitions (Maggs and Hurrelmann, 1998), they have much more of a risk effect in serious delinquent groups or youth gangs (Thornberry, 1998).

Neighbourhood and community factors

Since the area approach of Shaw and McKay (1942), it has been emphasised repeatedly that characteristics of the neighbourhood and wider community are risk factors for juvenile delinquency and violence (e.g., Attar *et al.*, 1994; Farrington *et al.*, 1993; Hawkins *et al.*, 1998; Reiss, 1995; Sampson and Lauritsen, 1994). Neighbourhood risk factors are, for example, a concentration of families living in economic deprivation or on social welfare, community disorganisation and low neighbourhood attachment, high crime and violence in the neighbourhood, availability of drugs, a high rate of new immigrants, and racial discrimination and prejudice (e.g., Brooks-Gunn *et al.*, 1993; Elliott *et al.*, 1989; Farrington, 1998; Gorman-Smith and Tolan, 1998; McCord and Ensminger, 1997; Reiss, 1995; Sampson and Laub, 1993; Seidman *et al.*, 1998; Wikström, 1991; Wikström and Loeber, 2000). These and other characteristics may impact directly on antisocial behaviour because they contribute to a stressful environment, concentrate deviant role models, offer situational opportunity structures, and so forth. Neighbourhoods may also have an indirect impact through interactions with individual, family, school, peer group, and other risks for antisocial behaviour.

Although Bronfenbrenner (1979) and others have emphasised the important role of ecological contexts for human development, most research in developmental psychopathology has focused on the individual or microsocial level. More studies on the wider social context and its linkage to individual development are needed (e.g., Cicchetti and Aber, 1998; Wikström and Loeber, 2000). This is particularly the case for potential protective effects of neighbourhood and community variables (Catalano *et al.*, 1998; Kupersmidt *et al.*, 1995). The protective model anticipates that positive characteristics of the wider social context may prevent or buffer negative influences at the individual or microsocial level.

Research on this issue is confronted with various problems, for example:

(a) In many studies on risk and protective factors, samples live in similar neighbourhoods. Thus, there is not enough ecological variation.
(b) If there is enough variation, characteristics of individuals, families, and so forth may be so closely related that it becomes difficult to separate a distinct community effect.
(c) There may be also a lack of connection between ecological or group correlations and correlations on the individual level (Robinson, 1950). This so-called ecological fallacy does not mean that ecological correlations cannot reveal causal mechanisms (e.g., Rutter, 1995). However, they need to be based on explicit hypotheses about important contextual domains, salient dimensions, and relations between the individual level and nested sets of ecosystems (Boyce *et al.*, 1998; Bronfenbrenner, 1979).
(d) Most ecological research designs are cross-sectional. However, the composition of neighbourhoods is not static and delinquency patterns may remain even after objective changes of such variables as the unemployment rate (Bursik and Grasmick, 1992).
(e) Some studies only use one data source. Thus, relations between perceived neigbourhood violence or disorganisation and self-reported problem behaviour may be confounded.
(f) Due to biopsychosocial dispositions, people also actively select and 'construct' their neighbourhoods. For example, neglecting and abusing parents are less interested in neighbourhood integration and move home more frequently than caring families (Creighton, 1985; Polansky *et al.*, 1985). They also describe their neighbourhoods as being more unfriendly and less helpful than normal families who live in the same area (e.g., Polansky *et al.*, 1985).
(g) Neighbourhoods may have influence by interactions with individual characteristics. However, such effects are difficult to replicate (Lynam *et al.*, in press).

Because of these and other problems, 'pure' community effects must be disentangled carefully. In the Pittsburgh Study, Peeples and Loeber (1994) analysed neighbourhoods that varied in their underclass composition (using census data on family poverty, male joblessness, family unemployment, single parenthood, female-headed families, welfare use, etc.). Living in an underclass neighbourhood correlated with self-reported delinquency of boys even after controlling for individual and family variables such as hyperactivity, parental supervision, single parenthood, and family poverty. Simcha-Fagan and Schwartz (1986) found that community disadvantage as defined at the census-tract level correlated with individual self-reported delinquency, when income, residential stability, and organisational participation on the family level had been controlled. However, such effects are small in magnitude when a broad selection of individual and microsocial variables is included. Loeber *et al.* (1998) reported that there was little tendency for macrovariables to predict outcome after controlling for child and family variables. The relations also varied across outcome measures and samples. Bad neighbourhood was an independent predictor of delinquency in the youngest sample, of covert behaviour in the middle sample, and of delinquency and physical aggression in the oldest sample. Interestingly, in the middle sample, living in a bad neighbourhood suppressed the risk effect of HIA problems. Whereas Stouthamer-Loeber *et al.* (1993) found only a risk effect of the amount of neighbourhood crime, Farrington (1994) reported that being away from London at age 18 protected against adult offending. However, this effect was relatively weak.

In an analysis of data from the Pittsburgh Study, Wikström and Loeber (2000) asked whether onset and prevalence of serious juvenile offending vary across advantaged, middle-range and disadvantaged neighbourhoods when individual sets of risk and protective factors are controlled. Low/high hyperactivity-impulsivity-attention problems, guilt/lack of guilt, good/poor parental supervision, high/low school motivation, few/many peer delinquents, and negative/positive perception of antisocial behaviour were used as variables to form an overall risk-protective score. Youngsters with a high score offended seriously at a similar rate across all neighbourhoods. Neighbourhood socioeconomic context also had no impact on the early onset of serious offending (before age 13). However, neighbourhood had a direct influence on the late onset of offending for those youngsters who scored high on protective factors. Boys with a balanced score of risk and protective factors showed a similar effect. Within disadvantaged neighbourhoods, public housing resulted in particularly bad outcomes. Altogether, these results suggest a direct effect of neighbourhood disadvantage only on well-adjusted children when they reach adolescence. Perhaps, weaker informal social control due to a stronger impact of public settings and peers may be a key mediator in this process.

Lack of informal social control also seems to be an explanation for results on the interaction of impulsivity and neighbourhood (Lynam *et al.*, 2001). In two studies, these authors applied both a cross-sectional and a longitudinal design as well as objective and subjective measures of neighbourhood disadvantage. They found a stronger effect of impulsivity on juvenile offending in poorer neighbourhoods. However, non-impulsive boys in worse neighbourhoods showed no greater risk for delinquency than non-impulsive boys in better neighbourhoods.

As neighbourhood influences may operate in rather different ways, Kupersmidt *et al.* (1995) tested four models: risk, protective, potentiator, and person-environment fit. The authors compared the relations of three risk factors (ethnicity, income, and family structure) with childhood aggression and peer relations. Their study of 1,271 ten-year-olds from a small Southern US city addressed the individual and the neighbourhood level as well as interactions between the two. Through cluster analyses of census data, they derived two distinct types of neighbourhood: the first cluster were middle-SES neighbourhoods primarily composed of whites with a minimum of college education and a higher per capita income than persons living in the second cluster of low-SES neighbourhoods with a larger percentage of residents who were separated or divorced, below the poverty level, receiving public assistance, and without a high school diploma. Families were classified according to the eight possible combinations of low- versus middle-income; black versus white; and single- versus two-parent family.

There was no main effect of neighbourhood type on peer-rated childhood aggression. However, the main effect of family type was qualified by a significant family x neighbourhood interaction. Results suggest a protective effect of middle-SES neighbourhoods on the aggressive behaviour of black children from low-income, single-parent homes. In addition to this direct protective effect on high-risk families, neighbourhoods also interacted with family type to produce a poor person-environment fit or to potentiate positive effects. In middle-SES neighbourhoods, children from low-income, white, single-parent families were rejected more often by their peers; and children from middle-income, white, two-parent families had more home play companions than in low-SES neighbourhoods. These findings show that the same neighbourhood may be protective for one aspect of adjustment or family type, but may function as a risk or neutral factor for others. Furthermore, they suggest that neighbourhood variables are particularly relevant for high-risk families in that they enhance or reduce risk accumulations in the development of antisocial behaviour.

With respect to causal mechanisms, relations between neighbourhood variables and childrearing seem to be particularly important. For example, Simons *et al.* (1996) have found that effects of tract-level community disadvantage on self-reported delinquency of boys (but not girls) were mediated through low parental warmth and harsh discipline. Various studies have shown that poverty in the neighbourhood is related to child maltreatment (e.g., Korbin *et al.*, 1998). Exposure to community violence has a similar effect (e.g., Lynch and Cicchetti, 1998). However, according to Richters and Martinez (1993), exposure to community violence was not a general predictor of adaptational failures of children. The risk of failure increased substantially when the environmental adversities coincided with instability and unsafeness of children's homes. Lynch and Cicchetti (1998) found that maltreatment enhanced the risk for later antisociality and had a joint effect with community violence. The negative effect of maltreatment in the family was not moderated or buffered by a low level of community violence.

Gorman-Smith and Tolan (1998) reported a main effect of exposure to community violence on aggressive behaviour in juveniles one year later. Family variables such as cohesion, shared beliefs, structure, monitoring, and discipline had less influence. Only perceived family structure interacted with exposure to community violence. McLoyd (1990) found that economic hardship had an impact on a parent's behaviour and thus affected children's socioemotional development. Low-income, single, black mothers who lived in low-SES neighbourhoods provided a low level of support and supervision but more coercive forms of parenting. As mentioned above, deficits in parental support and supervision do not just link up directly with antisocial behaviour. They may also enhance opportunities for wandering and associating with deviant peers, and this risk may be potentiated in low-SES neighbourhoods with a higher concentration of negative role models or youth gangs (Johnstone, 1983; Reiss and Farrington, 1991; Stoolmiller, 1994; Thornberry, 1998). Thus, neighbourhoods with a more heterogeneous composite of risks can have a protective function.

Growing up in a ghetto-like underclass neighbourhood with low achievement and labour force attachment may lead to low feelings of self-efficacy that are mutually reinforced by similarly situated neighbours (Wilson, 1991). However, many poor neighbourhoods exhibit both poverty-related risks and relatively cohesive social networks (Wilson, 1996). The latter configuration could be a protective factor or a risk (in the case of antisocial networks). Due to social comparison processes, experiences of disadvantage and individual failure may be more negative for individuals who are confronted with neighbours with a higher SES. Relations between the degree of social inequality (the gap between winners and losers) and juvenile violence at the society level point in this direction (James, 1995). However, neighbourhood influences depend on more or less complex and subjective moderators.

Garbarino and Kostelny (1992), for example, compared low SES neighbourhoods in Chicago that varied widely in rates of child maltreatment. In those neighbourhoods in which child abuse was particularly high, people found it hard to think of anything good to say about their situation, the community environment looked dark and uncared for, and criminality was highly visible. In contrast, in low-SES neighbourhoods with low child abuse and neglect, people were eager to talk about their communities, felt that they were poor but decent places, had enough services available, and a strong and appreciated political leadership. Aneshensel and Sucoff (1996) found that underclass African American neighbourhoods were associated with high levels of self-reported conduct disorder. After controlling for this effect, perceived ambient hazards, but not social cohesion, still had a strong effect on conduct disorders.

In a study of various cohorts of students from Baltimore, New York City, and Washington DC, Seidman *et al.* (1998) differentiated between structural and experiential neighbourhood characteristics. Structural neighbourhood risk was operationalised by a combination of poverty and violence data at the census-tract level. Experiential profiles were measured by instruments on neighbourhood daily hassles, participation, and cohesion. Adolescents residing in moderate-structural-risk neighbourhoods reported more antisociality than those in high-structural-risk neighbourhoods. However, this relation held only for youngsters in middle (not early) adolescence and was stronger for those who perceived their neighbourhoods as more hassling. The age effect can be explained by more unsupervised peer contacts in mid-adolescence. There was also a subgroup of youngsters who experienced themselves as disconnected from the neighbourhood and who exhibited less antisociality than most other clusters. This may be a protective effect of the family actively restricting of social involvement in a disadvantaged or risky neighbourhood.

As most of these data are cross-sectional and focus on risks, we can only speculate about potential protective mechanisms. More longitudinal studies are needed to disentangle proximal (microsystem) effects from distal (exosytem) effects of neighbourhood (e.g., Lynch and Cicchetti, 1998). As Pagani *et al.* (1996) have shown, it is also important to differentiate categories like poverty and family status according to their duration and stability in development. In a sample from low-SES neighbourhoods, previous family poverty did not have an effect on theft, substance abuse, or physical violence in boys at age 16. It only predicted extreme delinquency. However, it was not persistent poverty but variations in financial hardship at two or more assessments over a six-year period that were particularly risky. Interestingly, this unstable pattern of poverty had an impact above and beyond family status and processes like child monitoring.

Conclusions and perspectives

The present overview suggests numerous factors that may protect at-risk youngsters from the onset or persistence of antisocial behaviour. It also demonstrated how underlying protective mechanisms and causal processes may function. However, knowledge in this field is still rudimentary. Much more research is needed on the various areas of natural protective factors and resilience. Due to conceptual and methodological problems, we need more studies that are adequate to detect moderating protective mechanisms. This also involves more replications, multi-method/multi-informant approaches, and analyses of complex patterns of variables. Differences in protective mechanisms between overt and covert forms of antisocial behaviour, age-groups, and gender are rarely studied and could not be addressed here in detail. As sketched in the closing chapter of this volume, accelerated longitudinal designs would be powerful instruments to address the various knowledge gaps.

Our analysis of basic issues has shown that factors may be protective within one context or against one behaviour problem, but may have risk effects under different conditions or for other outcomes. The protective function of an influence may also depend on its dosage. Thus, we should not speak too generally about protective factors, but always ask: risk for, and protection against, what? In improving our knowledge of the underlying processes, studies on protective factors are not the 'counterpart' of traditional risk research. In contrast, they are integrated elements of differentiated explanations of the natural history of deviant or nondeviant behaviour.

As we have seen, protective processes against antisocial development in the face of various risks may take place on and between biological, psychological, and social levels. Although the research we have reviewed was only partially designed to detect protective mechanisms, the following factors may be protective at various ages: genetic dispositions and high autonomic arousal; an easy or inhibited temperament; characteristics of ego resiliency; above-average intelligence and good planning;

emotionally secure bonds to the mother or other caregivers inside or outside the family; supportive relations to nondeviant friends and heterosexual partners; consistency, warmth, and acceptance as well as supervision and control of childrearing in the family, at school, or in potential welfare institutions; adult role models of prosocial behaviour and resilience under difficult circumstances; success at school and bonding to school; vocational achievement and employment stability; satisfying social support from outside the family and close, nondeviant friends; affiliation to nondelinquent peers and (for specific risk groups) some social isolation; experiences of self-efficacy in nondeviant activities and a good but not inflated self-esteem; cognitive schemata, beliefs, and information processing that are not aggression-prone; experiences of meaning and structure in one's life; and neighbourhoods that do not concentrate too many high-risk families, are nonviolent, and are socially integrated in a nondeviant mode. Protective functions may also be transferred to the next generation.

Numerous relations between these levels became apparent. Nonetheless, our discussion could only address a selection of potential protective factors. A comprehensive perspective would have to include more levels or areas of influence. These are shown in Table 5.1.

Unfortunately, there is insufficient empirical support for all areas of such multilevel concepts of protection against antisocial behaviour. Although there is increasing evidence for relations and interactions between the various levels, it is still difficult to link them together in a theoretically sound way. As our discussion of biological, family, and community factors has shown, we need more research designs that disentangle as well as integrate developmental influences at the individual, microsystem, exosystem, and macroystem levels. A pragmatic middle-range theory of protective processes against antisociality may already be based on current concepts from developmental criminology (LeBlanc and Loeber, 1993; Moffitt, 1993a). Within such a framework, a basic principle of protective mechanisms is: interrupting chain reactions in the development of persistent antisociality and providing opportunities that otherwise would have been 'knived off' (e.g., Caspi and Moffitt, 1995; Yoshikawa, 1994).

Sound knowledge on resilience and natural protective factors is not only important for more differentiated and better explanations of antisociality, but is also useful for improving our programmes of prevention and intervention. As reviews have shown, prevention programmes that promote cognitive and social competencies in the individual, childrearing practices in the family, school bonding and organisation, and neighbourhood integration may work (Beelmann *et al.*, 1994; Catalano *et al.*, 1998; Farrington and Welsh, 1999; Gottfredson, 2001; Tremblay and Craig,

Table 5.1 *Multilevel examples of potential protective factors against antisocial behaviour*

Level	Examples
Genetics	Nondeviant close relatives; no molecular genetic defects
Pre- and perinatal	Nonalcoholic mother; no maternal smoking during pregnancy; no birth complications
Psychophysiology	High arousal; low testosterone; normal neurological functioning
Temperament/personality	Inhibition; flexibility; task orientation; ego-resiliency
Cognitive competencies	Intelligence; verbal skills; planning for the future
Interactional competencies	Self-control; victim awareness; nondeviant problem-solving
Emotion	Secure attachment; feelings of guilt; anger control
Motivation	School and work motivation; special interests or hobbies; resistance to drugs
Social cognitions	Perspective taking; nonhostile attributions; nonaggressive response schemata; negative evaluation of antisocial reactions
Self-related cognitions	Self-efficacy in prosocial behaviour; realistic self-esteem; sense of coherence
Family	Harmony; acceptance; supervision; consistency; positive role models; continuity of caretaking; no disadvantage
School	Achievement and bonding; climate of acceptance, organisation, and supervision
Peer group	Nondelinquent peers; support from close, prosocial friends
Intimate partner	Supportive, prosocial partner; harmonious marriage
Spiritual	Religious orientation; moral beliefs
Economic	Middle SES; income stability; low disparity between poor and rich
Community	Advantaged socioeconomic context; integrated and nonviolent neighbourhood
Mass media	Low exposure to violence in the media; consumption integrated into family life
Situational	Target hardening; victim assertiveness; formal and informal social control
Legal	Effective firearm and drug control; effective criminal justice interventions
Cultural	Low violence; tradition of prosocial values; shame- and guilt-orientation; morality of co-operation

1995; Tremblay *et al.*, 1999). The same holds for later interventions that address thinking patterns, social skills, self-control, support networks, and criminogenic needs in other areas (Andrews and Bonta, 1994; Lipsey and Wilson, 1998; Lösel, 1995). Integrated preventive concepts such as

Communities that Care seem to be promising (e.g., Catalano *et al.*, 1998; Hawkins *et al.*, 1992). However, many prevention studies still contain problems with respect to control groups, effect size, measurement issues, units of analysis, programme integrity, generalisability across populations and contexts, alongside other threats to internal and external validity. Surprisingly, there is not much overlap between correlational-longitudinal research on risk and protective factors and experimental evaluation research on prevention and intervention. More combined designs would be highly welcome (Loeber and Farrington, 1994).

Research on protective factors cannot just contribute to improving prevention programmes. It also may help in decisions on resource allocation. For example, where individual strengths and natural social resources are available, programmes can rely more on providing conditions for self-help than in cases of cumulated adversities without protective mechanisms. As our review has shown, we should not be too optimistic about breaking chain reactions of antisociality in youngsters with extreme risk. However, the bar for defining resilience must not be set too high (Robinson, 2000). Bringing these children to more normal levels of functioning can already be a success. Last but not least, being aware of protective processes and resilience may help practitioners or policymakers to counter the pessimism and resignation associated with a 'nothing-works' ideology.

Acknowledgements Preparation of this chapter was supported by grants from the German Federal Ministry for the Interior and the German Federal Ministry for Family, Women, Seniors, and Juveniles. We are also grateful to Jonathan Harrow for his help in translation and David Farrington for his editorial advice.

REFERENCES

Aber, J. L., Jones, S. M., Brown, J. L., Chaudry, N. and Samples, F. (1998) Resolving conflict creatively: Evaluating the developmental effects of a school-based violence prevention program in neighborhood and classroom context. *Development and Psychopathology*, *10*, 187–213.

Achenbach, T. M. and Edelbrock, C. (1987) *Manual for the Youth Self-Report and Profile*. Burlington, VT: University of Vermont, Department of Psychiatry.

Achenbach, T. M., McConaughy, S. H. and Howell, C. T. (1987) Child/adolescent behavioral and emotional problems: Implications of cross-informant correlations for situational specifity. *Psychological Bulletin*, *101*, 213–32.

Ainsworth, M. D. (1990) Some considerations regarding theory and assessment relevant to attachments beyond infancy. In M. T. Greenberg, D. Cicchetti and E. M. Cummings (eds.), *Attachment in the Preschool Years: Theory, Research and Intervention* (pp. 463–88). University of Chicago Press.

Ainsworth, M. D. S. (1991) Attachments and other affectional bonds across the life cycle. In C. M. Parkes, J. Stevenson-Hinde and P. Marris (eds.), *Attachment Across the Life Cycle* (pp. 33–51). London: Routledge.

Andrews, D. A. and Bonta, J. (1994) *The Psychology of Criminal Conduct*. Cincinnati, OH: Anderson.

Aneshensel, C. S. and Sucoff, C. A. (1996) The neighborhood context of adolescent mental health. *Journal of Health and Social Behavior, 37*, 293–310.

Anthony, E. J. (1974) The syndrome of the psychologically invulnerable child. In E. J. Anthony and C. Koupernik (eds.), *The Child in His Family, vol. 3: Children at Psychiatric Risk* (pp. 529–44). New York: Wiley.

(1987) Risk, vulnerability, and resilience: An overview. In E. J. Anthony and B. J. Cohler (eds.), *The Invulnerable Child* (pp. 3–48). New York: Guilford Press.

Antonovsky, A. (1987) *Unraveling the Mystery of Health: How People Manage Stress and Stay Well*. San Francisco: Jossey-Bass.

Archer, J. (1991) The influence of testosterone on human aggression. *British Journal of Psychology, 82*, 1–28.

Asendorpf, J. B., Banse, R., Wilpers, S. and Neyer, F. J. (1997) Beziehungsspezifische Bindungsskalen für Erwachsene und ihre Validierung durch Netzwerk- und Tagebuchverfahren [Relation-specific attachment scales for adults and their validation by network and diary data]. *Diagnostica, 43*, 289–313.

Attar, B., Guerra, N. and Tolan, P. (1994) Neighborhood disadvantage, stressful life events, and adjustment in urban elementary-school children. *Journal of Clinical Child Psychology, 23*, 391–400.

Baldwin, A. L., Baldwin, C. and Cole, R. E. (1990) Stress-resistant families and stress-resistant children. In J. Rolf, A. Masten, D. Cicchetti, K. Nuechterlein and S. Weintraub (eds.), *Risk and Protective Factors in the Development of Psychopathology* (pp. 257–80). Cambridge University Press.

Bandura, A. (1986) *Social Foundations of Thought and Action*. Englewood Cliffs, NJ: Prentice Hall.

(1997) *Self-efficacy: The Exercise of Control*. New York: Freeman.

Basic Behavioral Science Task Force (1996) Vulnerability and resilience. *American Psychologist, 51*, 22–8.

Bates, J. E. (1989) Concepts and measures of temperament. In G. A. Kohnstamm, J. E. Bates and M. K. Rothbart (eds.), *Temperament in Childhood* (pp. 3–26). New York: Wiley.

Battin, S. R., Hill, K. G., Abbott, R. D., Catalano, R. F. and Hawkins, J. D. (1998) The contribution of gang membership to delinquency beyond delinquent friends. *Criminology, 36*, 367–88.

Baumeister, R. F., Smart, L. and Boden, J. M. (1996) Relation of threatened egotism to violence and aggression: the dark side of high self-esteem. *Psychological Bulletin, 103*, 5–33.

Baumrind, D. (1989) Rearing competent children. In W. Damon (ed.), *Child Development Today and Tomorrow* (pp. 349–78). San Francisco: Jossey-Bass.

Beardslee, W. R. (1989) The role of self-understanding in resilient individuals: The developmental perspective. *American Journal of Orthopsychiatry, 59*, 266–78.

Beelmann, A., Bliesener, T. and Lösel, F. (2000). Dimensions of impulsivity and their relation to antisocial behavior. In A. Czerederecka, T. Jaskiewicz-Obydzinska and J. Wojcikiewicz (eds.), *Forensic Psychology and Law* (pp. 49–57). Krakow: Institute of Forensic Research.

Beelmann, A., Pfingsten, U. and Lösel, F. (1994) Effects of training social competence in children: A meta-analysis of recent evaluation studies. *Journal of Clinical Child Psychology*, *23*, 260–71.

Belsky, J., Fish, M. and Isabella, R. (1991) Continuity and discontinuity in infant negative and positive emotionality: Family and attachment consequences. *Developmental Psychology*, *27*, 421–31.

Belsky, J., Hsieh, K.-H. and Crnic, K. (1998) Mothering, fathering, and infant negativity as antecedents of boys' externalizing problems and inhibition at age 3 years: Differential susceptibility to rearing experience? *Development and Psychopathology*, *10*, 301–19.

Bender, D., Bliesener, T. and Lösel, F. (1996) Deviance or resilience? A longitudinal study of adolescents in residential care. In G. Davies, S. Lloyd-Bostock, M. McMurran and C. Wilson (eds.), *Psychology, Law, and Criminal Justice: International Developments in Research and Practice* (pp. 409–23). Berlin: De Gruyter.

Bender, D. and Lösel, F. (1996) *Effects of intelligence in the development of antisocial behavior: Results from a study of high-risk adolescents*. Paper presented at the XIVth Biennial Meetings of International Society for the Study of Behavioral Development, August 12–16, Québec City, Canada.

(1997) Protective and risk effects of peer relations and social support on antisocial behaviour in adolescents from multi-problem milieus. *Journal of Adolescence*, *20*, 661–78.

(1998a) Protektive Faktoren der psychisch gesunden Entwicklung junger Menschen: Ein Beitrag zur Kontroverse um saluto- versus pathogenetische Ansätze [Protective factors of mental health in young people: A contribution to the controversy on salutogenetic versus pathogenetic approaches]. In J. Margraf, S. Neumer and J. Siegrist (eds.), *Gesundheits- oder Krankheitstheorie? Saluto- versus pathogenetische Ansätze im Gesundheitswesen* (pp. 119–45). Berlin: Springer.

(1998b) *Protective and risk effects of personal resources*. Paper presented at the XVth Biennial Meetings of the International Society for the Study of Behavioral Development, July 1–4, Berne, Switzerland.

Bergman, L. R. and Magnusson, D. (1997) A person-oriented approach in research on developmental psychopathology. *Development and Psychopathology*, *9*, 291–319.

Berman, M. E., Kavoussi, R. J. and Coccaro, E. F. (1997) Neurotransmitter correlates of human aggression. In D. M. Stoff, J. Breiling and J. D. Maser (eds.), *Handbook of Antisocial Behavior* (pp. 305–13). New York: Wiley.

Bettelheim, B. (1943) Individual and mass behavior in extreme situations. *Journal of Abnormal and Social Psychology*, *38*, 417–52.

Biederman, J., Newcorn and Sprich, S. (1991). Comorbidity of attention-deficit hyperactivity disorder with conduct, depressive, anxiety, and other disorders. *American Journal of Psychiatry*, *148*, 564–77.

Bierman, K. L. and Wargo, J. B. (1995) Predicting the longitudinal course associated with aggressive-rejected, aggressive (nonrejected), and rejected (nonaggressive) status. *Development and Psychopathology, 7*, 669–82.

Blackburn, R. (1993) *The Psychology of Criminal Conduct: Theory, Research, and Practice*. Chichester: Wiley.

Block, J. (1971) *Lives Through Time*. Berkeley, CA: Bancroft Books.

(1995) On the relation between IQ, impulsivity, and delinquency: Remarks on the Lynam, Moffitt, and Stouthamer-Loeber (1993) interpretation. *Journal of Abnormal Psychology, 104*, 395–8.

Block, J. H. and Block, J. (1980) The role of ego-control and ego-resiliency in the organization of behavior. In W. A. Collins (ed.), *The Minnesota Symposia on Child Psychology, vol. 13* (pp. 39–101). Hillsdale, NJ: Erlbaum.

Bowlby, J. (1969/1982) *Attachment*. New York: Basic Books.

Boyce, W. T., Frank, E., Jensen, P. S., Kessler, R. C., Nelson, C. A., Steinberg, L. and The MacArthur Foundation Research Network on Psychopathology and Development (1998) Social context in developmental psychopathology: Recommendations for future research from the MacArthur Network on Psychopathology and Development. *Development and Psychopathology, 10*, 143–64.

Brain, P. F. and Susman, E. J. (1997) Hormonal aspects of aggression and violence. In D. M. Stoff, J. Breiling and J. D. Maser (eds.), *Handbook of Antisocial Behavior* (pp. 314–23). New York: Wiley.

Brennan, P. A., Mednick, S. A. and Raine, A. (1997) Biosocial interactions and violence: A focus on perinatal factors. In A. Raine, P. A. Brennan, D. P. Farrington and S. A. Mednick (eds.), *Biosocial Bases of Violence* (pp. 163–74). New York: Plenum Press.

Bronfenbrenner, U. (1979) *The Ecology of Human Development: Experiments by Nature and Design*. Cambridge, MA: Harvard University Press.

Brook, J. S., Whiteman, M. and Cohen, P. (1995) Stage of drug use, aggression, and theft/vandalism. In H. B. Kaplan (ed.), *Drugs, Crime, and Other Deviant Adaptations: Longitudinal Studies* (pp. 83–96). New York: Plenum Press.

Brooks-Gunn, J., Duncan, G. J., Klebanov, K. and Sealand, N. (1993) Do neighborhoods influence child and adolescent development? *American Journal of Sociology, 99*, 353–94.

Brooks-Gunn, J., Graber, J. and Paikoff, R. (1994) Studying links between hormones and negative affect: Models and measures. *Journal of Research on Adolescence, 4*, 469–86.

Brown, G. W. and Harris, T. O. (1978) *Social Origins of Depression*. New York: The Free Press.

Bursik, R. J., Jr. and Grasmick, H. G. (1992) Longitudinal neighborhood profiles in delinquency: The decomposition of change. *Journal of Quantitative Criminology, 8*, 247–63.

Bushman, B. and Baumeister, R. F. (1998) Threatened egotism, narcissism, self-esteem, and direct and displaced aggression: Does self-love or self-hate lead to violence? *Journal of Personality and Social Psychology, 75*, 219–29.

Buss, A. H. and Plomin, R. (1975) *A Temperament Theory of Personality Development*. New York: Wiley.

Cairns, R. B. and Cairns, B. D. (1991) Social cognition and social networks: A developmental perspective. In D. J. Pepler and K. H. Rubin (eds.), *The Development and Treatment of Childhood Aggression* (pp. 249–76). Hillsdale, NJ: Erlbaum.

Cairns, R. B., Cairns, B. D., Neckerman, H. J., Ferguson, L. L. and Gariepy, J. L. (1988) Social networks and aggressive behavior: Peer support or peer rejection? *Developmental Psychology, 24*, 815–23.

Caron, C. and Rutter, M. (1991) Comorbidity in child psychopathology: concepts, issues and research strategies. *Journal of Child Psychology and Psychiatry, 32*, 1063–80.

Caspi, A. and Herbener, E. S. (1990) Continuity and change: Assortative marriage and the consistency of personality in adulthood. *Journal of Personality and Social Psychology, 58*, 250–8.

Caspi, A., Lynam, D., Moffitt, T. E. and Silva, P. A. (1993) Unraveling girls' delinquency: Biological, dispositional, and contextual contributions to adolescent misbehavior. *Developmental Psychology, 29*, 19–30.

Caspi, A. and Moffitt, T. E. (1995) The continuity of maladaptive behavior: From description to understanding in the study of antisocial behavior. In D. Cicchetti and D. J. Cohen (eds.), *Developmental Psychopathology, vol. 2, Risk, Disorder, and Adaptation* (pp. 472–511). New York: Wiley.

Caspi, A. and Silva, P. A. (1995) Temperamental qualities at age 3 predict personality traits in young adulthood: Longitudinal evidence from a birth cohort. *Child Development, 66*, 486–98.

Cassidy, J., Scolton, K. L., Kirsh, S. J. and Parke, R. D. (1996) Attachment and representations of peer relationships. *Developmental Psychology, 32*, 892–904.

Catalano, R. F., Arthur, M. W., Hawkins, J. D., Berglund, L. and Olson, J. J. (1998) Comprehensive community- and school-based interventions to prevent antisocial behavior. In R. Loeber and D. P. Farrington (eds.), *Serious and Violent Juvenile Offenders: Risk Factors and Successful Interventions* (pp. 248–83). Thousand Oaks: Sage.

Catalano, R. F. and Hawkins, J. D. (1996) The social developmental model: A theory of antisocial behavior. In J. D. Hawkins (ed.), *Delinquency and Crime: Current Theories* (pp. 149–97). New York: Cambridge University Press.

Cauce, A. M., Felner, R. D. and Primavera, J. (1982) Social support in high-risk adolescents: Structural components and adaptive impact. *American Journal of Community Psychology, 10*, 417–28.

Chess, S. and Thomas, A. (1985) *Origins and Evolution of Behavior Disorders*. New York: Bruner/Mazel.

Ciba Foundation (ed.) (1996) *Genetics of Criminal and Antisocial Behavior*. Chichester: Wiley.

Cicchetti, D. and Aber, J. L. (1998) Editorial: Contextualism and developmental psychopathology. *Development and Psychopathology, 10*, 137–41.

Cicchetti, D. and Garmezy, N. (1993) Editorial. Prospects and promises in the study of resilience. *Development and Psychopathology, 5*, 497–502.

Cicchetti, D. and Rogosch, F. A. (1996) Equifinality and multifinality in developmental psychopathology. *Development and Psychopathology, 8*, 597–600.

(1977) The role of self-organisation in the promotion of resilience in maltreated children. *Development and Psychopathology, 9*, 797–815.

Cicchetti, D., Rogosch, F. A., Lynch, M. and Holt, K. D. (1993) Resilience in maltreated children: Processes leading to adaptive outcome. *Development and Psychopathology*, 5, 629–47.

Cloninger, C. R., Svrakic, D. M. and Przybeck, T. R. (1993) A psychobiological model of temperament and character. *Archives of General Psychiatry*, *50*, 975–90.

Cloninger, C. R., Svrakic, D. M. and Svrakic, N. M. (1997) A multidimensional psychobiological model of violence. In A. Raine, P. A. Brennan, D. P. Farrington and S. A. Mednick (eds.), *Biosocial Bases of Violence* (pp. 39–54). New York: Plenum Press.

Cohen, J. M. (1977) Sources of peer group homogeneity. *Sociology of Education*, *50*, 227–41.

Coie, J. D. and Dodge, K. A. (1998) Aggression and antisocial behavior. In W. Damon and N. Eisenberg (eds.), *Handbook of Child Psychology, 5th ed., vol. 3: Social, Emotional, and Personality Development* (pp. 779–862). New York: Wiley.

Coie, J., Terry, R., Lenox, K., Lochman, J. and Hyman, C. (1995) Childhood peer rejection and aggression as predictors of stable patterns of adolescent disorder. *Development and Psychopathology*, *7*, 697–713.

Comer, J. (1988) *Maggies's American Dream*. New York: New American Library.

Compas, B. E. (1987) Coping with stress during childhood and adolescence. *Psychological Bulletin*, *101*, 393–403.

Compas, B. E. and Phares, V. (1991) Stress during childhood and adolescence: Sources of risk and vulnerability. In E. M. Cummings, A. L. Greene and K. H. Karraker (eds.), *Life-span Developmental Psychology* (pp. 111–30). Hillsdale, NJ: Erlbaum.

Conrad, M. and Hammen, C. (1993) Protective and resource factors in high- and low-risk children: A comparison of children with unipolar, bipolar, medically ill, and normal mothers. *Development and Psychopathology*, *5*, 593–607.

Costello, E. J. and Angold, A. (1995) Developmental epidemiology. In D. Cicchetti and D. J. Cohen (eds.), *Developmental Psychopathology*, vol. 1 (pp. 23–56). New York: Wiley.

Cowen E. L., Wyman, P. A., Work, W. C., Kim, J. Y., Fagen, D. B. and Magnus, K. B. (1997) Follow-up study of young stress-affected and stress-resilient urban children. *Development and Psychopathology*, *9*, 565–677.

Cowen, E. L., Wyman, P. A., Work, W. C. and Parker, G. R. (1990) The Rochester Child Resilience Project: Overview and summary of first year findings. *Development and Psychopathology*, *2*, 193–212.

Coyne, J. C. and Downey, G. (1991) Social factors and psychopathology: Stress, social support, and coping processes. *Annual Review of Psychology*, *16*, 401–25.

Creighton, S. (1985) Epidemiological study of abused children and their families in the United Kingdom between 1977 and 1982. *Child Abuse and Neglect*, *9*, 441–8.

Crick, N. R. and Dodge, K. A. (1994) A review and reformulation of social information–processing mechanisms in children's social adjustment. *Psychological Bulletin*, *115*, 74–101.

Crick, N. R. and Grotpeter, J. K. (1995) Relational aggression, gender, and social psychological adjustment. *Child Development*, *66*, 710–22.

Crittenden, P. M. (1992) The quality of attachment in the preschool years. *Development and Psychopathology*, *4*, 209–41.

Cummings, E. M. and Davies, P. (1996) Emotional security as a regulatory process in normal development and the development of psychopathology. *Development and Psychopathology*, *8*, 123–39.

Cutrona, C. E. (1989) Ratings of social support by adolescents and adult informants: Degree of correspondence and prediction of depressive symptoms. *Journal of Personality and Social Psychology*, *57*, 723–30.

Dabbs, J. M. and Hopper, C. H. (1990) Cortisol, arousal, and personality in two groups of normal men. *Personality and Individual Differences*, *11*, 931–5.

Dabbs, J. M., Jurkovic, G. J. and Frady, R. L. (1991) Salivary testosterone and cortisol among late adolescent offenders. *Journal of Abnormal Child Psychology*, *19*, 469–78.

Denno, D. W. (1990) *Biology and Violence: From Birth to Adulthood*. Cambridge University Press.

Dishion, T. J., Capaldi, D., Spracklen, K. M. and Li, F. (1995) Peer ecology of male adolescent drug use. *Development and Psychopathology*, *7*, 803–24.

Dishion, T. J., Patterson, G. R. and Griesler, P. C. (1994) Peer adaptations in the development of antisocial behavior. A confluence model. In L. R. Huesmann (ed.), *Aggressive Behavior: Current Perspectives* (pp. 61–95). New York: Plenum Press.

Dodge, K. A., Pettit, G. S., McClaskey, C. L. and Brown, M. (1986) Social competence in children. *Monographs of the Society for Research in Child Development*, *51 (2, No. 213)*.

Dodge, K. A., Price, J. M., Bachorowski, J. A. and Newman, J. P. (1990) Hostile attributional biases in severely aggressive adolescents. *Journal of Abnormal Psychology*, *99*, 385–92.

Dolan, B. and Coid, J. (1993) *Psychopathic and Antisocial Personality Disorders*. London: Gaskell.

Egeland, B., Carlson, E. and Sroufe, L. A. (1993) Resilience as process. *Development and Psychopathology*, *5*, 517–28.

Egeland, B., Jacobvitz, D. and Sroufe, L. A. (1988) Breaking the cycle of abuse. *Child Development*, *59*, 1080–8.

Elder, G. H. (1986) Military times and turning points in men's lives. *Developmental Psychology*, *22*, 233–45.

Elder, G. H., Jr., Caspi, A. and Nguyen, T. van (1986) Resourceful and vulnerable children: Family influence in hard times. In R. K. Silbereisen, K. Eyferth and G. Rudinger (eds.), *Development as Action in Context* (pp. 167–86). Berlin: Springer.

Elder, G. H., Liker, K. and Cross, C. E. (1984) Parent-child behavior in the Great Depression: Life course and intergenerational influences. In T. B. Baltes and O. G. Brim, Jr. (eds.), *Lifespan Development and Behavior* (pp. 109–58). New York: Academic Press.

Elliott, D. S. (1994) Serious violent offenders: Onset, developmental course, and termination – The American Society of Criminology 1993 presidential address. *Criminology*, *32*, 1–21.

Elliott, D. S., Huizinga, D. and Ageton, S. S. (1985) *Explaining Delinquency and Drug Use*. Beverly Hills, CA: Sage.

Elliott, D. S., Huizinga, D. and Menard, S. (1989). *Multiple Problem Youth*. New York: Springer.

Emery, R. E. and Laumann-Billings, L. (1998) An overview of the nature, causes, and consequences of abusive family relationships. *American Psychologist, 53*, 121–35.

Engfer, A. (1991) Prospective identification of violent mother-child relationships. Child outcomes at 6.3 years. In G. Kaiser, H. Kury and H.-J. Albrecht (eds.), *Victims and Criminal Justice* (pp. 415–58). Freiburg i.Br.: Max-Planck-Institut für ausländisches und internationales Strafrecht.

Ensminger, M. E., Kellam, S. G. and Rubin, B. R. (1983) School and family origins of delinquency: Comparison by sex. In K. T. Van Dusen and S. A. Mednick (eds.), *Prospective Studies of Crime and Delinquency* (pp. 73–97). Boston: Kluwer-Nijhoff.

Eysenck, H. J. (1977) *Crime and Personality* (3rd ed.). St Albans: Paladin.

Fagot, B. I. and Pears, K. C. (1996) Changes in attachment during the third year: Consequences and predictions. *Development and Psychopathology, 8*, 325–44.

Farber, E. A. and Egeland, B. (1987) Invulnerability among abused and neglected children. In E. J. Anthony and B. J. Cohler (eds.), *The Invulnerable Child* (pp. 253–88). New York: Guilford Press.

Farrington, D. P. (1987) Early precursors of frequent offending. In J. Q. Wilson and G. C. Loury (eds.), *From Children to Citizens*, vol. 3 (pp. 27–50). New York: Springer.

(1989) Later adult life outcomes of offenders and nonoffenders. In M. Brambring, F. Lösel and H. Skowronek (eds.), *Children at Risk: Assessment, Longitudinal Research, and Intervention* (pp. 220–44). Berlin: de Gruyter.

(1990) Age, period, cohort, and offending. In D. M. Gottfredson and R. V. Clarke (eds.), *Policy and Theory in Criminal Justice: Contributions in Honour of Leslie T. Wilkins* (pp. 51–75). Aldershot: Avebury.

(1992) Psychological contributions to the explanation, prevention, and treatment of offending. In F. Lösel, D. Bender and T. Bliesener (eds.), *Psychology and Law: International Perspectives* (pp. 35–51). Berlin, New York: De Gruyter.

(1994) *Protective factors in the development of juvenile delinquency and adult crime*. Invited lecture at the 6th Scientific Meeting of the Society for Research in Child and Adolescent Psychopathology. London, June 1994.

(1997a) Early prediction of violent and nonviolent youthful offending. *European Journal on Criminal Policy and Research, 5*, 51–66.

(1997b) The relationship between low resting heart rate and violence. In A. Raine, P. A. Brennan, D. P. Farrington and S. A. Mednick (eds.), *Biosocial Bases of Violence* (pp. 89–105). New York: Plenum Press.

(1998) Predictors, causes, and correlates of youth violence. In M. Tonry and M. H. Moore (eds.), *Youth Violence* (pp. 421–75). University of Chicago Press.

Farrington, D. P., Gallagher, B., Morley, L., St Ledger, R. J. and West, D. J. (1988) Are there any successful men from criminogenic backgrounds? *Psychiatry, 51*, 116–30.

Farrington, D. P. and Loeber, R. (2001) Summary of key conclusions. In R. Loeber and D. P. Farrington (eds.), *Child Delinquents* (pp. 359–84). Thousand Oaks, CA: Sage.

Farrington, D. P., Loeber, R., Elliott, D. S., Hawkins, J. D., Kandel, D. B., Klein, M. W., McCord, J., Rowe, D. C. and Tremblay, R. E. (1990) Advancing knowledge about the onset of delinquency and crime. In B. B. Lahey and A. E. Kazdin (eds.), *Advances in Clinical and Child Psychology*, vol. 13 (pp. 283–342). New York: Plenum.

Farrington, D. P., Sampson, R. J. and Wikström, P.-O. (eds.)(1993) *Integrating Individual and Ecological Aspects of Crime*. Stockholm: Liber.

Farrington, D. P. and Welsh, B. C. (1999) Delinquency prevention using family-based interventions. *Children and Society*, *13*, 287–303.

Felsman, K. H. and Vaillant, G. E. (1987) Resilient children as adults: A 40-year study. In E. J. Anthony and B. J. Cohler (eds.), *The Invulnerable Child* (pp. 289–314). New York: Guilford Press.

Fergusson, D. M., Woodward, L. J. and Horwood, J. (1998) Maternal smoking during pregnancy and psychiatric adjustment in late adolescence. *Archives of General Psychiatry*, *55*, 721–7.

Fisher, L., Kokes, R. F., Cole, R. E., Perkins, P. M. and Wynne, L. C. (1987) Competent children at risk: A study of well-functioning offspring of disturbed parents. In E. J. Anthony and B. J. Cohler (eds.), *The Invulnerable Child* (pp. 211–28). New York: Guilford Press.

Freedman, M. (1993) *The Kindness of Strangers*. San Francisco: Jossey-Bass.

Garbarino, J. (1990) Youth in dangerous environments: Coping with the consequences. In K. Hurrelmann and F. Lösel (eds.), *Health Hazards in Adolescence* (pp. 193–218). Berlin: De Gruyter.

Garbarino, J. and Kostelny, K. (1992) Child maltreatment as a community problem. *Child Abuse and Neglect*, *16*, 455–64.

Garmezy, N. (1985) Stress resistant children: The search for protective factors. In J.E. Stevenson (ed.), *Recent Research in Developmental Psychopathology. Journal of Child Psychology and Psychiatry*, Book Supplement (vol. 4, pp. 213–33). Oxford: Pergamon Press.

(1987) Stress, competence, and development: Continuities in the study of schizophrenic adults, children vulnerable to psychopathology, and the search for stress-resistant children. *American Journal of Orthopsychiatry*, *57*, 159–74.

(1991) Resiliency and vulnerability to adverse developmental outcomes associated with poverty. *American Behavioral Scientist*, *34*, 416–30.

Garmezy, N., Masten, A. S. and Tellegen, A. (1984) Studies of stress-resistant children: A building block for developmental psychopathology. *Child Development*, *55*, 97–111.

Garmezy, N. and Nuechterlein, K. (1972) Invulnerable children: The fact and fiction of competence and disadvantage. *American Journal of Orthopsychiatry*, *42*, 328–9.

Ge, X., Cadoret, R. J., Conger, R. D., Neiderhiser, J. M., Yates, W., Troughton, E. and Stewart, M. A. (1996) The developmental interface between nature and nurture: A mutual influence model of child antisocial behavior and parent behaviors. *Developmental Psychology*, *32*, 574–89.

Gest, S. D., Neeman, J., Hubbard, J. J., Masten, A. S. and Tellegen, A. (1993) Parenting quality, adversity, and conduct problems in adolescence: Testing process-oriented models of resilience. *Development and Psychopathology, 5*, 663–82.

Glueck, S. and Glueck, E. (1950) *Unraveling Juvenile Delinquency*. Cambridge, MA: Harvard University Press.

Gordon, E. W. and Wang, M. C. (1994) Epilogue: Educational resilience: Challenges and prospects. In M. C. Wang and E. W. Gordon (eds.), *Educational Resilience in Inner-city America: Challenges and Prospects* (pp. 191–4). Hillsdale, NJ: Erlbaum.

Gorman-Smith, D. and Tolan, P. (1998) The role of exposure to community violence and developmental problems among inner-city youth. *Development and Psychopathology, 10*, 101–16.

Gottfredson, D. C. (2001) *Schools and Delinquency*. Cambridge University Press.

Gottfredson, M. and Hirschi, T. M. (1990) *A General Theory of Crime*. Stanford University Press.

Gottman, J. M. and Katz, L. F. (1989) Effects of marital discord on young children's peer interaction and health. *Developmental Psychology, 25*, 373–81.

Gray, J. A. (1987) *The Psychology of Fear and Stress*. New York: Cambridge University Press.

Greenberg, M. T., Speltz, M. L. and DeKlyen, M. (1993) The role of attachment in the early development of disruptive behavior problems. *Development and Psychopathology, 5*, 191–213.

Grossmann, K. E. and Grossmann, K. (1991) Attachment quality as an organizer of emotional and behavioral responses in a longitudinal perspective. In C. M. Parkes, J. Stevenson-Hinde and P. Marris (eds.), *Attachment Across the Life Cycle* (pp. 93–114). London: Routledge.

Guerra, N. and Slaby, R. (1990) Cognitive mediators of aggression in adolescent offenders: II. Intervention. *Developmental Psychology, 26*, 269–77.

Haapasalo, J. and Tremblay, R. E. (1994) Physically aggressive boys from ages 6 to 12: Family background, parenting behavior, and prediction of delinquency. *Journal of Consulting and Clinical Psychology, 62*, 1044–52.

Hämäläinen, M. and Pulkkinen, L. (1996) Problem behavior as a precursor of male criminality. *Development and Psychopathology, 8*, 443–55.

Hall, G. C. N. (1995) Sexual offender recidivism revisited: A meta-analysis of recent treatment studies. *Journal of Consulting and Clinical Psychology, 63*, 802–9.

Hare, R. D. (1995) Psychopathy: A clinical construct whose time has come. *Criminal Justice and Behavior, 23*, 25–54.

Hawkins, J. D., Catalano, R. F. and Miller, J. Y. (1992) Risk and protective factors for alcohol and other drug problems in adolescence and early adulthood: Implications for substance abuse prevention. *Psychological Bulletin, 112*, 64–105.

Hawkins, J. D., Herrenkohl, T., Farrington, D. P., Brewer, D., Catalano, R. F. and Harachi, T. W. (1998) A review of predictors of youth violence. In R. Loeber and D. P. Farrington (eds.), *Serious and Violent Juvenile Offenders* (pp. 106–46). Thousand Oaks, CA: Sage.

Henry, B., Caspi, A., Moffitt, T. E. and Silva, P. A. (1996) Temperamental and familial predictors of violent and nonviolent criminal convictions: Age 3 to age 18. *Developmental Psychology, 32*, 614–23.

Hetherington, E. M. (1989) Coping with family transitions: Winners, losers, and survivors. *Child Development, 60*, 1–14.

Hinde, R. A. (1992) Developmental psychology in the context of other behavioral sciences. *Developmental Psychology, 28*, 1018–29.

Hinshaw, S. P., Lahey, B. B. and Hart, E. L. (1993) Issues of taxonomy and comorbidity in the development of conduct disorder. *Development and Psychopathology, 5*, 31–49.

Hirschi, T. (1969) *Causes of Delinquency*. Berkeley: University of California Press.

Hirschi, T. and Hindelang, M. J. (1977) Intelligence and delinquency: A revisionist review. *American Sociological Review, 42*, 571–87.

Hodgins, S. Coté, G. and Toupin, J. (1998) Major mental disorder and crime: An etiological hypothesis. In D. J. Cooke, A. E. Forth and R. D. Hare (eds.), *Psychopathy: Theory, Research, and Implications for Society* (pp. 231–56). Dordrecht, NL: Kluwer.

Hoge, R. D., Andrews, D. A. and Leschied, A. W. (1996) An investigation of risk and protective factors in a sample of youthful offenders. *Journal of Child Psychology and Psychiatry, 37*, 419–24.

Holler-Nowitzki, B. (1994) *Psychosomatische Beschwerden im Jugendalter [Psychosomatic disorders in adolescence]*. Weinheim: Juventa.

Hoza, B., Molina, B. S. G., Bukowski, W. M. and Sippola, L. K. (1995) Peer variables as predictors of later childhood adjustment. *Development and Psychopathology, 7*, 787–802.

Huesmann, L. R. (1997) Observational learning of violent behavior: Social and biosocial processes. In A. Raine, P. A. Brennan, D. P. Farrington and S. A. Mednick (eds.), *Biosocial Bases of Violence* (pp. 69–88). New York: Plenum Press.

Huesmann, L. R., Eron, L. D. and Yarmel, P. W. (1987) Intellectual functioning and aggression. *Journal of Personality and Social Psychology, 52*, 232–40.

Hughes, J. N., Cavell, T. A. and Grossman, P. B. (1997) A positive view of self: Risk or protection for aggressive children? *Development and Psychopathology, 9*, 75–94.

Hunter, R. and Kilstrom, N. (1979) Breaking the cycle in abusive families. *American Journal of Psychiatry, 136*, 1320–2.

James, O. (1995) *Juvenile Violence in a Winner-loser-culture: Socio-economic and Familial Origins of the Rise of Violence Against the Person*. London: Free Association Books.

Jenkins, J. M. and Smith, M. A. (1990) Factors protecting children living in disharmonious homes: Maternal reports. *Journal of the American Academy of Child and Adolescent Psychiatry, 29*, 60–9.

Jessor, R., Donovan, J. E. and Costa, F. M. (1991) *Beyond Adolescence: Problem Behavior and Young Adult Development*. Cambridge University Press.

Johnstone, J. W. C. (1983) Recruitment to a youth gang. *Youth and Society, 14*, 281–300.

Junger, M., Terlouw, G. J. and van der Heijden, P. G. M. (1995) Crime, accidents, and social control. *Criminal Behaviour and Mental Health, 5*, 386–410.

Kagan, J. (1994) *Galen's Prophecy*. New York: Basic Books.

Kagan, J., Reznick, J. S. and Snidman, N. (1988) Biological bases of childhood shyness. *Science, 240*, 167–71.

Kandel, D. B. (1996) The parental and peer contexts of adolescent deviance: An algebra of interpersonal influences. *Journal of Drug Issues, 26*, 289–315.

Kandel, E., Mednick, S. A., Kirkegaard-Sorensen, L., Hutchings, B., Knop, J., Rosenberg, R. and Schulsinger, F. (1988) IQ as a protective factor for subjects at high risk for antisocial behavior. *Journal of Consulting and Clinical Psychology, 56*, 224–6.

Kaplan, H. B. (1999) Toward an understanding of resilience: A critical review of definitions and models. In M. D. Glantz and J. R. Johnson (eds.), *Resilience and Development: Positive Life Adaptations* (pp. 17–83). New York: Plenum.

Kaufman, J., Cook, A., Arny, L., Jones, B. and Pittinsky, T. (1994) Problems defining resiliency: Illustrations from the study of maltreated children. *Development and Psychopathology, 6*, 215–29.

Keenan, K., Loeber, R., Zhang, Q., Stouthamer-Loeber. M. and Van Kammen, W. B. (1995) The influence of deviant peers on the development of boys' disruptive and delinquent behavior: A temporal analysis. *Development and Psychopathology, 7*, 715–26.

Kellam, S. G., Ling, X., Merisca, R., Brown, C. H. and Ialongo, N. (1998) The effect of the level of aggression in the first grade classroom on the course and malleability of aggressive behavior into middle school. *Development and Psychopathology, 10*, 165–85.

Kemper, T. D. (1990) *Social Structure and Testosterone: Explorations of the Socio-bio-social Chain*. New Brunswick: Rutgers University Press.

Kerner, H.-J., Weitekamp, E. G. M., Stelly, W. and Thomas, J. (1997) Patterns of criminality and alcohol abuse: results of the Tuebingen Criminal Behaviour Development Study. *Criminal Behaviour and Mental Health, 7*, 401–20.

Kindlon, D. J., Tremblay, R. E., Mezzacappa, E., Earls, F., Laurent, D. and Schaal, B. (1995) Longitudinal patterns of heart rate and fighting behavior in 9- through 12-year-old boys. *Journal of the American Academy of Child and Adolescent Psychiatry, 34*, 371–7.

Klinteberg, B. af (1996) The psychopathic personality in a longitudinal perspective. *European Journal of Adolescent Psychiatry, 5*, 57–63.

Kolvin, I., Charles, G., Nicholson, R., Fleeting, M. and Fundudis, T. (1990) Factors in prevention in inner-city deprivation. In D. Goldberg and D. Tantum (eds.), *Public Health Impact of Mental Disorder* (pp. 115–23). Stuttgart: Hogrefe and Huber.

Kolvin, I., Miller, F. J. W., Fleeting, M. and Kolvin, P. A. (1988) Risk/protective factors for offending with particular reference to deprivation. In M. Rutter (ed.), *Studies of Psychosocial Risk: The Power of Longitudinal Data* (pp. 77–95). Cambridge University Press.

Kolvin, I., Miller, F. J. W., Scott, D. McI., Gatzanis, S. R. M. and Fleeting, M. (1990). *Continuities of Deprivation? The Newcastle 1000 Family Study*. Aldershot: Avebury.

Köferl, P. (1988) *Invulnerabilität und Stressresistenz: Theoretische und empirische Befunde zur effektiven Bewältigung von psychosozialen Stressoren [Invulnerability and stress-resistance]. Doctoral Dissertation.* Universität Bielefeld, Fakultät für Psychologie und Sportwissenschaft.

Korbin, J. E., Coulton, C. J., Chard, S., Platt-Houston, C. and Su, M. (1998) Impoverishment and child maltreatment in African American and European American Neighborhoods. *Development and Psychopathology, 10*, 215–33.

Kraemer, G. W. (1997) Social attachment, brain function, aggression, and violence. In A. Raine, P. A. Brennan, D. P. Farrington and S. A. Mednick (eds.), *Biosocial Bases of Violence* (pp. 207–29). New York: Plenum Press.

Kupersmidt, J. B., Griesler, P. C., DeRosier, M. E., Patterson, C. J. and Davis, P. W. (1995) Childhood aggression and peer relations in the context of familiy and neighborhood factors. *Child Development, 66*, 360–75.

LeBlanc, M. (1998) Screening of serious and violent juvenile offenders: Identification, classification, and prediction. In R. Loeber and D. P. Farrington (eds.), *Serious and Violent Juvenile Offenders: Risk Factors and Successful Interventions* (pp. 167–93). Thousand Oaks, CA: Sage.

LeBlanc, M. and Loeber, R. (1993) Precursors, Causes and the development of offending. In D. F. Hale and A. Angold (eds.), *Precursors, Causes and Psychopathology* (pp. 233–64). New York: Wiley.

Lipsey, M. W. and Derzon, J. H. (1998) Predictors of violent or serious delinquency in adolescence and early adulthood: A synthesis of longitudinal research. In R. Loeber and D. P. Farrington (eds.), *Serious and Violent Juvenile Offenders* (pp. 86–105). Thousand Oaks, CA: Sage.

Lipsey, M. W. and Wilson, D. B. (1998) Effective intervention for serious juvenile offenders: A synthesis of research. In R. Loeber and D. P. Farrington (eds.), *Serious and Violent Juvenile Offenders* (pp. 313–45). Thousand Oaks, CA: Sage.

Lochman, J. E. and Dodge, K. A. (1998) Distorted perceptions in dyadic interactions of aggressive and nonaggressive boys: Effects of prior expectations, context, and boy's age. *Development and Psychopathology, 10*, 495–512.

Loeber, R. (1990) Development and risk factors of juvenile antisocial behavior and delinquency. *Clinical Psychology Review, 10*, 1–41.

Loeber, R., Brinthaupt, V. P. and Green, S. M. (1990) Attention deficits, impulsivity, and hyperactivity with or without conduct problems: Relationship to delinquency and unique contextual factors. In R. J. McMahon and R. DeV. Peters (eds.), *Behavior Disorders of Adolescence: Research, Intervention, and Policy in Clinical and School Settings* (pp. 39–61). New York: Plenum.

Loeber, R. and Dishion, T. J. (1983) Early predictors of male delinquency: A review. *Psychological Bulletin, 94*, 68–99.

Loeber, R. and Farrington, D. P. (1994) Problems and solutions in longitudinal and experimental treatment studies of child psychopathology and delinquency. *Journal of Consulting and Clinical Psychology, 62*, 887–900.

Loeber, R. and Farrington, D. (eds.) (1998) *Serious and Violent Juvenile Offenders: Risk Factors and Successful Interventions*. Thousand Oaks, CA: Sage.

Loeber, R., Farrington, D. P., Stouthamer-Loeber, M. and Van Kammen, W. B. (1998) *Antisocial Behavior and Mental Health Problems*. Mahwah, NJ: Lawrence Erlbaum.

Loeber, R. and Hay, D. (1994) Developmental approaches to aggression and conduct problems. In M. Rutter and D. F. Hay (eds.), *Development Through Life: A Handbook for Clinicians* (pp. 488–516). Oxford: Blackwell.

(1997) Key issues in the development of aggression and violence from childhood to early adulthood. *Annual Review of Psychology*, *48*, 371–40.

Loeber, R., Keenan, K. and Zhang, Q. (1997) Boys' experimentation and persistance in developmental pathways toward serious delinquency. *Journal of Child and Family Studies*, *6*, 321–57.

Loeber, R., Russo, M. F., Stouthamer-Loeber, M. and Lahey, B. B. (1994) Internalizing problems and their relation to the development of disruptive behaviors in adolescence. *Journal of Research on Adolescence*, *4*, 615–37.

Loeber, R. and Stouthamer-Loeber, M. (1986) Family factors as correlates and predictors of juvenile conduct problems and delinquency. In M. Tonry and N. Morris (eds.), *Crime and Justice: An Annual Review of Research* (vol. 7, pp. 219–339). University of Chicago Press.

(1998) Development of juvenile aggression and violence: Some common misconceptions and controversies. *American Psychologist*, *53*, 242–59.

Loeber, R., Wung, P., Keenan, K., Giroux, B., Stouthamer-Loeber, M., Kammen, W. B. van and Maughan, B. (1993) Developmental pathways in disruptive child behavior. *Development and Psychopathology*, *5*, 103–33.

Lösel, F. (1975) *Handlungskontrolle und Jugenddelinquenz [Action control and juvenile delinquency]*. Stuttgart: Enke.

(1991) Meta-analysis and social prevention: Evaluation and a study of the family hypothesis in developmental psychopathology. In G. Albrecht and H.-U. Otto (eds.), *Social Prevention and the Social Sciences* (pp. 305–32). Berlin: De Gruyter.

(1994) Protective effects of social resources in adolescents at high risk for antisocial behavior. In H.-J. Kerner and E. G. M. Weitekamp (eds.), *Cross-national Longitudinal Research on Human Development and Criminal Behavior* (pp. 283–301). Dordrecht, Netherlands: Kluwer.

(1995) The efficacy of correctional treatment: A review and synthesis of meta-evaluations. In J. McGuire (ed.), *What Works: Reducing Reoffending* (pp. 79–111). Chichester: Wiley.

(1996) Working with young offenders: The impact of meta-analysis. In C. R. Hollin and K. Howells (eds.), *Clinical Approaches to Working With Young Offenders* (pp. 57–82). Chichester: Wiley.

(1998) Treatment and management of psychopaths. In D. J. Cooke, A. E. Forth and R. B. Hare (eds.), *Psychopathy: Theory, Research, and Implications for Society* (pp. 303–54). Dordrecht, Netherlands: Kluwer.

(2002) Risk/need assessment and prevention of antisocial development in young people. In R. R. Corrado, R. Roesch, S. D. Hart and J. K. Gierowski (eds.), *Multi-Problem Violent Youth* (pp. 35–57). Amsterdam: IOS Press/NATO Science Series.

Lösel, F. and Bender, D. (1997) Heart rate and psychosocial correlates of antisocial behavior in high-risk adolescents. In A. Raine, D. P. Farrington,

P. Brennan and S. A. Mednick (eds.), *Biosocial Bases of Violence* (pp. 321–4). New York: Plenum Press.

Lösel, F., Bender, D. and Bliesener, T. (1998) *Biosocial risk and protective factors for antisocial behavior in juveniles: Heart rate and family characteristics*. Paper presented at the XVth Biennial Meetings of the International Society for the Study of Behavioral Development, July 1–4, 1998, Berne, Switzerland.

Lösel, F. and Bliesener, T. (1990) Resilience in adolescence: A study on the generalizability of protective factors. In K. Hurrelmann and F. Lösel (eds.), *Health Hazards in Adolescence* (pp. 299–320). Berlin: De Gruyter.

(1994) Some high-risk adolescents do not develop conduct problems: A study of protective factors. *International Journal of Behavioral Development*, *17*, 753–77.

(1998) Zum Einfluss des Familienklimas und der Gleichaltrigengruppe auf den Zusammenhang zwischen Substanzengebrauch and antisozialem Verhalten von Jugendlichen [Co-occurence and single occurence of substance abuse and antisocial behavior in adolescents: Influences of family climate and peer group.] *Kindheit und Entwicklung*, *7*, 208–20.

(1999a) Germany. In P. K. Smith, Y. Morita, J. Junger-Tas, D. Olweus, R. Catalano and P. Slee (eds.), *The Nature of School Bullying: A Cross-national Perspective* (pp. 224–49). London: Routledge.

(1999b) Aggressive conflict behavior and social information processing in juveniles. In I. Sagel-Grande and M. V. Polak (eds.), *Models of Conflict Resolution* (pp. 61–78). Antwerp: Maklu.

(in press) *Aggression und Delinquenz unter Jugendlichen* [*Aggression and Delinquency in Adolescence*]. Neuwied: Luchterhand.

Lösel, F., Bliesener, T. and Bender, D. (2001) Social information processing, experiences of aggression in social contexts, and aggressive behavior in adolescents. Ms. submitted for publication.

Lösel, F., Bliesener, T. and Köferl, P. (1989) On the concept of 'invulnerability': Evaluation and first results of the Bielefeld project. In M. Brambring, F. Lösel and H. Skowronek (eds.), *Children at Risk: Assessment, Longitudinal Research, and Intervention* (pp. 186–219). Berlin, New York: De Gruyter.

Lösel, F., Kolip, P. and Bender, D. (1992) Stress-Resistenz im Multiproblem-Milieu: Sind seelisch widerstandsfähige Jugendliche 'Superkids' [Stress-resistance in a multiproblem milieu: Are resilient juveniles 'superkids'?]. *Zeitschrift für Klinische Psychologie*, *21*, 48–63.

Luthar, S. S. (1991) Vulnerability and resilience: A study of high-risk adolescents. *Child Development*, *62*, 600–16.

(1993) Annotation: methodological and conceptual issues in research on childhood resilience. *Journal of Child Psychology and Psychiatry*, *34*, 441–53.

Luthar, S. S., Cicchetti, D. and Becker, B. (2000a) The construct of resilience: A critical evaluation and guidelines for future work. *Child Development*, *71*, 543–62.

(2000b) Research on resilience: Response to commentaries. *Child Development*, *71*, 573–5.

Luthar, S. S. and Zigler, E. (1991) Vulnerability and competence: A review of research on resilience in childhood. *American Journal of Orthopsychiatry*, *6*, 6–22.

Luthar, S., Zigler, E. and Goldstein, D. (1992) Methodological and conceptual issues in research on childhood resilience. *Journal of Child Psychology and Psychiatry*, *33*, 361–73.

Lynch, M. and Cicchetti, D. (1998) An ecological-transactional analysis of children and contexts: The longitudinal interplay among child maltreatment, community violence, and children's symptomatology. *Development and Psychopathology*, *10*, 235–57.

Lynam, D. R. (1996) Early identification of chronic offenders: Who is the fledgling psychopath? *Psychological Bulletin*, *120*, 209–34.

Lynam, D. R., Caspi, A., Moffitt, T. E., Wikström, P.-O. H., Loeber, R. and Novak, S. (2001). The interaction between impulsivity and neighborhood context on offending: The effects of impulsivity are stronger in poor neighborhoods. *Journal of Abnormal Psychology*, *109*, 563–74.

Lynam, D. R. and Moffitt, T. E. (1995) Delinquency and impulsivity and IQ: A reply to Block (1995). *Journal of Abnormal Psychology*, *104*, 399–401.

Lynam, D. R., Moffitt, T. E. and Stouthamer-Loeber, M. (1993) Explaining the relation between IQ and delinquency: Class, race, test motivation, school failure, or self-control? *Journal of Abnormal Psychology*, *102*, 187–96.

Maggs, J. L. and Hurrelmann, K. (1998) Do substance use and delinquency have different implications for adolescents' peer relations? *International Journal of Behavioural Development*, *22*, 367–88.

Magnusson, D. and Bergman, L. R. (1988) Individual and variable-based approaches to longitudinal research on early risk factors. In M. Rutter (ed.), *Studies of Psychosocial Risk: The Power of Longitudinal Data* (pp. 45–61). Cambridge University Press.

Maguin, E., Hawkins, J. D., Catalano, R. F., Hill, K., Abbott, R. and Herrenkohl, T. (1995) *Risk factors measured at three ages for violence at age 17–18*. Paper presented at the American Society of Criminology, November 1995, Boston.

Masten, A. S. (1986) Humor and competence in school-aged children. *Child Development*, *57*, 461–73.

(1989) Resilience in development: Implications of the study of successful adaptation for developmental psychopathology. In D. Cicchetti (ed.), *The Emergence of a Discipline: Rochester Symposium on Developmental Psychopathology*, vol. 1 (pp. 261–94). Hillsdale, NJ: Erlbaum.

Masten, A. S., Best, K. M. and Garmezy, N. (1990) Resilience and development: Contributions from the study of children who overcome adversity. *Development and Psychopathology*, *2*, 425–44.

Masten, A. S. and Coatsworth, J. D. (1995) Competence, resilience, and psychopathology. In D. Cicchetti and D. J. Cohen (eds.), *Developmental Psychopathology, vol. 2: Risk, Disorder, and Adaptation* (pp. 715–52). New York: Wiley.

Masten, A. S. and Garmezy, N. (1985) Risk, vulnerability, and protective factors in developmental psychopathology. In B. B. Lahey and A. E. Kazdin (eds.), *Advances in Clinical Child Psychology* (vol. 8, pp. 1–52). New York: Plenum Press.

Masten, A. S., Garmezy, N., Tellegen, A., Pellegrini, D. S., Larkin, K. and Larsen, A. (1988) Competence and stress in school children: The moderating effects of individual and family qualities. *Journal of Child Psychology and Psychiatry, 29*, 745–64.

Mawson, A. R. (1987) *Transient Criminality: A Model of Stress-induced Crime*. New York: Praeger.

McBurnett, K., Lahey, B. B., Capasso, L. and Loeber, R. (1996) Aggressive symptoms and salivary cortisol in clinic-referred boys with conduct disorder. *Annals of the New York Academy of Science, 794*, 169–78.

McBurnett, K., Lahey, B. B., Frick, P. J., Risch, S. C., Loeber, R., Hart, E. L., Christ, M. A. G. and Hanson, K. S. (1991) Anxiety, inhibition, and conduct disorder in children: II. Relation to salivary cortisol. *Journal of the American Academy of Child and Adolescent Psychiatry, 30*, 192–6.

McCall, R. B. (1981) Nature-nurture and the two realms of development: A proposed integration with respect to mental development. *Child Development, 52*, 1–12.

McCord, J. and Ensminger, M. E. (1997) Multiple risks and comorbidity in an African-American population. *Criminal Behaviour and Mental Health, 7*, 339–52.

McLloyd, V. C. (1990) The impact of economic hardship on Black families and children: Psychological distress, parenting, and socioemotional development. *Child Development, 61*, 311–46.

Meaney, M. J., Mitchell, J. B., Aitken, D. H., Bhatnagar, S., Bodnoff, S. R., Iny, L. J. and Sarrieau, A. (1991) The effects of neonatal handling on the development of the adrenocortical response to stress: Implications for neuropathology and cognitive deficits in later life. *Psychoneuroendocrinology, 16*, 85–103.

Megargee, E. I. (1966) Undercontrolled and overcontrolled personality types in extreme antisocial aggression. *Psychological Monographs, 80*, Whole No. 611.

Moffitt, T. E. (1993a) Adolescence-limited and life-course-persistent antisocial behavior: A developmental taxonomy. *Psychological Review, 100*, 674–701.

(1993b) Neuropsychology of conduct disorder. *Development and Psychopathology, 5*, 135–51.

Moffitt, T. E., Caspi, A., Dickson, N., Silva, P. and Stanton, W. (1996) Childhood-onset versus adolescent-onset antisocial conduct problems in males: natural history from ages 3 to 18 years. *Development and Psychopathology, 8*, 399–424.

Moffitt, T. E., Caspi, A., Fawcett, P. Brammer, G. L., Raleigh, M., Yuwiler, A. and Silva, P. (1997) Whole blood serotonin and family background relate to male violence. In A. Raine, P. A. Brennan, D. P. Farrington and S. A. Mednick (eds.), *Biosocial Bases of Violence* (pp. 231–49). New York: Plenum Press.

Mortimore, P. (1995) The positive effects of schooling. In M. Rutter (ed.), *Psychosocial Disturbances in Young People: Challenge for Prevention* (pp. 333–63). New York: Cambridge University Press.

Murphy, L. B. and Moriarty, A. E. (1976) *Vulnerability, Coping, and Growth*. New Haven, CT: Yale University Press.

Nagin, D. S., Farrington, D. P. and Pogarsky, G. (1997) Adolescent mothers and the criminal behavior of their children. *Law and Society Review, 31*, 137–62.

Nagin, D. and Tremblay, R. E. (1999) Trajectories of boys' physical aggression, opposition, and hyperactivity on the path to physically violent and nonviolent juvenile delinquency. *Child Development, 70*, 1181–96.

Neighbors, B., Forehand, R. and McVicar, D. (1993) Resilient adolescents and interparental conflict. *American Journal of Orthopsychiatry, 63*, 462–71.

Newcomb, M. D. (1997) General deviance and psychological distress: impact of family support/bonding over 12 years from adolescence to adulthood. *Criminal Behaviour and Mental Health, 7*, 349–400.

Olweus, D. (1979) Stability of aggressive reaction patterns in males: A review. *Psychological Bulletin, 86*, 852–75.

(1993) *Bullying at School*. Oxford: Blackwell.

Orlinsky, D. E., Grawe, K. and Parks, B. K. (1994) Process and outcome in psychotherapy: In A. E. Bergin and S. L. Garfield (eds.), *Handbook of Psychotherapy and Behavior Change* (4th ed., pp. 270–376). New York: Wiley.

Osborn, A. F. (1990) Resilient children: a longitudinal study of high achieving socially disadvantaged children. *Early Child Development and Care, 62*, 23–47.

O'Grady, D. and Metz, J. R. (1987) Resilience in children at high risk for psychological disorder. *Journal of Pediatric Psychology, 12*, 3–23.

Pagani, L., Boulerice, B., Tremblay, R. E. and Vitaro, F. (1996) *Effects of poverty on academic failure and delinquency in boys: A change and process model approach*. Paper presented at the 19th Biennial Meeting of the International Society for the Study of Behavioral Development, August 1996, Québec, Canada.

Parker, G. R., Cowen, E. L., Work, W. C. and Wyman, P. A. (1990) Test correlates of stress resilience among urban school children. *Journal of Primary Prevention, 11*, 19–35.

Parker, J. G., Rubin, K. H., Price, J. M. and DeRosier, M. E. (1995) Peer relationships, child development, and adjustment: A developmental psychopathology perspective. In D. Cicchetti and D. J. Cohen (eds.), *Developmental Psychopathology, vol. 2: Risk, Disorder, and Adaptation* (pp. 96–161). New York: Wiley.

Patterson, G. R., Capaldi, D. M. and Bank, L. (1991) An early starter model for predicting delinquency. In D. J. Pepler and K. H. Rubin (eds.), *The Development and Treatment of Childhood Aggression* (pp. 139–68). Hillsdale, NJ: Erlbaum.

Patterson, G. R., Forgatch, M. S., Yoerger, K. L. and Stoolmiller, M. (1998) Variables that initiate and maintain an early-onset trajectory for juvenile offending. *Development and Psychopathology, 10*, 531–47.

Patterson, G. R., Reid, J. B. and Dishion, T. J. (1992) *Antisocial Boys*. Eugene, OR: Castalia.

Peeples, F. and Loeber, R. (1994) Do individual factors and neighborhood context explain ethnic differences in juvenile delinquency? *Journal of Quantitative Criminology, 10*, 141–57.

Perry, D. G., Perry, L. C. and Rasmussen, P. (1986) Cognitive social learning mediators of aggression. *Child Development, 57*, 700–11.

Pianta, R. C., Egeland, B. and Sroufe, L. A. (1990) Maternal stress and children's development: Prediction of school outcomes and identification of protective factors. In J. Rolf, A. Masten, D. Cicchetti, K. Nuechterlein and

S. Weintraub (eds.), *Risk and Protective Factors in the Development of Psychopathology* (pp. 215–35). Cambridge University Press.

Pickles, A. and Rutter, M. (1991) Statistical and conceptual models of 'turning points' in developmental processes. In D. Magnusson, L. R. Bergman, G. Rudinger and B. Törestad (eds.), *Problems and Methods in Longitudinal Research: Stability and Change* (pp. 133–65). Cambridge University Press.

Pike, A., McGuire, S., Hetherington, E. M., Reiss, D. and Plomin, R. (1996) Family environment and adolescent depressive symptoms and antisocial behavior: A multivariate genetic analysis. *Developmental Psychology, 32*, 590–603.

Pliszka, S. R. (1989) Effect of anxiety on cognition, behavior, and stimulant response in ADHD. *Journal of the American Academy of Child and Adolescent Psychiatry, 28*, 882–7.

Plomin, R. (1994) *Genetics and Experience*. Newbury Park, CA: Sage.

Polansky, N. A., Gaudin, J. M., Ammons, P. W. and Davis, K. B. (1985) The psychological ecology of the neglectful mother. *Child Abuse and Neglect, 9*, 265–75.

Price, J. M. and Dodge, K. A. (1989) Peers' contribution to children's social maladjustment: Description and intervention. In T. J. Berndt and G. W. Ladd (eds.), *Peer Relations in Child Development* (pp. 341–70). New York: Wiley.

Quay, H. C. (1993) The psychobiology of undersocialized aggressive conduct disorder: A theoretical perspective. *Development and Psychopathology, 5*, 165–80.

Quinton, D., Pickles, A., Maughan, B. and Rutter, M. (1993) Partners, peers and pathways: Assortive pairing, and continuities in conduct disorder. *Development and Psychopathology, 5*, 763–83.

Quinton, D., Rutter, M. and Liddle, C. (1984) Institutional rearing, parenting difficulties, and marital support. *Psychological Medicine, 14*, 107–24.

Quinton, D. and Rutter, M. (1988) *Parenting Breakdown: The Making and Breaking of Intergenerational Links*. Aldershot, Hants: Avebury.

Radke-Yarrow, M. and Brown, E. (1993) Resilience and vulnerability in children of multiple-risk families. *Development and Psychopathology, 5*, 581–92.

Radke-Yarrow, M. and Sherman, T. (1990) Hard growing: Children who survive. In J. Rolf, A. Masten, D. Cicchetti, K. Nuechterlein and S. Weintraub (eds.), *Risk and Protective Factors in the Development of Psychopathology* (pp. 97–119). Cambridge University Press.

Rae-Grant, N., Thomas, B. H., Offord, D. R. and Boyle, M. H. (1989) Risk, protective factors, and prevalence of behavioral and emotional disorders in children and adolescents. *Journal of the American Academy of Child and Adolescent Psychiatry, 28*, 262–8.

Raine, A. (1993) *The Psychopathology of Crime*. San Diego: Academic Press.

Antisocial behavior and psychophysiology: A biosocial perspective and a prefrontal dysfunction hypothesis. In D. M. Stoff, J. Breiling and J. D. Maser (eds.), *Handbook of Antisocial Behavior* (pp. 289–304). New York: Wiley.

Raine, A., Farrington, D. P., Brennan, P. and Mednick, S. A. (eds.) (1997) *Biosocial Bases of Violence*. New York: Plenum Press.

Raine, A., Reynolds, C., Venables, P. H. and Mednick, S. A. (1997) Biosocial bases of aggressive behavior in childhood: Resting heart rate, skin conductance orienting, and physique. In A. Raine, P. A. Brennan, D. P. Farrington and S. A. Mednick (eds.), *Biosocial Bases of Violence* (pp. 107–26). New York: Plenum.

Raine, A. and Venables, P. H. (1981) Classical conditioning and socialization – A biosocial interaction? *Personality and Individual Differences*, *2*, 273–83.

Raine, A., Venables, P. H. and Williams, M. (1990) Relationships between CNS and ANS measures of arousal at age 15 and criminality at age 24. *Archives of General Psychiatry*, *47*, 1003–7.

(1995) High autonomic arousal and electrodermal orienting at age 15 years as protective factors against criminal behavior at age 29 years. *American Journal of Psychiatry*, *152*, 1595–600.

(1996) Better autonomic conditioning and faster electrodermal half-recovery time at age 15 years as possible protective factors against crime at age 29 years. *Developmental Psychology*, *32*, 624–30.

Räsänen, P., Hakko, H., Isohanni, M., Hodgins, S., Järvelin, M.-R. and Tiihonen, J. (1999) Maternal smoking during pregnancy and risk of criminal behavior among adult male offspring in the northern Finland 1966 birth cohort. *American Journal of Psychiatry*, *156*, 857–62.

Reiss, A. J., Jr. (1995) Community influences on adolescent behavior. In M. Rutter (ed.), *Psychosocial Disturbances in Young People: Challenges for Prevention* (pp. 305–32). New York: Cambridge University Press.

Reiss, A. J. and Farrington, D. P. (1991) Advancing knowledge about co-offending: Results from a prospective longitudinal survey of London males. *Journal of Criminal Law and Criminology*, *82*, 360–95.

Rende, R. D. and Plomin, R. (1992) Relations between first grade stress, temperament, and behavior problems. *Journal of Applied Developmental Psychology*, *13*, 435–46.

Renshaw, P. D. and Asher, S. R. (1983) Children's goals and strategies for social interaction. *Merrill-Palmer-Quarterly*, *29*, 353–74.

Richters, J. E. and Martinez, P. E. (1993) Violent communities, family choices, and children's chances: An algorithm for improving the odds. *Development and Psychopathology*, *5*, 609–27.

Robins, L. N. (1966) *Deviant Children Grown up: A Sociological and Psychiatric Study of Sociopathic Personality*. Baltimore: Williams & Wilkins.

(1978) Sturdy childhood predictors of adult antisocial behavior: Replications from longitudinal studies. *Psychological Medicine*, *8*, 611–22.

Robins, R. W., John, O. P., Caspi, A., Moffitt, T. T. and Stouthamer-Loeber, M. (1996) Resilient, overcontrolled, and undercontrolled boys: Three replicable personality types. *Journal of Personality and Social Psychology*, *70*, 157–71.

Robins, L. N. and Price, R. K. (1991) Adult disorders predicted by childood conduct problems: Results from the NIMH epidemiologic catchment area project. *Psychiatry*, *54*, 116–32.

Robins, L. N. and Ratcliff, K. S. (1980) Childhood conduct disorders and later arrest. In L. N. Robins, P. J. Clayton and J. K. Wing (eds.), *The Social Consequences of Psychiatric Illness* (pp. 1–12). New York: Brunner/Mazel.

Robinson, J. A. L. (2000) Are there implications for prevention research from studies of resilience? *Child Development*, *71*, 570–2.

Robinson, N. S. and Garber, J. (1995) Social support and psychopathology across the life span. In D. Cicchetti and D. J. Cohen (eds.), *Developmental*

Psychopathology, vol. 2: Risk, Disorder, and Adaptation (pp. 162–209). New York: Wiley.

Robinson, W. S. (1950) Ecological correlations and the behavior of individuals. *American Sociological Review, 15*, 351–7.

Rowe, D. C. (1994) *The Limits of Family influence: Genes, Experience, and Behavior*. New York: Guilford.

Rubin, K. H., Bream, L. A. and Krasnor, L. R. (1991) Social problem solving and aggression in childhood. In D. J. Pepler and K. H. Rubin (eds.), *The Development and Treatment of Childhood Aggression* (pp. 219–48). Hillsdale, NJ: Lawrence Erlbaum.

Rubin, K. H., Chen, X., McDougall, P., Bowker, A. and McKinnon, J. (1995) The Waterloo Longitudinal Project: Predicting internalizing and externalizing problems in adolescence. *Development and Psychopathology, 7*, 751–64.

Rutter, M. (1979) Protective factors in children's responses to stress and disadvantage. In M. W. Kent and J. E. Rolf (eds.), *Primary Prevention in Psychopathology* (vol. 3, pp. 49–74). Hanover, NH: University Press of New England.

(1985) Resilience in the face of adversity. Protective factors and resistance to psychiatric disorder. *British Journal of Psychiatry, 147*, 598–611.

(1987) Psychosocial resilience and protective factors. *American Journal of Orthopsychiatry, 57*, 316–31.

(1990) Psychosocial resilience and protective mechanisms. In J. Rolf, A. Masten, D. Cicchetti, K. Nuechterlein and S. Weintraub (eds.), *Risk and Protective Factors in the Development of Psychopathology* (pp. 181–214). Cambridge University Press.

(1995) Causal concepts and their testing. In M. Rutter and D. J. Smith (eds.), *Psychosocial Disorders in Young People: Time Trends and Their Causes* (pp. 7–34). Chichester: Wiley.

(1996) Psychosocial adversity: risk, resilience, and recovery. In L. Verhofstadt-Denève, I. Kienhorst and C. Braet (eds.), *Conflict and Development in Adolescence* (pp. 21–33). Leiden, Netherlands: DSWO Press.

(1997) Comorbidity: concepts, claims and choices. *Criminal Behaviour and Mental Health, 7*, 265–85.

Rutter, M., Giller, H. and Hagell, A. (1998) *Juvenile Delinquency: Trends and Perspectives*. New York: Guilford.

Rutter, M., Maughan, B., Mortimore, P. and Ouston, J. (1979) *Fifteen Thousand Hours: Secondary Schools and Their Effects on Children*. Cambridge, MA: Harvard University Press.

Rutter, M. and Quinton, D. (1984) Long term follow-up of women institutionalized in childhood: Factors promoting good functioning in adult life. *British Journal of Developmental Psychology, 18*, 225–34.

Rutter, M. and Rutter, M. (1993) *Developing Minds: Challenge and Continuity Across the Lifespan*. Harmondsworth: Penguin.

Sampson, R. J. and Laub, J. H. (1993) *Crime in the Making: Pathways and Turning Points Through Life*. Cambridge, MA: Harvard University Press.

Sampson, R. and Lauritsen, J. (1994) Violent victimization and offending: Individual-, situational-, and community-level risk factors. In A. J. Reiss and J. A. Roth (eds.), *Understanding and Preventing Violence, vol. 3: Social Influences* (pp. 1–115). Washington, DC: National Academy Press.

Scerbo, A. S. and Kolko, D. J. (1994) Salivary testosterone and cortisol in disruptive children: Relationship to aggressive, hyperactive, and internalizing behaviors. *Journal of the American Academy of Child Psychiatry*, *33*, 1174–84.

Schneider-Rosen, K. and Cicchetti, D. (1984) The relationship between affect and cognition in maltreated infants: Quality of attachment and the development of visual self-recognition. *Child Development*, *55*, 648–58.

Schwartz, C. E., Snidman, N. and Kagan, J. (1996) Early childhood temperament as a determinant of externalizing behavior in adolescence. *Development and Psychopathology*, *8*, 527–37.

Schwarzer, R. and Leppin, A. (1991) Social support and health: A theoretical and empirical overview. *Journal of Social and Personal Relationships*, *8*, 99–127.

Seidman, E., Yoshikawa, H., Roberts, A., Chesir-Teran, D., Allen, L., Friedman, J. L. and Aber, J. L. (1998) Structural and experimental neighborhood contexts, developmental stage, and antisocial behavior among urban adolescents. *Development and Psychopathology*, *10*, 259–81.

Seifer, R. and Sameroff, A. J. (1987) Multiple determinants of risk and invulnerability. In E. J. Anthony and B. J. Cohler (eds.), *The Invulnerable Child* (pp. 51–69). New York: Guilford Press.

Shaw, C. R. and McKay, H. D. (1942) *Juvenile Delinquency and Urban Areas*. University of Chicago Press.

Silbereisen, R. K. and Kracke, B. (1993) Variation in maturational timing and adjustment in adolescence. In S. Jackson and H. Rodriguez-Tomé (eds.), *Adolescence and Its Social Worlds* (pp. 67–94). Hove: Erlbaum.

Silbereisen, R. K. and Noack, P. (1990) Adolescents' orientations for development. In H. A. Bosma and A. E. Jackson (eds.), *Coping and Self-concept in Adolescence* (pp. 111–27). Heidelberg, Germany: Springer.

Simcha-Fagan, O. and Schwartz, J. E. (1986) Neighborhood and delinquency: An assessment of contextual effects. *Criminology*, *24*, 667–99.

Simons, R. L., Johnson, C., Beaman, J., Conger, R. D. and Whitbeck, L. B. (1996) Parents and peer group as mediators of the effect of community structure on adolescent problem behavior. *American Journal of Community Psychology*, *24*, 145–71.

Spencer, M. B., Cole, S. P., DuPree, D., Glymph, A. and Pierre, P. (1993) Self-efficacy among urban African American early adolescents: Exploring issues of risk, vulnerability, and resilience. *Development and Psychopathology*, *5*, 719–39.

Stattin, H., Romelsjö, A. and Stenbacka, M. (1997) Personal resources as modifiers of the risk for future criminality. *British Journal of Criminology*, *37*, 198–223.

Stattin, H. and Magnusson, D. (1990) *Pubertal Maturation in Female Development*. Hillsdale, NJ: Erlbaum.

(1996) Antisocial development: A holistic approach. *Development and Psychopathology*, *8*, 617–45.

Steinhausen, H.-Ch., Willms, J. and Spohr, H. (1993) Long-term psychopathological and cognitive outcome of children with fetal alcohol syndrome. *Journal of the American Academy of Child and Adolescent Psychiatry*, *32*, 990–4.

Stoolmiller, M. (1994) Antisocial behavior, delinquent peer association, and unsupervised wandering for boys: Growth and change from childhood to early adolescence. *Multivariate Behavioral Research*, *29*, 263–88.

Stouthamer-Loeber, M., Loeber, R., Farrington, D. P., Zhang, Q., van Kammen, W. and Maguin, E. (1993) The double edge of protective and risk factors for delinquency: Interrelations and developmental patterns. *Development and Psychopathology*, *5*, 683–701.

Susman, E. J. and Ponirakis, A. (1997) Hormones-context interactions and antisocial behavior in youth. In A. Raine, P. A. Brennan, D. P. Farrington and S. A. Mednick (eds.), *Biosocial Bases of Violence* (pp. 251–69). New York: Plenum.

Tarter, R. E. and Vanyukov, M. (1999) Re-visiting the validity of the construct of resilience. In M. D. Glantz and J. L. Johnson (eds.), *Resilience and Development: Positive Life Adaptations* (pp. 85–100). New York: Plenum.

Thomas, A. and Chess, S. (1977) *Temperament and Development*. New York: Bruner/Mazel.

Thornberry, T. P. (1998) Membership in youth gangs and involvement in serious and violent offending. In R. Loeber and D. P. Farrington (eds.), *Serious and Violent Juvenile Offenders: Risk Factors and Successful Interventions* (pp. 147–66). Thousand Oaks, CA: Sage.

Thornberry, T. P. and Krohn, M. D. (1997) Peers, drug use, and delinquency. In D. Stoff, J. Breiling and J. D. Maser (eds.), *Handbook of Antisocial Behavior* (pp. 218–33). New York: Wiley.

Tolan, P. H. (1996) How resilient is the concept of resilience? *The Community Psychologist*, *29*, 12–15.

Tremblay, R. E. (2000) The development of aggressive behavior during childhood: What have we learned in the past century? *International Journal of Behavioral Development*, *24*, 129–41.

Tremblay, R. E. and Craig, W. M. (1995) Developmental crime prevention. In M. Tonry and D. Farrington (eds.), *Building a Safer Society: Strategic Approaches to Crime Prevention. Crime and Justice: An Annual Review of Research*, vol. 19. (pp. 151–236). University of Chicago Press.

Tremblay, R. E., LeMarquand, D. and Vitaro, F. (1999) The prevention of ODD and CD. In H. C. Quay and A. E. Hogan (eds.), *Handbook of Disruptive Behavior Disorders* (pp. 525–55). New York: Kluwer/Plenum.

Tremblay, R. E., Masse, E., Perron, D., LeBlanc, M., Schwartzman, A. E. and Ledingham, J. E. (1992) Early disruptive behavior, poor school achievement, delinquent behavior and delinquent personality: Longitudinal analyses. *Journal of Consulting and Clinical Psychology*, *60*, 64–72.

Tremblay, R. E., Masse, L. C., Vitaro, F. and Dobkin, P. L. (1995) The impact of friends' deviant behavior on early onset of delinquency: Longitudinal data from 6 to 13 years of age. *Development and Psychopathology*, *7*, 649–67.

Tremblay, R. E., Schaal, B., Boulerice, B., Arsenault, L., Soussignan, R. and Pérusse, D. (1997) Male physical aggression, social dominance, and testorone levels at puberty: A developmental perspective. In A. Raine, P. A. Brennan, D. P. Farrington and S. A. Mednick (eds.), *Biosocial Bases of Violence* (pp. 271–91). New York: Plenum Press.

Tress, W., Reister, G. and Gegenheimer, L. (1989) Mental health in spite of stressful childhood. In M. Brambring, F. Lösel and H. Skrowronek (eds.), *Children at Risk: Assessment, Longitudinal Research, and Intervention* (pp. 173–85). Berlin: De Gruyter.

Tschann, J. M., Kaiser, P., Chesney, M. A., Alkon, A. and Boyce, W. T. (1996) Resilience and vulnerability among preschool children: Family functioning, temperament, and behavior problems. *Journal of the American Academy of Child and Adolescent Psychiatry*, *35*, 184–92.

Virkkunen, M., Rawlings, R., Tokola, R., Poland, R. E., Guidotti, A., Nemeroff, C., Bissette, G., Kalogeras, K., Karonen, S. L. and Linnoila, M. (1994) CSF biochemistries, glucose metabolism, and diurnal activity rhythms in alcoholic, violent offenders, impulsive fire setters, and healthy volunteers. *Archives of General Psychiatry*, *51*, 20–7.

Eye, A. von and Schuster, C. (2000) The odds of resilience. *Child Development*, *71*, 563–6.

Wadsworth, M. E. J. (1976) Delinquency, pulse rates, and early emotional deprivation. *British Journal of Criminology*, *16*, 245–56.

Ward, D. A. and Tittle, C. R. (1994) IQ and delinquency: A test of two competing explanations. *Journal of Quantitative Criminology*, *10*, 189–212.

Waters, E., Weinfeld, N. S. and Hamilton, C. E. (2000) The stability of attachment security from infancy to adolescence and early adulthood: General discussion. *Child Development*, *71*, 703–6.

Werner, E. E. (1989) High-risk children in young adulthood: A longitudinal study from birth to 32 years. *American Journal of Orthopsychiatry*, *59*, 72–81.

(1990) Antecedents and consequences of deviant behavior. In K. Hurrelmann and F. Lösel (eds.), *Health Hazards in Adolescence* (pp. 219–31). Berlin, New York: De Gruyter.

(1993) Risk, resilience, and recovery: Perspectives from the Kauai longitudinal study. *Development and Psychopathology*, *5*, 503–15.

Werner, E. E. and Smith, R. S. (1982) *Vulnerable But Invincible*. New York: McGraw-Hill.

(1992) *Overcoming the Odds*. Ithaca, NY: Cornell University Press.

Wertlieb, D., Weigel, C. and Feldstein, M. (1989) Stressful experiences, temperament, and social support: Impact on children's behavior symptoms. *Journal of Applied Developmental Psychology*, *10*, 487–503.

West, D. J. and Farrington, D. P. (1973) *Who Becomes Delinquent?* London: Heinemann.

White, J. L., Moffitt, T. E., Caspi, A., Bartusch, D. J., Needles, D. J. and Stouthamer-Loeber, M. (1994) Measuring impulsivity and examining ist relationship to delinquency. *Journal of Abnormal Psychology*, *103*, 192–205.

White, J. L., Moffitt, T. E. and Silva, P. A. (1989) A prospective replication of the protective effects of IQ in subjects at high risk for delinquency. *Journal of Consulting and Clinical Psychology*, *37*, 719–24.

Wikström. P.-O. (1991) *Urban Crime, Criminals, and Victims: The Swedish Experience in an Anglo-American Comparative Perspective*. New York: Springer.

Wikström, P.-O. (2000) Do disadvantaged neighborhoods cause well-adjusted children to become adolescent delinquents? A study of male juvenile serious offending, individual risk and protective factors, and neighborhood context. *Criminology, 38*, 1109–42.

Williams, J. H. (1994) *Understanding substance use, delinquency involvement, and juvenile justice system involvement among African-American and European-American adolescents. Dissertation.* University of Washington, Seattle.

Williams, T. and Kornblum, W. (1985) *Growing Up Poor.* Lexington, MA: D. C. Heath.

Wilson, J. Q. (1991) Studying inner city social dislocations: the challenge of public agenda research. *American Sociological Review, 56*, 1–14.

Wilson, W. J. (1996) *When Work Disappears: The World of the New Urban Poor.* New York: Alfred Knopf.

Windle, R. C., and Windle, M. (1995) Longitudinal patterns of physical aggression: Associations with adult social, psychiatric, and personality functioning and testosterone levels. *Development and Psychopathology, 7*, 563–85.

Wyman, P. A., Cowen, E. L., Work, W. C. and Kerley, J. H. (1993) The role of children's future expectations in self-system functioning and adjustment to life-stress: A prospective study of urban at-risk children. *Development and Psychopathology, 5*, 649–61.

Wyman, P. A., Cowen, E. L., Work, W. C. and Parker, G. R. (1991) Developmental and family milieu correlates of resilience in urban children who have experienced major life stress. *American Journal of Community Psychology, 19*, 405–26.

Yoshikawa, H. (1994) Prevention as cumulative protection: Effects of early family support and education on chronic delinquency and its risks. *Psychological Bulletin, 115*, 28–54.

Zentner, M. R. (1993) Temperament, psychische Entwicklung und Psychopathologie [Temperament, psychological development, and psychopathology). *Zeitschrift für Klinische Psychologie, Psychopathologie und Psychotherapie, 41*, 43–68.

Zigler, E. and Farber, E. A. (1985) Commonalities between the intellectual extremes: Giftedness and mental retardation. In F. Horowitz and M. O'Brien (eds.), *The Gifted and Talented: Developmental Perspectives* (pp. 387–408). Washington, DC: American Psychological Association.

Zuckerman, M. (1994) *The Psychobiology of Sensation Seeking.* Cambridge University Press.

Zumkley, H. (1994) The stability of aggressive behavior: A meta-analysis. *German Journal of Psychology, 18*, 273–81.

6 Prevention during pregnancy, infancy, and the preschool years

Richard E. Tremblay and Christa Japel

Much attention has been paid to the increase in delinquent behaviour from pre-adolescence to the middle of adolescence, followed by its decrease from late adolescence to early adulthood (Elliott, 1994; Farrington, 1986). Using official statistics, the director of the Brussels Observatory in the early nineteenth century, Quetelet (1833), described this phenomenon and concluded that 'This fatal propensity seems to develop in proportion to the intensity of physical strength and passions in man'. More recently, Ellis and Coontz (1990) concluded that this crime bell curve could be explained by the increase of testosterone levels during puberty.

Surprisingly little attention has been paid to the link between the 'strength of passions' during early childhood and later delinquency. There is evidence that the most disruptive toddlers are at highest risk of becoming the most deviant adolescents and adults (Caspi, Moffitt, Newman and Silva, 1996; Stattin and Klackenberg-Larsson, 1993; White, Moffitt, Earls, Robins and Silva, 1990). Furthermore, there is evidence that the peak frequency of physical aggression during an individual's life is generally attained at around 24 months after birth (see Figure 6.1, and Tremblay *et al.*, 1996; Tremblay, Mâsse, Pagani and Vitaro, 1996) and not during mid- or late adolescence. Observational studies of the frequency of physical aggression between toddlers count the number of physical aggressions within a fifteen or thirty minute period (e.g., Hay and Ross, 1982), while studies during adolescence generally count the frequency of aggressions over a twelve-month period.

The lack of attention to toddlers' physical aggression as a crucial step in the development of chronic physical aggression appears to indicate that scholars in the field of antisocial behaviour have followed Jean-Jacques Rousseau in believing that children are born with prosocial tendencies and learn antisocial behaviour from their environment. The description that Thomas Hobbes made of children as self-centred machines who need to learn to take others into account appears to fit better with present day observations.

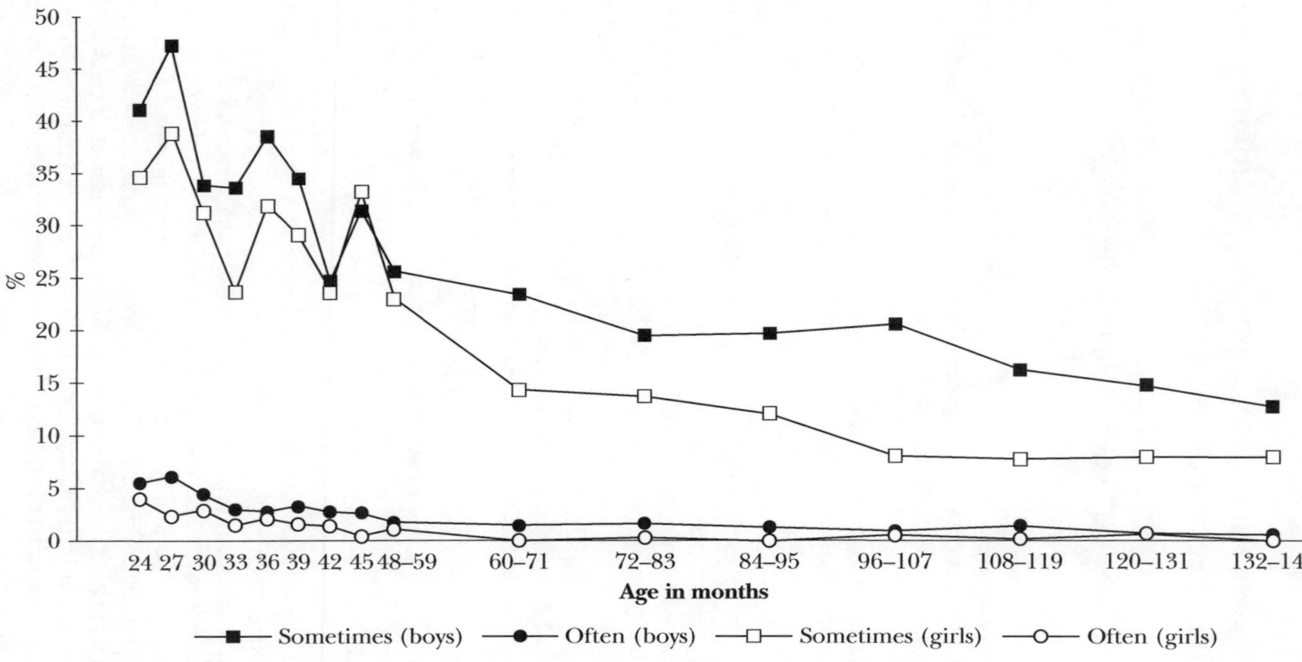

Figure 6.1. Frequency of hitting, biting, and kicking for boys and girls aged 2 to 11 years

The age 2 peak in the frequency of physical aggression is followed by a steep decline up to age 5 and a steady decline up to adolescence (Cairns and Cairns, 1994; Tremblay *et al.*, 1996). This is an indication that most humans learn to control the use of physically aggressive behaviour before they enter the school system. It can be assumed that brain maturation, language development, emotional regulation, parenting practices, and experience with peer interactions all play an important role in this socialisation process. Those who have not learned to control their aggressive reactions by the time they enter the school system enter a vicious circle of negative interactions, where rejection from their peers, because of their aggressive behaviour, leads to more reasons for aggression (Boivin and Vitaro, 1995; Vitaro, Tremblay, Gagnon and Boivin, 1992).

This developmental perspective argues in favour of prevention programmes during early childhood for high-risk families. This essay reviews prevention experiments with pregnant women and young children targetting important risk and protective factors in the development of antisocial behaviour. The aim was to review prevention experiments with pregnant women and preschool children to understand the extent to which they indicate the possibility of preventing criminal behaviour and contribute to our understanding of its development. Although a relatively large number of prevention experiments have addressed risk and protective factors for delinquency with children, there are few which assessed their impact on delinquent behaviour. Thus, the aim of the review is not to quantify the impact of these prevention experiments on delinquent behaviour, but rather to describe the types of studies which have been conducted, identify those that appear to give the most promising results, and suggest what further types of studies are needed to contribute to a science of developmental crime prevention.

Developmental prevention refers to interventions aiming to reduce risk factors and increase protective factors which are hypothesised to have a significant impact on an individual's adjustment at later points of his development. Childhood experiences have been identified as key predictors of later life events at least since the Greek philosophers (McCord, 1993). The unique contribution of the twentieth century has been the use of longitudinal and experimental studies to test these ideas.

Figure 6.2 is a representation of a number of possible links between manipulated factors and outcomes from the prenatal period to adulthood. Each arrow represents one or a series of experiments where the variable at the beginning of the arrow is the manipulated factor, and the variable at the end of the arrow is the assessed outcome of that manipulation. Arrows which link the same variable at two points in time (horizontal arrows) indicate that the experiment simply assessed whether the manipulation

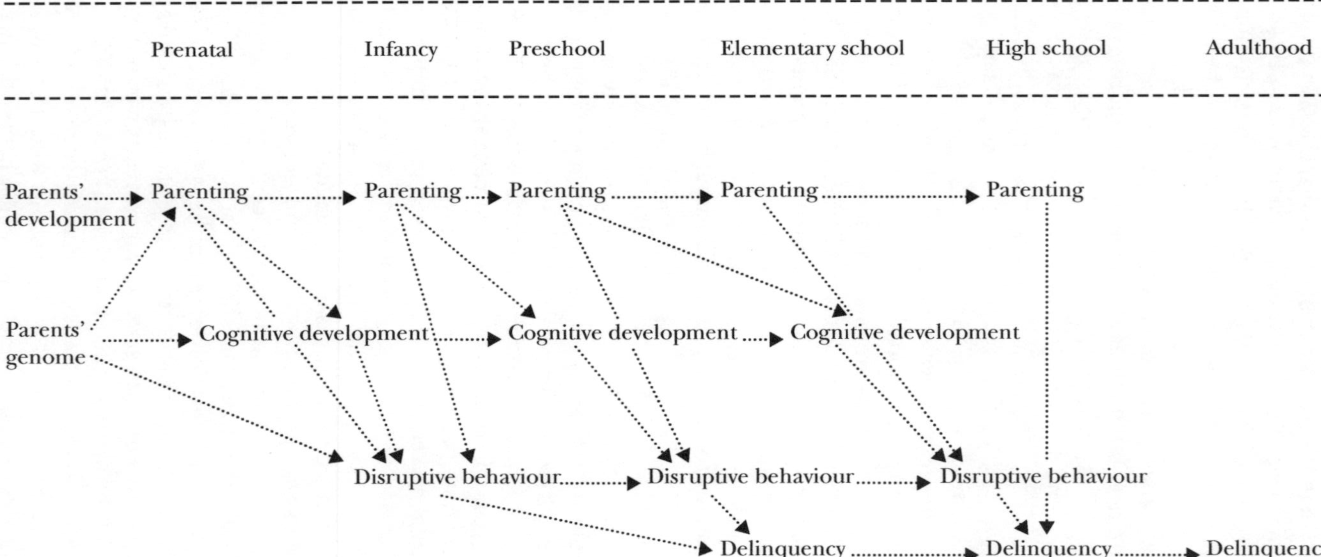

Figure 6.2. Possible links between manipulated factor and outcome for developmental prevention experiments

of a given variable created change in the variable over a defined period of time. For example, a parent training programme for parents of infants could assess two years later whether the manipulation of parenting during infancy had an impact on parenting at age 3. Similarly, training children for anger control in preschool could be followed by an assessment of anger control at the end of elementary school.

Arrows which link two different variables at two points in time (diagonal arrows) indicate that the experiment manipulated the first variable, and assessed its later impact on another variable. For example, an experiment could assess whether a prenatal parent training programme had an impact on children's cognitive performance and/or disruptive behaviour three years later. For simplicity, Figure 6.2 does not attempt to represent studies that manipulate more than one variable at the same time. However, it will be seen that most experiments with preschool children have been manipulating more than one risk or protective factor at a time.

Each of the following sections focuses on a given outcome. The order of presentation was based on the conceptual proximity of the variables to delinquent behaviour. The first section presents experiments with delinquency as an outcome. It is followed by experiments with socially disruptive behaviour as an outcome, then cognitive skills, and parenting. Because our interest was in long-term effects of interventions, experiments were selected for the review only if they had at least a one year follow-up after the end of the intervention. With one exception, we selected experiments only if they used a randomised procedure to allocate subjects to treatment and control conditions.

Tables 6.1, 6.2, 6.3, and 6.4 present summary information for all studies in each of the sections. Because the main focus of this review was crime prevention, and there exist few studies with delinquency as an outcome, these few studies are presented in some detail. In the other sections, only a few examples of prevention studies are presented in some detail to give the reader an overview of the types of experiments involved.

Prevention of delinquency

The prevention studies described in Table 6.1 assessed the extent to which treated subjects were less involved in criminal activity during adolescence and adulthood compared to control subjects. It should be noted that none of these studies were undertaken with the specific aim to prevent delinquent behaviour. Their aim was much more proximal, that is, they targetted quality of parenting, cognitive development, or early school achievement. However, because these studies had long-term follow-ups they eventually assessed criminal involvement.

Table 6.1 *Studies with juvenile delinquency as an outcome*

Authors	Age at treatment (in yrs)	Type	Risk factors manipulated	Context of intervention	# of subjects	Length of treatment	Type of treatment	Length of follow-up	Results at post-test or follow-up	
									Delinquency	Others
1. Schweinhart *et al.* (1993)	3–4 yrs	Selective	Cognitive development	Day care Home	72 boys 51 girls	1–2 years	Day care programme Home visits	24 years	Police arrests +(.54)[a]	IQ+ School achievement+ High school graduation+ Social services+ Wages+
2. Schweinhart and Weikart (1997)	3–4 yrs	Selective	Cognitive development	Day care Home	31 boys 37 girls	1–2 years	Three day care programmes (DI, HS, NS) Home visits	18 years	Self-reported delinquency+ HS versus DI and NS (.22)[a] Lifetime arrests+ HS versus DI and NS (.21)[a]	School achievement+ Social adjustment+ Interpersonal relationships+ HS < DI
3. Clarke and Campbell (1997)	$M = 4.4$ months	Selective	Cognitive development	Day care	486 boys 499 girls	5 years	Day care programme	13 years	Criminal charges and arrests0	IQ+School achievement+
4. Lally *et al.* (1988)	Birth	Selective	Education Nutrition Family Environment	Day care Home	82 children	5 years	Parent training Education Nutrition Health & safety Mother-child relationship	10 years	Court records+ (.48)[a]	IQ+Social behaviour+ School achievement+
5. Olds *et al.* (1986, 1990, 1997, 1998)	Prenatal	Indicated	Parenting Family planning	Home	400 families	2 years	Parent education Parent support Community support Family planning	15 years	Self-reports of: Running away + (.24)[a] Police arrests+ (.37)[a] Convictions and probation violations+ (.44)[a]	IQ+ Parenting+ Maternal adjustment+ Alcohol and tobacco use+ No. of sexual partners+

\+ = Positive intervention effect
− = Negative intervention effect
0 = No intervention effect
[a] = Effect size

The High/Scope Perry Preschool Project

Background

The High/Scope Perry Preschool Project (Schweinhart, Barnes and Weikart, 1993) was implemented in the 1960s in the early period of the Head Start programmes for disadvantaged children. The general hypothesis underlying these programmes was that preschool programmes could have a significant impact on later school achievement of children from economically deprived families in the USA. The High/Scope Project was more specifically influenced by studies of environmental enrichment to stimulate the development of animals, and by studies showing the importance of the preschool years for children's cognitive development. The programme was not meant to prevent juvenile delinquency, but it can be argued, from most social and psychological theories of delinquency, that a programme which increases children's' cognitive development and school achievement should have a preventive impact on juvenile delinquency.

Method

The High/Scope programme was implemented in a poor African-American neighbourhood of Ypsilanti, Michigan. Most of the subjects' parents had not completed high school (79 per cent) and close to half were single-parent families. A total of 123 children were selected for the study. They entered the programme by small groups between 1962 and 1965. A sample of thirteen subjects attended the programme from age 4 to 5 while all the other participants (N = 45) attended the programme from age 3 to 5. Subjects were first paired on IQ and then randomly allocated to two groups. After some modifications of group assignment to match the groups on sex and socioeconomic status, and to assign siblings to the same group, the membership of the treatment group was decided by flipping a coin.

After five years fifty-eight subjects had received the experimental programme and sixty-five had been placed in the control group. Children attended the preschool daily for 2.5 hours on weekday mornings, and teachers visited each mother and child for 1.5 hours a week in the afternoon. The programme lasted thirty weeks a year and its content aimed at stimulating cognitive development by active learning based on Piaget's (1960) work. The programme evolved over the five years, but remained focused on a daily routine of active learning with systematic assessment of individual needs and interests. Subjects were followed up to age 27. There were yearly assessments from age 3 to 11 and assessments at age 14, 15, 19, and 27.

Table 6.2 *Studies with socially disruptive behaviour as an outcome*

Authors	Age at treatment (in yrs)	Type	Risk factors manipulated	Context of intervention	# of subjects	Length of treatment	Type of treatment	Length of follow-up	Results: Delinquency	Results: Others
6. McNeil *et al.* (1991)	$M = 4.9$	Indicated	Parenting	Home	30 children	14 weeks	Parent training	0	Inattention0 Aggression+ Appropriate behaviour+ Compliance+ Oppositional+	Peer relations0
7. Packard *et al.* (1983)	$M = 4.3$	Indicated	Parenting	Home	34 mother-child pairs	2 weeks	Parent training	11 weeks	Problem behaviour+	Positive behaviours0
8. Shure and Spivack (1979)	$M = 4.3$	Indicated	Interpersonal cognitive problem solving	Home	10 boys 10 girls	3 months	Social problem solving Parent training	0	Impulsivity+	Withdrawal+ Problem solving+
9. Webster-Stratton *et al.* (1988, 1990)	$M = 4.5$	Indicated	Parenting	Home	101 mothers 70 fathers	4 months	Parent training	3 years	Externalising problems+ Total behaviour problems+ Hyperactivity+	Parenting+
10. Strain *et al.* (1982)	3–5	Indicated	Parenting	Home	33 males 7 females	17 weeks	Individual parent training	3–9 years	Compliance+ Oppositional behaviour+	Positive behaviours+
11. Dadds *et al.* (1987)	$M = 4.2$	Indicated	Parent training Marital satisfaction	Home	24 families	6 weeks	Parent training Problem solving	6 months	Compliance+ Oppositional behaviour+	Marital satisfaction+
12. Strayhorn and Weidman (1991)	$M = 3.7$	Selective	Parenting	Home	36 boys 48 girls	5 months	Parent training	1 year	Hostility0 Hyperactivity+	Parenting+ Attention+

13. Seitz *et al.* (1985)	2.5	Selective	Family support	Home Day care	36 infants	2.5 years	Education Medical support Parent training Day care	10 years	Antisocial behaviour+	Service usage+ SES+ Parenting style+ School attendance+ Academic achievement+ Learning patterns+
14. Johnson (1990)	1	Indicated	Parenting Cognitive development	Home Day care	47 girls 41 boys	2 years	Education Parent training	8 years	Antisocial behaviour+ Impulsivity+	School achievement+ Cognitive development+
15. McCarton *et al.* (1997)	Birth	Selective	Parenting Cognitive development	Home Day care	985 infants	3 years	Parent training Day care	5 years	Behaviour problems0	Health status+ Cognition+ IQ+

+ = Positive intervention effect
− = Negative intervention effect
0 = No intervention effect

Table 6.3 *Studies with cognitive skills as an outcome*

Authors	Age at treatment (in yrs)	Type	Risk factors manipulated	Context of intervention	# of subjects	Length of treatment	Type of treatment	Length of follow-up	Results	
									Delinquency	Others
13. Seitz *et al.* (1985)	2.5 yrs	Selective	Family support	Home Day care	36 children	2.5 years	Education Medical support Parent training Day care	10 years	Academic achievement+ School attendance+ Learning patterns+	Antisocial behaviour+ Parenting style+ SES+ Service usage+
16. Madden *et al.* (1984)	21–33 months	Selective	Cognitive development	Home	164 families	2 years	Home visits Parent training	0–2 years	Cognitive+ IQ+	Positive mother interactions+ School problems0
14. Johnson (1990)	1 year	Indicated	Parenting Cognitive development	Home Day care	47 girls 41 boys	2 year	Education Parent training	8 years	School achievement+ Cognitive development+	Impulsivity+ Antisocial behaviour+
17. Garber (1988)	3–6 months	Selective	Education Parenting	Home Day care	11 girls 9 boys	18 months	Education Parent training	10 years	IQ+ Language+ School placement+	Sibling+ Parenting+
18. Wasik *et al.* (1990)	6 weeks to 3 months	Selective	Parenting Cognitive development	Day care Home	62 families	3 years	Cognitive and social development Language development Parent training	4 years	Cognitive+	Family environment0 Family characteristics0 Attitudes to parenting+

15. McCarton *et al.* (1997)	Birth	Selective	Parenting Cognitive development	Home Day care	985 infants	3 years	Parent training Day care	5 years	Cognition+ IQ+	Behaviour problems0 Health status+ Child abuse+Child neglect + Punishment+
19. Barrera *et al.* (1986)	Birth	Selective	Parenting	Home	83 infants	1 year	Parent training	1.3 years	Mental and motor scores+	Parent-child interaction+
20. Ross (1984)	Birth	Indicated	Parenting	Home	80 infants	1 year	Home visits Parent education Parent training	0	Mental and psychomotor development+	Home environment+ Parent-child interactions+
21. Achenbach *et al.* (1990)	Birth	Selective	Parenting	Home	93 infants	3 months	Parent training	7 years	School achievement+ Cognitive development+	Mother confidence+ Mother satisfaction+ Health0
22. Pollitt *et al.* (1993)	Prenatal to 2 years	Primary	Diet	Home	1410 children	3 years	Diet high protein substitute	10 years	Cognitive+	Reaction time+
23. Booth *et al.* (1992)	Prenatal	Indicated	Parenting Mother support	Home	147 mothers	1.5 years	Home visits Mother support Information	1.5 years	Attachment0 IQ0 Motor0	Mother-child relationship+ Mother competence+

\+ = Positive intervention effect
− = Negative intervention effect
0 = No intervention effect

Table 6.4 *Studies with family characteristics as an outcome*

Authors	Age at treatment (in yrs)	Type	Risk factors manipulated	Context of intervention	# of subjects	Length of treatment	Type of treatment	Length of follow-up	Results	
									Delinquency	Others
7. Packard *et al.* (1983)	$M = 4.3$ yrs	Indicated	Parenting	Home	34 mother-child pairs	2 weeks	Parent training	11 weeks	Mother attitudes to child+ Commands+ Praise0[c]	Problem behaviour+ Positive behaviour0
9. Webster-Stratton *et al.* (1988, 1990)	$M = 4.5$yrs	Indicated	Parenting	Home	101 mothers 70 fathers	4 months	Parent training	3 years	Parenting+	Externalising problems+ Total behaviour problems+ Hyperactivity+
11. Dadds *et al.* (1987)	$M = 4.2$yrs	Indicated	Parenting Marital satisfaction	Home	24 families	6 weeks	Parent training	6 months	Marital satisfaction+	Compliance+ Oppositional behaviour+
12. Strayhorn and Weidman (1991)	$M = 3.7$ yrs	Selective	Parenting	Home	36 boys 48 girls	5 months	Parent training	1 year	Parenting+	Hostility0 Attention+ Hyperactivity+
13. Seitz *et al.* (1985)	2.5 yrs	Selective	Family support	Home Day care	36 infants	2.5 years	Education Medical support Parent training Day care	10 years	Service usage+ SES+ Parenting style+	Antisocial behaviour+ School attendance+ Academic achievements+ Learning patterns+
14. Johnson (1990)	2yrs	Indicative	Parenting Cognitive development	Home Day care	47 girls 41 boys	1 year	Education Parent training	8 years	Parenting+	School achievement+ Antisocial behaviour+ Impulsivity+ Cognitive development+

17. Garber (1988)	3–6 months	Selective	Parenting Education	Home Day care	11 girls 9 boys	1.5 years	Education Parent training	10 years	Parenting+	Sibling+ IQ+ Language+ School placement+ Cognitive+
18. Wasik *et al.* (1990)	6 weeks to 3 months	Selective	Parenting Education	Home Day care	62 families	3 years	Cognitive & social development Language development Parent training	4 years	Family environment0 Family characteristics0 Attitudes to parenting+	Cognitive+
15. McCarton *et al.* (1997)	Birth	Selective	Parenting Cognitive development	Home Day care	985 infants	3 years	Parent training Day care	5 years	Child abuse+ Child neglect+ Punishment+	Health status+ Cognition+ I.Q.+ Behaviour problems0
19. Barrera *et al.* (1986)	Birth	Selective	Parenting	Home	59 preterm 24 full term infants	1 year	Parenting skills	1.3 years	Parent-child interaction+	Mental & motor scores+
24. Field *et al.* (1982)	Birth	Selective	Parenting Schooling	Home School	120 mothers	6 months	Parent training Job training	1.5 years	Pregnancy rates+ Return to work+	Cognitive+ Motor+
25. Jacobson and Frye (1991)	Birth	Selective	Social support	Home	46 mothers	1 year	Social support Education Child development	14 months	Stimulation0 Play0	Attachment+
21. Achenbach *et al.* (1990)	Birth	Selective	Parenting	Home	93 infants	3 months	Parent training	7 years	Mother confidence+ Mother satisfaction+ Health0	Achievement+ Cognitive+ Motor skills+

(*cont.*)

Table 6.4 (*cont.*)

Authors	Age at treatment (in yrs)	Type	Risk factors manipulated	Context of intervention	# of subjects	Length of treatment	Type of treatment	Length of follow-up	Results: Delinquency	Results: Others
20. Ross (1984)	Birth	Indicated	Parenting	Home	80 infants	1 year	Home visits Parent education Parent training	0	Home environment+ Parent-child interactions+	Mental & psychomotor development+
26. Stone *et al.* (1988)	Birth	Selective	Parenting	Home Nursery	131 infants	8 months	Parent education	5–8 years	Maternal self-esteem0 Parenting stress0	Academic achievement0 Social-emotional adjustment0
27. Larson (1980)	Prenatal	Selective	Social environment	Home	115 mother – infant dyads	1.5 years	Parent education Parent support	0	Positive interactions+ Father participation+ Medical+ Accidents+ Feeding +	
23. Booth *et al.* (1992)	Prenatal	Indicated	Parenting Mother support	Home	147 mothers	1.5 years	Home visits Mother support Information	1.5 years	Mother-child relationship+ Mother competence+	Attachment0 IQ0 Motor0
28. Barth *et al.* (1988)	Prenatal	Selective	Social support	Home	50 mothers	6 months	Parent training Home visits Parent education	0	Child welfare calls+ Child abuse+ Well being- Prenatal care + Birth outcomes+	

\+ = Positive intervention effect
− = Negative intervention effect
0 = No intervention effect

Results

The study documented the subjects' development in many areas, including educational performance, delinquency, and economic status. Results for cognitive development showed that the treated group scored higher than the control group on IQ tests from the end of the first year of treatment to age 7. That significant difference disappeared from age 8 onwards, but by age 14 the treated subjects were performing significantly better than the controls on reading, arithmetic, and language achievement; by age 27 significantly more treated subjects had finished high school (71 per cent) compared to controls (54 per cent). The treated subjects by age 27 were also earning significantly more money per year, a significantly higher percentage were home owners, and a lower percentage had received social services. The delinquency data indicated that the treated subjects had significantly less lifetime arrests (mean = 2.3) compared to the controls (mean = 4.6). The difference in arrests was observed mainly for adult arrests (adult misdemeanours and drug related arrests). There were no significant differences for self-report measures of total acts of misconduct.

The High/Scope Preschool Curriculum Study

Background

Conducted by the High/Scope Educational Research Foundation since 1967, the High/Scope Preschool Curriculum Comparison Study (Schweinhart and Weikart, 1997) set out to study which of three theoretically distinct preschool curriculum models had the most beneficial effects on children's cognitive development.

Method

Sixty-eight children born in poverty and at high risk of failing in school were selected for this study. The children, 65 per cent of whom were African-American, were randomly assigned at ages 3 and 4 to one of three groups, each experiencing a different curriculum model: (a) In the Direct Instruction model, teachers followed a script to directly teach children academic skills, rewarding them for correct answers to the teacher's questions; (b) In the High/Scope model, teachers set up the classroom and the daily routine so children could plan, do, and review their own activities and engage in key active learning experiences; (c) In the traditional Nursery School model, teachers responded to children's self-initiated play in a loosely structured, socially supportive setting. Programme staff implemented the curriculum models independently over two years in $2\frac{1}{2}$-hour classes held five days a week and $1\frac{1}{2}$-hour home visits every two weeks, when the children were 3 and 4 years old. The subjects were assessed annually from 3 to 8 years of age, and subsequently at age 10, 15, and 23.

Results

Only one curriculum group difference was discernible as the preschool programmes ended: the average IQ of the Direct Instruction group was significantly higher than the average IQ of the Nursery School group (103 versus 93). However, by age 10, it was apparent that, regardless of their theoretical orientation, all three preschool programmes had similar effects on children's intellectual and academic performance. The overall average IQ of the three curriculum groups rose 27 points from a borderline impairment level of 78 to a normal level of 105 after one year of their preschool programme and subsequently settled in at an average of 95, still at the normal level. Throughout their school years, curriculum groups did not differ significantly in school achievement or in their rate of high school graduation. By age 23, however, the High/Scope and Nursery School groups showed significant advantages over the Direct Instruction group, while the Direct Instruction group had no significant advantages over them. The High/Scope group, for example, had less felony arrests than the Direct Instruction group, no arrests for property crimes, and fewer acts of teen misconduct reported at age 15. Fewer High/Scope than Direct Instruction students needed treatment during their schooling or indicated that people gave them a hard time. By age 23, more High/Scope students were living with their spouses, had done volunteer work, and planned to graduate from college.

The Abecedarian Project

Background

The Abecedarian Project (Campbell and Ramey, 1995; Clarke and Campbell, 1997) was implemented in the 1970s and intended to test the degree to which continual, consistent enrichment of the early environments might alter the negative trend toward developmental retardation among children growing up in poverty. Since most existing early childhood programmes were of short duration and enrolled youngsters aged 3 years and older, and the long-term results of these programmes generally appeared to be disappointing, the Abecedarian Project wanted to examine if a systematic educational intervention beginning in early infancy and continuing up to the point of kindergarten entry would have long-lasting effects on the intellectual development and academic achievement of poor children. Like the High/Scope Perry Preschool Project, this programme was not meant to prevent juvenile delinquency. However, improved school performance could reduce juvenile delinquency as well as youth crime by reducing the children's frustration with school and increasing their self-esteem. Furthermore, the positive bonds formed with the adult staff of the preschool project could have an effect on later delinquency by teaching the children more effective ways to handle angry feelings and more appropriate social skills.

Method

This study was a randomised clinical trial of early childhood education aimed at healthy infants born to impoverished families living in a small North Carolina town. To be admitted to the study, families of the target children had to qualify as likely to have a child at high risk of suboptimal cognitive development based on family demographic characteristics and psychological risk indicators. The original group included 111 infants born between 1972 and 1977, and their mean age on entry to treatment was 4.4 months. Ninety-eight percent of the selected participants were African-American.

Systematic educational intervention was provided in a day care setting from infancy until children entered public kindergarten at age 5. The child care centre operated full days, year round. The caregiver to infant ratio was 1:3. An infant curriculum was developed, covering four major domains: cognitive and fine motor development, social and self-help skills, language, and gross motor skills. Child ratios gradually increased from 1:3 to 1:6 as children moved from the nursery into toddler and preschool groupings. The preschool resembled other high quality programmes, with special emphasis placed on language development and preliteracy skills. Parents of treated youngsters served on the day care centre's advisory board and were provided a series of informative programmes on parenting topics. Since treated children received their primary medical care at the centre, parents were also counselled by the medical staff about child health and development. Children were evaluated throughout the treatment phase, and follow-ups were conducted at age 8, 12, 15, 18, and 19.

Results

With regard to IQ, the preschool treatment group tested higher than did the control group at age 3 (Stanford-Binet) and at age 8 (WISC-R). The mean difference between the two groups over all measurements was 8.8 IQ points. At age 15, the preschool intervention was still associated with gains in intellectual development; the mean WISC-R Full Scale IQ score was 95.0 for the preschool group and 90.3 for controls. The preschool intervention was also associated with higher academic achievement at age 15. The intervention group obtained significantly higher scores on standardised reading and mathematics tests than did the control group. Furthermore, the proportion of students repeating a grade at least once or transferred to special education classes was significantly less for the preschool group than for the no-preschool group. At age 18, fewer preschool programme participants than control group subjects had dropped out of school.

The degree to which the project had an impact on criminal charges filed through the state of North Carolina was assessed when the subjects were 16 and 17 years of age (Clarke and Campbell, 1997). The rate of arrests for the combined treatment and control group was 24.8 per cent, compared to a rate of 17.5 per cent for the total state population of 16- and 17-year-olds in 1994. No significant differences were observed between the treatment and the control groups. Furthermore, the two groups did not differ with respect to the proportion of individuals receiving charges of any kind or the mean number of charges and arrests. These results are surprising and suggest that the pathway so often postulated from better school achievement to better social adjustment and reductions in criminal behaviour is not guaranteed.

The Syracuse University Family Development Research Programme

Background

This prevention intervention was an attempt to break the link between poor education of parents and children's educational difficulties. The programme was first implemented in 1969 (Lally, Mangione and Honig, 1988). It was aimed at poor pregnant young girls (mean age 18 years) without a high school education. Five different theoretical perspectives were used to plan the intervention. Piaget's (1960) equilibration and active child participation theory was used to guide the development of a home and day-care centre curriculum for the child. Language theories (Bernstein, 1954) were used to focus part of the programme on language skills acquisition. Erikson's (1950) theory of personality development was used to focus the programme on the child's development of trust in his abilities and environment. Help was given to the families only to the extent that they were stimulated to be active participants, according to Alinsky's (1971) theory of community organisation. Finally, from John Dewey, the programme staff took the idea of the importance of freedom of choice for the children, the stimulation of creativity, and the organisation of an environment that stimulates exploration.

Method

The programme was meant to help the families for the first five years of the child's life. A total of 108 pregnant women (mostly African-American) were recruited in the programme over a three-year period. When the programme children were 36 months old, a longitudinal control group was established. The control children were matched in pairs with programme children with respect to sex, ethnicity, birth order, age, family income, family marital status, maternal age, and maternal education status (no high-school diploma) at the time of the infant's birth. Over 85 per cent of the women were single parents and all families had an income of less than $5,000 per year (in 1970 US dollars).

The intervention programme was based on the premise that the parent was the primary caregiver and teacher of the child. Paraprofessionals were used for weekly home visits focused on parent-child interaction. Piagetian sensorimotor games were taught to the parents, nutrition and neighbourhood services information was provided, and links with the day-care staff were maintained. When the child entered the school system, mothers learned how to make contact with the teachers. From 6 months of age to 60 months, the children were taken daily by bus to a day-care centre at the university. The centre had been specialising in preschool education since 1964. Special programmes were developed for the children at different ages, using the concepts described in the background section above. Assessments of the children's development were made at different points in time up to age 15.

Results

The five-year programme was completed by 82 (76 per cent) of the 108 children who started the programme, and 74 (69 per cent) of the matched controls remained in the study up to the fifth year. For the follow-up study, ten years after the end of treatment, 65 treated (60 per cent) and 54 controls (50 per cent) gave informed consent. The authors reported no bias caused by attrition. At age 3, the treated subjects had significantly higher IQ scores than control subjects. However, that difference had disappeared by age 5 at the end of the programme. Data on delinquency when the children were between ages 13 and 16 were available from the probation department and court records. There were 6 per cent of the treated children (4 of 65) and 22 per cent of the untreated children (12 of 54) who had been probation cases (chi-square $= 6.54$, $p < .01$).

The Elmira Prenatal/Early Childhood Project

Background

Olds *et al.* (1998) examined the effects of a home visit intervention in Elmira, New York, as a means of preventing child maltreatment and a range of childhood health and developmental problems. The randomised trial was an effort to prevent the development of long-term negative outcomes and increase our understanding of underlying causal influences on maternal and child outcomes. Nurse home care visitors are in an optimal position to identify and change factors in the family environment that interfere with maternal health habits, infant care-giving, and personal accomplishments in the areas of work, education, and family planning. The intervention was designed to address these processes.

Method

Women were recruited if they had no previous live births and had one or more of the following problems that predispose to infant health and developmental problems: young age, single-parent status, or low socioeconomic status. To avoid the programme being perceived as exclusively for the poor, all women with no previous live births who asked to participate were accepted. Of the 400 participants, 85 per cent had one of the three risk factors. All the subjects were randomly assigned to one of four conditions.

In the first treatment condition services were provided for sensory and developmental screening at 12 and 24 months after birth (N = 94). In the second condition, families (N = 90) were provided with the screening services and transportation for prenatal and infant medical visits up to age 24 months. In the third condition (N = 100), a nurse home-visitor was provided during pregnancy, in addition to screening and transportation. The nurses visited on average every two weeks. In the fourth condition, families (N = 116) received the same treatment as in the third condition, but in addition the nurse continued to visit until the child was 24 months old. The nurses provided parent education regarding fetal and infant development, the involvement of family members and friends, and the linkage of family members with other health and human services.

Data were collected during the intervention at the 30th week of pregnancy, at 6, 10, 22 months after birth, at the end of the intervention (24 months), and for follow-ups when the children were 4 and 15 years old. Sources of information included medical records of the infant, social services records, criminal records, maternal reports of child behaviour, standardised testing (i.e., Bayley, Cattell), observations (i.e., Caldwell Home Observation checklist), interviews, self-reports, and state records.

Results

There were no differences across treatments in the rate of attrition. The results indicated significant group differences at the 46-month follow-up (Olds, Henderson, Chamberlin and Talelbaum, 1986; Olds and Kitzman, 1990) for reported child abuse and neglect, infant temperament, behavioural problems, conflict, use of punishment, play materials, developmental quotients, emergency room visits, and maternal sense of control. Infants in intervention conditions 3 and 4 had fewer problems than infants in the other conditions. For example, the nurse-visited mothers were less likely to restrict and punish their children, visited the emergency room fewer times, and had fewer episodes of child maltreatment than those in the control condition. In addition, the nurse-visited mothers showed an increase in the number of months they were employed and fewer had subsequent pregnancies.

The results from the follow-up when the children were 15 years old indicated important positive effects of the prenatal to age 2 nurse visiting programme on teen mothers who were both unmarried and poor during pregnancy. Compared to mothers of the first two conditions (N = 62), the mothers with the extended nurse visiting programme (N = 38) were found to be significantly different on the following variables: number of subsequent pregnancies, number of subsequent births, number of months between birth of first and second child, number of months on 'Aid to Families with Dependent Children', and number of months receiving Food Stamps. Mothers visited during pregnancy and infancy also showed less behavioural impairment due to use of alcohol and other drugs and were less frequently arrested by the police than mothers who had not benefitted from the home visits by nurses. Furthermore, the children of nurse-visited women were less often the object of substantiated reports of child abuse and neglect. However, this intervention did not significantly reduce child maltreatment among mothers reporting a high incidence of domestic violence (Eckenrode *et al.*, 2000).

While prenatal home visitation by itself was not associated with any of the postnatal maternal adjustment benefits observed among mothers visited during pregnancy and infancy, the fifteen-year follow-up revealed that both prenatal as well as extended nurse home visits were effective in preventing criminal behaviour among children born to unmarried and low-SES women. Compared to their counterparts whose mothers had not received any nurse home visits, adolescents of nurse-visited mothers reported fewer episodes of running away from home, arrests, convictions, and violations of probation. In addition, the latter also reported a lower incidence of substance use, and their parents reported that they had fewer behavioural problems related to their use of drugs and alcohol. Adolescents of mothers visited during pregnancy and infancy also had fewer sexual partners than the adolescents in the comparison group. There were, however, no programme effects on more normative types of disruptive behaviour among young adolescents.

The pattern of results from this study provides evidence that nurse home-visitors are capable of preventing a large number of care-giving dysfunctions, including child abuse and neglect. Frequent home visits designed to establish a rapport with families and to identify and reinforce family strengths, combined with parent education, improved not only the quality of care-giving, but pregnancy outcomes, and maternal life course development, such as rates of fertility, substance abuse, and criminal involvement. Moreover, there were demonstrable improvements in child functioning, thereby reducing the risk of unfavourable outcomes such as serious forms of antisocial behaviour leading to arrests and convictions.

Preventing socially disruptive behaviours

A large number of the prevention experiments with children were attempts to prevent patterns of behaviour considered disruptive at school and in the home: aggression, opposition, bullying, truancy, lying, hyperactivity, and impulsivity. These behaviours lead to frequent consultations with child specialists (Earls, 1986; Mrazek and Haggerty, 1994), and they are the best predictors of juvenile delinquency. The following is an experiment aiming to prevent these disruptive behaviours, but which did not assess the impact on delinquency.

The Houston Parent-Child Development Centre Project

Background

This programme was aimed at helping children develop optimal school performance (Johnson, 1990). Intermediate goals were to reduce behaviour problems and to promote self-esteem and social skills development. The programme was designed in the tradition of other early childhood programmes such as the Consortium for Longitudinal Studies (Lazar, Darlington, Murray, Royce and Snipper, 1982) and the High/Scope Perry Preschool Project.

Method

Families were recruited from low-income Mexican-American families who had one-year-old children, and were randomly allocated to treatment conditions. Approximately 100 families met the selection criteria each year from 1970 to 1978. The intervention was conducted over a two-year period. In the first year, paraprofessionals made home visits and provided information on child development, health, and safety. A significant part of the programme was directed at promoting language development, curiosity, and inquiry. During the second year, mothers and children attended the Parent-Child Development Centre four mornings a week for four hours each morning. At the Centre, mothers and their children attended separate sessions, in addition to joint sessions. The nursery school programme was based on a Piagetian perspective (similar to the Perry Preschool Project), with an emphasis on the exploration of toys and the development of relationships with others. The mother training component focused on managing problem behaviours and developing an authoritative parenting style. Assessments were carried out at pre-intervention, post-intervention, at preschool-age, and at elementary school-age.

Results

Approximately 50 per cent of the subjects completed the two-year intervention. Mother reports from preschool indicated that the intervention boys were less destructive and overactive than the control boys. Teacher ratings in primary school indicated that the boys and girls in treatment were less impulsive, obstinate, restless, disruptive, hostile, and aggressive than the control group. Twenty-four control children were classified as 'referable' compared to only five experimental children. In addition, the experimental subjects performed better on school achievement tests than did the controls. The results of this study suggest that this intervention successfully improved the behaviour and school achievement of children from economically and educationally disadvantaged families. Furthermore, the effects of the programme persisted for five to eight years following the intervention.

Preventing cognitive deficits

Cognitive deficits of all kinds are associated with criminal behaviour (Buikhuisen, 1987; Moffitt, 1993; Séguin, Pihl, Harden, Tremblay and Boulerice, 1995). Longitudinal studies have shown that preschoolers' and elementary school children's cognitive deficits predict later criminal behaviour (e.g., Farrington, 1991; Moffitt, 1990; Stattin and Klackenberg-Larsson, 1993). One would expect that preventive interventions which increase children's cognitive skills would have a reductive impact on delinquency. This hypothesis was supported by four of the five preschool prevention experiments presented in section I above. While all five had an impact on early cognitive development, all but one had also an impact on later delinquency. To understand the extent to which the positive outcomes of these experiments could be replicated, this section presents other studies aimed at fostering cognitive development. These experiments did not assess delinquency as an outcome, but a positive impact on cognitive skills would support the idea that this important precursor of delinquency can be modified.

Project CARE

Background

Project CARE (Wasik, Ramey, Bryant and Sparling, 1990) provided a multi-context intervention (home and day care) designed to promote preschool children's cognitive and behavioural development. This project was for families in North Carolina judged at risk for delayed development because of the disadvantaged educational or social circumstances of the parents. Children who grow up in poverty are at increased risk for school failure and lower cognitive performance. The combination of a home and day-care intervention was designed to address a larger range of environmental variables that influence children's and parents' behaviour. The study was in part based on the premise that parent-child interactions are influenced by the parent's knowledge and skill, as well as by the parent's own needs and coping strategies. By providing a family education programme as well as a day-care programme it was expected that the impact on children's development would be greater.

Method

Over an eighteen-month period beginning in July 1978, families were screened for an indication of risk through an interview and a psychological assessment. The sixty-two families who met the risk criteria were randomly assigned at the time of the child's birth to one of the two interventions and control groups. In this study, one intervention group received a day-care programme aimed at enhancing both cognitive and social development with a systematic curriculum, as well as a family education programme. In this intervention, children regularly attended day care. The curriculum emphasised activities which supported intellectual/creative, social, and emotional development. Language development was also a focus through promoting verbal interaction and modelling of what a nurturant and developmentally encouraging mother might do. Teachers provided opportunities for communication and for social, representational, syntactic, and semantic competence.

The family education programme was a home-based parent training programme with the specific goals of providing information, promoting effective coping, enhancing parent problem solving, and encouraging positive parent-child interactions. Home visitors facilitated the development of positive parenting practices and were advocates for the families in the community. In addition, the home visitor tried to help parents learn specific problem-solving strategies. Finally, the basic child curriculum taught in the day-care centre was also taught in the home. The home visits occurred on average 2.5 times a month for 3 years. During years 4 and 5, there were an average of 1.4 home visits per month. The second intervention group received only the family education intervention, while the control group received neither of the interventions.

There were fifteen subjects in the day-care plus family education intervention, twenty-four in the family-education alone intervention, and twenty-three in the control group. Outcome measures included assessments of children's cognitive abilities and observations of the following: the quality of the mother-child relationship, the quality of the environment in the home, the types of parenting strategies, attitudes to parenting, and parent responsiveness. Assessments were conducted regularly over a fifty-four-month period during which the intervention was implemented.

Results

A repeated multivariate analysis of variance assessed the group differences over time. Children in the educational day-care programme with the family education component responded significantly better on measures of cognitive performance than the other groups. The family intervention group did not differ significantly from the control group on measures of parenting, parent responsiveness, quality of mother-child relationship, and parent satisfaction. Thus, overall, the family education component did not affect the home environment, nor did it change the parents' or child's behaviours in the home. This experiment supports the effectiveness of high quality day care with a family support programme in improving children's cognitive development, but the value of the family support programme to change the parents' or child's behaviour in the home was not supported. The researchers suggested that the lack of success of the family support programme may be in part a consequence of design variables such as not enough intensive training and supervision of home visitors, and not initiating home services in the prenatal period. The latter explanation tends to be confirmed by the Elmira experiment which is reported in section I (Olds *et al.*, 1998).

The Vermont Intervention Project (Achenbach, 1989)

Background

This experiment for low birth weight infants (LBW) was implemented in the Vermont Hospital Medical Centre between April 1980 and December 1981. These children were followed for seven years. It has been repeatedly documented that low birth weight infants tend to manifest biological, cognitive, and psychosocial disabilities in their development. The risk for cognitive deficits is present throughout the full spectrum of birth weights less than or equal to 2,500 grams, although the risk increases as birth weight decreases. The likelihood of adverse developmental and scholastic outcomes is further increased by low socioeconomic status.

This intervention, the Mother-Infant Transactional Programme (MITP), was designed to enhance the mother's adjustment to the care of a LBW infant by educating the mother on the infant's specific behavioural and temperamental characteristics. The MITP was aimed at sensitising the mother to the infant's cues, such as stimulus overload, stress, and readiness for interaction, and at teaching the mother to respond appropriately to the infant's specific cues. A neonatal care nurse worked with the mother daily prior to discharge from the hospital and in four home sessions at 3, 14, 30, and 90 days after discharge. The intervention took place in the home. Achenbach and his colleagues hypothesised that increasing the mother's knowledge, skill, confidence, and satisfaction through contact with the nurse would improve the mother-child interactions and consequently reduce the risk of later developmental delays and problems.

Method

Subjects were eligible for the study if they were born between April 1980 and December 1981, weighed less than 2,250 grams, and were free from congenital anomalies and neurological deficits. Subjects were randomly assigned to either the LBW experimental or LBW control conditions. A control group of normal birth weight infants was also used. One of the important measured outcomes of the programme was academic progress. The infants were followed up at ages 6 and 12 months and ages 4 and 7 years (adjusting for the short gestations of the LBW children). At the seven-year follow-up, there were twenty-four LBW children in the experimental condition, thirty-seven LBW control children, and thirty-seven normal birth weight children (NBW). At this follow up, children were assessed with the Kaufman Assessment Battery for Children and the Peabody Picture Vocabulary Test.

Results

Seven years following treatment, the LBW children who received the experimental intervention programme performed significantly better than LBW controls on the Kaufman Mental Processing Achievement scales and the Peabody Picture Vocabulary Test. Compared to the LBW control children, the LBW experimental group did not differ from the

NBW children on any of these measures. The results of this intervention suggest that an intervention designed to enhance the skill and confidence of mothers significantly improves the cognitive development of LBW children. Achenbach and his colleagues provided support for their transactional model of development, whereby changing the mother's behaviours and attitudes contributed to more favourable transactional patterns between mothers and their children, which optimised children's cognitive development.

Preventing inadequate parenting

The quality of parenting has been systematically associated with delinquent behaviour over the past century (Carpenter, 1851; Healy and Bronner, 1936; Loeber and Stouthamer-Loeber, 1986; McCord, 1979). Interventions have attempted to support families (Cabot, 1940) and train parents (Patterson, Reid, Jones and Conger, 1975) to help prevent onset of serious delinquent behaviour. Section I presented four of these studies with follow-ups assessing delinquency outcomes (see Table 6.1). Other experiments have aimed at preventing inadequate parenting but without a follow-up on delinquency. Eighteen of these studies are summarised in Table 6.4.

Most of these experiments (twelve) were carried out with parents starting before the child had reached 6 months of age: three during the prenatal period, seven from birth, and two studies between birth and six months. The six remaining studies were implemented when the children were between ages two and five. As we have seen in other sections, many intervention experiments with preschool children included parent training. However, few of those studies focused on parenting skills as the outcome. The situation is different with perinatal studies, where parenting is the main manipulated variable and one of the main immediate outcomes. Interestingly, although the perinatal parenting interventions are 'early' forms of intervention, they are relatively intensive. (It should be noted that the term 'early' refers here to the age of the child; the intervention can be considered 'late' if we refer to the aim of changing the parents' behaviour.) Two-thirds of the interventions starting before the baby was 6 months old lasted at least one year. The shortest interventions (ranging from 2 weeks to 5 months) were with the parents of the oldest children (3- and 4-year-olds). It is of interest to note that interventions with parents of pre- and early disruptive adolescents tend to be comparatively much shorter (e.g., Dishion, Patterson and Kavanagh, 1992).

Outcome assessments were made at times varying from a few months to almost ten years after treatment. The parent interventions were generally implemented in the family home. These interventions included information programmes, education programmes, parent training, job training, medical support, and family support. Two of these interventions were described earlier (Achenbach, Phares and Howell, 1990; Olds *et al.*, 1998). One more is described in detail below.

The Infant Health and Development Programme

Background

This study (McCarton *et al.*, 1997) was an eight-site clinical trial designed to evaluate the effectiveness of an early intervention aimed at reducing the developmental and health problems of low birth weight premature infants (LBW). As already mentioned, compared to normal birth weight infants, LBW infants are at increased risk for developmental delay, a variety of medical complications, cognitive functioning difficulties, low scholastic achievement, and behavioural problems. The Infant Health and Development Programme combined medical, child, and family services in an effort to reduce developmental, behavioural, and health problems among LBW premature infants.

Method

A total of 985 infants were randomly assigned to treatment and control groups. The intervention programme was initiated on discharge from the neonatal nursery and continued until the infants were 3 years old. Both groups participated in the same pediatric follow-up, which comprised medical, developmental, and social assessments. In addition, the intervention group received home visits, attended a child developmental centre, and participated in parent group meetings. The home visitor provided families with health and developmental information, family support, and family education on parent management and understanding of developmental issues. In the child development centres, educational and learning activities were provided five days a week. Finally, every second month parents attended parent group meetings that provided information on child-rearing, health and safety, and other parent concerns. Infants were assessed at 4, 8, 12, 18, 24, 30 and 36 months. Sources of information included mother reports (about health and developmental functioning and family sociographic and demographic information), physical measurements, cognitive assessments, and behavioural and observational data. Outcome measures included cognitive development, behavioural competence, health status, and quality of care-giving (e.g., child abuse and neglect).

Results

Ninety-three per cent of subjects were assessed at the 36-month follow-up. The results indicated that there was a reduction in the incidence of care-giving dysfunction for the intervention groups. The incidence of verified cases of child abuse and neglect was also reduced. The incidence of maltreatment increased in the comparison group (to 19 per cent), but not in the nurse-visited group (remaining at 4 per cent). The nurse-visited high-risk mothers were observed to restrict and punish their children less frequently than those in the control group. In addition, at 36 months of age, the intervention infants had significantly higher cognitive scores, fewer maternally reported behaviour problems, and a small but significant increase in maternally reported morbidity than those in the control group. The largest treatment effect was the significantly higher cognitive scores obtained by the intervention group. At age 8 years, 874 children were assessed: 336 in the intervention group and 538 in the follow-up only group. Although there were modest intervention-related differences in the cognitive and academic skills of heavier LBW premature children, the results showed an attenuation of the large favourable intervention effects seen at age 3. These results suggest that LBW premature children require additional interventions to ensure that the benefits of early interventions are sustained.

Summary of results and discussion

i Impact of preventive interventions on parenting

The eighteen studies described in Table 6.4 attempted to assess the impact of experimental interventions on family characteristics. To the extent that family characteristics are important factors in the development of criminal behaviour (Loeber and Stouthamer-Loeber, 1986; Yoshikawa, 1994), the results of these experiments are useful to understand the possibility of a developmental prevention approach to crime. From the Table 6.4 studies it can be seen that a large number of perinatal and preschool experiments have shown that interventions with high-risk families can change the parenting behaviour which many theories identify as the first step of a chain of events that lead to antisocial behaviour.

Positive effects of the interventions were observed for a variety of outcomes: from attitudes to parenting, mother satisfaction, family communication and father participation to child abuse and neglect, as well as return to work, pregnancy rates, substance abuse and police arrests. To the extent that these effects can be maintained over long periods of time, one would expect that they would have a significant impact on children's development. Most studies had small samples (twelve of the eighteen studies had fewer than one hundred subjects), and most of the significant positive effects were of a moderate to low magnitude. It is important to emphasise that interventions which target the behaviours of infants' parents can be considered early interventions only from the perspective of the children's development. From the perspective of the parent's development, these interventions start late. Their effectiveness could be due to the fact that adults who give birth to a child, especially a first born, are in a sensitive period which makes them more amenable to change.

ii Impact of interventions to foster children's cognitive development

It is important to realise that all of the eleven studies aimed at facilitating the cognitive development of preschool children started before the children were 34 months old. In fact, eight studies targeted children before they were 6 months old. The rationale for these early interventions is that cognitive skills are very stable from early childhood on (McCall and Carriger, 1993). Most of these studies are thus based on the hypothesis that interventions must stimulate cognitive development early to obtain a significant impact.

Two complementary intervention strategies have been used to achieve this aim. The first is parent training to foster adequate caring behaviours. The second is day care to offer a stimulating environment to the child. Results from studies using one or both of these strategies show positive long-term outcomes. These studies are, however, difficult to compare because the subjects are from different populations. Some studies aim at premature children, some aim at high-risk pregnant teenagers, and others aim at immigrant families. The majority of these studies had fewer than 100 subjects, but one experiment with a large sample and low attrition (McCarton *et al.*, 1997) had significant positive effects.

If cognitive skills are a protective factor for criminal behaviour, these experiments indicate that helping at-risk families around the birth period should have a positive long-term impact. The results from the Elmira Prenatal/Early Childhood Project appear to confirm this hypothesis. However, findings from the High/Scope Perry Preschool Study and the High/Scope Preschool Curriculum Study demonstrate that such interventions could also be effective with 3-year-old children from deprived environments. There is clearly an interaction between cognitive and behavioural problems throughout development. It appears wiser to prevent early negative interactive effects between these two dimensions than to wait for one of the dimensions to have a negative impact on the other. Fostering adequate parenting starting from the prenatal period and providing quality day care appear to be sound investments.

iii Impact of interventions on disruptive behaviour

Prevention experiments with infants and preschool children with disruptive behaviour as an outcome (Table 6.2) all tend to show some beneficial impact. A number of these studies aimed at more than one risk factor, but some targetted only one risk factor and showed some positive impact. Because chronic offenders appear to have a history of problem behaviour during early childhood (Moffitt, 1993), one would expect that preventing problem behaviours during early childhood would also prevent chronic offending. However, providing continued support for the children from the highest risk families during the elementary school years and early adolescence would probably be a good investment.

iv Impact of interventions on criminal behaviour

Four of the five prevention experiments with pregnant mothers, infants and preschool children which assessed the impact on criminal activity had impressive long-term effects during adolescence and early adulthood. These interventions lasted for a relatively long period of time, namely from one to five years. The four interventions which had an impact on self-reported delinquency and/or official crime records (Lally *et al.*, 1988; Olds *et al.*, 1998; Schweinhart *et al.*, 1993; Schweinhart and Weikart, 1997) included intensive day-care programmes and/or parent training. The intervention which did not have an impact on official delinquency (Campbell and Ramey, 1995; Clarke and Campbell, 1997) had a five-year day-care programme with minimal support to parents. This intervention was successful in increasing cognitive abilities and school success, but appears to have had no impact on official crime records.

It is difficult to understand why the Abecedarian experiment did not have an impact on delinquency. One could have expected that it would have had a greater impact on delinquency than the High/Scope Perry Preschool Project (Schweinhart *et al.*, 1993) and the High/Scope Preschool Curriculum Study (Schweinhart and Weikart, 1997), since it had an important impact on cognitive development and school success, it started earlier in the children's life, and it lasted three years longer. Clarke and Campbell (1997) suggested that the absence of a strong parenting programme in the Abecedarian Project could explain why the programme failed to have an impact on delinquent behaviour. In the High/Scope Preschool Curriculum Study all three preschool programmes included the same parenting component. Yet only those who attended the High/Scope programme had significantly lower levels of criminality at follow-up when the participants were 23 years old. This suggests that the content of the preschool programme rather than the parenting component is the active preventive ingredient for delinquency. On the other hand, the Elmira Prenatal/Early Childhood Project provides evidence that pre- and postnatal support to vulnerable mothers yields positive results with respect to the adolescents' delinquency, even in the absence of any particular day-care intervention.

These results suggest that some parent and preschool programmes have an impact on antisocial behaviour which is independent of the impact on IQ and school success. The main differentiating characteristic of the successful High/Scope curriculum was that teachers set up the classroom and the daily routine so children could plan, do, and review their own activities. This description comes close to what would be referred to in present day terms as 'training of executive functions'. Séguin *et al.* (1995) showed that executive functions, after having controlled for IQ, discriminated between physically aggressive and not physically aggressive adolescents. The description of the content of the Syracuse University Family Development Research Programme (Lally *et al.*, 1988), which was also successful in preventing delinquency, also emphasised active child and parent participation in the choice of means and ends. It is intriguing, however, that the Elmira Prenatal/Early Childhood Project by itself was effective in preventing criminal behaviour among children born to at-risk women. Nurse home visits during pregnancy, present in both the prenatal and extended intervention programme, may have had the positive effect of altering maternal prenatal health and the children's corresponding neuropsychological functioning. In other words, improving the mother's prenatal health may have had a beneficial effect on the neuromotor development of the fetus, thus making the individual more amenable to the 'training of executive functions'.

If preschool programmes can have differential impacts on the development of executive functions, one would expect that they will have differential impacts on the development of antisocial behaviour. All of the experimental preschool programmes were aiming to have an impact on school performance by increasing cognitive abilities, but they mostly monitored changes in IQ. New experiments need to monitor a wider range of cognitive and social abilities to identify the mechanisms through which some preschool programmes have a positive impact on delinquent behaviour.

The general impression from the review of the twenty-eight prevention experiments is that early childhood interventions can have a positive impact on the three most important risk factors for juvenile delinquency: disruptive behaviour, cognitive skills, and parenting. Furthermore, experiments with long-term follow-ups which have targeted at least two of these risk factors in childhood have shown a significant impact on criminal behaviour. From these results it can be concluded that early and intensive preventive interventions can have the desirable impact which appears to be so difficult to achieve with disruptive elementary school children and juvenile delinquents.

Unfortunately, this conclusion is based on a very small set of studies. Increasing the number of these long-term follow-up studies to obtain a better assessment of their impact on crime does not mean that we have to start new interventions with babies and wait eighteen years for the outcome. Criminologists could study the criminal records of the experimental and control subjects from the numerous intervention experiments of the 1970s and 1980s which were aiming to improve parenting and cognitive skills or reduce disruptive behaviours.

We also need to assess to what extent the relatively small-scale and well-controlled prevention experiments can be integrated in the service delivery systems and how we can maintain their effectiveness before we confidently conclude that interventions during pregnancy, infancy, and preschool will have a substantial impact on a society's crime rate.

REFERENCES

Achenbach, T. M. (1989) Empirically based assessment of child and adolescent disorders: Implications for diagnosis, classification, epidemiology, and longitudinal research. In M. Brambring, F. Losel and H. Skowronek (eds.), *Children at Risk: Assessment, Longitudinal Research, and Intervention* (pp. 24–45). Berlin: Gruyter.

Achenbach, T. M., Phares, V. and Howell, C. T. (1990) Seven-year outcome of the Vermont intervention program for low-birthweight infants. *Child Development, 61*, 1672–81.

Alinsky, S. D. (1971) *Rules for Radicals*. New York: Random House.

Barrera, M. E., Rosenbaum, P. L. and Cunningham, C. E. (1986) Early home intervention with low-birth-weight infants and their parents. *Child Development, 57*, 20–33.

Barth, R. P., Hacking, S. and Ash, J. R. (1988) Preventing child abuse: An experimental evaluation of the child parent enrichment project. *Journal of Primary Prevention, 8*, 201–17.

Bernstein, B. (1954) Social class, speech systems and psycho-therapy. In F. Riessman, J. Cohen and A. Pearls (eds.), *Mental Health of the Poor* (pp. 194–204). New York: Free Press of Glencoe.

Boivin, M. and Vitaro, F. (1995) The impact of peer relationships on aggression in childhood: Inhibition through coercion or promotion through peer support. In J. McCord (ed.), *Coercion and Punishment in Long-term Perspectives* (pp. 183–97). New York: Cambridge University Press.

Booth, C. L., Spieker, S. J., Barnard, K. E. and Morisset, C. E. (1992) Infants at risk: The role of prevention intervention in deflecting a maladaptive developmental trajectory. In J. McCord and R. E. Tremblay (eds.), *Preventing Antisocial Behavior: Interventions From Birth to Adolescence* (pp. 21–42). New York: Guilford.

Buikhuisen, W. (1987) Cerebral dysfunctions and persistent juvenile delinquency. In S. A. Mednick, T. E. Moffitt and S. A. Stack (eds.), *The Causes of Crime: New Biological Approaches* (pp. 168–84). New York: Cambridge University Press.

Cabot, P. S. d. Q. (1940) A long-term study of children: The Cambridge-Somerville Youth Study. *Child Development*, *11*, 143–51.

Cairns, R. B. and Cairns, B. D. (1994) *Life Lines and Risks: Pathways of Youth in our Time*. New York: Cambridge University Press.

Campbell, F. A. and Ramey, C. T. (1995) Cognitive and school outcomes for high-risk African-American students at middle adolescence: Positive effects of early intervention. *American Educational Research Journal*, *32*, 743–72.

Carpenter, M. (1851) *Reformatory Schools for the Children of the Perishing and Dangerous Classes and for Juvenile Offenders*. London: The Woburn Press (1968).

Caspi, A., Moffitt, T. E., Newman, D. L. and Silva, P. A. (1996) Behavioral observations at age 3 years predict adult psychiatric disorders. Longitudinal evidence from a birth cohort. *Archives of General Psychiatry*, *53*, 1033–9.

Clarke, S. H. and Campbell, F. A. (1997) *The Abecedarian Project and youth crime*. Paper presented at the Biennial Meeting of the Society for Research in Child Development, Washington, DC.

Dadds, M. R., Schwartz, S. and Sanders, M. (1987) Marital discord and treatment outcome in behavioral treatment of child conduct disorders. *Journal of Consulting and Clinical Psychology*, *55*, 396–403.

Dishion, T. J., Patterson, G. R. and Kavanagh, K. A. (1992) An experimental test of the coercion model: Linking theory, measurement, and intervention. In J. McCord and R. E. Tremblay (eds.), *Preventing Antisocial Behavior: Interventions from Birth Through Adolescence* (pp. 253–82). New York: Guilford.

Earls, F. (1986) Epidemiology of psychiatric disorders in children and adolescents. In G. L. Klerman, M. M. Weissman, P. S. Appelbaum and L. H. Roth (eds.), *Psychiatry: Social, Epidemiologic, and Legal Psychiatry* (vol. 5, pp. 123–52). New York: Basic Books.

Eckenrode, J., Ganzel, B., Henderson, Jr., C. R., *et al.* (2000) Preventing child abuse and neglect with a program of nurse home visitation: the limiting effects of domestic violence. *Journal of the American Medical Association*, *284*, 1385–91.

Elliott, D. S. (1994) Serious violent offenders: Onset, developmental course and termination: The American Society of Criminology 1993 Presidential Address. *Criminology*, *32*, 1–21.

Ellis, L. and Coontz, P. D. (1990) Androgens, brain functioning, and criminality: The neurohormonal foundations of antisociality. In L. Ellis and H. Hoffman (eds.), *Crime in Biological, Social and Moral Contexts* (pp. 162–93). New York: Praeger.

Erikson, E. (1950) *Childhood and Society*. New York: W.W. Norton.

Farrington, D. P. (1986) Stepping stones to adult criminal carreers. In D. Olweus, J. Block and M. Radke-Yarrow (eds.), *Development of Antisocial and Prosocial Behavior* (pp. 359–84). New York: Academic Press.

(1991) Childhood aggression and adult violence: Early precursors and life outcomes. In D. J. Pepler and K. H. Rubin (eds.), *Development and Treatment of Childhood Aggression* (pp. 5–29). Hillsdale, NJ: Erlbaum.

Field, T., Widmayer, S., Greenberg, R. and Stoller, S. (1982) Effects of parent training on teenage mothers and their infants. *Pediatrics*, *69*, 703–4.

Garber, H. L. (1988) *The Milwaukee Project: Preventing Mental Retardation in Children at Risk*. Washington, DC: American Association on Mental Retardation.

Hay, D. F. and Ross, H. S. (1982) The social nature of early conflict. *Child Development*, *53*, 105–13.

Healy, H. and Bronner, A. F. (1936) *New Light on Delinquency and its Treatment: Results of a Research Conducted for the Institute of Human Relations*. Yale University: Greenwood Press.

Jacobsen, S. and Frye, K. (1991) Effect of maternal social support on attachment: Experimental evidence. *Child Development*, *62*, 572–82.

Johnson, D. L. (1989) The Houston Parent-Child Development Centre Project: Disseminating a viable program for enhancing at-risk families. *Prevention in Human Serices*, *7*, 89–108.

(1990) The Houston Parent-Child Development Centre Project: Dissemination of a viable program for enhancing at-risk families. In R. P. Lorion (ed.), *Protecting the Children: Strategies for Optimizing Emotional and Behavioral Development* (pp. 89–108). London: Haworth Press.

Lally, J. R., Mangione, P. L. and Honig, A. S. (1988) The Syracuse University Family Development Research Program: Long-range impact of an early intervention with low-income children and their families. In D. R. Powell (ed.), *Advances in Applied Developmental Psychology: Parent Education as Early Childhood Intervention: Emerging Directions in Theory, Research, and Practice* (pp. 79–104, vol. 3). Norwood, NJ: Ablex Publishing.

Larson, C. P. (1980) Efficacy of prenatal and post partum home visits on child health and development. *Pediatrics*, *66*, 191–7.

Lazar, I., Darlington, R., Murray, H., Royce, J. and Snipper, A. (1982) Lasting effects of early education :A report from the Consortium for Longitudinal Studies. *Monographs of the Society for Research in Child Development*, *47*(2–3, Serial No. 195).

Loeber, R. and Stouthamer-Loeber, M. (1986) Family factors as correlates and predictors of juvenile conduct problems and delinquency. In M. Tonry and N. Morris (eds.), *Crime and Justice: An Annual Review of Research* (vol. 7, pp. 29–149). University of Chicago Press.

Madden, J. O'Hara, J. and Levenstein, P. (1984) Home again: Effects of the mother-child home program on mother and child. *Child Development, 55,* 636–47.

McCall, R. B. and Carriger, M. S. (1993) A meta-analysis of infant habituation and recognition memory performance as predictors of later IQ. *Child Development, 64,* 57–79.

McCarton, C. M., Brooks-Gunn, J., Wallace, I. F., Bauer, C. R., Bennett, F. C., Bernbaum, J. C., Broyles, R. S., Casey, P. H., McCormick, M. C., Scott, D. T., Tyson, J., Tonascia, J. and Meinert, C. L. (1997) Results at age 8 years of early intervention for low-birth-weight premature infants. The Infant Health and Development Program. *Journal of the American Medical Association, 277,* 126–32.

McCord, J. (1993) Conduct disorder and antisocial behavior: Some thoughts about processes. *Development and Psychopathology, 5,* 321–9.

McNeil, C. B., Eyberg, S., Eisenstadt, T. H., Newcomb, K. and Funderburk, B. (1991) Parent-child interaction therapy with behavior problem children: Generalization of treatment effects to the school setting. *Journal of Clinical Child Psychology, 20,* 140–51.

Moffitt, T. E. (1990) Juvenile delinquency and attention deficit disorder: Developmental trajectories from age 3 to age 15. *Child Development, 61,* 893–910.

(1993) Adolescence-limited and life-course persistent antisocial behavior: A developmental taxonomy. *Psychological Review, 100,* 674–701.

Mrazek, P. J. and Haggerty, R. J. (eds.) (1994) *Reducing Risks for Mental Disorders: Frontiers for Preventive Intervention Research.* Washington: National Academy Press.

Olds, D. L., Henderson, C. R., Chamberlin, R. and Talelbaum, R. (1986) Preventing child abuse and neglect: A randomized trial of nurse home visitation. *Pediatrics, 78,* 65–78.

Olds, D. L., Henderson, C. R., Cole, R., Eckenrode, J., Kitzman, H., Luckey, D., Pettitt, L., Sidora, K., Morris, P. and Powers, J. (1998) Long-term effects of nurse home visitation on children's criminal and antisocial behavior. *Journal of the American Medical Association, 280,* 1238–44.

Olds, D. L., Eckenrode, J. and Henderson, C. R., et al. (1997) Long-term effects of home visitation on maternal life course and child abuse and neglect: fifteen-year follow-up of a randomized trial. *Journal of the American Medical Association, 278,* 637–43.

Olds, D. L. and Kitzman, H. (1990) Can home visitation improve the health of women and children at environmental risk? *Pediatrics, 86,* 108–16.

Packard, T., Robinson, E. A. and Grove, D. (1983) The effect of training procedures on the maintenance of parental relationship building skills. *Journal of Clinical Child Psychology, 12,* 181–6.

Patterson, G. R., Reid, J. B., Jones, R. R. and Conger, R. R. (1975) *A Social Learning Approach to Family Intervention: Families with Aggressive Children.* (vol. 1) Eugene, OR: Castalia.

Piaget, J. (1960) *The Psychology of Intelligence.* Totowa, NJ: Littlefield, Adams.

Pollitt, E., Gorman, K. S., Engle, P. L., Martorell, R. and Rivera, J. (1993) Early supplementary feeding and cognition. *Monographs of the Society for Research in Child Development, 58* (7, Serial No. 235).

Ross, G. S. (1984) Home intervention for premature infants of low-income families. *American Journal of Orthopsychiatry*, *54*, 263–70.

Schweinhart, L. L., Barnes, H. V. and Weikart, D. P. (1993) *Significant Benefits: The High/Scope Perry School Study Through Age 27*. Ypsilanti, MI: High/Scope Press.

Schweinhart, L. L. and Weikart, D. P. (1997) *Lasting Differences: The High/Scope Preschool Curriculum Comparison Study Through Age 23*. Ypsilanti, MI: High/Scope Press.

Séguin, J. R., Pihl, R. O., Harden, P. W., Tremblay, R. E. and Boulerice, B. (1995) Cognitive and neuropsychological characteristics of physically aggressive boys. *Journal of Abnormal Psychology*, *104*, 614–24.

Seitz, V., Rosenbaum, L. K. and Apfel, H. (1985) Effects of family support intervention: A ten-year follow-up. *Child Development*, *56*, 376–91.

Shure, M. B. and Spivack, G. (1979) Interpersonal problem solving thinking and adjustment in the mother-child dyad. In M. W. Kent and J. E. Rolf (eds.), *Primary Prevention of psychopathology* (vol. III, pp. 201–19). Hanover, NH: University Press of New England.

Stattin, H. and Klackenberg-Larsson, I. (1993) Early language and intelligence development and their relationship to future criminal behavior. *Journal of Abnormal Psychology*, *102*, 369–78.

Stone, W. L., Bendell, R. D. and Field, T. M. (1988) The impact of socioeconomic status on teenage mothers and children who received early intervention. *Journal of Applied Developmental Psychology*, *9*, 391–408.

Strain, P. S., Steele, P., Ellis, T. and Timm, M. A. (1982). Long-term effects of oppositional child treatment with mothers as therapists and therapist trainers. *Journal of Applied Behavior Analysis*, *15*, 163–9.

Strayhorn, J. M. and Weidman, C. (1991) Follow-up one year after parent-child interaction training: Effects on behavior of preschool children. *Journal of the American Academy of Child and Adolescent Psychiatry*, *30*, 138–43.

Tremblay, R. E., Boulerice, B., Harden, P. W., McDuff, P., Pérusse, D., Pihl, R. O. and Zoccolillo, M. (1996) Do children in Canada become more aggressive as they approach adolescence? In Human Resources Development Canada & Statistics Canada (eds.), *Growing Up in Canada: National Longitudinal Survey of Children and Youth* (pp. 127–37). Ottawa: Statistics Canada.

Tremblay, R. E., Mâsse, L. C., Pagani, L. and Vitaro, F. (1996) From childhood physical aggression to adolescent maladjustment: The Montréal Prevention Experiment. In R. D. Peters and R. J. McMahon (eds.), *Preventing Childhood Disorders, Substance Abuse and Delinquency* (pp. 268–98). Thousand Oaks, CA: Sage.

Vitaro, F., Tremblay, R. E., Gagnon, C. and Boivin, M. (1992) Peer rejection from kindergarten to grade 2: Outcomes, correlates, and prediction. *Merrill-Palmer Quarterly*, *38*, 382–400.

Wasik, B. H., Ramey, C. T., Bryant, D. M. and Sparling, J. J. (1990) A longitudinal study of two early intervention strategies: Project CARE. *Child Development*, *61*, 1682–96.

Webster-Stratton, C. (1990) Long-term follow-up of families with young conduct problem children: From preschool to grade school. *Journal of Clinical Child Psychology*, *19*, 144–9.

Webster-Stratton, C., Kolpacoff, M. and Hollinsworth, T. (1988) Self-administered videotape therapy for families with conduct-problem children: Comparison with two cost-effective treatments and a control group. *Journal of Consulting and Clinical Psychology*, *56*, 558–66.

White, J. L., Moffitt, T. E., Earls, F., Robins, L. and Silva, P. A. (1990) How early can we tell? Predictors of childhood conduct disorder and adolescent delinquency. *Criminology*, *28*, 507–33.

Yoshikawa, H. (1994) Prevention as cumulative protection: Effects of early family support and education on chronic delinquency and its risks. *Psychological Bulletin*, *115*, 28–54.

7 Prevention through family and parenting programmes

David Utting

No single topic has received more attention in recent political debate about antisocial behaviour and its prevention than the role of families. Public opinion in Britain, as measured in surveys, has scarcely faltered in asserting the prime responsibility of parents for offspring who turn to crime, drugs, and other misconduct. More recently, policy makers have focused their attention on the part that parenting may play in making it more or less likely that children will exhibit problem behaviour in adolescence and as adults (Straw and Anderson, 1996; Home Office, 1997). In the words of a government consultation paper:

> *Children who grow up in stable, successful families are less likely to become involved in offending. Helping parents to exercise effective care and supervision of their young children can achieve long-term benefits by reducing the risk that children will become involved in delinquent or offending behaviour.* (Home Office, 1998)

While in tune with popular sentiment, this interest is also an acknowledgement of research messages that not only identify parental style as part of the problem, but also view parenting education and family support as among the more promising potential contributors to a solution.

- Longitudinal and other studies in Britain, the United States, and other western nations have consistently placed family and parenting variables among the most significant risk factors for childhood and adolescent antisocial behaviour as the precursor of adult antisocial behaviour (Robins, 1978; Farrington, 1995a).
- Parent training therapy, functional family therapy, and multisystemic therapy have achieved positive outcomes in treating antisocial children and adolescents (Kazdin, 1997; Mrazek and Haggerty, 1994; Howell *et al.*, 1995; Henggeler *et al.* 1995).
- A wide range of family-based interventions has shown promise in enhancing protective factors and reducing the known risks of antisocial behaviour in childhood and beyond (Mrazek and Haggerty, 1994; Farrington, 1996).

- There are indications from the United States that parent training therapy and multisystemic therapy are cost-effective ways of preventing criminal offences, especially when compared with increasing levels of incarceration (Greenwood *et al.*, 1996; Henggeler *et al.*, 1992; Walsh, this volume).

Risk and protective factors

Risk and protective factors for antisocial behaviour are reviewed elsewhere in this book, as is the crucial question of continuities between conduct problems in childhood, adolescence, and adulthood. Among the most significant family-based risk factors are:

poor parental supervision;
harsh or erratic discipline;
parental conflict;
separation from a biological parent;
having an antisocial parent.

Investigation of the mechanisms involved suggest that while children's behaviour is directly influenced by the supervision and discipline provided by parents, the adverse influence of parental conflict or separation from a biological parent can be indirect and flow from the stress it places on the parent-child relationship (Utting *et al.*, 1993; Junger-Tas, 1994; Yoshikawa, 1994). In the context of lone-parenthood and family reordering especially, there is evidence that the quality of parenting is of more consequence than the quantity of parents (McCord, 1982; Junger-Tas, 1994). The link between childhood antisocial behaviour and socio-economic risk factors, notably low family income, can also be mediated through parenting (Larzelere and Patterson, 1990). A number of important protective factors known to help children and young people to negotiate exposure to risk also relate to families. They include sharing warm, supportive, affectionate relationships with parents and other family members and having parents who set clear standards for pro-social behaviour (Brewer *et al.*, 1995, Pettit *et al.*, 1997).

Evidence that persistence into late adolescence and adulthood in chronic offending, violence, and other chronic forms of antisocial behaviour problems is associated with an early age of onset underlines the potential preventive benefits of tackling family risk factors (Wilson and Herrnstein, 1985; Loeber and LeBlanc, 1990; Sampson and Laub, 1993; Farrington, 1995b). In the Cambridge Study in Delinquent Development, boys who experienced extremes of poor parenting, harsh discipline, and low family income were over-represented among the most persistent offenders (Osborn and West, 1978). Patterson and Yoerger (1997) using longitudinal data on boys from the Oregon Youth Survey, have since argued that the paths leading to early-onset delinquency (by age 14) are not only different, but also more predictable than juvenile offending in general. Disrupted parenting practices are accorded a key role in their models for both early and late-onset arrest, but the former is seen as following a coercive family process that produces high levels of antisocial behaviour in early childhood and sets the scene for training in delinquent activities by deviant peers.

Patterson, whose clinical and cohort studies have included measures of parent-child interactions directly observed in the home, suspects that the most severe behaviour problems start early with the combination of temperamentally difficult toddlers and inexperienced parents. He describes a downward spiral for early onset, where parents' ineffective monitoring and discipline inadvertently reinforce their preschool child's discovery that whining, temper tantrums, hitting, and other aggressive behaviours are successful strategies for gaining attention. At primary school age, the child's repertoire of (for them) functional behaviours expands to include lying, stealing, cheating, and truancy. Because they lack pro-social skills, such children also tend to be rejected by most other children and to gravitate into the company of similarly antisocial peers (Patterson, 1994). By contrast, parents in the homes of late-onset delinquents are more likely to reward pro-social behaviour (although not so much as parents of non-delinquent boys). An increase in 'covert' antisocial behaviour (for example, truancy or substance use) follows from a much later disruption in parental monitoring, discipline, family problem solving, and reinforcement during early adolescence (Patterson and Yoerger, 1997).

Using data from a sub-sample of at-risk families in the longitudinal Oregon Youth Study, Patterson and colleagues reject the late-onset pathway to offending as an alternative predictor of chronic adult offending and other long-term negative outcomes. By contrast, their analysis endorses the predictive strength of a three-point, early-onset trajectory towards adult antisocial behaviour, as defined by measures of childhood antisocial behaviour at ages 9 and 10, age of first arrest up to the age of 14, and frequency of arrests before the age of 18. A majority (52 per cent) of adult recidivist offenders in the Oregon Study had travelled through all three points in the sequence. The influence during the second and third stages of deviant peers and contextual factors, such as social disadvantage and family restructuring is emphasised. However, the authors also conclude that children who experience the highest levels of disrupted parenting are the most likely to progress through the entire trajectory (Patterson *et al.*, 1998).

Prevention experiments

Researchers who have considered causal processes do not always place Patterson's degree of emphasis on the primacy of disrupted parenting among risk factors (for example, Hawkins and Catalano, 1992; Moffitt, 1993). There is, however, general agreement on the value of improving knowledge about the developmental phases leading to childhood, adolescent and adult antisocial behaviour, and about the ages at which causal factors and processes are most susceptible to preventive interventions (Farrington, 1995a). Clinical experiments conducted at the Oregon Social Learning Center have been among the first to provide evidence that children's antisocial conduct can be controlled by teaching family management strategies to their parents. The therapy evolved there is based on encouraging parents to monitor their children's behaviour, enabling them to provide attention, praise and other rewards for positive behaviour. Negative behaviour is, where possible, denied attention or else dealt with by time out and other non-violent but contingent sanctions. Patterson and colleagues (1982) reported that two-thirds of an experimental group of out-of-control children aged 3 to 12 were brought within the normal range of behaviour for children of their age, compared with one third of a control group who received other treatments. Behavioural improvements persisted for at least a year. Oregon researchers subsequently showed that the magnitude of improvement in parental discipline practices among clinical groups was linked (negatively) to out-of-home placements and the number of times that young people were arrested two years after treatment (Patterson and Forgatch, 1995).

Elsewhere in the United States, results from a non-experimental study showed that improvements in the independently-assessed behaviour of non-compliant and aggressive children following parent training therapy were sustained for as long as 10 and 14 years after treatment (Forehand and Long, 1988; Long *et al.*, 1994). Webster-Stratton and colleagues have, meanwhile, demonstrated the effectiveness, in different contexts, of a group-based parenting programme, now known as The Incredible Years, in which video vignettes of parent-child interactions provide the models for discussion. Experiments with parents of 3- to 8-year-olds referred for conduct problems found significant improvements in parenting behaviour and reductions in child non-compliance being maintained at one year follow-up. Her studies also suggest that a ten to twelve-week course using videotape modelling can achieve results comparable to many more hours of more expensive, individual therapy (Webster-Stratton, 1984; Webster-Stratton *et al.*, 1988 and 1989). The programme has subsequently been expanded to address a wider range of parental problems including anger management, depression, and marital distress, with evidence of increased effectiveness (Webster-Stratton, 1997a).

A version for use as a community-based method for preventing conduct problems in young children has also been positively evaluated. A study involving low-income mothers and children taking part in the Head Start preschool programme found that those assigned to the parenting intervention used less harsh discipline and were more positive, reinforcing and competent in their parenting than a control group. Their children were observed to show fewer conduct problems, less non-compliance and more positive affect, with most improvements being maintained a year later (Webster-Stratton, 1998a). The study is of interest not least because of its success in achieving and maintaining the involvement of socially-disadvantaged families (a group who have classically been regarded as both high risk and hard to reach) (Kazdin, 1997; Webster-Stratton, 1998b).

In Oregon, working with the families of older children, Dishion and colleagues (1992) carried out a four-way random assignment of antisocial 11 to 14-year-olds and their parents to:

- a parent focus group attending weekly sessions targetting family management practices and communication skills;
- a teen focus group attending sessions targetting the young peoples' self-regulation, pro-social and problem solving skills;
- a combined parent and teen focus group where both the young people and their parents were targetted;
- a self-directed change group in which parents and young people only received the intervention newsletters and videos.

A quasi-experimental comparison group of families who received no intervention was also studied. Measurements immediately following a twelve-week intervention showed that parent training therapy had produced modest but significant reductions in young peoples' antisocial behaviour and that the degree of improvement in parenting behaviour was significantly correlated with the level of improvement in their children's behaviour rated by teachers. A one-year follow-up found that coercive interactions between mothers and teenagers involved in either the parent or teen focus groups had reduced significantly. This compared with no change or deterioration among families where there had been no active intervention. However, it was also found that participation in the teen focus groups was linked to negative outcomes. Young people's attitudes were more favourable to substance use, self-reported smoking was higher and there were more teacher-rated behaviour problems than for those in other groups. The researchers concluded that interventions involving parents, extended family and other concerned adults are promising prevention strategies. In an important, cautionary rider, they added that interventions where the by-product is an abnormal level of contact between high-risk youths should probably be avoided (Dishion and Andrews, 1995).

Reviewing current treatments of antisocial behaviour, including those for children and adolescents with diagnosed conduct disorders, Kazdin (1987, 1997) has identified functional family therapy (FFT) as a further promising technique in the family domain. It relates child and adolescent conduct problems to beliefs and behaviour within the family system, including interactions between other family members as well as interactions with the child giving immediate cause for concern. Treatment aims to improve communication and behaviour management within the family, involving all family members in reinforcing and rewarding positive behaviour. Supporting evidence for this approach comes from experiments in Utah a quarter of a century ago when adolescents referred to the juvenile court for minor offences were assigned to FFT, psychodynamic family therapy, client-centred family groups, or no treatment. The (time-limited) FFT group achieved significant changes in family communication and a reduction in court appearances by the focus teenager up to eighteen months after treatment. The proportion of younger siblings from the FFT families who had been referred to court two and a half years later was 20 per cent – less than half the proportion in other groups (Alexander and Parsons, 1973, 1980; Klein *et al.*, 1977).

Multisystemic Therapy (MST) is even more broadly-based, combining strategies drawn from family and behavioural therapy with external family support services. School, work, peers, and the wider community are viewed among the interconnected systems that influence child and family behaviour. A 15-year-old boy's persistent stealing and aggression could be variously related to living in a neighbourhood without constructive youth activities, association with a delinquent peer group, low achievement and disruptive behaviour in school, and having a socially-isolated mother who lacks basic parenting skills and is clinically depressed (Henggeler *et al.*, 1995). Treatment aims to eliminate the barriers to effective parenting for example, by treating depression, providing parent skills training and developing a support network of neighbours and friends. Once there is progress, it seeks to introduce strategies to improve parental monitoring and discipline and to draw young people away from delinquent peers. A randomised trial in which 176 juvenile offenders were allocated to MST or individual therapy showed that the former was more effective in improving family correlates of antisocial behaviour. Four years later, recorded rates of violent and other crime among the young MST participants were substantially lower than for the comparison group (Borduin *et al.*, 1995).

A community-based trial randomly assigned eighty-four serious juvenile offenders to MST or to standard processing by the criminal justice system, including curfew orders and school attendance orders. Attrition among the sample a year after referral was higher than desired. Even so, the researchers demonstrated that young offenders who had taken part in the MST intervention had fewer arrests and reported lower levels of offending. They had also spent an average of ten fewer weeks in custody. It was argued that multisystemic therapy, lasting an average three months, offered a cost-effective alternative to conventional psychotherapy as well as to youth custody (Henggeler *et al.*, 1992). MST has demonstrated additional promise in reducing re-offending among substance abusing or dependent delinquents (Schoenwald *et al.*, 1996) and adolescent sex offenders (Borduin *et al.*, 1990).

Combined interventions

Further evidence concerning the effectiveness of family-focused interventions comes from programmes in which they have been combined with other approaches to target a wider range of risk factors. Many of the best-evaluated prevention programmes focused on pregnancy, infancy, and preschool children have been combined interventions. Even the frequently-cited High/Scope Perry Preschool Programme should be viewed, in part, as a family support initiative given its home visiting component, enlisting support from parents to reinforce their children's learning. As Schweinhart and colleagues (1993) observed, the benefits of a good preschool programme on children's later years probably depend on having immediate effects on families as well as children.

Tremblay and colleagues in Montreal (1992, 1995), tested a bimodal intervention during which aggressive and hyperactive boys from low socio-economic status families were trained, between the ages of 7 and 9, in anger management and other interpersonal and social skills. Their parents were taught family management skills along lines developed by the Oregon Social Learning Centre. An experimental group was compared with an observation group (attention but no intervention) and a control group. A three-year follow-up at age 12 found that teacher-rated fighting had decreased significantly among the experimental group compared with the other two and that they were less likely to have been held back in school, show serious school adjustment problems or have started delinquent behaviour. Follow up at age 15 found that the treated boys themselves reported less delinquent behaviour in annual assessments and that teachers had rated them less disruptive than members of the control group up to the age of 13. However, there was no significant difference in the proportion of boys who had been arrested and referred to the juvenile court. The authors concluded that the impact of the intervention might have been improved if the boys and their parents had received booster sessions between the ages of 12 and 15.

Their findings chime with Kazdin's suggestion (1987) that severe antisocial behaviour leading to diagnosable conduct disorder can usefully be viewed as a chronic condition that can best be contained by regular treatment. But they also indicate that 'more of the same' is unlikely to be an appropriate prescription and that different interventions become appropriate at different developmental stages. Training programmes for parents of preschoolers will not be of equal relevance to the parents of troublesome adolescents. Moreover, the evidence concerning the growing influence of peers suggests that interventions targetted on parents will, in isolation, yield diminishing returns as children grow older.

The Seattle Social Development Project and the North Carolina Abecedarian Experiment are examples of an attempt to sustain primary prevention programmes by adjusting the ingredients in a multicomponent intervention to children's changing circumstances and developmental needs. The Seattle experiment combined cognitive-based social competence training for elementary school pupils, parenting skills training for their parents and training in proactive classroom management for their teachers. Over six years of elementary schooling, the focus of the parenting and social skills elements switched from encouragement of pro-social behaviour to skills for reducing family conflict and helping children to recognise and resist negative peer pressure (Hawkins *et al.*, 1991, 1992; O'Donnell *et al.*, 1995). A six-year follow-up study, when the participating students were aged 18, found a number of enduring, positive effects. In particular, those who had received the full intervention were significantly less likely than a control group to report violent criminal behaviour, heavy drinking, multiple sexual partners, pregnancy or causing pregnancy. No equivalent effects were observed for cannabis use or heavy smoking. However, the intervention group were distinguished by greater commitment and attachment to school, less school misbehaviour and better self-reported academic achievement. Another finding with practice implications was that a 'late intervention' programme provided for children in grades 5 and 6 and their families did not produce the significant, long-term effects achieved by the full intervention. The Seattle researchers are committed to following their sample beyond school, exploring the potential influence of their early intervention on adult outcomes such as employment, crime, problem drug use, relationship stability, and parenting (Hawkins *et al.*, 1999). In the Abecedarian experiment, a high quality day-care programme for infants from socially disadvantaged families (including parenting support) gave way to more structured nursery education and was succeeded by a programme to stimulate parental interest and involvement in their education at elementary school. Children who took part in both the preschool and elementary school programmes showed the greatest educational gains at age 8 (Ramey and Campbell, 1991).

Given that some researchers emphasise the individual child's cognitive processes in explaining the development of antisocial behaviour (Moffitt, 1993), while others give pride of place to disordered parenting (Patterson and Yoerger, 1997), it is worth noting the intervention described by Kazdin and colleagues (1992). Children aged 7 to 13 referred for severe antisocial behaviour were randomly assigned to three groups: one where they received training in problem solving skills; one where parents received training in parent management skills; and one where both children and parents were treated. A year after the conclusion of treatment, it was the *combined* treatment group that had the highest proportion of children whose behaviour had been brought within the normal range. In a similar way, an experiment by Webster-Stratton and Hammond (1997) tested the individual and combined effects of parent training and a child-training programme (known as 'Dinosaur School') which used videotape modelling and fantasy play to develop interpersonal skills. A one-year follow up of participating families of children with early-onset conduct problems found that the combined intervention produced the most significant improvements in child behaviour.

Research findings from other combined interventions are no less instructive for the fact that their results have been more equivocal. These include programmes devised for 5-year-old children in Worcester, Massachusetts, who had been screened from the general preschool population for symptoms of behavioural and emotional problems, including ADHD. A four-way research design allocated families to: a parent training course over ten weeks followed by monthly booster sessions, an intensive full-day special classroom programme for children, a combination of parent training and the classroom programme, and an untreated control group. Preliminary results from the evaluation found significant reductions in attention problems, and aggressive and externalising behaviour at school after nine months among children who took part in the classroom programme. However, a lack of improvement in various measures of behaviour at home was attributed to implementation setbacks, in the shape of low attendance rates for the parenting groups (Barkley *et al.*, 2000). On an even larger scale, the Fast Track Programme has operated in four sites within the United States with almost 900 children found to be within the top 10 per cent for antisocial behaviour when screened at kindergarten. Children were allocated either to a no intervention control group, or to a 'unified model of prevention' that was explicitly designed to build on the work of Tremblay and colleagues in Montreal (see above). In their first year of elementary schooling this experimental package included parent training, home visiting, parent and child 'sharing' groups, a cognitive and social skills curriculum at school, classroom management training for teachers, one-to-one tutoring for literacy, additional social skills groups for the high-risk children, and a peer friendship programme that paired high-risk and low-risk children. Initial results from the first year of a ten-year intervention identify moderate positive effects on some measures of the experimental children's behaviour and social, emotional and academic skills compared with the control group. Parents in the experimental group also demonstrated more warmth and positive involvement, more appropriate and consistent discipline, and more positive involvement with school. The researchers argue that even an accumulation of modest effects over the lifetime of the programme should make it less likely that children will face serious and chronic adjustment problems as adults (Conduct Problems Prevention Research Group, 1999). However, critics insist that replicability and cost-effectiveness are already major considerations that can only become more pressing if Fast Track does not demonstrate greater changes for the (huge) resources invested in the programme (Scott, in press).

The United Kingdom

Comparable parenting and family support programmes to those so far described exist in the UK, but have not, in many cases, been rigorously evaluated (Utting *et al.*, 1993; Smith and Pugh, 1996; Barlow, 1999). The Child Development Programme, based on home visiting for parents of infants during the first year, is an exception. The programme uses visiting to explore a range of health, development, and diet issues, with the emphasis on enabling parents to build on their own skills and strengths. One version of the programme intensified the number of visits to families with new babies by professional health visitors, who are trained nurses. A randomised controlled trial found that children aged three and under showed greater concentration and more positive social behaviour than those in a control group whose families received conventional postnatal care. Children's diets and and general health were also better in the experimental group (Barker, 1988). Prevention of child abuse was not an aim of the programme; however, a subsequent study of 30,000 programme children in twenty-four health authority areas found substantially lower rates of physical abuse and registration on Child Protection Registers compared with the normal levels for those areas (Barker, 1994a, 1994b). A second version of the programme that used experienced and purpose-trained parents as 'community mothers' was evaluated using a randomised controlled trial in the Irish Republic. This found that programme children were more likely to have received all their immunisations and been breastfed during the first six months of life than control group children. They were also more likely to have been read to regularly by their parents and less likely to have mothers who reported feeling tired and miserable (Johnson *et al.*, 1993).

Health visitors play a central part in another promising programme devised for hyperactive children under 10 and their parents. The training materials and curriculum for the eight-week course are designed to improve parents' understanding of Attention Deficit Hyperactivity Disorder (ADHD) while suggesting behaviour modification strategies that can help them to gain their child's attention, remain calm, avoid confrontation and deal effectively with tantrums (Weeks *et al.*, 1999). An evaluation study divided a sample of eighty hyperactive children at random between a behaviour modification group who were visited at home by two purpose-trained health visitors, a group where parents were offered counselling and support and a waiting-list control group. This found that improvements in children's behaviour reported by parents of children in the behaviour modification group were far greater at the end of the course than those for the other two groups (Sonuga-Barke *et al.*, 2001).

A number of parent training approaches that were devised and evaluated in the United States have been replicated in the UK. The Child and Adolescent Psychiatry Unit at the Maudsley Hospital has, for some years, been applying the 'Parent-Child Game' training therapy first tested at the University of Georgia (Forehand and McMahon, 1981). An unpublished pilot study showed improvements in children's behaviour being maintained up to two years after treatment (Whild, 1991). More recently, the unit has been responsible for an experimental trial of a group-based parent training programme, administered over thirteen to sixteen weeks, which used the video-modelling vignettes devised by Webster-Stratton and colleagues. The study of 141 children aged 3 to 8, all displaying high levels of aggression and other behaviour problems, found that up to seven months after entering the trial there was a large reduction in antisocial behaviour among those whose parents took part in the parenting programme. This compared with no change among children in a waiting-list control group. Parents in the experimental group gave their children much more praise for positive behaviour and were more effective in gaining compliance from their children when needed. Other promising features of the study were that the therapists were existing staff in Child and

Adolescent Mental Health Services who were trained to administer the programme and that the attendance levels among socially-disadvantaged parents were good. The costs of the programme per child were similar to those for six sessions of 'normal' individual therapy (Scott *et al.*, 2001).

Webster-Stratton's method has been adopted by practitioners in Liverpool, in Sheffield and in Oxford where it is applied by the Family Nurturing Network with parents and preschool children referred with behaviour problems – including parents of children at risk of physical abuse. When working with parents of older children, aged 4 to 12, the Network also uses materials derived from a nurturing programme devised in the United States by Bavolek (1984). A small controlled study of the UK programme, carried out for a doctoral thesis, found significant improvements in parenting attitudes, emotional well-being and relationships with children (Braffington, 1996).

Parenting Positively, a programme designed for use by health and other professionals working with families of preschool and primary school age children, emphasises strategies for reinforcing positive behaviour and reducing negative behaviour by ignoring it or using effective, non-violent sanctions. A small-scale randomised controlled trial showed improvements in programme children's behaviour being maintained up to eighteen months after their parents took part. The improvements in comparison with the control group applied whether parents had received support and advice during home visits or by telephone (Sutton, 1992). A second small-scale trial, which replicated the telephone training method, showed similar, positive results (Sutton, 1995).

The national voluntary organisation Parentline Plus offers its 'Parenting Matters' (formerly 'Parent-Link') courses to parents irrespective of their circumstances and the age of their children. A non-experimental evaluation comparing fifty-nine participating parents with forty-two similar non-participants found significant improvements in family relationships and well-being over the twelve to thirteen-week duration of the course. Children's behaviour, assessed on the Achenbach checklist, also improved, including a number who had displayed severe problems at the start of the course that moved within the normal range (Davis and Hester, 1996). A degree of promise has also been demonstrated by the Mellow Parenting programme running in Scotland and South London. Referrals include parents of children registered at risk of abuse and of children with persistent behaviour problems. A distinctive feature of the group-based approach is the use (with consent) of parent-child interaction videoed in the home as a tool for discussion and evaluation. A Department of Health funded research evaluation is in progress.

However, a pilot study in Alloa found improvements in before-and-after observations of parenting behaviour and a higher rate of de-registration by social services compared with other 'at risk' children in the area (Puckering *et al.*, 1994).

The preventive focus of many of the more intensive parenting and family support initiatives in Britain is on reducing child abuse and the need for children to be taken into care (Utting, 1996). There is no UK equivalent of the Tacoma Homebuilders and other family preservation schemes in the United States where multi-disciplinary professional teams provide time-limited intensive care in homes where serious consideration is being given to placing a child in care (Nelson, 1991; Feldman, 1991). However, the Radford Shared Care Project in Nottingham uses purpose-trained carers to provide up to four hours a week support in the homes of children at risk of being accommodated by the local authority. Part of their role is to model parenting skills, including stimulating play, and consistent, non-violent discipline. This programme met its target of keeping more than 80 per cent of children safe from abuse and living at home (Fleming and Ward, 1992). Another project, in East Leeds, provided time-limited support for families of at risk children with paraprofessional family aides. Of twenty-seven high risk families who received help during a three-year study period, thirteen families remained intact a year after the intervention (Leeds Family Service Unit, 1987).

The preventive emphasis of the 1989 Children Act has stimulated interest in a tier of less intensive family support services whose aim is, in plain terms, to intervene before problems develop into crises (Hardiker *et al.*, 1991). Family centres run by local authorities or in partnership with voluntary organisations provide a local focus for services that range from parenting groups and group or family therapy to money advice, toy libraries and crèche facilities. Studies suggest that open-access centres, available to anyone living in their catchment area, can attract disadvantaged users without the stigma associated with centres serving only clients of the social services (Holman, 1988; Gibbons *et al.*, 1990, Smith, 1995). Home Start, a national voluntary organisation with more than 280 autonomous, local schemes, is another example of a neighbourhood support service for families under stress, including parents with mental and physical health problems as well as children with behavioural difficulties. It uses trained volunteers, who are also experienced parents, as regular visitors providing friendship and practical support in homes that include at least one preschool child. Studies using before and after measurements have shown that parents generally welcome Home Start and consider that they and their children have benefitted and that the visiting complements the work of the statutory services (Gibbons and Thorpe, 1989;

Frost *et al.*, 1996). An evaluation comparing outcomes for children and families participating in Home Start with non-participants is in progress.

This chapter began by noting the attention that British politicians have given to issues of parental responsibility and the potential role that parenting education might play in a strategy for preventing adolescent and adult antisocial behaviour. The turn of the century (and millennium) has seen their interest translate into policy and practice that, in turn, carry implications for research. The 'On Track' initiative, established by the Home Office as part of its overall Crime Reduction Strategy, is paying for parenting and other early intervention programmes to be implemented and evaluated in a number of social disadvantaged areas with high levels of crime. As with projects supported by a much larger Family Fund, it has been placed under the aegis of the cross-departmental Children and Young People's Unit where the focus is on preventive work with children aged 5 to 13 and their families.

Arguably the most interesting UK development in terms of learning about long-term prevention, is the commitment to a longitudinal, national evaluation of Sure Start. This government programme, which is partly modelled on the Head Start programme in the United States, was established in 1998 to offer comprehensive support services to parents-to-be and families of children under 4 in disadvantaged neighbourhoods. By 2004 it is expected to be active in 500 local areas whose population includes a third of young children living in government-defined poverty. The core services that each local programme is expected to provide include 'outreach and home visiting', 'befriending and social support' and 'parenting information and support' (Sure Start, 2001). The longitudinal design agreed for the national evaluation, raises the tantalising possibility that, in time, it could be possible to link the support that children received through parenting programmes and other family services with outcomes during adulthood.

Conclusions

There is a persuasive case, on the available evidence, for regarding parent-child relationships as the mediator between a range of risk factors and children's social (or antisocial) behaviour. Conflict between parents and low family income are important examples of risk factors. Parenting can also be viewed as the primary force capable of compounding or ameliorating the risks associated with temperament, including the hyperactivity / impulsivity / attention-deficit syndrome. Well-structured parenting education programmes based on behavioural principles are, as Scott (in press) observes, the most widely-researched psychological intervention in child and adolescent mental health and also the single most effective approach to treating child conduct disorders. This does not imply, however, that primary prevention – whether of adult behaviour problems or the more widespread conduct problems during adolescence – can be boiled down to a need for parent training therapy ('parenting education' in the UK context) and nothing else. On the contrary, the message from studies on both sides of the Atlantic is that efforts to work with parents are less likely to succeed if implemented in isolation from action to tackle the factors that have placed their parenting under stress. As Rutter (1974) told a Department of Health conference in London more than a quarter of a century ago: 'Good parenting requires certain permitting circumstances'.

A more specific, but related issue is the need to improve current understanding of how to gain the co-operation and involvement of those socially disadvantaged, isolated, and vulnerable parents whose children will, often, be most at risk. Attrition, even among those prepared to be recruited, has been an issue for clinical studies and programmes in the US and UK alike. There is more to be learned, but experience does suggest that parents are most likely to engage with programmes that avoid stigmatising them and that actively seek to recognise and develop their existing strengths (Pugh *et al.*, 1994). The transatlantic practice messages of Webster-Stratton's The Incredible Years programme in reaching out to vulnerable parents and tailoring delivery to the needs of intended participants deserve wide dissemination (Webster-Stratton, 1997b, 1998b; Scott *et al.*, 2001). While the long-term goal may be to reduce the risks associated with chronic antisocial behaviour, it should also be remembered that a more immediate aim must always be that of enabling parents to build happier, healthier relationships with their children.

Parenting and family support, on the available evidence, cannot be provided in isolation from economic and other pressures that make it harder for parents to be warm, loving, attentive, consistent, and fair in dealings with their children. Nor can its effectiveness be maintained if other influences on children – notably at school and from peers are ignored. If continuity between childhood, adolescent, and adult conduct problems is characterised as a chronic condition (Kazdin, 1987), then it is one in which combination therapies are increasingly indicated. The components of those treatments will need to vary according to changing circumstances and developmental needs. There is reason to believe that interventions helping parents to exert a positive influence over their children's lives, should form part of the prescription for healthy, pro-social adulthood as well as childhood and adolescence. The ingredients will, however, need to be different and the strength of their relative contribution to each preventive package is unlikely to remain the same.

There is still much to be learned about the combinations that work best and about the 'dosage' of preventive programmes needed to produce significant reductions in risk across a community or population as a whole. The possibility that an apparently effective combination may include treatments whose contribution is at best neutral cannot be ignored (Kazdin, 1997). Nor can the dangers that some ingredients will prove positively counter-productive (Dishion and Andrews, 1995– see above). Even when the content of a multiple intervention appears to draw meticulously on existing knowledge concerning 'what works' there is always the risk that failures of implementation will produce the unexpected in the shape of poor results. The most promising of parenting curricula will have little influence on children's lives if too few parents can be persuaded to attend.

In Britain, one glaring gap in existing provision has been the lack of parenting programmes that are purpose-designed and proven to meet the needs of adolescents and their parents; let alone the families of persistent young offenders or those with diagnosed conduct disorders. The need for such programmes has become pressing, given provision in the Crime and Disorder Act 1998 for a parenting order, under which parents of juvenile offenders are required to attend counselling or guidance sessions. Among the parenting education and family support work that *does* exist in Britain, some of the most promising approaches are currently those that replicate programmes that have been rigorously evaluated in America. Others have demonstrated promise of a type that can only be confirmed through replication. For future interventions and for the many existing initiatives that lack a research warrant, an increasing commitment is needed to the three 'e's: 'evaluation, evaluation and evaluation'.

REFERENCES

Aldgate, J., Tunstill, J. and McBeath, G. (1994) *Implementing Section 17 of the Children Act – the first 18 months*. A Report for the Department of Health. University of Leicester.

Alexander, J. F. and Parsons, B. V. (1973) Short-term behavioral intervention with delinquent families: Impact on family process and recidivism. *Journal of Abnormal Psychology*, *18*, 219–25.

(1980) *Functional Family Therapy*. Monterey, California: Brooks/Cole Publishing.

Audit Commission (1994) *Seen But Not Heard. Co-ordinating Community Child Health and Social Services for Children in Need*. London: HMSO.

Barker, W. (1988) *The Child Development Programme: an Evaluation of Process and Outcomes*. Bristol: Early Childhood Development Centre.

(1994a) *Child Protection: the Impact of the Child Development Programme*. Bristol: Early Childhood Development Centre.

(1994b) *Empowering Parents: The Child Development Programme*. Bristol: Early Childhood Development Centre.

Barkley, R. A., Shelton, T. L., Crosswait, C., Moorehouse, M., Fletcher, K., Barrett, S., Jenkins, L. and Metevia, L. (2000) Multi-method psycho-educational intervention for preschool children with disruptive behaviour: preliminary results at post-treatment. *Journal of Child Psychology and Psychiatry*. *41*, 319–32.

Barlow, J. (1999) What works in parent education programmes. In E. Lloyd (ed.) *Parenting Matters: What Works in Parenting Education?* Barkingside, Essex: Barnardos.

Bavolek, J. S. (1984) An innovated program for reducing abusive parent-child interactions. *Child Resource World Review*, no. 2, 6–24.

Borduin, C. M., Henggeler, S. W., Blaske, D. M. and Stein, R. (1990) Multisystemic treatment of adolescent sexual offenders. *International Journal of Offender Therapy and Comparative Criminology*, *34*, 105–13.

Borduin, C. M., Mann, B. J., Cone, L. T., Henggeler, S. W., Fucci, B. R., Blaske, D. M. and Williams, R. A. (1995) Multisystemic treatment of serious juvenile offenders: Long-term prevention of criminality and violence. *Journal of Consulting and Clinical Psychology*, *63*, 560–78.

Braffington, S. (1996) *Evaluation of a Nurturing Programme*. Unpublished doctoral thesis (summary available from Family Nurturing Network, Oxford).

Brewer, D. D., Hawkins, J. D., Catalano, R. F. and Neckerman, H. J. (1995) Preventing serious, violent and chronic juvenile offending. A review of evaluations of selected strategies in childhood, adolescence and the community. In J. C. Howell, B. Krisberg, J. D. Hawkins and J. J. Wilson (eds.) *A Sourcebook Serious, Violent and Chronic Juvenile Offenders*. London: Sage.

Conduct Problems Prevention Group (1999) Initial impact of the fast track prevention trial for conduct problems: I. The high-risk sample. *Journal of Consulting and Clinical Psychology*, *67*, 631–47.

Davis, H. and Hester, P. (1996) *An Independent Evaluation of Parent-Link: A Parenting Education Programme*. London: Parent Network.

Dishion, T. J. and Andrews, D. W. (1995) Preventing escalation in problem behaviors with high-risk young adolescents: immediate and 1-year outcomes. *Journal of Consulting and Clinical Psychology*, *63*, 538–48.

Dishion, T. J., Patterson, G. R. and Kavanagh, K. A. (1992) An experimental test of the coercion model: linking theory, measurement and intervention. In J. McCord and R. Tremblay (eds.) *Preventing Antisocial Behavior* (pp. 253–82). New York: Guilford.

Farrington, D. P. (1995a) The challenge of teenage antisocial behavior. In M. Rutter (ed.) *Psychosocial Disturbances in Young People: Challenges for Prevention* (pp. 83–130). Cambridge University Press.

(1995b) The development of offending and antisocial behaviour from childhood. Key findings from the Cambridge Study in Delinquent Development. *Journal of Child Psychology and Psychiatry* *36*, 929–64.

(1996) *Understanding and Preventing Youth Crime*. York: Joseph Rowntree Foundation/York Publishing Services.

Feldman, L. H. (1991) Evaluating the impact of intensive family preservation services in New Jersey. In K. Wells and D. E. Biegel (eds.) *Family Preservation Services*. Newbury Park, CA: Sage.

Fleming, J. and Ward, D. (1992) '*For the Children to be Alright their Mothers Need to be Alright' An alternative to removing the child: The Radford Shared Care Project. An evaluation from the participants viewpoints*. Nottingham: Centre for Social Action, School of Social Studies, University of Nottingham.

Forehand, R. and Long, N. (1988) Outpatient treatment of the acting out child: procedures, long term follow-up data, and clinical problems. *Advances in Behaviour Research and Therapy*, *10*, 129–77.

Forehand, R. and McMahon, R. J. (1981) *Helping the Noncompliant Child: A Clinician's Guide to Parent Training*. NewYork: Guilford.

Frost, N., Johnson, L., Stein, M. and Wallis, L. (1996) *Negotiated Friendship – Home-Start and the Delivery of Family Support*. Leicester: Home-Start (UK).

Gibbons, J. and Thorpe, S. (1989) Can voluntary support projects help vulnerable families? The work of Home-Start. *British Journal of Social Work*, *19*, 189–202.

Gibbons, J. with Thorpe, S. and Wilkinson, P. (1990) *Family Support and Prevention*. London: National Institute for Social Work/HMSO.

Greenwood, P., Model, K. E., Rydell, C. P. and Chiesa, J. (1996) *Diverting Children from a Life of Crime. Measuring Costs and Benefits*. Santa Monica, CA: RAND.

Hardiker, P., Exton, K. and Barker, M. (1991) *Policies and Practices in Preventive Child Care*. Avebury: Gower.

Hawkins, J. D. and Catalano, R. F. (1992) *Communities that Care*. San Francisco, CA: Jossey-Bass.

Hawkins, J. D., Catalano, R. F., Kosterman, R., Abbott, R. and Hill, K. G. (1999) Preventing adolescent health-risk behaviors by strengthening protection during childhood. *Archives of Pediatrics & Adolescent Medicine*, *153*, 226–34.

Hawkins, J. D., Catalano, R. F., Morrison, D. M., O'Donnell, J., Abbott, R. D. and Day, L. E. (1992) The Seattle Development Project: Effects of the first four years on protective factors and problem behaviors. In J. McCord and R. Tremblay (eds.) *The Prevention of Antisocial Behavior in Children* (pp. 139–61). New York: Guilford.

Hawkins, J. D., Von Cleve, E. and Catalano, R. F. (1991) Reducing early childhood aggression: results of a primary prevention program. *Journal of the American Academy of Child and Adolescent Psychiatry*, *30*, 208–17.

Henggeler, S. W., Melton, G. B. and Smith, L. A. (1992) Family preservation using multisystemic therapy: an effective alternative to incarcerating serious juvenile offenders. *Journal of Consulting & Clinical Psychology*, *60*, 953–61.

Henggeler, S. W., Schoenwald, S. K. and Pickrel, S. G. (1995) Multisystemic therapy: bridging the gap between university and community-based treatment. *Journal of Consulting & Clinical Psychology*, *63*, 709–17.

Holman, B. (1988) *Putting Families First: Prevention and Child Care*. London: Children's Society/Macmillan.

Home Office (1997) *Preventing Children Offending. A Consultation Document.* London: HMSO.

(1998) *Supporting Families. A Consultation Document.* London: The Stationery Office.

Howell, J. C., Krisberg, B., Hawkins, J. D. and Wilson, J. J. (1995) *A Sourcebook: Serious, Violent & Chronic Juvenile Offenders.* London: Sage.

Johnson, Z., Howell, F. and Molloy, B. (1993) Community mothers programme: randomised controlled trial of non-professional intervention in parenting. *British Medical Journal, 306,* 1449–52.

Junger-Tas, J. (1994) Changes in the family and their impact on delinquency. *European Journal on Criminal Policy and Research, 1,* 27–51.

Kazdin, A. E. (1987) Treatment of antisocial behavior in children: current status and future directions. *Psychological Bulletin, 102,* 187–203.

(1997) Practitioner review: psychosocial treatments for conduct disorder in children. *Journal of Child Psychology and Psychiatry, 38,* 161–78.

Kazdin, A. E., Siegel, T. C. and Bass, D. (1992) Cognitive problem-solving skills training and parent management training in the treatment of antisocial behaviour in children. *Journal of Consulting and Clinical Psychology, 60,* 733–47.

Klein, N. C., Alexander, J. F. and Parsons, B. V. (1977) Impact of family systems intervention on recidivism and sibling delinquency: A model of Primary Prevention and program evaluation. *Journal of Consulting and Clinical Psychology, 45,* 469–74.

Larzelere, R. E. and Patterson, G. R. (1990) Parental management: mediator of the effect of socio-economic status on early delinquency. *Criminology, 28,* 301–24.

Leeds Family Services Unit (1987) *Can Family Aides Prevent Admission to Care? An Evaluation.*

Loeber, R. and LeBlanc, M. (1990) Toward a developmental criminology. In M. Tonry and N. Morris (eds.) *Crime and Justice, vol. 12* (pp. 375–473). University of Chicago Press.

Long, P., Forehand, R., Wierson, M. and Morgan, A. (1994) Does parent training with young noncompliant children have long-term effects? *Behaviour Research and Therapy,* 32, 101–7.

McCord, J. (1982) A longitudinal view of the relationship between paternal absence and crime. In J. Gunn and D.P. Farrington (eds.) *Abnormal Offenders, Delinquency and the Criminal Justice System* (pp. 113–28). Chichester: Wiley.

Moffitt, T. E. (1993) Adolescence-limited and life-course persistent antisocial behavior. A developmental taxonomy. *Psychological Review, 100,* 674–701.

Mrazek, P. J. and Haggerty, R. J. (eds.) (1994) *Reducing Risks for Mental Disorders. Frontiers for Preventive Intervention Research.* Washington DC: Institute of Medicine/National Academy Press.

Nelson, D. W. (1991) The public policy implications of family preservation. In K. Wells and D. E. Biegel (eds.) *Family Preservation Services.* Newbury Park, CA: Sage.

O'Donnell, J., Hawkins, J. D., Catalano, R. F., Abbott, R. D. and Day, L. E. (1995) Preventing school failure, drug use and delinquency among low-income children: long-term intervention in elementary schools. *American Journal of Orthopsychiatry*, *65*, 87–100.

Osborn, S. and West, D. J. (1978) Effectiveness of various predictors of criminal careers. *Journal of Adolescence*, *1*, 101–17.

Patterson, G. R. (1994) Some alternatives to seven myths about treating families of antisocial children. In C. Henricson (ed.) *Crime and the Family Conference Report. Proceedings of an International Conference Held in London 3 February 1994*. London: Family Policy Studies Centre.

Patterson, G. R., Chamberlain, P. and Reid, J. B. (1982) A comparative evaluation of a parent-training program. *Behavior Therapy*, *13*, 638–50.

Patterson, G. R. and Forgatch, M. S. (1995) Predicting future clinical adjustment from treatment outcomes and process variables. *Psychological Assessment*, *7*, 275–85.

Patterson, G. R. and Yoerger, K. (1997) A developmental model for late-onset delinquency. In D. W. Osgood (ed.) *Motivation and Delinquency: Nebraska Symposium on Motivation* (vol. 44, pp. 119–77). University of Nebraska Press.

Patterson, G. R., Forgatch, M. S., Yoerger, K. L. and Stoolmiller, M. (1998) Variables that initiate and maintain an early-onset trajectory for juvenile offending. *Development and Psychopathology*, *10*, 531–47.

Pettit, G. S., Bates, J. E. and Dodge, K. A. (1997) Supportive parenting, ecological context, and children's adjustment: A seven-year longitudinal study. *Child Development*, *68*, 908–23.

Puckering, C., Rogers, J., Mills, M., Cox, A. D. and Mattson-Graff, M. (1994) Mellow mothering: process and evaluation of group intervention for distressed families. *Child Abuse Review*, *3*, 299–310.

Pugh, G., DeAth, E. and Smith, C. (1994) *Confident Parents, Confident Children. Policy and Practice in Parent Education and Support*. London: National Children's Bureau.

Ramey, C. T. and Campbell, F. A. (1991) Poverty, early childhood education, and academic competence: The Abecedarian Experiment. In A. C. Huston (ed.) *Children in Poverty* (pp. 190–221) Cambridge University Press.

Reid, J. B., Eddy, M., Bank, L. and Fetrow, R. (1994) *A Universal Prevention Strategy for Conduct Disorder: Some Preliminary Findings*. Paper presented at Society for Research in Child and Adolescent Psychopathology Conference, London.

Robins, L. N. (1978) Sturdy childhood predictors of adult antisocial behaviour: replications from longitudinal studies. *Psychological Medicine*, *8*, 611–22.

Rutter, M. (1974) Dimensions of parenthood: some myths and some suggestions. In *The Family in Society: Dimensions of Parenthood*. London: Department of Health and Social Security/HMSO.

Sampson, R. J. and Laub, J. H. (1993) *Crime in the Making: Pathways and Turning Points Through Life*. Cambridge, MA: Harvard University Press.

Schoenwald, S. K., Ward, D. M., Henggeler, S. W., Pickrel, S. G. and Patel, H. (1996) MST treatment of substance abusing or dependent adolescent offenders: Cost of reducing incarceration, inpatient and residential placement. *Journal of Child and Family Studies*, *4*, 431–44.

Schweinhart, L. J., Barnes, H. V. and Weikart, D. P. (1993) *Significant Benefits. The High/Scope Perry Preschool Study Through Age 27*. Ypsilanti, MI: High/Scope Educational Foundation.

Scott, S. (in press) 'Parent training programmes'. In M. Rutter and E. Taylor (eds.) *Child and Adolescent Psychiatry*. Oxford: Blackwell Science.

Scott, S., Spender, Q., Doolan, M., Jacobs, B. and Aspland, H. (2001) Multicentre controlled trial of parenting groups for childhood antisocial behaviour in clinical practice. *British Medical Journal, 323*, 194–6.

Smith, C. and Pugh, G. (1996) *Learning to Be a Parent: A Survey of Group-Based Parenting Programmes*. London: Family Policy Studies Centre/Joseph Rowntree Foundation.

Smith, T. (1995) *Family Centres and Bringing up Children*. London: Department of Health / The Children's Society.

Sonuga-Barke, E., Daly, D., Thompson, M., Laver-Bradbury, C. and Weeks, A. (2001) Parent-based therapy for preschool attention deficit/hyperactivity disorder: a randomised controlled trial. *Journal of the American Academy of Child and Adolescent Psychiatry, 40* (4), 1–7.

Straw, J. and Anderson, J. (1996) *Parenting. A Discussion Paper*. London: The Labour Party.

Sure Start Unit (2001) *Sure Start. A Guide for Fourth-wave Programmes*. London: DfEE Publications.

Sutton, C. (1992) Training parents to manage difficult children: a comparison of methods. *Behavioural Psychotherapy, 20*, 115–39.

(1995) Parent training by telephone: a partial replication. *Behavioural and Cognitive Psychotherapy, 23*, 1–24.

Tremblay, R. E., Pagani-Kurtz, L., Mâsse, L. C., Vitaro, F. and Pihl, R. O. (1995) A bimodal preventive intervention for disruptive kindergarten boys: Its impact through mid-adolescence. *Journal of Consulting and Clinical Psychology, 63*, 560–68.

Tremblay, R. E., Vitaro, F., Bertrand, L., LeBlanc, M., Beauchesne, H., Boileau, H. and David, L. (1992) Parent and child training to prevent early onset of delinquency: The Montreal longitudinal-experimental study. In J. McCord and R.E. Tremblay (eds.) *Preventing Antisocial Behavior* (pp. 117–38). New York: Guilford.

Utting, D. (1996) *Reducing Criminality Among Young People: A Sample of Relevant Programmes in the United Kingdom*. London: Home Office (Research Study 161).

Utting, D., Bright, J. and Henricson, C. (1993) *Crime and the Family. Improving Child-rearing, Preventing Delinquency*. London: Family Policy Studies Centre.

Webster-Stratton, C. (1984) Randomized trial of two-parent-training programs for families with conduct-disordered children. *Journal of Consulting and Clinical Psychology, 52*, 666–78.

(1997a) Early intervention for families of preschool children with conduct problems. In M. J. Guralnick (ed.) *The Effectiveness of Early Intervention: Second Generation Research* (pp. 429–53). Baltimore: Paul H. Brookes.

(1997b) From parent training to community building. *Families in Society: The Journal of Contemporary Human Services*, March/April, 156–70.

(1998a) Preventing conduct problems in Head Start children: strengthening parenting competencies. *Journal of Consulting and Clinical Psychology, 66*, 715–30.

(1998b) Parent training with low-income families: promoting parental engagement through a collaborative approach. In J. R. Lutzker (ed.) *Handbook of Child Abuse Research and Treatment*. New York/London: Plenum Press.

Webster-Stratton, C. and Hammond, M. (1997) Treating children with early-onset conduct problems: a comparison of child and parent training interventions. *Journal of Consulting and Clinical Psychology, 65*, 93–109.

Webster-Stratton, C., Hollinsworth, T. and Kolpacoff, M. (1989) The long-term effectiveness and clinical significance of three cost-effective training programs for families with conduct-problem children. *Journal of Consulting and Clinical Psychology, 57*, 550–3.

Webster-Stratton, C., Kolpacoff, M. and Hollinsworth, T. (1988) Self-administered videotape therapy for families with conduct-problem children: comparison with two cost-effective treatments and a control group. *Journal of Consulting and Clinical Psychology, 56*, 558–66.

Weeks, A., Laver-Bradbury, C. and Thompson, M. (1999) *Information manual for professionals working with families with a child who has Attention Deficit Hyperactivity Disorder (ADHD) 2–9 years*. Southampton Community Health Services Trust.

Whild, P. (1991) *The Parent/child Game: A Pilot Study of Treatment Outcome and Consumer Satisfaction*. Unpublished, cited in Gent, M. (1992) Parenting assessment: The parent/child game. *Nursing Standard, 6*, (29), 31–5.

Wilson, J. Q. and Herrnstein, R. J. (1985) *Crime and Human Nature*. New York: Simon & Schuster.

Yoshikawa, H. (1994) Prevention as cumulative protection: effects of early family support and education on chronic delinquency and its risks. *Psychological Bulletin, 115*, 28–54.

8 Prevention in the school years

J. David Hawkins and Todd I. Herrenkohl

Prevention in the school years

The trajectories toward productive citizen and antisocial adult diverge dramatically from ages six to 17. During the school years, children who will grow up to be productive citizens make great strides, beginning by learning to read, compute, control impulses, and by making friends with other children. For many, this development culminates in a love of learning, high personal and moral expectations, and pleasure found in action that strengthens the bonds of human solidarity.

During this same period, those who will become antisocial adults have difficulty learning to recognise and control their impulses without intensive instruction and reinforcement. They often have difficulty academically beginning in the late elementary grades. They lose their commitment to getting an education as a way to personal success. They are likely to use tobacco, alcohol, and other drugs earlier than their age contemporaries. They are more likely to engage in early sexual activity and are more likely to fail to complete examinations or graduate from high school.

Three major risk factors for adult antisocial behaviour become observable in individuals in school settings during the elementary grades. These include persistent physically aggressive behaviour (including fighting and bullying) (Farrington, 1991; Mrazek and Haggerty, 1994; Kellam, Rebok, Ialongo and Mayer, 1994; Robins, 1978), academic failure, and low commitment to school (Dryfoos, 1990; Maguin and Loeber, 1996). All three of these risks can be affected by intentional alterations in schools and schooling. As students move from elementary to secondary schools, social influences and behavioural norms of school peers also contribute to risk for antisocial behaviour. Several effective curricula for students ages 11–16 focus on confronting and reducing these later appearing risks. This chapter reviews evidence about the effectiveness and promise of school-based interventions for children ages six to 17 in preventing antisocial behaviour in adulthood, noting gaps in knowledge where further research is needed, and briefly discussing interventions outside of schools focused on school aged youths.

We begin this review by exploring practices shown effective in promoting school success that show promise for reducing antisocial behaviour in adulthood. Some programmes reviewed here have not focused on adult antisocial behaviour as an outcome. Rather, they show effects on predictors of adult antisocial behaviour including earlier forms of antisocial behaviour, such as childhood aggression, adolescent delinquency, and substance use (Loeber, 1990; Loeber and Hay, 1996). Interventions implemented in the school years that prevent or reduce aggression, delinquency, and substance use should, in turn, reduce adult antisocial behaviour. However, these hypothesised long term effects must still be tested through extended follow up studies of these interventions.

Classroom organisation, management, and instructional strategies

Maguin and Loeber (1996) found that academic performance makes an independent contribution to delinquency even after the effects of socioeconomic status and prior conduct problems are controlled. This evidence linking poor academic performance to later antisocial behaviour is important in considering preventive interventions. Promoting academic success among students and assuring that they develop a commitment to schooling should be viewed as a fundamental goal for schools and an important objective for the prevention of antisocial behaviour.

Many changes in schools intended to promote academic success and reduce antisocial behaviour have been advocated. Those that have shown positive effects include improved classroom organisation, management, and instructional strategies (Kellam and Rebok, 1992; Slavin, Karweit and Wasik, 1994); behaviour management strategies; strategies for school organisation or reorganisation; and a range of curricula that teach skills deemed important to promote good citizenship in the classroom, on the playground, and beyond (Hawkins, Farrington and Catalano, 1998).

Brewer, Hawkins, Catalano and Neckerman (1995) summarised a variety of effective classroom practices shown to be effective in improving students' academic achievement in subject areas like reading and maths, and in diminishing co-occurring problem behaviours. These include substantial reductions in class size in the primary grades, ability grouping for instruction, proactive classroom management, co-operative learning, computer-assisted instruction, tutoring, and interactive teaching.

Good teaching begins with good classroom management. There is a long history of strong experimental evidence demonstrating that behavioural techniques for classroom management, such as the establishment of clear rules and directions, the use of contingent approval and reinforcement, and the involvement of students in specifying contingencies and reinforcing themselves can reduce antisocial behaviour in schools (O'Leary and O'Leary, 1977). Intervention studies have shown that the use of proactive classroom management practices produces less student misbehaviour in class and more on-task academically focused behaviour (Evertson, 1985; Evertson, Emmer, Sanford and Clements, 1983; Kellam and Rebok, 1992).

Kellam and Rebok's (1992) and Kellam, Rebok, Ialongo and Mayer's (1994) evaluations of the Good Behaviour Game, an intervention for elementary students, illustrate the promise of classroom management approaches using behavioural reinforcement. In an experimental study in the Baltimore schools, urban first grade students were assigned to heterogeneous groups that included equal numbers of aggressive and disruptive children. While the Good Behaviour Game was in progress, teachers monitored the behaviour of students in each group. Misbehaviour of any student in a group resulted in a check mark being placed on the chalkboard for that group. At the end of the session, groups with fewer than five check marks received a reward. In the beginning of the programme, game sessions were announced and tangible rewards (such as stickers) were given immediately following the session. As the programme became more familiar to students, sessions started unannounced and less tangible rewards were given (such as extended recess). In addition, the time between the session and the granting of rewards was extended. The programme lasted for two years, in grades one and two.

After one year, experimental students were rated as less aggressive and shy by teachers and peers when compared with control students. Positive effects of the programme were most evident among students rated highly aggressive at baseline. Positive effects of the intervention on aggressive behaviour were maintained through grade six for boys with the highest baseline ratings of aggression at first grade entry.

Methods of classroom management and instruction have been combined in comprehensive interventions during the elementary grades designed to improve academic achievement and reduce or prevent antisocial behaviour. Two examples are described here: Success for All (Madden, Slavin, Karweit, Dolan and Wasik, 1993; Slavin *et al.*, 1996), and the Seattle Social Development Project (Hawkins, Catalano, Kosterman, Abbott and Hill, 1999; Hawkins *et al.*, 1992).

The Success for All programme, focused on children in the primary grades, seeks to prevent learning and behaviour problems by providing children with effective classroom instruction and by engaging parents in support of their children's success. When learning problems do appear, corrective interventions are employed immediately to help students who are having difficulty keeping up academically before problems become significant. Students are assessed every eight weeks to determine whether they are making adequate progress in reading. Regrouping allows all children to continually progress at a challenging rate.

Success for All combines continuous progress instruction, one-to-one tutoring, and co-operative learning with other instructional methods in classrooms. A family support staff provides family assistance when there are indications that students are not working up to their full potential because of problems at home. For example, assistance is provided when students are not getting adequate sleep or nutrition, need glasses, are not attending school regularly, or are exhibiting serious behaviour problems. Referrals to appropriate community service agencies are facilitated, when appropriate.

Evaluation of the Success for All programme in Baltimore found that participating students scored significantly higher than control students on a variety of academic achievement tests (Slavin, Maden, Karweit, Liverman and Dolan, 1990). Subsequently, Success for All has been implemented in over eighty-five schools in thirty-seven school districts in nineteen states (Slavin *et al.*, 1994). Success for All schools are matched with control schools on indicators of poverty (percentage of students qualifying for free lunch), historical achievement level, and ethnicity of the student body, as well as other factors (Slavin *et al.*, 1996). Students in intervention and control schools are matched using achievement test scores. Slavin *et al.* (1996) reported significant positive effects in evaluations of Success for All programmes in nineteen schools representing nine cities and eight states: Baltimore, Maryland; Philadelphia, Pennsylvania; Charleston, South Carolina; Memphis, Tennessee; Fort Wayne, Indiana; Montgomery, Alabama; Caldwell, Idaho; Modesto, California; and Riverside, California. Success for All was successful in increasing reading achievement among bilingual and ESL students, as well as students eligible for special education (Slavin *et al.*, 1996).

The Seattle Social Development Project (SSDP) is a multi-component intervention designed specifically to prevent antisocial behaviour by promoting academic achievement and commitment to schooling during the elementary grades. The intervention employed a package of classroom management and instruction methods in the elementary grades, including proactive classroom management, interactive teaching, and co-operative learning, as well as an interpersonal skills training curriculum.

The programme also included a parenting component, which provided behaviour management and academic support skills training for adult caregivers (Hawkins *et al.*, 1992; O'Donnell, Hawkins, Catalano, Abbott and Day, 1995).

Two intervention conditions were created. The first consisted of students who received the intervention package from grade 1 through grade 6 (full intervention). The second consisted of students who received the intervention package in grades 5 and 6 only (late intervention). A control condition received no special intervention.

Each year, teachers of intervention classrooms received five days of inservice training to strengthen their knowledge of proactive classroom management, interactive teaching, and co-operative learning methods. Control teachers did not participate in this training. However, both intervention and control teachers were observed to document their use of targeted teaching strategies. Greater use of these strategies was observed in intervention classrooms (Abbott *et al.* 1998).

First grade teachers of the full intervention condition also received instruction in the use of a cognitive and social skills training curriculum, Interpersonal Cognitive Problem Solving (Shure and Spivak, 1980, 1988), which teaches problem-solving skills to children so as to avoid violent or aggressive interactions with peers. This curriculum was used to develop children's skills for involvement in co-operative learning groups and other social activities without antisocial behaviours.

In addition, when students in both intervention conditions were in grade 6, they received four hours of training from project staff in skills to recognise and resist social influences to engage in problem behaviour and to generate and suggest positive alternatives in order to stay out of trouble while keeping friends.

The parenting component of the intervention offered classes to parents on a voluntary basis. Parents of children in the full intervention condition were trained in the use of child behaviour management strategies when their children were in the first and second grades through a seven session curriculum, 'Catch 'Em Being Good' (Hawkins, Catalano, Jones and Fine, 1987). In the spring of second grade and again in the third grade, parents of children in the full intervention were offered a four session curriculum, 'How to Help Your Child Succeed in School', to strengthen their skills for supporting their children's academic development. When their children were in grades 5 and 6, parents of children in both the full and late intervention conditions were offered a five session curriculum, 'Preparing for the Drug (Free) Years', (Hawkins *et al.*, 1988) to strengthen their skills to reduce their children's risks for drug use. Professional multi-ethnic project staff provided parenting workshops in collaboration with participating schools and parent councils. Parents of 43 per cent of children in the full intervention condition attended parenting classes.

The intervention was tested with a multi-ethnic urban sample. Positive effects of the full intervention on behaviour were shown early. By the end of grade 2, boys in the full intervention classrooms were rated by teachers as significantly less aggressive than boys in control classrooms (Hawkins, Von Cleve and Catalano, 1991). By the beginning of grade 5, full intervention students were significantly less likely to have initiated delinquent behaviour and alcohol use than controls (Hawkins *et al.*, 1992). By the end of grade 6, full intervention boys from low income families had significantly greater academic achievement, better teacher-rated behaviour, and lower rates of delinquency initiation than did control boys from low income families (O'Donnell *et al.*, 1995). A six-year follow up at age 18 found significantly higher achievement and lower rates of life-time violent delinquent behaviour among children exposed to the full intervention compared with controls (Hawkins *et al.*, 1999). The late intervention in grades 5 and 6 only did not significantly reduce later violent behaviour. These results indicate that interventions that promote academic achievement and commitment to schooling throughout the elementary grades can reduce antisocial behaviour through to age 18.

An important emerging task for schools is to integrate the teaching of academic and social/emotional skills in the classroom (Battistich, Schaps, Watson and Solomon, 1996). Recent longitudinal studies indicate that this can be done successfully in the elementary grades and that this approach can affect achievement and behaviour. Two initiatives currently underway, the Child Development Project, and Raising Healthy Children, seek to accomplish this goal.

The Child Development Project uses co-operative learning and proactive classroom management methods that seek to foster responsibility, establish prosocial norms, and strengthen conflict resolution skills; classroom and school-wide community building activities; activities for students and parents to do at home together; and a literature-based language arts programme that emphasises students' critical thinking about relevant social and ethical issues.

A longitudinal, multi-site quasi-experimental test of the Child Development Project involving twelve intervention and twelve comparison elementary schools across the US found significant increases in student attachment and commitment to school and academic achievement, increases in conflict resolution skills and prosocial behaviours, and significant reductions in alcohol use among fifth and sixth grade students (Battistich *et al.*, 1996; Battistich, Solomon, Watson and Schaps, 1997). Longer term effects on antisocial behaviour remain to be studied.

Raising Healthy Children (RHC) is a third generation intervention study growing out of the Seattle Social Development Project. The RHC project is designed to promote academic, social, and emotional growth through the use of integrated classroom curricula. The experimental project is following a panel of children from first and second grade in five experimental and five control schools. The intervention strategies include (a) proactive classroom management; (b) use of effective instructional techniques including motivational methods and active student involvement in learning activities; (c) interpersonal and social problem solving skills training; (d) co-operative learning methods; and (e) reading strategies that balance guided reading, shared reading, reading aloud and reading alone.

Because children often come to the classroom unprepared for the social environment in which learning occurs, and because co-operative learning techniques require interpersonal and problem solving skills for successful implementation, a major focus of the teacher training intervention is on helping teachers to integrate social and emotional skills training into the classroom environment and curricula. During teaching workshops, teachers identify how to integrate interpersonal and problem solving skills training into the daily schedule.

After one and a half years of exposure to these integrated teaching practices, academic and behaviour outcomes of the experimental students have been examined, using hierarchical linear modeling of growth and level differences between experimental and control groups. Students in the experimental condition have shown significantly higher commitment to school and academic achievement. Social competency and appropriate social interaction have both shown growth and level changes favouring intervention students. Measures of antisocial behaviour also have shown significant level and growth differences favouring the intervention group. Experimental students have shown lower levels and decreasing growth rates of antisocial behaviour while control students showed increasing growth rates of antisocial behaviour (Catalano, Harachi, Haggerty and Abbott, 1996).

The results of the Child Development Project and RHC indicate that the teaching of academic and social and emotional skills can be integrated in the classroom with positive effects on academic achievement, skill development, and student behaviour. The best practice is likely to integrate the teaching of both academic and emotional skills in planned developmental sequences that complement each other.

School behaviour management strategies

Behavioural interventions have been used in schools to improve behaviour and achievement. These interventions seek directly to reduce persistent aggressive behaviours in school that predict antisocial behaviour in adulthood. A wide range of behaviour management programmes has been evaluated. Structured playground activities, behavioural monitoring and reinforcement, and special educational placements for disruptive, disturbed, and learning disabled students in the secondary grades have been found effective over varying periods of time.

Some of these interventions are applied universally. For example, structured playground activities before school and during recess provide stimulating supervised play opportunities for children with appropriate and consistent punishment for aggressive behaviour (such as a two-minute time out sitting on a bench). These changes in the playground environment have produced large decreases in disruptive and aggressive playground incidents in schools (Murphy, Hutchinson & Bailey, 1983).

Behavioural reinforcement methods have also been used effectively to reduce aggressive behaviours among school-aged children. These methods have typically been applied selectively to children with behaviour or attendance problems (Barber and Kagey, 1977; Brooks, 1975). Bry (1982) evaluated a two-year behavioural intervention focused on low achieving, disruptive seventh grade students with low bonding to family. The intervention included a weekly report card completed for each participating student, which rated student's behaviour in the classroom. Students met in small groups where the report cards were distributed and discussed. Positive reports elicited praise and approval from staff. Negative reports elicited discussions of how to gain more positive opinions from teachers. Points, that could be used toward an extra field trip, were given or taken away on the basis of the weekly reports. Parents were kept informed of students' progress through phone calls, letters, and home visits.

At the end of the programme, participants had significantly better grades and attendance and fewer behavioural problems at school than matched and randomly assigned controls (Bry and George, 1979, 1980). Five years after the programme, participants were 66 per cent less likely than control youths to have a delinquency record in juvenile court (Bry, 1982). Programme effects were uniform across race and socioeconomic groups.

Special education and alternative schools

Special education placements have sometimes been used for students with early aggressive or disruptive behaviours. Safer (1982) reviewed evaluations of special education placements, including self-contained classes and resource rooms for disruptive, emotionally disturbed, learning disabled, and/or educable developmentally disabled elementary students. He found that they have no effects or only marginally positive effects on academic achievement and school behaviour during the programme and no lasting effects after students leave the programme. These results, coupled with the positive results reported for Success for All and the Seattle Social Development Project, indicate that during the elementary grades, the greatest positive effects on achievement, school commitment and behaviour are likely to be achieved by altering teaching and management strategies in regular classrooms and allocating intensive resources such as tutoring to ensure skill development for all, rather than by segregating aggressive and disruptive students in self-contained classes or resource rooms.

However, there is some evidence that special educational placements and alternative schools for disruptive secondary school students can have benefits. Safer (1990) evaluated a programme in which seventh to ninth grade students who had been suspended from school multiple times were placed into a special classroom section for the school day. At each grade level, a regular teacher and an aide led classes of ten to fifteen youths in four major academic subjects during consecutive morning periods using small group and individualised instruction. The programme used a token economy for reinforcing good classroom behaviour. Points could be used to earn early release from school (at approximately 1:00 pm), gain access to play in an afternoon recreation room, study in an academic resource room, or buy items such as food or dance tickets. Other school reinforcers included daily, weekly, and monthly recognition of good behaviour in the form of certificates and cash awards. Grades also were partially based on attendance. Programme staff had regular meetings with youths' parents to develop home-based reinforcement contracts that specified the rewards that would be provided to youths for their good school reports. Students who broke more than one class rule during the same period were expelled from the class until they spent time in school detention or renegotiated their home reinforcement contracts. Virtually all programme students were returned to regular classes three months before the end of ninth grade.

The evaluation compared one experimental junior high school with two comparison junior high schools in suburban, working-class areas. In each of the three study schools, study youths who had been suspended multiple times were selected by the school's assistant principal. Prior to entry to the study, experimental and comparison youths were similar in terms of intelligence, socioeconomic status, family structure, academic achievement, and school misconduct. The programme operated for seven years.

During the programme, intervention youths had significantly fewer expulsions from the classroom, fewer school suspensions, and better grades than comparison youths. However, the groups did not differ significantly on standardised achievement tests or in school attendance during the programme. After the programme's completion, intervention youths were significantly more likely to enter high school and had significantly better attendance rates and school behaviour than comparisons. Comparison youths were significantly more likely to drop out of school than programme youths. However, similar proportions of both groups ultimately graduated from high school.

Gold and Mann (1984) studied three alternative schools in Detroit for disruptive and delinquent juveniles which aimed to increase their success experiences through individualised curricula and grades based on a student's own progress. They found that students assigned to the alternative schools showed less disruptive behaviour than controls assigned to regular high schools.

Special educational placements do not appear effective during the elementary grades for disruptive, disturbed, learning disabled, and educable developmentally disabled students. However, there is evidence that special education and alternative placements for disruptive secondary school students can help these adolescents remain in school and enhance their achievement, attendance, and behaviour.

Organisational change in schools

In communities lacking an effective partnership between schools, parents, and the larger community where significant numbers of students are falling behind academically, fundamental changes in how schools are organised and function may be needed. Several approaches have changed the organisation of schools to make them more effective.

Working originally with two inner-city elementary schools serving 90 per cent African-American students and characterised by poor attendance, low achievement, discipline problems, and high teacher turnover, James Comer (1988) developed a comprehensive elementary school intervention involving four components: (a) a social calendar that integrated arts and athletic programmes into school activities; (b) a parent programme in support of school academic and extracurricular activities which fostered interaction among parents, teachers, and other school staff; (c) a multi-disciplinary mental health team that provided consultation for school staff in managing student behaviour problems; and (d) a representative governance and management team composed of school administrators, teachers, support staff, and parents that oversaw the implementation of the other three components.

Follow up studies of students from the original intervention elementary schools and matched comparison subjects showed significantly better middle school grades, achievement test scores, and self-rated social competence when compared with matched comparison students (Cauce, Comer and Schwartz, 1987; Comer, 1988).

Gottfredson (1986) evaluated a comprehensive school organisation intervention for secondary schools in low-income, predominantly African-American areas in Charleston County, South Carolina. The six main components were: (a) teams composed of teachers, other school staff, students, parents, and community members that designed, planned, and implemented school improvement programmes, with the assistance of two full-time project staff; (b) curriculum and discipline policy review and revision, including student participation in the development of school and classroom rules, and ongoing in-service training for teachers in instructional and classroom management practices; (c) school-wide academic innovations, including study skills programmes and co-operative learning methods; (d) school-wide climate innovations, including expanded extracurricular activities, peer counselling, and a school pride campaign intended to improve the overall image of the school; (e) career-oriented innovations, including a job-seeking skills programme and a career exploration programme; and (f) special academic and counselling services for low-achieving and disruptive students.

Because of the design used, it is difficult to ascertain the effects of the school wide intervention. However, the low-achieving and disruptive students in intervention schools who received special academic and counselling services scored significantly higher on standardised tests of basic academic skills and were significantly less likely to report drug involvement or repeat a grade than were control group students. High school seniors who received these services were significantly more likely to graduate (76 per cent) than were seniors in the corresponding control group (42 per cent). However, there were no significant differences between students who received special services and their controls on delinquency, court contacts or other educational or behavioural measures.

Probably the clearest implication from the Gottfredson (1986) study is that, in the context of a whole school improvement effort, preventive interventions with students at risk of school failure can have beneficial effects on academic success and on high school completion, even when implemented late in development.

In 1987, Gottfredson reported results of a school-wide intervention that consisted of training teachers in classroom management techniques and co-operative learning as well as a parent volunteer programme, a community support and advocacy programme, and other components from the earlier Charleston project. The evaluation indicated that where the intervention was well implemented, students reported significantly more rewards from academic involvement and less delinquent behaviour than did comparison school students.

Robert Felner and his colleagues (1993) also have sought to reorganise schools as a preventive strategy. Felner's School Transitional Environment Project sought to ease the transition to high school among students from disadvantaged low-income backgrounds. Students entering ninth grade were assigned to units of 65 to 100 students in a 'school within a school'. Homeroom and academic classes were composed only of students in the same unit, and classrooms for the same unit were located in close proximity to each other. Academic subject teachers also served as homeroom teachers and as the main administrative and counselling link between the students, their parents, and the rest of the school. Homeroom teachers contacted parents before the school year and also held brief individual check-in sessions with each homeroom student once a month.

Experimental students had significantly more positive perceptions of school, teachers, and other school personnel than did comparison students at the end of the one year intervention. Intervention students also showed significantly smaller decreases in academic performance and attendance during the transition between junior and senior high school. Intervention students had a significantly lower school drop out rate (24 per cent) than did comparison students (43 per cent).

The Comer, Gottfredson and Felner studies provide evidence that elementary and secondary schools serving disadvantaged and minority populations can be reorganised to promote achievement and decrease antisocial behaviour.

School-based prevention curricula

Numerous school curricula have been developed to promote norms against aggressive, violent or other antisocial behaviour and to help students develop problem solving, anger management, and refusal skills to avoid antisocial behaviour. Some of these are social and emotional competence curricula that aim to counteract and prevent early antisocial behaviour by teaching basic interpersonal skills. Examples of effective interventions of this type for early elementary grades are the Interpersonal Cognitive Problem-Solving (ICPS) and the PATHS curricula. A second approach aims to prevent antisocial behaviour by teaching peer influence resistance and life skills to older children as illustrated by the life skills training curriculum developed by Gilbert Botvin and his colleagues and the Social-Competence Promotion Programme for Young Adolescents developed by Roger Weissberg and his colleagues.

The ICPS curriculum consists of daily lessons in the form of games for preschool and kindergarten children focused on generating alternative solutions to interpersonal problems, consequential thinking, and recognising and being sensitive to others' feelings. In tests with children from low-income urban families, the programme produced significant and durable effects on aggressive and socially inappropriate behaviours (Shure and Spivack, 1980, 1982, 1988).

The PATHS curriculum enhances instruction by integrating emotional, cognitive, and behavioural skill development in young children. An innovation of PATHS is its focus on recognising and regulating emotions for effective self-management. The PATHS curriculum was first shown to be effective in improving deaf children's social skills and reading achievement (Greenberg and Kusche, 1993). Subsequent tests of PATHS in randomised clinical trials with regular education and special needs classes have shown significant effects on teacher-rated and self-reported conduct problems, and teacher ratings of adaptive behaviour (Greenberg, 1996).

Currently, PATHS is being tested as the universal component of the Fast Track Program, a randomised clinical trial involving fifty elementary schools in four sites across the US. Use of the curriculum has been found to reduce teacher ratings of classroom conduct problems and reduce student sociometric ratings of peer aggression in grade 1 (Conduct Problems Prevention Research Group, 1999a, 1999b; Weissberg and Greenberg, 1997).

Botvin Baker, Dusenbury, Botvin and Diaz (1995) evaluated a multi-site classroom-based life skills training programme designed to teach middle school students life skills including skills for resisting social influences to use drugs. The programme was structured around fifteen class sessions in the seventh grade and booster sessions in the eight and ninth grades. Students were taught skills to enhance self-esteem, manage anxiety, improve interpersonal communication, and increase assertiveness. The programme also focused on skills to resist social pressure to use drugs, such as tobacco, alcohol, and marijuana, and students were given knowledge about the immediate consequences of drug use. Frequency of tobacco, alcohol, and marijuana use was assessed through student self-reports in the twelfth grade. Lower prevalences of monthly and weekly cigarette smoking, weekly cigarette smoking and alcohol use, and weekly tobacco and marijuana use were found among experimental students when compared with controls five years after the initial intervention.

The Social-Competence Promotion Programme for Young Adolescents taught cognitive, behavioural and affective skills to middle school students through classroom instruction (Weissberg, Barton and Shriver, 1997; Weissberg and Greenberg, 1997). The forty-five session programme sought to promote social competency (self-control, stress management, responsible decision making, social problem solving, and communication skills), improve communication between school personnel and students, and prevent antisocial behaviour such as aggression and substance use, as well as high-risk sexual behaviour (Weissberg *et al.*, 1997). Evaluations of the programme have shown positive effects on students' skills for problem-solving, managing stress, resolving conflicts constructively, and controlling impulses (Weissberg and Greenberg, 1997). Positive effects of the programme were also shown in reducing levels of student antisocial behaviour (Weissberg and Greenberg, 1997).

Conflict resolution and violence prevention curricula

Aggressive and nonaggressive youths differ in their approval of violence (Slaby and Guerra, 1988). Violence prevention curricula seek to promote the development of norms against the use of violence in conflict situations. Conflict resolution and violence prevention curricula seek to improve students' social, problem solving, and anger management skills, and promote norms favourable to nonviolence. These curricula typically teach skills in empathy, appropriate social behaviour, interpersonal problem solving, and anger management using discussion, modelling, and role-play methods to ensure skill acquisition. Topics and sessions are developmentally adjusted for the grade and age of children and vary in duration from ten to thirty sessions and in length from thirty minutes to one hour.

Evaluated conflict resolution and violence prevention curricula generally have found improvements in students' skills to provide nonviolent solutions to hypothetical social conflict situations (Bretherton, Collins and Ferretti, 1993; Committee for Children, 1988, 1989, 1990, 1992; Hammond and Yung, 1991, 1992, 1993; Marvel, Moreda and Cook, 1993). However, of the four quasi-experimental studies that investigated the effects of conflict resolution and violence prevention curricula on norms toward violence, only one has demonstrated a positive impact on these norms (Gainer, Webster and Champion, 1993).

Perhaps the best evidence of effectiveness of a classroom violence prevention curriculum comes from Grossman *et al.*'s (1997) experimental evaluation of the Committee on Children's Second Step curriculum. The Second Step curriculum teaches elementary students skills for anger management, impulse control, and empathy. A randomised controlled trial was used to evaluate the programme across twelve elementary schools. Positive effects of the curriculum were shown in lower levels of observed aggressive behaviour and higher levels of neutral and prosocial behaviour among second and third grade students when compared with controls. Intervention students exhibited less physical aggression in the lunchroom and on the playground immediately following the programme. Many effects were maintained six months later. Students in the experimental condition also reported higher levels of empathy, interpersonal problem solving, anger management, and behavioural social skills than those in the control condition.

Peer mediation and counselling

Peer mediation programmes, sometimes operated in conjunction with conflict resolution curricula, are another school-based approach to preventing violence. In these programmes, students involved in a conflict agree to use a trained peer mediator to help them resolve their dispute. Peer mediators help the disputants examine various aspects of the problem, recommend compromises, and assist in developing a mutually agreed solution. Peer mediators are trained in problem-solving, active listening, communication skills, taking command of adversarial situations, identifying points of agreement, and maintaining confidentiality and a nonjudgemental stance (Goleman, 1995).

Two quasi-experimental evaluations of peer mediation programmes that operated in tandem with conflict resolution curricula have shown positive effects on attitudes toward conflict and violence (Benenson, 1988; Jenkins and Smith, 1987). However, only one study with an adequate design has indicated a decrease in aggressive behaviour associated with peer mediation (Tolson, McDonald and Moriarty, 1992). That study found that high school students who participated as disputants in peer mediation were less likely to be referred to school officials for interpersonal conflicts during a two-and-half-month follow up period than were controls.

Peer counselling (also called guided group interaction, peer culture development, or positive peer culture) also has been implemented in schools as a strategy for preventing or reducing violent and other delinquent behaviour. Peer counselling typically involves an adult leader guiding group discussion in which participants are encouraged to recognise problems with their behaviour and attitudes. The approach seeks to shift participants' attitudes or norms so that they become unfavourable to antisocial behaviour and to provide peer group support for this shift. Peer counselling has been used in elementary and secondary schools as a preventive intervention, and frequently involves students at high risk for delinquency and violence mixed with prosocial student leaders and others. Unfortunately, the available evidence indicates that peer counselling in schools has no, or even undesirable, effects on delinquency and attitudes toward violence (Gottfredson, 1987). In short, while peer counselling attempts to change norms, it does not appear to be an effective strategy for doing so.

In summary, there is evidence that schools can promote the development of skills to avoid antisocial behaviour through the use of classroom curricula that seek to promote social and emotional competence (Goleman, 1995). There is some evidence that conflict resolution and violence prevention curricula positively affect students' skills for resolving conflict situations non-violently. There is also some evidence that peer mediation programmes can encourage the development of norms against violent solutions to conflict situations. Unfortunately, some studies of these types of intervention have not revealed positive results (Hausman, Spivak, Prothrow-Stith and Loeber, 1992). More rigorous evaluations of peer mediation, conflict resolution, and violence prevention curricula are needed. In contrast, the evidence does not support the use of peer counselling as a strategy for developing norms of non-violence or reducing violent behaviour.

Bullying prevention

Programmes designed to reduce bullying in schools can be targetted on bullies, victims, or schools, or on some combination. For example, Lowenstein (1991) proposed making bullies aware of victims' feelings, punishing bullies, providing opportunities for bullies to behave positively, and rewarding desirable behaviour by bullies (e.g., using tokens that could be exchanged for extrinsic rewards such as candy and privileges).

The most important evaluation of a school-based anti-bullying programme was conducted in Bergen, Norway by Olweus (1991). This programme aimed to increase awareness and knowledge of bullying by teachers, parents, and students. Booklets were distributed to schools and parents describing what was known about bullying and what steps could be taken to reduce it. Students completed anonymous self-report questionnaires about the prevalence of bullies and victims, in a specially arranged school conference day. Teachers were encouraged to develop explicit rules about bullying (e.g., bullying will not be tolerated, tell someone when bullying happens, try to help victims), and to discuss bullying in class using a video and role-playing exercises. Also, teachers were encouraged to improve monitoring and supervision of children, especially on the playground.

The programme was evaluated using before-and-after measures of bullying and victimisation of children at each age. For example, the self-reported prevalence of bullies and victims among 13-year-olds before the programme was compared with the prevalence of bullies and victims among (different) 13-year-olds twenty months after the programme. Generally, the percentage of students reporting being bullied or bullying others decreased by approximately 50 per cent or more in most comparisons (Olweus, 1994). In most cases, the reductions in bullying and victimisation corresponded to large effect sizes (a *d* value of 1.0 or greater; see Cohen, 1988).

A similar programme was implemented in 1992 in twenty-three Sheffield, England schools by Smith and Sharp (1994). The core programme involved establishing a 'whole-school' anti-bullying policy, increasing awareness of bullying, and clearly defining roles and responsibilities of teachers and students, so that everyone knew what bullying was and what they should do about it. In addition, there were optional interventions tailored to particular schools: curricula, work (e.g., reading books, watching videos), direct work with students (e.g., assertiveness training for victims), and playground work (e.g., training lunch-time supervisors). This programme was successful in reducing bullying among younger children, but had relatively small effects on older children.

Gang prevention programmes

In schools, as gangs have become an increasing problem, (Kodluboy and Evenrud, 1993) a number of strategies have been proposed to reduce gang activity, including: gang prevention curricula; dress codes or school uniforms, prohibiting gang clothing and insignia; gang reporting hotlines; support and protection for victims of gang violence; parent notification of gang activity; and visitor screening (Stephens, 1993).

Unfortunately, the effectiveness of most of these measures in reducing antisocial behaviour has not yet been tested. However, there are examples of promising programmes. Thompson and Jason (1988) evaluated the combination of a gang prevention curriculum and after-school recreational activities provided to eighth-grade students in lower income areas with high gang activity in Chicago. The twelve-session curriculum included classroom sessions on gang violence, substance abuse in gangs, gang recruitment and methods of resisting recruitment, consequences of gang membership, and values clarification. After the curriculum was taught, youths considered at risk for joining a gang were invited to participate in after-school recreational activities, including organised sports clinics, job skills/training workshops, educational assistance programmes, and social activities.

A nonequivalent comparison group design involved three pairs of public middle schools matched on the basis that the same gang actively recruited members from both schools in a pair. Youths in the intervention schools were less likely to become gang members over the course of the eighth grade. Unfortunately, the evaluation was limited by the short follow-up period and a relatively small sample size, given the low prevalence of gang membership. Four of the forty-three comparison youths in the study had joined gangs by the end of the school year, compared with one of the seventy-four youths exposed to the intervention.

After-school recreation programmes

Though not, of necessity, conducted in schools, after-school recreation programmes for youths have been widely recommended, but not well evaluated. Evidence suggesting that crime peaks during the late afternoon hours when children are not in school (Snyder, Sickmund and Poe-Yamagata, 1996) has strengthened support for providing opportunities for involvement with prosocial youths and adults, skills for leisure activities, and bonding to prosocial others through after-school recreation programmes.

The strongest evidence in support of this approach comes from Jones and Offord's (1989) evaluation of the effects of an after-school recreation programme that targetted low-income children ages five to 15 residing in a public housing project in Ottawa, Ontario. Programme staff actively recruited all children in the housing development to participate in structured after-school courses for improving skills in sports, music, dance, scouting, and other nonsport areas. After children reached a certain skill level, they were encouraged to participate in on-going leagues or other competitive activities in the surrounding community. The thirty-two-month long programme was evaluated using a nonequivalent comparison group design comparing the experimental housing project with another public housing project, which had only minimal city-provided recreational services.

The programme was fairly successful in recruiting project youths. Between 49 to 71 per cent of age-eligible children in the experimental complex participated in at least one programme course during each of the three years of the programme.

The number of arrests of juveniles residing in the experimental complex during the programme declined significantly from the two years before the intervention relative to arrests of youths in the comparison project. There was a 75 per cent decrease in juvenile crime in the experimental project, but a 67 per cent increase in the comparison project. No such differences were observed in the number of arrests for adults, strengthening the plausibility that changes in juvenile crime were related to the youth-focused after school programme. In addition, the number of security reports due to juveniles at the experimental complex declined significantly after the intervention began in contrast to the comparison complex. Sixteen months after the programme had ended, these positive changes had diminished significantly.

After-school recreation programmes may be a promising intervention for preventing antisocial behaviour, but should be evaluated further with strong research designs.

Vocational training and employment

Evidence is clear that, in the US, early involvement in employment during the years of school attendance increases risk for school failure and drug use (Steinberg and Cauffman, 1995). However, later in adolescence, vocational training and employment programmes are primarily intended to increase youth employment and participants' earnings, though secondary objectives frequently include the improvement of educational functioning and reduction of antisocial behaviour.

Youth employment and training programmes have successfully recruited participants from hard to reach populations. Programme effects on employment and earnings outcomes have typically been positive, although the effects tended to last only for short periods during and immediately after the programme. Substantial improvements in educational outcomes appeared only when the programme included a significant educational component (Cave, Bos, Doolittle and Toussaint, 1993; Cave and Quint, 1990; Corporation for Public/Private Ventures, 1983; Mallar, Kerachsky, Thornton and Long, 1982; Shapiro, Gaston, Hebert and Guillot, 1986; Walker and Vilella-Velez, 1992).

Nine evaluations of youth employment programmes have specifically assessed the impact on crime and delinquency. Six showed no significant effects, and one (Bloom *et al.*, 1994) indicated an undesired increase in criminal behaviour. For the two that reported positive effects, crime reduction was restricted to the period when participants were involved in intensive, largely educationally-oriented programmes which offered a comprehensive array of services to school dropouts (Cave *et al.*, 1993; Mallar *et al.*, 1982). Although the Mallar *et al.* (1982) evaluation indicated long-term reductions in some crime outcomes, the initial crime prevention effect reported in the Cave *et al.* (1993) evaluation disappeared by the four year follow-up.

Conclusion

During the school years, the experiences of developing children help to shape their futures. Important malleable risk and protective factors for future behaviour problems stabilise during this period. Children who do not learn to control aggression, who do not succeed academically, who do not develop a commitment to learning and educational success, who do not develop personal standards of disapproval for antisocial behaviour, and who do not develop the skills to resist social influences to engage in antisocial behaviour are at risk for antisocial behaviour in adulthood. From a developmental perspective, the school years appear to be an ideal time to seek to prevent adult antisocial behaviour. Because all children are expected to attend school during these years, school-based interventions have the potential to reach the entire population, including those at highest risk for antisocial behaviour.

In the last two decades, school-based interventions have been tested and shown to be effective in addressing each of the predictors of later antisocial behaviour listed here. Tested approaches include:

- improving the management of schools and classrooms to provide more opportunities and reinforcement for prosocial behaviour and engagement in learning;
- using classroom instructional practices shown to promote academic achievement with tutoring for those who need it;
- engaging families in supporting student achievement;
- reorganising schools to increase opportunities for learning and bonding to school and to develop consistency of support and recognition from school and parents;
- teaching emotional and social skills for self-control and social interaction across the school years through developmentally appropriate curricula;
- integrating the teaching of academic and social and emotional skills in elementary classrooms;

- promoting norms antithetical to violence and other forms of antisocial behaviour through school curricula and peer mediation.

In addition, programmes that provide opportunities to become involved in positive activities in the after school hours and that teach young people skills to succeed in these activities may also hold promise, though these have not been well tested yet. Finally, youth employment and training programmes that help to promote the educational success of those in their late teens may also hold promise for preventing later antisocial behaviour.

These interventions hold promise for reducing the prevalence of adult antisocial behaviours through preventive applications. While the empirical evidence regarding the effectiveness of these programmes in reducing risk and enhancing protection is growing, longer follow up studies of most of these interventions are needed to determine their effects on antisocial behaviour in adulthood. It is important to learn whether interventions focused exclusively on promoting academic achievement or interventions that help students control aggressive behaviours in the elementary grades can reduce or prevent antisocial behaviour in adulthood. It is also important to learn whether combinations of the efficacious interventions reviewed here, implemented at developmentally appropriate stages across the school years would have synergistic effects in preventing antisocial behaviour.

Much remains to be learned about the relative costs and benefits of providing interventions selectively to individuals at greatest risk for future antisocial behaviours compared with interventions with an entire classroom or school or community. During the elementary years from ages 6 to 11 or 12, interventions with whole classrooms to improve the academic success of all children have been more effective than special education or pull out programmes for children with academic or behavioural problems when implemented in schools serving populations at risk for academic failure. The long term implications for preventing adult antisocial behaviour remain to be explored.

It is clear that it is possible to reduce antisocial behaviour in childhood and adolescence through the school-based interventions reviewed here. Ascertaining the potential of these interventions to prevent adult antisocial behaviour should be a top research priority.

Acknowledgements

This research was supported by research grant #1R01DA09679 from the National Institute on Drug Abuse, and #1R24MH56587 from the National Institute for Mental Health. Herrenkohl, T. I., Hawkins, J. D.,

Chung, I.-J., Hill, K. G., and Battin-Pearson, S. R. (2000) School and community risk factors and interventions. In R. Loeber and D. P. Farrington (eds.), *Child Delinquents: Development, Intervention, and Service Needs* (pp. 211–46). Thousand Oaks, CA: Sage Publications. Excerpts from pages 223–44, copyright 2000 by Sage Publications, Inc. Reprinted by permission of Sage Publications, Inc.

REFERENCES

Abbott, R. D., O'Donnell, J., Hawkins, J. D., Hill K. G., Kosterman, R. and Catalano, R. F. (1998) Changing teaching practices to promote achievement and bonding to school. *American Journal of Orthopsychiatry*, *68*(4), 542–52.

Barber, R. M. and Kagey, J. R. (1977) Modification of school attendance for an elementary population. *Journal of Applied Behavior Analysis*, *10*, 41–8.

Battistich, V., Schaps, E., Watson, M. and Solomon, D. (1996) Prevention effects of the Child Development Project: Early findings from an ongoing multisite demonstration trial. *Journal of Adolescent Research*, *11*, 12–35.

Battistich, V., Solomon, D., Watson, M. and Schaps, E. (1997) Caring school communities. *Educational Psychologist*, *32*(3), 137–51.

Benenson, W. (1988) *Assessing the effectiveness of a peer based conflict management program in elementary schools*. Unpublished doctoral dissertation, University of Idaho.

Bloom, H. S., Orr, L. L., Cave, G., Bell, S. H., Doolittle, F. and Lin, W. (1994) *The National JTPA Study: Overview: Impacts, Benefits, and Costs of Title II-A*. Bethesda, MD: Abt Associations, Inc.

Botvin, G. J., Baker, E., Dusenbury, L., Botvin, E. M. and Diaz, T. (1995) Long-term follow-up results of a randomized drug abuse prevention trial in a white middle-class population. *Journal of the American Medical Association*, *273*, 1106–12.

Bretherton, D., Collins, L. and Ferretti, C. (1993) Dealing with conflict: Assessment of a course for secondary school students. *Australian Psychologist*, *28*, 105–11.

Brewer, D. D., Hawkins, J. D., Catalano, R. F. and Neckerman, H. J. (1995) Preventing serious, violent, and chronic juvenile offending: A review of selected strategies in childhood, adolescence, and the community. In J. C. Howell, B. Krisberg, J. D. Hawkins and J. J. Wilson (eds.), *A Sourcebook: Serious, Violent, and Chronic Juvenile Offenders* (pp. 61–141). Thousand Oaks, CA: Sage Publications.

Brooks, B. D. (1975) Contingency management as a means of reducing school truancy. *Education*, *95*, 206–11.

Bry, B. H. (1982) Reducing the incidence of adolescent problems through preventive intervention: One- and five-year follow-up. *American Journal of Community Psychology*, *10*, 265–76.

Bry, B. H. and George, F. E. (1979) Evaluating and improving prevention programs: A strategy from drug abuse. *Evaluation and Program Planning*, *2*, 127–36.

(1980) The preventive effects of early intervention on the attendance and grades of urban adolescents. *Professional Psychology, 11*(2), 252–60.

Catalano, R. F., Harachi, T. W., Haggerty, K. P. and Abbott, R. D. (1996 August) Proximal effects of a comprehensive risk and protective factor prevention strategy. In *School-based risk and protective factor-focused drug abuse prevention.* Symposium conducted at the 104th Annual Convention of the American Psychological Association, Toronto, Canada.

Cauce, A. M., Comer, J. P. and Schwartz, D. (1987) Long-term effects of a systems-oriented school prevention program. *American Journal of Orthopsychiatry, 57*, 127–31.

Cave, G., Bos, H., Doolittle, F. and Toussaint, C. (1993) *JOBSTART: Final Report on a Program for School Dropouts*. New York: Manpower Demonstration Research Corporation.

Cave, G. and Quint, J. (1990) *Career Beginnings Impact Evaluation: Findings From a Program for Disadvantaged High School Students.* New York: Manpower Demonstration Research Corporation.

Cohen, J. (1988) *Statistical Power Analysis for the Behavioral Sciences* (2nd ed.). New Jersey: Lawrence Erlbaum.

Comer, J. P. (1988) Educating poor minority children. *Scientific American, 259*, 42–8.

Committee for Children (1988) *Second Step, grades 1–3, pilot project 1987–88, summary report*. Seattle, WA: Author.

(1989) *Second Step, grades 4–5, pilot project 1988–89, summary report*. Seattle, WA: Author.

(1990) *Second Step, grades 6–8, pilot project 1989–90, summary report*. Seattle, WA: Author.

(1992) *Evaluation of Second Step, preschool-kindergarten, a violence-prevention curriculum kit*. Seattle, WA: Author.

Conduct Problems Prevention Research Group (1999a) Initial impact of the Fast Track Prevention Trial for conduct problems: I. The high-risk sample. *Journal of Consulting and Clinical Psychology, 67*, 631–47.

(1999b) Initial impact of the Fast Track Prevention Trial for conduct problems: II. Classroom effects. J*ournal of Consulting and Clinical Psychology, 67*, 648–57.

Corporation for Public/Private Ventures (1983) *Longer Term Impacts of Pre-employment Services on the Employment and Earnings of Disadvantaged Youth.* Philadelphia: Corporation for Public/Private Ventures.

Dryfoos, J. G. (1990) *Adolescents at Risk: Prevalence and Prevention.* New York: Oxford University Press.

Evertson, C.M. (1985) Training teachers in classroom management: An experimental study in secondary school classroom. *Journal of Educational Research, 79*(1), 51–8.

Evertson, C. M., Emmer, E. T., Sanford, J. P. and Clements, B. S. (1983) Improving classroom management: An experiment in elementary school classrooms. *Elementary School Journal, 84*(2), 173–88.

Farrington, D. P. (1991) Childhood aggression and adult violence: Early precursors and later-life outcomes. In D. J. Pepler and K. H. Rubin (eds.), *The*

Development and Treatment of Childhood Aggression (pp. 5–29). Hillsdale, NJ: Erlbaum.

Felner, R. D., Brand, S., Adan, A. M., Mulhall, P. F., Flowers, N., Sartain, B. and DuBois, D. L. (1993) Restructuring the ecology of the school as an approach to prevention during school transitions: Longitudinal follow-ups and extensions of the School Transition Environment Project (STEP). *Prevention in Human Services, 10*, 103–36.

Gainer, P. S., Webster, D. W. and Champion, H. R. (1993) A youth violence prevention program: Description and preliminary evaluation. *Archives of Surgery, 128*, 303–8.

Gold, M. and Mann, D. W. (1984) *Expelled to a Friendlier Place: A Study of Effective Alternative Schools*. Ann Arbor, MI: University of Michigan.

Goleman, D. (1995) *Emotional Intelligence*. New York: Bantam Books.

Gottfredson, D. C. (1986) An empirical test of school-based environmental and individual interventions to reduce the risk of delinquent behavior. *Criminology, 24*, 705–31.

(1987) An evaluation of an organization development approach to reducing school disorder. *Evaluation Review, 11*, 739–63.

Greenberg, M. T. (1996) *The PATHS project: Preventive intervention for children – A final report to NIMH (Grant No. RO1MH42131)*. University of Washington: Author.

Greenberg, M. T. and Kusche, C. A. (1993) *Promoting Social and Emotional Development in Deaf Children: The PATHS Project*. Seattle: University of Washington Press.

Grossman, D. C., Neckerman, H. J., Koepsell, T., Asher, K., Liu, P. Y., Beland, K., Frey, K. and Rivara, F. P. (1997) A randomized controlled trial of a violence prevention curriculum among elementary school students. *Journal of the American Medical Association, 277*, 1605–11.

Hammond, W. R. and Yung, B. R. (1991) Preventing violence in at-risk African-American youth. *Journal of Health Care for the Poor and Underserved 2*, 359–73.

(1992) *Evaluation and activity report: Positive Adolescents Choices Training (PACT) program*. (Grant No. MCJ-393A1501-0. Ohio Governor's Office of Criminal Justice Services). Dayton, OH: Wright State University. School of Professional Psychology.

(1993) Psychology's role in the public health response to assaultive violence among young African-American men. Special Issue: Adolescence. *American Psychologist, 48*(2), 142–54.

Hausman, A. J., Spivak, H., Prothrow-Stith, D. and Loeber, J. (1992) Patterns of teen exposure to a community-based violence prevention project. *Journal of Adolescent Health, 13*, 668–75.

Hawkins, J. D., Catalano, R. F., Brown, E. O., Vadasy, P. F., Roberts, C., Fitzmahan, D., Starkman, N. and Ransdell, M. (1988) Preparing for the drug (free) years: A family activity book. Seattle, WA: Comprehensive Health Education Foundation.

Hawkins, J. D., Catalano, R. F., Jones, G and Fine, D. N. (1987) Delinquency prevention through parent training: Results and issues from work in progress, in J. Q. Wilson and G. C. Loury (eds.), *From Children to Citizens*: vol. 3. *Families, Schools, and Delinquency Prevention* (pp. 186–204). New York: Springer-Verlag.

Hawkins, J. D., Catalano, R. F., Kosterman, R., Abbott, R. D. and Hill, K. G. (1999) Preventing adolescent health-risk behaviors by strengthening protection during childhood, *Archives of Pediatrics & Adolescent Medicine, 153*, 226–34.

Hawkins, J. D., Catalano, R. F., Morrison, D. M., O'Donnell, J., Abbott, R. D. and Day, L. E. (1992) The Seattle Social Development Project: Effects of the first four years on protective factors and problem behaviors. In J. McCord and R. Tremblay (eds.), *The Prevention of Antisocial Behavior in Children* (pp. 139–61). New York: Guilford.

Hawkins, J. D., Farrington, D. P. and Catalano R. F. (1998) Reducing violence through the schools. In D. S. Elliott, B. A. Hamburg and K. R. Williams (eds.), *Violence in American Schools* (pp. 188–216). New York: Cambridge University Press.

Hawkins, J. D., Von Cleve, E. and Catalano, R. F. (1991) Reducing early childhood aggression: Results of a primary prevention program. *Journal of the American Academy of Child and Adolescent Psychiatry, 30*, 208–17.

Jenkins, J. and Smith, M. (1987) *Mediation in the Schools: 1986–87 Program Evaluation*. Albuquerque: New Mexico Center for Dispute Resolution.

Jones, M. B. and Offord, D. R. (1989) Reduction of antisocial behavior in poor children by nonschool skill-development. *Journal of Child Psychology and Psychiatry, 30*(5), 737–50.

Kellam, S. G. and Rebok, G. W. (1992) Building developmental and etiological theory through epidemiologically based preventive intervention trials. In J. McCord and R. E. Tremblay (eds.), *Preventing Antisocial Behavior: Interventions From Birth Through Adolescence* (pp. 162–95). New York: Guilford.

Kellam, S. G., Rebok, G. W., Ialongo, N. and Mayer, L. S. (1994) The course and malleability of aggressive behavior from early first grade into middle school: Results of a developmental epidemiology-based preventive trial. *Journal of Child Psychology and Psychiatry, 35*(2), 259–81.

Kodluboy, D. W. and Evenrud, L. A. (1993) School-based interventions: Best practices and critical issues. In A. P. Goldstein and C. R. Huff (eds.), *The Gang Intervention Handbook*. Champaign, IL: Research Press.

Loeber, R. (1990) Development and risk factors of juvenile antisocial behavior and delinquency. *Clinical Psychology Review, 10*, 1–41.

Loeber, R. and Hay, D. (1996) Key issues in the development of aggression and violence from childhood to early adulthood. *Annual Review of Psychology, 48*, 371–410.

Lowenstein, L. F. (1991) The study, diagnosis and treatment of bullying in a therapeutic community. In M. Elliott (ed.), *Bullying: A Practical Guide to Coping for Schools*. Harlow: Longman.

Madden, N. A., Slavin, R. F., Karweit, N. K., Dolan, L. J. and Wasik, B. A. (1993) Success for All. Longitudinal effects of a restructuring program for inner-city elementary schools. *American Educational Research Journal, 30*, 123–48.

Maguin, E. and Loeber, R. (1996) Academic performance and delinquency. In M. Tonry (ed.), *Crime and Justice: A Review of Research*, vol. 20, (pp. 145–264). University of Chicago Press.

Mallar, C., Kerachsky, S., Thornton, C. and Long, D. (1982) *Evaluation of economic impact of the Job Corps program, third follow-up report*. Princeton, NJ: Mathematica Policy Research.

Marvel, J., Moreda, I. and Cook, I. (1993) *Developing Conflict Resolution Skills in Students: A Study of the Fighting Fair Model*. Miami, FL: Peace Education Foundation.

Mrazek, P. J. and Haggerty, R. J. (eds.) (1994) *Reducing Risks for Mental Disorders: Frontiers for Preventive Intervention Research*. Washington, DC: National Academy Press.

Murphy, H. A., Hutchinson, J. M. and Bailey, J. S. (1983) Behavioral school psychology goes outdoors: The effect of organized games on playground aggression. *Journal of Applied Behavioral Analysis*, *16*, 29–35.

O'Donnell, J., Hawkins, J. D., Catalano, R. C., Abbott, R. D. and Day, L. E. (1995) Preventing school failure, drug use, and delinquency among low-income children: Long-term intervention in elementary schools. *American Journal of Orthopsychiatry*, *65*, 87–100.

O'Leary, K. D. and O'Leary, S. G. (1977) *Classroom Management: The Successful Use of Behavior Modification* (2nd ed.) New York: Pergamon.

Olweus, D. (1991) Bully/victim problems among schoolchildren: Basic facts and effects of an intervention program. In K. Rubin and D. Pepler (eds.), *The Development and Treatment of Childhood Aggression*, (pp. 411–48). Hillsdale, NJ: Erlbaum.

(1994) Bullying at schools: Basic facts and effects of a school-based intervention program. *Journal of Child Psychology and Psychiatry*, *35*, 1171–90.

Robins, L. N. (1978) Sturdy childhood predictors of adult anti-social behavior: Replications from longitudinal studies. *Psychological Medicine*, *8*, 611–22.

Safer, D. J. (1982) Special education and programs for behavior problem youth. In D. J. Safer (ed.), *School Programs for Disruptive Adolescents*. Baltimore: University Park Press.

(1990) A school intervention for aggressive adolescents. In L. J. Hertzberg, G. F. Ostrum and J. R. Field (eds.), *Violent Behavior, Volume 1: Assessment and Intervention*. Great Neck, NY: PMA Publishing Corporation.

Shapiro, J. Z., Gaston, S. N., Hebert, J. C. and Guillot, D. J. (1986) *LSYOU (Louisiana State Youth Opportunities Unlimited) Project Evaluation*. Baton Rouge, LA: College of Education, Louisiana State University.

Shure, M. D. and Spivack, G. (1980) Interpersonal problem solving as a mediator of behavioral adjustment in preschool and kindergarten children. *Journal of Applied Developmental Psychology*, *1*, 29–44.

(1982) Interpersonal problem-solving in young children: A cognitive approach to prevention. *American Journal of Community Psychology*, *10*, 341–56.

(1988) Interpersonal cognitive problem solving. In R. H. Price, E. L. Cowen, R. P. Lorion and J. Ramos-McKay (eds.), *14 Ounces of Prevention: A Casebook for Practitioners* (pp. 69–82). Washington, DC: American Psychological Association.

Slaby, R. and Guerra, N. (1988) Cognitive mediators of aggression in adolescent offenders. *Developmental Psychology, 24,* 580–8.

Slavin, R. E., Karweit, N. L. and Wasik, B. A. (1994) *Preventing Early School Failure.* Needham Heights, MA: Allyn & Bacon.

Slavin, R. E., Madden, N. A., Dolan, L. J., Wasik, B. A., Ross, S., Smith, L. and Dianda, M. (1996) Success for All: A summary of research. *Journal of Education for Students Placed At Risk, 1*(1), 41–76.

Slavin, R. E., Madden, N. A., Karweit, N. I., Liverman, B. J. and Dolan, N. (1990) Success for All: First year outcomes of a comprehensive plan for reforming urban education. *American Educational Research Journal, 27,* 255–78.

Smith, P. K. and Sharp, S. (1994) *School Bullying.* London: Routledge.

Snyder, P. K., Sickmund, M. and Poe-Yamagata, E. (1996) *Juvenile Offenders and Victims: 1996 Update on Violence.* Washington DC: Office of Juvenile Justice and Delinquency Prevention.

Steinberg, L. and Cauffman, A. (1995) The impact of employment on adolescent development. In V. Ross, *et al.* (eds.), *Annals of Child Development: A Research Annual. vol. 11,* (pp. 131–66). London, England, UK: Jessica Kingsley Publishers, Ltd.

Stephens, R. J. (1993) School-based interventions: Safety and security. In A. P. Goldstein and C. R. Huff (eds.), *The Gang Intervention Handbook* (pp. 219–56). Champagne, IL.: Research Press.

Thompson, D. W. and Jason, L. A. (1988) Street gangs and preventive interventions. *Criminal Justice and Behavior, 15,* 323–33.

Tolson, E. R., McDonald, S. and Moriarty, A. R. (1992) Peer mediation among high school students: A test of effectiveness. *Social Work in Education, 14,* 86–93.

Walker, G. and Vilella-Velez, F. (1992) *Anatomy of a Demonstration: STEP From Pilot Through Replication and Postprogram Impacts.* Philadelphia: Public/Private Ventures.

Weissberg, R. P., Barton, H. A. and Shriver, T. P. (1997) The Social-Competence Promotion Program for Young Adolescents. In G. W. Albee, Gulotta, T. P. *et al.* (eds), *Primary Prevention Works. Issues in Children's and Families' Lives, vol. 6* (pp. 268–290). Thousand Oaks, CA: Sage Publications, Inc.

Weissberg, R. P. and Greenberg, M. T. (1997) School and community competence-enhancement and prevention programs. In W. Damon (Series ed.), I. E. Sigel and K. A. Renninger (vol. eds.), *Handbook of Child Psychology: vol. 5. Child Psychology in Practice* (5th ed., pp. 877–954). New York: John Wiley & Sons.

9 Prevention of antisocial behaviour in females

Deborah Gorman-Smith

Sound preventive interventions to target antisocial behaviour among girls depends on reliable empirical data to address three primary questions. First, what are the rates and patterns of involvement in antisocial behaviour among females? Second, what are the predictors and correlates of involvement in antisocial behaviour among females? Third, is there any evidence of programme impact of interventions for females and is there any evidence of differential impact due to gender? In this chapter, I review the available empirical literature to summarise the state of our knowledge to address these questions to guide prevention efforts.

However, it is clear that the ability of the review to be informative for guiding prevention is constrained because there are limited data available that focus specifically on girls. Also, there are several issues that limit the ability to interpret much of the data that do exist. Therefore, the first part of the chapter focuses on three major issues that have constrained the state of knowledge regarding antisocial behaviour and girls: (1) lack of inclusion of girls in studies of antisocial behaviour, (2) differences in the behaviours that might define antisocial behaviour among girls and the long-term outcomes associated with antisocial behaviour in childhood for women and (3) the inclusion of gender in theory development. The second part of the chapter proposes an approach that can overcome these limitations and through which the development of antisocial behaviour for both males and females might be understood. This model permits consideration of similarities as well as differences across gender without assuming male-developed models are directly transferable to females *or* that male-developed models are irrelevant. Finally, with these issues in mind, the three initial questions (i.e, rates, correlates, and treatment impact) are addressed and implications for prevention of antisocial behaviour among females are discussed.

Exclusion of females from studies

Most of the early empirical work on antisocial behaviour and delinquency excluded females or considered them marginally important to understanding delinquent behaviour (Shaw and McKay, 1942; Glueck and Glueck, 1950; Hirschi, 1969), aggression, and conduct disorder (Robins, 1986; Zoccolillo, 1993). Essentially, because these problems were thought to be rare among females, girls and women were simply not included in most risk, developmental, and intervention outcome studies. Thus, data to understand course and outcome were simply not gathered, leaving much understanding of female antisocial behaviour to speculation or generalisation.

When females were mentioned in studies, they were often relegated to a footnote about a need for cross-validation at some future point or data were collapsed with that of males (Chesney-Lind, 1989; Robins, 1986). For example, in *Causes of Delinquency*, Hirschi (1969) wrote in a footnote, 'in the analyses that follows, the "non-Negro" becomes "white" and the girls disappear'. Another strain of literature, however, focused on delinquent behaviour of girls as being comprised primarily as sexual misconduct, a role which was not considered in male delinquency (Chesney-Lind, 1989; Chesney-Lind and Brown, 1998). That is, most of girls' delinquency was considered to be confined to sexual acts (e.g., promiscuity, prostitution), while boys' delinquency was measured as involvement in aggressive and criminal acts (Calhoun, Jurgens and Chen, 1993; Chesney-Lind and Sheldon, 1992). In this strain of studies were those that focused primarily on status offences such as running away from home, being in need of supervision, or being 'incorrigible' to measure girls' delinquency; assuming no need to consider aggressive and violent behaviours. These two strains were rarely integrated. However, both promoted a view that antisocial behaviour, when defined as robbery, assault, and other criminal acts, was rare enough among females not to need study.

The belief that boys and girls got involved in different types of delinquent behaviour and that 'male types' of antisocial behaviour were uncommon among females was based primarily on official delinquency arrest data that showed large numbers of girls arrested and referred for status offences (Chesney-Lind, 1989). This statistical difference appears to have been due in large part to differential treatment of boys and girls by the juvenile justice system (Chesney-Lind, 1973, 1989; Figueira-McDonough, 1985; Poe-Yamagata and Butts, 1996). That is, boys were less often charged for the same types of offences as girls and girls were charged for behaviours for which boys would not have been charged. This difference has not disappeared into history. In a review of delinquency referrals made to the juvenile courts in the 1980s, Snyder, Finnegan, Nimick, Sickmund, *et al.* (1989) found that while 81 per cent of all delinquency referrals were male, 46 per cent of all of the status offenders were female. Thus, official data still suggests that females are disproportionately involved in status offences. Self-report data, however, do not reflect this significant difference in per cent of girls involved in status offences. Rather, self-report data suggest that there is no evidence of girls being more involved than boys in any type of delinquent behaviour, including status offences (Canter, 1982; Elliott, 1994; Figueira-McDonough, 1985; Steffensmeier and Allan, 1996). Thus, use of official data only appears to distort the nature of female involvement in antisocial behaviour.

The belief that girls' delinquency involved status offences primarily had two implications for theory development of antisocial and delinquent behaviour among females. By having separate and incomparable definitions of antisocial and delinquent behaviour of males and females, this view promoted the exclusion of females as subjects in studies of serious delinquency and gender as a variable in most empirical studies and theory development. As most theories of delinquency and antisocial behaviour largely discounted status offences in understanding the development of delinquent careers, it biased theory development to be male-based. Because those types of behaviours were often not considered as critical in understanding delinquent and criminal careers, women, even if in the sample, were left out of analyses. When there was some recognition that there might be something different about girls' involvement in delinquency or antisocial behaviour, little empirical work was conducted to understand these differences through full gender comparisons.

Antisocial behaviour among women

Recent research suggests that it is not that female antisocial behaviour is wholly different from male antisocial behaviour, but rather, if we are to adequately understand the role of gender in antisocial behaviour and such behaviour among women, a more complex set of behaviours may need to be included in any assessment than has traditionally been considered in most studies. Particularly for females, aggression and antisocial behaviour may not be represented by the overt and criminal behaviours that have traditionally been measured when referring to males (Bjorkqvist and Niemela, 1992; Crick, Wellman, Casas, O'Brien, Nelson, Grotpeter and Markon, in press; Zoccarillo, 1993). For example, evaluating gender differences in aggression, Crick and colleagues (Crick, Bigbee and Howes in press; Crick and Groteper, 1995) challenge the belief that females are not as aggressive as males by suggesting that females may exhibit forms of aggression that are not common in males. They note that these forms have been overlooked in much of the previous research. These researchers argue that while aggression is defined as behaviours that are intended to hurt or harm others, there are ways to inflict harm on another person other than through physical aggression. They suggest that the ways in which people aggress may be related to their social role, which is a function of gender. The methods of aggression preferred are those that best prevent others from reaching goals that are valued by the aggressive person's gender. Because girls often emphasise qualities of interpersonal relations more than boys, girls' aggression focuses on relational issues. Thus, girls would be more likely to harm peers through damage or the threat of damage to interpersonal relationships. In contrast, boys would be most likely to harm peers through physical forms of aggression. Examples of relational aggressive behaviours include using social exclusion from a peer group, giving someone the 'silent treatment', or threatening to stop being friends (Crick, Bigbee and Howes, 1996). In contrast, physical aggression harms through damage to another's physical well-being, such as hitting, kicking, or threatening to beat up.

As a test of this theory, both physical and relational aggression were measured among a sample of third to sixth grade children using peer nominations (Crick and Grotpeter, 1995). These investigators found that approximately equal numbers of boys and girls were classified as nonaggressive (73 per cent of the boys and 78 per cent of the girls). Sixteen percent of the boys but only 0.4 per cent of the girls were classified as overtly aggressive (physically and verbally aggressive). Similarly, 17 per cent of the girls but only 2 per cent of the boys were classified as relationally aggressive. Interestingly, 9 per cent of the boys and 4 per cent of the girls were classified as both relationally and overtly aggressive. Thus, when both types of aggression were considered, gender differences were not large, but when considering only physically aggressive behaviour they were.

Other researchers have reported similar findings. Cairns and colleagues (Cairns and Cairns, 1994; Cairns *et al.*, 1989) also found girls to use high rates of relational aggression (ostracism and social sabotage) as a way to retaliate against others, particularly other girls. They also found greater use of this form of aggression by girls as they got older (Cairns and Cairns, 1986). In addition to supporting the finding of gender differences in the use of relational aggression, these data suggest that there may also be a developmental shift in the expression of aggression for girls to increasing covertly aggressive behaviour over time.

Even if there is evidence of females relying more on relational aggression, it can be argued that the harm caused is not as 'serious' as physical aggression. Therefore, it should not be considered a part of aggressive behaviour or of equal concern. However, as with other forms of aggression, relationally aggressive children appear to be at risk for serious adjustment problems. Crick and Grotpeter (1995) found that relationally aggressive children were significantly more disliked and rejected by other children. These children also had significantly elevated rates of depression and reported being lonely and socially isolated. Relational aggression was associated with depression among youth adult women (MacDonald and O'Laughlin, 1997). Associations between relational aggression and delinquency (MacDonald and O'Laughlin, 1997; Morey, 1991) and some features of antisocial personality disorder (stimulus-seeking, egocentricity; Morey, 1991; Wellman and Crick, 1998) have been found for both men and women, even after controlling for the contribution of physical aggression. These findings suggest that relational aggression is a serious problem that is associated with other types of disorders during childhood and is related to increased risk for serious psychosocial problems in adolescence and youth adulthood.

As relational aggression is associated with serious psychosocial problems in childhood and is related to many forms of antisocial behaviour in adulthood, it seems clear that definitions of aggression and antisocial behaviour should be expanded to encompass a wider variety of methods of acting aggressively. Both relational and physical aggression need to be considered as early forms of antisocial behaviour. In addition, developmental models of antisocial behaviour need to be expanded to include gender as a major consideration. Specifically, models need to be able to include how development and risk for antisocial behaviour may be related to gender roles and related social expectations. For example, theories of the development of antisocial behaviour should include the centrality of greater relational concerns observed among women and the way those concerns may affect development. This needs to be the case for both men and women, so that the focus is not biased in studies of males or 'male types' of aggression.

These findings can have important implications for prevention programmes targetting antisocial behaviour. For example, general programmes might need to be expanded to target these types of aggression. A greater focus on relational issues, between family members, siblings and peers, may be warranted. In addition, for targetted or indicated prevention programmes, it may be important to expand the selection criteria for participant inclusion. If participants are screened only for physical or verbal aggression, a large percentage of children who are at risk, particularly girls, may be missed.

Adult outcomes of antisocial behaviour among girls

In addition to data suggesting that antisocial behaviour among girls may include additional types of behaviours than have been traditionally considered for boys, research on the long-term outcomes of children and youth with aggression and conduct problems suggest that adult outcomes for females may be more complex than have been considered for boys. Early studies of the adult consequences of aggression in childhood (based on overt aggression) suggested that the outcomes for antisocial behaviour among girls might be better than for antisocial boys. For example, Kellam, Simon and Ensminger (1983) found aggression in first grade was more predictive of delinquency before age 17 for boys than for girls. Havighurst and colleagues (1962) found that aggressive girls were less likely to have bad outcomes than aggressive boys among a sample followed from seventh grade to adulthood. Lefkowitz, Eron, Walder and Huesmann (1977) found that aggression in third grade was more predictive of aggression at age 19 for males than for females. However, each of these studies focused on the types of outcomes that are usually associated with antisocial behaviour among males such as physical aggression, delinquency, adult criminality and violence. This focus seems to have resulted in obscuring the fact that long-term outcomes of antisocial behaviour in childhood for females may be different than that of males.

When the outcomes of focus are expanded beyond aggression and criminality, data suggest that the adult outcomes for girls may not be so benign (Pajer, 1998; Robins, 1986). For example, using data from the Epidemiological Catchment Area Study (ECA), Robins (1996) found that when the outcome of interest was expanded beyond externalising problems, girls appeared to do at least as poorly as boys, if not worse. She found that the development of externalising problems in adulthood was dependent on the number of conduct problems in childhood for both men and women. For men, the average proportion ever having one of these disorders rose from 14 per cent for those with a history of no conduct problems to 84 per cent for those with a history of at least seven conduct problems. For women, it rose from 4 per cent for those with a history of no conduct problems to 64 per cent for those with at least seven conduct problems. When internalising disorders were considered as well as externalising disorders, women's history of conduct problems was associated with an increased rate of almost every disorder. This association with internalising problems was not found with men.

Consistent findings were also obtained using data from the Dunedin Mutidisciplinary Health and Development Study. Young adult women with a history of adolescent conduct disorder were found to have more medical problems, poorer self-reported overall health, lower body mass index, alcohol and/or marijuana dependence, tobacco dependence, more life-time sexual partners, sexually transmitted diseases, and early pregnancy compared with healthy controls, girls with depression, and girls with anxiety (Bardone, Moffitt, Caspi, Dickson, Stanton and Silva, 1998). Girls with depression or anxiety during adolescence did not have such broad risk associated.

Other studies suggest that at least 25 per cent to 50 per cent of antisocial girls engage in criminal behaviour as adults (Pajer, 1998; Robins and Price, 1991; Zoccolillo and Rogers, 1991; Zoccolillo *et al.*, 1992). They are at increased risk for psychiatric problems with rates ranging between 21 and 90 per cent (Lewis *et al.*, 1991; Robins, 1966; Zoccolillo *et al.*, 1992). Studies have found deficits in parenting, with 33 to 36 per cent of conduct disordered or delinquent girls having either a family court record or children placed outside of the home because of abuse or neglect (Lewis *et al.*, 1991; Robins, 1966; Werner and Smith, 1992). Adult women with a history of conduct disorder or delinquency had higher rates of dysfunctional and often violent intimate relationships (Bardone *et al.*, 1996; Lewis *et al.*, 1991; Robins, 1966; Werner, 1992) and high rates of service utilisation as adults (Bardone *et al.*, 1996; Robins, 1966). Thus, these data suggest that there are serious long-term risks for girls with antisocial behaviour or conduct disorder in childhood and that there may be a broader array of risk associated for girls than for boys.

Taken together, these data point to the serious problems associated with childhood antisocial behaviour for girls. It can no longer be assumed that girls will 'outgrow' their antisocial behaviour. Rather, girls appear to be as at risk for problems in adulthood as boys and the types of problems associated appear to be less predictable than have been found for boys. Research is needed to understand these divergent patterns in outcome. However, these data clearly point to the critical need for prevention and intervention programmes for girls as well as for boys. In addition, they punctuate the need for broader consideration of gender in the theory of the development of antisocial behaviour.

Can there be a unified theory of antisocial behaviour?

Most theories of antisocial behaviour have been developed to explain male antisocial behaviour with little attention to explaining female antisocial behaviour or understanding gender differences in rates or patterns of behaviour. When discussions of female delinquency occur, it has often been assumed that the same theories can be used to explain female antisocial behaviour as are used explain male antisocial behaviour (without considering gender) or that completely different models need to be developed. Discussions of a unified theoretical framework to describe the development of antisocial behaviour in both males and females that includes the specific ways in which differences in the lives of males and females relate to differences in the type, frequency and context of involvement are rare (see Steffensmeier and Allan, 1996 for an exception). As discussed previously, because female involvement in antisocial behaviour was considered unusual, there seemed to be no need to attend to issues of gender. When attention was paid to females, the focus was on theory to explain the gender gap in involvement in crime.

Researchers began to strongly challenge the assumption that antisocial behaviour was essentially a male problem in the 1970s and began to focus empirically and theoretically on the study of sex differences in antisocial behaviour, primarily delinquent behaviour (Adler, 1975; Canter, 1982; Chesney-Lind, 1973; Simon, 1975). Little empirical attention was given to evaluating causes or correlates of the behaviour among women or to understanding differences in rates in how risk develops. Initially, the increased interest in studying the problem among women was due to an increase in female involvement in delinquent and criminal behaviour beginning in the 1950s. In addition, there was a general social change occurring such that there was greater sensitivity to issues of gender. There was particular interest in the effects of greater equality of opportunities and ascribed social roles across genders. Theories to explain this increased involvement in antisocial behaviour among women were proposed which suggested this increase was a by-product of the women's movement and their departure from traditionally female roles (Adler, 1975; Simon, 1975). That is, as women were becoming more 'equal' in social status and role expectations to men, this included less disparity in prevalence of involvement in criminal behaviour. Empirical tests did not support this perspective, although it permeated much of the discussion of and literature about female antisocial behaviour (see Chesney-Lind and Brown, 1998; Steffensmeier and Allan, 1996 for further discussion of these issues) and continues to have influence on some theories of gender and crime today (e.g., Hagan, Gillis and Simpson, 1993).

There has now been a substantial body of research that has demonstrated that a gender equality theory may not provide the best explanation of female antisocial behaviour (Jensen and Eve, 1976; Chesney-Lind,

1989; Morash and Chesney-Lind, 1991; Steffensmeier and Allan, 1996; Steffensmeier and Allan, 1995; Steffensmeier, Allan and Streifel, 1989). First, rates of female participation in antisocial and criminal behaviour remain significantly lower than rates of men's involvement. A gender equality theory would lead to the expectation that women's involvement would have increased substantially and would have come closer to the level of male involvement. Although female involvement in delinquency and crime have increased, male involvement has also increased so the difference in male and female involvement has not changed substantially. Using Uniform Crime Reports of adult crimes from 1960 to 1990, Steffensmeier and Allan (1996) report that significant increases in female percentage of arrests are found mainly for minor property crimes (larceny, fraud, forgery, and embezzlement). Small increases (1 per cent to 3 per cent are found for major property crimes and malicious mischief offences (auto theft, vandalism). No clear trends were found for crimes against persons and sex-related crimes. Across this time, the female share of arrests for most offence categories was 15 per cent or less and was smallest for the most serious crimes.

There have been greater increases in adolescents' involvement in delinquency and crime, although this increase has been more recent. Using data from FBI reports from 1985 to 1994, rates of adolescent and young adult girls arrested for violent crimes have increased substantially. Arrests of females for murder were up 64 per cent, robbery 114 per cent and aggravated assaults were up 137 per cent over this ten-year period. However, these changes in arrest rates were similar to those found for males, suggesting overall changes in youth violence over this time rather than merely reflecting changes in violence among women. Importantly, violence continues to be a small proportion of the types of antisocial or delinquent behaviour for which girls are arrested. In 1985, 2 per cent of girls' arrests were for serious crimes of violence versus 3.4 per cent in 1994. Again, a gender equality hypothesis theory would lead to the expectation that there would have been a greater increase in female crime relative to male involvement. Thus, the existing data do not appear to support the idea that female involvement in crime is 'catching up' to male involvement. Rather, girls' involvement is still considerably less than boys' involvement.

Even for those types of crimes for which there has been a relatively greater increase in female involvement compared to males, a variety of alternatives to a gender equality explanation can be identified to explain these trends. Steffensmeier (1993) points out that increases in property crimes are less likely to result from increases in women's involvement in the workforce than from economic pressures on women that have been heightened by increasing rates of divorce and female-headed households, together with increasing responsibility for children. That is, other social or economic forces may provide the explanation for change. In addition, changes in law enforcement practices and record keeping and the increase in women's drug use may also explain the increase in petty property crime (Steffensmeier, 1993). Female involvement in drug use has increased since the 1960s (Anglin and Hser, 1987; Steffensmeier and Allan, 1996). For both men and women, drug use appears to exacerbate involvement in crime. For women in particular, burglary and robbery typically occurs after addiction and are likely to cease after the woman stops using drugs (Anglin and Hser, 1987). In addition to these potential explanations and the data suggesting that, for most types of crimes, female involvement has not been increasing, some investigators have noted the contradiction of considering 'a hypothesis that assumed improving girls' and women's economic conditions would lead to an increase in female crime when almost all the existing criminological literature stresses the role played by discrimination and poverty (and unemployment and underemployment) in the creation of crime' (p. 77, Chesney-Lind and Sheldon, 1992). Some investigators have suggested that the over-reliance on the gender equality hypothesis to explain female antisocial behaviour has suppressed theory building in this area and the development of a multivariate framework for explaining the gender differences found (Steffensmeier and Allan, 1996; Steffensmeier and Allan, 1995).

A gendered approach

Although general theories of delinquency do not specifically exclude females, they often do not include gender issues in the understanding of the development, frequency, seriousness, and context of involvement in antisocial and delinquent behaviour. For example, a developmental life course perspective on crime focuses on career trajectories marked by 'turning points' (a change in the life course) from conventional to criminal behaviour or vice versa (Sampson and Laub, 1994). Transitions such as school to work or being single to married are opportunities for change in behaviour. Data suggest that, for men, involvement in a stable live-in relationship with a woman decreases risk for continued criminal behaviour (Farrington and West, 1995; Sampson and Laub, 1994) whether this is because of social bonding (Sampson and Laub, 1994) or decreased involvement with delinquent peers (Warr, 1998). However, it is not clear what effect this type of transition might have for a woman. There is some evidence to suggest that adolescent girls' involvement with male peers serves to increase their risk for antisocial behaviour (Caspi *et al.*, 1993).

The role of men in initiating women into crime, particularly serious crime, is a consistent finding in the literature (Gilfus, 1992; Pettiway, 1997; Steffensmeier, 1983). Thus, what may be a protective factor for men may, in fact, be a risk factor for women. This does not mean that a developmental life course perspective might not be useful for understanding antisocial behaviour among women. However, it does point to the fact that most theories of delinquent and antisocial behaviour fail to consider how risk factors may vary in impact by gender.

Steffensmeier and Allan (1996) point out several key elements that should be included in a gendered approach to understanding antisocial behaviour. Although their work refers more specifically to adult involvement in crime, some elements are transferable to a developmental understanding of antisocial behaviour and adolescent delinquency as well. Theory should help explain both male and female involvement by revealing how the organisation of gender deters or encourages antisocial behaviour in both males and females. 'Organisation of gender' refers broadly to things such as 'norms, identities, arrangements, institutions, and relations by which human sexual dichotomy is transformed into something physically and socially different' (p. 474).

For prevention utility, risk theory should not just function as a sophisticated tabulation of gender differences in type and frequency of crime, but should also provide an understanding of the developmental and contextual influences that relate gender to antisocial behaviour. Although the contexts in which mild forms of delinquent behaviour occur seem similar for males and females, the context for more serious behaviours, particularly violence, are quite different. For example, females are more likely than males to murder family members and very young victims (Kruttschnitt, 1993; Loper and Cornell, 1996). When involved in peer homicide, girls are more likely to have killed as a result of interpersonal conflict and are more likely to kill alone. Boys are more likely to kill with an accomplice (Loper and Cornell, 1996). These variations need to be understandable or related to gender as an important aspect of development and maintenance of antisocial behaviour. On that basis, sound gender encompassing prevention can occur.

Developmental-ecological model

One model that can provide such a gendered approach to understanding antisocial behaviour is developmental-ecological theory. It can also provide a framework to unify prediction and prevention efforts (Tolan, Guerra and Kendall, 1995). The numerous risk and protective factors associated with antisocial behaviour indicates a need for a conceptual/

theoretical framework to effectively organise them into a multi-level, multivariate model that is developmental but also takes into account social-ecological variations including gender (Brook, Nomura and Cohen, 1989; Szapocznik and Coatsworth, 1999; Szapocznik, Gorman-Smith, Coatsworth and Tolan, 1998; Tolan *et al.*, 1995). Such models permit the needed consideration of the multiple social contexts influencing development, the interrelations among those contexts, the changing nature of the contexts, and how these elements affect risk for the development of problem behaviours over time (Cicchetti and Aber, 1998; Richters and Cicchetti, 1993).

Developmental-ecological theory is influenced strongly by Urie Bronfenbrenner's work on the social ecology of human development (Bronfenbrenner, 1979, 1986). *Social ecological theory* proposes that the social domains for human development can be represented by a set of nested social structures (Bronfenbrenner, 1979, 1986). These social systems include social settings in which the child participates directly (e.g., family, peer), the interaction between systems (e.g., family/peer relationships, parent/school relationships), and the political, social, and cultural ideologies that shape individual development by enriching or impoverishing the other systems in which the child functions. Developmental-ecological theory is concerned with the change in youth behaviour and dynamic changes in the characteristics of social ecosystems across time (Boyce *et al.*, 1998). Thus, an important element of developmental-ecological theory is understanding what changes in the structure, organisation, integration, and functioning of the child's social ecology over time has for the development of antisocial behaviour (Cairns, Elder and Costello, 1996; Szapocznik *et al.*, 1998). This developmental perspective also emphasises that an individual develops as an integrated whole through continual transactions with a comparably developing social context (Bronfenbrenner, 1979; 1986; Cairns *et al.*, 1996). Developmental-ecological theory then, refers to the complex set of features that emerge over time within the child *and* in the child's social ecosystems, and the nature of the interactions within and among these systems as they change and influence each other reciprocally over time.

Implicit in this approach is the idea that the social role and behaviours associated with gender affect the nature and impact of these relationships. For example, parental monitoring has been identified as an important risk factor for delinquency (Gorman-Smith, Tolan, Zelli and Huessman, 1996; Patterson, Reid and Dishion, 1992; Loeber and Stouthamer-Loeber, 1986). However, monitoring may vary as a function of the gender of the child independent of the general quality of parenting. Because of increased concerns about girls' safety, parents are likely to monitor female children more closely than their male children. This increased monitoring results in decreased risk for girls.

The developmental-ecological model also emphasises the importance of considering individual risk factors within a larger context (Gorman-Smith, Tolan and Henry, 1999; Gorman-Smith, Tolan and Henry, 2000; Wikstrom and Loeber, 2000). That is, the impact of an individual risk factor may vary depending on other contextual factors. For example, for girls, early onset of puberty is related to increased risk for problem behaviours (Caspi and Moffitt, 1991; Stattin and Magnusson, 1990). However, the impact of this individual risk factor is likely moderated by context. Caspi, Lynam, Moffitt and Silva (1993) evaluated delinquent behaviour within four groups of girls: early-maturing girls attending mixed-sex schools, early maturing girls attending same sex schools, later maturing girls attending mixed-sex schools and later-maturing girls attending same sex schools. They found that the early maturing girls attending mixed-sex schools were at greatest risk for delinquent behaviour. Early maturing girls who attended all-girl schools were not at any greater risk for delinquent involvement. In addition, later maturing girls attending mixed-sex schools appeared to 'catch up' with their early maturing peers in their level of delinquent involvement after menarche. Thus, the school context (and likely greater exposure to delinquent peers) moderated the impact of this individual risk factor. The predictive value of an individual risk factor, and the use for aiding in the development of preventive interventions, is greatly increased when variation by gender and context are understood. A developmental-ecological model provides a frame for evaluation of these relations and a framework to unify prediction and prevention efforts (Tolan, Guerra and Kendall, 1995).

What about prevention?

In the beginning of this chapter, three questions were proposed as important to address to inform prevention efforts for female antisocial behaviour. What are the rates and patterns of involvement in antisocial behaviour among females? What are the predictors and correlates of involvement in antisocial behaviour among females? Is there any evidence of programme impact of interventions for females and is there any evidence of differential impact due to gender? Some aspects of these questions have been addressed through the discussion on constraints. However, in the next section, the current state of information available to address each of these questions is organised and summarised from a developmental-ecological perspective with particular attention to the issues discussed earlier regarding gender.

What are the rates and patterns of involvement among females?

It is clear that males are at greater risk for involvement in most types of antisocial behaviour, other than for relational aggression (Crick and Grotpeter, 1995; Cairns and Cairns, 1986). Boys are consistently rated as more physically aggressive in childhood (Lefkowitz, Eron, Walder and Huesmann, 1977; Kellam, Simon and Ensminger, 1983), more boys are diagnosed with conduct disorder (Cohen, Cohen, Kasen, Velez, Hatmark, Johnson, Rojas, Brook and Steuning, 1993; Robbins, 1986), and males have a higher rate of involvement in delinquent and violent offending (Elliott, 1994; Loeber and Farrington, 1998). In addition to differences in rates of disorders, longitudinal analyses suggest age differences in onset and desistance by gender, particularly for violent offenders (Cohen *et al.*, 1993; Elliott, 1994; Sommers and Baskin, 1992). The careers of violent females both begin and peak a little earlier than those of males. For example, Elliott (1994) found the peak age in prevalence of violent offending to be earlier for females than males (15 versus 17) and the decline to be steeper for females.

Gender differences in rates and onset and desistance patterns of delinquent and violent offending are found for both self-reported and official records (Cernkovich and Giordano, 1979; Elliott, Huizinga and Ageton, 1985; Figueira-McDonough, 1985; Laub and McDermott, 1985). These differences tend to be greater for more serious than for minor offences. For example, based on National Youth Survey data for White adolescents in 1980, Huizinga and Elliott (1986) reported male-female prevalence ratios of approximately 1.2 for status offences, 2.5 for minor theft and 4.5 for robbery. Elliott (1994) reported that the gender differential for self-reported participation in violence increases over development. At age 12, the male-to-female differential is 2 to 1; by 18 it has increased to 3 to 1; by age 21, it is 4 to 1. Official arrest statistics reflect similar rate gender differentials. In 1992, the rate for female offenders between the ages of 10 and 17 was approximately one-fourth the rate of offending by same age males for crimes against persons, crimes against property, drugs and public order offences (Snyder and Sickmund, 1995). Similar increases in the gender differential in violent offending are found by examining official juvenile homicide offending rates. At age 13, the male homicide rate is 6.3 times greater than the female rate; by age 17 the male rate is 11.5 times greater (Snyder and Sickmund, 1995). As adults, the male rates of arrest for homicide, robbery, and burglary are about eighteen, twelve and fourteen times higher respectively, than the female rates (Sommers and Baskin, 1992).

In examining these rates, there are several issues that are important to note and have implications for prevention. First, there is a change in the relation of boys' and girls' involvement in antisocial behaviour over the course of development. The gap in prevalence becomes greater as children get older. There are also differences in the onset and desistance of delinquent behaviour for boys and girls. Girls tend to start somewhat younger, peak earler and desist earlier. This change may reflect differences in roles and expectations across development. It may also reflect the greater range of outcomes associated with problem behaviours among girls (Pajer, 1998; Robins, 1986). Girls may develop other types of problems in adolescence and young adulthood and there is a need to be cognisant of the multiple range of problems for girls across development.

It is also important to note contextual differences between male and female offences. The context of offending refers to things such as whether the offence was committed with others, the offender's role in initiating and committing the offence, the type of victim, the victim-offender relationship, the value or type of property stolen or damaged, and whether a weapon was used (Daly, 1994; Steffensmeier, 1983, 1993; Steffensmeier and Allan, 1996; Triplett and Myers, 1995). Even when males and females participate in the same types of behaviours, they may differ substantially in quality and these differences appear to be greater for more violent offences.

For minor forms of delinquency such as hitting others or stealing from stores or schools, girls' prevalence of involvement approaches that of boys. However, girls are less likely to use a weapon or to intend serious injury to their victims (Kruttschnitt, 1994). They are also less likely to break into buildings to steal or to steal things that they cannot use (Steffensmeier and Allan, 1996). Girls are more likely to steal from somewhere familiar, like a residence when no one is at home or from work and they are more likely to steal alone (Steffensmeier, 1993). When female offenders do steal with others, they usually act as accomplices (e.g., driving the car) and are less likely to get an equal share of what is taken (Steffensmeier, 1983).

As discussed earlier, there are greater contextual differences between male and female violence. Females are more likely than males to kill someone they know intimately such as a spouse, child or other family member. Girls are more likely than boys to murder very young victims (24 per cent of girls' victims are under age 3 compared with 1 per cent of boys' victims; Loper and Cornell, 1996). Girls are more likely to use a knife than a gun and to murder someone as the result of conflict, rather than in a commission of a crime (Chesney-Lind and Brown, 1998). Thus, although committing the same violent offence, there are often significant differences in the nature and quality of the crime committed. Thus, while it is important to understand the rates and patterns of girls' involvement in antisocial behaviour, it is important to consider these statistics within the context of development as well as the context within which the crime occurs. These differences have important implications for prevention of both male and female delinquent and violent offending.

What are the predictors of female antisocial behaviour?

Recent research suggests that many of the same predictors of antisocial behaviour among males relate to antisocial behaviour among females. Family, peer, and community factors are all related to increased risk (Canter, 1982; Chesney-Lind, 1989; Figueira-McDonough, 1985; Giordano *et al.*, 1986; Steffensmeier and Allan, 1996). So, in reviewing the literature, the same list of risk factors appears for girls as appears for boys. However, the nature and quality of how these factors relate to risk may be different for boys and girls. There are certain important ways in which gender is implicated in social relationships that can be obscured or missed when simply looking at whether variables relate. For example, because female adolescents are more invested in interpersonal relationships than male adolescents (Block, 1983; Crick *et al.*, in press; Giordano *et al.*, 1986), girls are more likely to get involved in or be affected by parental conflict (Henggeler, Edwards and Borduin, 1987) or may be pulled into delinquent behaviour through involvement in intimate relationships with delinquent men (Steffensmeier and Allan, 1996). Given the strong social sanctions against girls' involvement in antisocial behaviour, data suggest that it may take a particularly deviant family to impact risk among girls. Although both family and peer influences are related to female antisocial behaviour, the nature of the relation may be different and reflect gender differences in relationship development, norms and values, and social control. For example, the greater supervision and control of girls by parents reduces female risk-taking and increases attachment to parents, teachers, and conventional friends, which in turn reduces influence by delinquent peers (Giordano, Cerkovich and Pugh, 1986). Gender organises the proximal risk factor of the family and results in different relationships with other significant social systems. Thus, when evaluating psychosocial predictors of antisocial behaviour, particularly in regard to informing prevention, elements of social expectations, role and power as a function of gender need to be considered. Even though the same factors relate to risk, the nature and power of those associations may vary for boys and girls.

Victimisation

One of the primary differences in discussions of predictors of girls' antisocial behaviour versus boys' antisocial behaviour is the role of victimisation. Although it is clear that boys are also at risk, victimisation has been given a much more central role in risk for antisocial behaviour among girls than boys (Howing, Wodarski, Kurtz, Gaudin and Herbst, 1990; Kelley, Thornberry and Smith, 1997; McCord, 1982; Scudder, Blount, Heide and Silverman, 1993; Smith and Thornberry, 1995; Zingraff, Leiter, Myers and Johnsen, 1993). In addition to increased risk for involvement in general, some research suggests a link between more serious types of crime and violence (Avery and Gorman-Smith, 1998; Doerner, 1987; Smith and Thornberry, 1995). This research suggests some differences by gender. However, these findings are somewhat inconsistent. Some have found no differences in relations by gender (Smith and Thornberry, 1995). That is, maltreatment is related to involvement in more serious forms of delinquency, including violent, serious and moderate forms of delinquency and not related to minor delinquency for both males and females. Others have found a relation to violence only for males (Avery and Gorman-Smith, 1998; Widom, 1989) and others only for females (Widom and White, 1997). Part of what may be contributing to these differences is a difference in the relation between types of abuse and outcome for males and females. Some studies combined both physical and sexual abuse to evaluate the relation between 'abuse' or 'maltreatment' and others have focused on specific types of abuse. There are important differences in the nature and impact of each that are related to the gender of the victim.

For example, when the focus becomes sexual victimisation, differences related to gender are complex. A number of studies have found a relation between history of sexual abuse and antisocial behaviour (Chesney-Lind and Rodriguez, 1983; Phelps *et al.*, 1982; Snell and Morton, 1994; Widom, 1988). Girls, however, are significantly more likely to be sexually abused as children and adults. Rates of sexual abuse among women range from 25 to 35 per cent, representing about 70 per cent of all sexual abuse victims (Finkelhor and Baron, 1986). There are also qualitative differences in the experience of sexual abuse by males and females. Girls' sexual abuse tends to start earlier than boys and they are more likely to be assaulted by a family member (Finkelhor and Baron, 1986).

The abuse tends to last longer and is more likely to last into adulthood (DeJong, Hervada and Emmett, 1983; Snell and Morton, 1994). All of these factors (relationship with perpetrator, onset and length of victimisation) are associated with more severe trauma (Browne and Finkelhor, 1986; Spaccarelli, 1994). In addition to different qualities of the abuse, girls may react differently than boys. Girls are more likely to run away than boys in an attempt to escape continued abuse. Once on the street, they may be forced into delinquent or criminal behaviour to survive (Chesney-Lind, 1989). Thus, both girls' victimisation and their response to it are influenced by their status as female. However, it is clear that victimisation is related to increased risk for boys as well. Only by including both males and females in studies of antisocial behaviour can we begin to have a gendered understanding of risk.

Are there differential prevention effects? And what works?

Several excellent reviews of prevention of antisocial behaviour, delinquency and violence have been conducted over the past few years (see Farrington and Welsh, 1999; Tolan and Guerra, 1994; Wasserman and Miller, 1998). Readers are referred to those reviews for specific programme effects. Programmes that appear to have the greatest impact tend to target multiple aspects of risk (e.g., family, peers, school). In general, programmes that include the family have shown the most promise, particularly those that focus on improving parent behaviour and management skills, promoting emotional cohesion within the family, and aiding family problem solving (Tolan and Guerra, 1994). In addition, those targetting academic achievement and school bonding are also among the most successful (Farrington and Welsh, 1999; Hawkins *et al.*, 1992).

However, limited attention has been paid to the specific needs or concerns of girls. Wasserman and Miller (1998) acknowledge that the problem may be very different for boys and girls and may require different programme targets. As with other research in this area, most preventive interventions appear to have been designed based on male models and boys' risk, and not girls', in mind. In fact, many programmes have been applied only to boys. In an exhaustive review of all programme evaluation studies conducted since 1950, Lipsey (1992) found that only 8.2 per cent of the surveyed programmes served girls or mostly girls. Often when girls have been included, overall effects are reported and analyses are completed by gender. Some studies report no differences in effects for boys and girls. In some cases, when girls have been included, programmes have been less effective with girls than boys (e.g., Farrell and Meyer, 1997; Kellam, Mayer, Rebok and Hawkins, 1998). Other programmes have reported some differential effects for boys and girls (e.g., Hawkins, Von Cleve and Catalano, 1991). That is, different behavioural outcomes were found or different moderators of risk were changed. However, there has been little discussion of the meaning of these potential differences.

There are several potential explanations for these differences. Some of the programmes that have been less effective may not have targetted those risk factors that are most likely to affect change for girls or may not have attended to the particular ways that gender may be a part of the relation. For example, programmes that do not focus on management of relationship issues may not be salient for girls and may miss an important path toward modifying risk (Capaldi and Gorman-Smith, in press). In addition, research has demonstrated that programmes that include the family as part of the intervention are likely to have the most powerful effects (Tolan and Guerra, 1994; Wasserman and Miller, 1998). This is true of girls, as well as boys, but may even be more important given the research suggesting that girls tend to be more involved with their families and that antisocial girls' families are more dysfunctional than families of antisocial boys. The increased prevalence of victimisation among girls and the extensive research on the long-term effects of such abuse suggest that programmes should be prepared to address these issues (Chesney-Lind, 1997).

Second, it is possible that programmes have been effective, but that programmes have not evaluated change in multiple types of outcomes. A focus only on physical aggression or other types of externalising problems could result in missing important intervention effects. For example, by not considering types of relational aggression, intervention effects (particularly for girls) could be missed. As research suggests that the long-term outcomes for girls with antisocial behaviour might be more complex than that of boys, additional outcomes such as internalising disorders and other indicators of well-being, should be considered. Attention to these other types of problems might also result in finding that these outcomes have been affected for boys as well as girls.

If we are to understand why programmes are effective for one group and not another or why programmes impact different types of behaviours, gender must be included in analyses. In addition, programme evaluation should examine mediators of risk and targets of intervention by gender. The same programme may decrease risk for both boys and girls, but might do so through different processes. These differences may be important for understanding basic risk processes, and are critical for understanding how to develop appropriate and effective intervention programmes. Thus, while it may be possible to design a programme that is applicable for both boys and girls, this will only be accomplished by attending to some of the ways in which risk and intervention effects may vary in impact by gender.

Preparation of this chapter was supported by NICHD grant HS35415, CDC grant R14/CCR512739 and a Faculty Scholar Award from the William T. Grant Foundation. Special thanks to Patrick Tolan and David Farrington for comments on an earlier draft of this chapter and to Marlita White for research assistance.

REFERENCES

Adler, F. (1975) *Sisters in Crime*. New York: McGraw-Hill.

Anglin, D. and Hser, Y. (1987) Addicted women and crime. *Criminology, 25*, 359–97.

Avery, L. and Gorman-Smith, D. (1998) *Child Abuse, Neglect, and Violence*. Unpublished manuscript.

Bardone, A. M., Moffitt, T. E., Caspi, A., Dickson, N., Stanton, W. R. and Silva, P. A. (1996) Adult mental health and social outcomes of adolescent girls with depression and conduct disorder. *Developmental Psychopathology, 8*, 811–29.

Adult physical health outcomes of adolescent girls with conduct disorder, depression, and anxiety. *Journal of the American Academy of Child Adolescent Psychiatry, 37*, (6), 594–601.

Bjorkqvist, K. and Niemela, P. (1992) New trends in the study of female aggression. In K. Bjorkqvist and P. Niemala. (eds.), *Of Mice and Women: Aspects of Female Aggression*. (pp. 1–16). San Diego, CA: Academic Press.

Block, J. (1983) Differential premises arising from differential socialization of the sexes: Some conjectures. *Child Development, 54*, 1335–54.

Boyce, W. T., Frank, E., Jensen, P. S., Kessler, R. C., Nelson, C. A. and Steinberg, L. (1998) Social context in developmental psychopathology: Recommendations for future research from the MacArthur Foundation Research Network on Psychopathology and Development. *Development and Psychopathology, 10*, (2), 143–64.

Bronfenbrenner, U. (1979) *The Ecology of Human Development: Experiments by Nature and Design*. Cambridge, MA: Harvard University Press.

(1986) Ecology of the family as a context for human development. *American Psychologist, 32*, 513–31.

Brook, J. S., Nomura, C. and Cohen, P. (1989) A network of influences on adolescent drug involvement: Neighborhood, school, peer, and family. *Genetic, Social, and General Psychology Monographs, 115*, (1), 125–45.

Browne, A. and Finklehor, D. (1986) Impact of child sexual abuse: A review of Research. *Psychological Bulletin, 99*, 66–77.

Cairns, R. B. and Cairns, B. D. (1986) The developmental-interactional view of social behavior: Four issues of adolescent aggression. In D. Olweus J. Block, and M. Radke-Yarrow (eds.), *Development of Antisocial and Prosocial Behavior* (pp. 315–42). New York: Academic Press.

(1994) *Lifelines and Risk: Pathways of Youth in Our Time*. Cambridge University Press.

Cairns, R. B., Cairns, B. D., Neckerman, H. J., Ferguson, L. L. and Gariepy, J. L. (1989) Growth and aggression: I. Childhood to early adolescence. *Developmental Psychology*, *25*, 320–30.

Cairns, R. B., Elder, G. H. and Costello, E. J. (1996) *Developmental Science*. New York: Cambridge University Press.

Calhoun, G., Jurgens, J. and Chen, F. (1993) The neophyte female delinquent: A review of the literature. *Adolescence*, *28*, (110), 461–71.

Canter R. J. (1982) Family correlates of male and female delinquency. *Criminology*, *20*, 149–67.

Capaldi, D. and Gorman-Smith, D. (in press) Physical and psychological aggression in male/female adolescent and young adult couples. In P. Florsheim, (ed.) *Adolescent Romance and Sexual Behavior: Theory, Research and Practical Implications*. Los Angeles: LEA associates.

Caspi, A. and Moffitt, T. E. (1991) Individual differences are accentuated during periods of social change: The sample case of girls at puberty. *Journal of Personality and Social Psychology*, *61*, 157–68.

Caspi, A., Lynam, D., Moffitt, T. E. and Silva, P. A. (1993) Unraveling girls' delinquency: Biological, dispositional, and contextual contributions to adolescent misbehavior. *Developmental Psychology*, *29*, 19–30.

Cernkovich, S. A. and Giordano, P. C. (1979) A comparative analysis of male and female delinquency. *Sociological Quarterly*, *20*, 131–45.

Chesney-Lind, M. (1973) Judicial enforcement of the female sex role. *Issues in Criminology*, *3*, 51–71.

(1989) Girls' crime and woman's place: Toward a feminist model of female delinquency. *Crime and Delinquency*, *35*, (1), 5–29.

(1997) *The Female Offender: Girls, Women and Crime*. Thousand Oaks, CA: Sage Publications.

Chesney-Lind, M. and Brown, M. (1998) Girls and violence. In Flannery, D. J. and Huff. C. R. (eds.). *Youth Violence: Prevention, Intervention, and Social Policy*. (pp. 171–99). Washington, DC: American Psychiatric Press.

Chesney-Lind, M. and Rodriquez, N. (1983) Women under lock and key. *Prison Journal*, *63*, 47–65.

Chesney-Lind, M. and Shelden, R. G. (1992) *Girls, Delinquency, and Juvenile Justice*. Pacific Grove, CA: Brooks/Cole.

Cicchetti, D. and Aber, J. L. (1998) Contextualism and developmental psychopathology. *Development and Psychopathology*, *4*, 489–93.

Cohen, P., Cohen, J., Kasen, S., Velez, C. N., Hartmark, C., Johnson, J. Rojas, M., Brook, J. and Streuning, E. L. (1993) An epidemiological study of disorders in late childhood and adolescence- I. age- and gender-specific prevalence. *Journal of Child Psychology and Psychiatry*, *34*, 851–67.

Crick, N. R. and Grotpeter, J. K. (1995) Relational aggression, gender, and social-psychological adjustment. *Child Development*, *66*, (3), 710–22.

Crick, N. R., Bigbee, M. and Howes, C. (1996) Gender differences in children's normative beliefs about aggression: How do I hurt thee? Let me count the ways. *Child Development*, *67*, 1003–14.

Crick, N. R., Wellman, N. E., Casas, J. F., O'Brien, K. M., Nelson, D. A., Grotpeter, J. K. and Markon, K. (in press). Childhood aggression and gender: A new look at an old problem. In D. Berstein (ed.), *Nebraska Symposium on Motivation*, vol. 45.

Daly, K. (1994) *Gender, Crime, and Punishment*. New Haven, CT: Yale University Press.

DeJong, A. R., Hervada, A. R. and Emmett, G. A. (1983) Epidemiologic variations in childhood sexual abuse. *Child Abuse and Neglect*, *7*, 155–62.

Doerner, W. G. (1987) Child maltreatment seriousness and juvenile delinquency. *Youth and Society*, *19*, (2), 197–224.

Elliott, D. S. (1994) Serious violent offenders: Onset, developmental course, and termination-the American society of criminology 1993 presidential address. *Criminology*, *32*, 1–21.

Elliott, D. S., Huizinga, D. A. and Ageton, S. S. (1985) *Explaining Delinquency and Drug Use*. Beverly Hills, CA: Sage.

Farrell, A. D. and Meyer, A. L. (1997) The effectiveness of a school-based curiculum for reducing violence among urban sixth-grade students. *American Journal of Public Health*, *87*, 979–84.

Farrington, D. P. and Welsh, B. C. (1999) Delinquency prevention using family-based interventions. *Children and Society*, *13*, 287–303.

Farrington, D. P. and West, D. J. (1995) Effects of marriage, separation, and children on offending by adult males. In Z. Blau Smith and J. Hagan (eds.), *Current Perspectives on Aging and the Life Cycle*. vol. 4. (pp. 249–81). Greenwich, CT: JAI Press.

Figueira-McDonough, J. (1985) Are girls different? Gender discrepancies between delinquent behavior and control. *Child Welfare*, *64*, 273–89.

Finklehor, D. and Baron, L. (1986) Risk factors for child sexual abuse. *Journal of Interpersonal Violence*, *1*, 43–71.

Gilfus, M. (1992) From victims to survivors to offenders: Women's routes of entry and immersion into street crime. *Women Crim. Justice*, *4*: 63–89.

Giordano, P. C., Cernkovich, S. A. and Pugh, M. D. (1986) Friendships and delinquency. *American Journal of Sociology*, *91*, 1170–202.

Glueck, S. and Glueck, E. (1950) *Unraveling Juvenile Delinquency*. New York: Commonwealth Fund.

Gorman-Smith, D., Tolan, P. H. and Henry, D. (1999) The relation of community and family to risk among urban poor adolescents. In P. Cohen and L. N. Robins, C. Slomkowski (eds.), *Historical and Geographical Influences on Psychopathology* (pp. 349–67). Mahwah, NJ: Erlbaum.

(2000) A developmental-ecological model of the relation of family functioning to patterns of delinquency. *Journal of Quantitative Criminology*, *16*, 169–98.

Gorman-Smith, D., Tolan, P. H., Zelli, A. and Huesmann, L. R. (1996) The relation of family functioning to violence among inner-city minority youth. *Journal of Family Psychology*, *10*, 115–29.

Hagan, J., Gillis, A. and Simpson, J. (1993) The power of control in sociological theories of delinquency. In F. Adler and W. Laufer (eds.), *Advances in Criminological Theory*. New Brunswick, NJ: Transaction.

Havighurst, R. J., Bowman, P. H., Liddle, G. P., Matthews, C. V. and Pierce, J. V. (1962) *Growing Up in River City*. New York: John Wiley.

Hawkins, J. D., Von Cleve, E. and Catalano, R. F. (1991) Reducing early childhood aggression: Results of a primary prevention program. *Journal of the American Academy of Child and Adolescent Psychiatry*, *30*, 208–17.

Henggeler, S. W., Edwards, J. and Borduin, C. M. (1987) The family relations of female juvenile delinquents. *Journal of Abnormal Child Psychology*, *15*, 199–209.

Hirschi, T. (1969) *Causes of Delinquency*. Berkeley: University of California Press.

Howing, P., Wodarski, J. S., Kurtz, P. D., Gaudin, Jr., J. M. and Herbst, E. N. (1990) Child abuse and delinquency: The empirical and theoretical links. *Social Work*, *35*, 244–9.

Huizinga, D. and Elliott, D. (1986) Reassessing the reliability and validity of self-report delinquency measures. *Journal of Quantitative Criminology*, *2*, 293–327.

Jensen, G. J. and Eve, R. (1976) Sex differences in delinquency: an examination of popular sociological explanations. *Criminology: An Interdisciplinary Journal*, *13* (4), 427–48.

Kellam, S. G., Mayer, L. S., Rebok, G. W. and Hawkins, W. E. (1998) Effects of improving achievement on aggressive behavior and of improving aggressive behavior on achievement through two preventive interactions: An investigation of causal paths. In B. Dohrenwend (ed.), *Adversity, Stress, and Psychopathology* (pp. 486–505). New York: Oxford University Press.

Kellam, S. G., Simon, M. and Ensminger, M. (1983) Antecedents in first grade of teenage substance abuse and psychological well being. In D. Ricks and B. Dohrenwend (eds.), *Origins of psychopathology*. Cambridge, MA: Cambridge University Press.

Kelley, B. T., Thornberry, T. P. and Smith, C. A. (August, 1997) *In the wake of Childhood Maltreatment*. Washington, DC: Juvenile Justice Bulletin.

Kruttschnitt, C. (1993) Violence by and against women: A cooperative and cross-national analysis. *Violence and Victims*, *vol. 8* (3), 253–70.

(1994) Gender and interpersonal violence. In J. Roth and A. Reiss (eds.), *Understanding and Preventing Violence: vol. 3: Social Influences* (pp. 293–376). Washington, DC: National Academy Press.

Laub, J. H. and McDermott, M. J. (1985) An analysis of serious crime by young black women. *Criminology*, *23*, 81–98.

Lefkowitz, M. M., Eron, L. D., Walder, L. O. and Huesmann, L. R. (1977) *Growing Up to Be Violent*. New York: Pergamon.

Lewis, D. O., Yeager, C. A., Cobham-Portorreal, C. S., Klein, N., Showalter, C. and Anthony, A. (1991) A follow-up of female delinquents: Maternal contributions to the perpetuation of deviance. *Journal of the American Academy of Child and Adolescent Psychiatry*, *30*, 197–201.

Lipsey, M. (1992) Juvenile delinquency treatment: A meta-analytic inquiry in the variability of effects. In T. A. Cook, H. Cooper, D. S. Corday, H. Hartmann, L. V. Hedges, R. J. Light, T. A. Louis and F. Mosleller (eds.) *Meta-analysis for Explanation: A Casebook* (pp. 83–126). New York: Russell Sage.

Loeber, R. and Farrington, D. P. (1997) Strategies and yields of longitudinal studies on antisocial behavior. In D. M. Stoff, J. Breiling and J. D. Maser (eds.), *Handbook of Antisocial Behavior*. (pp. 125–39). New York: Wiley.

(1998) Conclusions and the way forward. In Loeber, R. and Farrington, D. P. (eds), *Serious and Violent Juvenile Offenders: Risk Factors and Successful Interventions* (pp. 405–27). Thousand Oaks, CA: Sage.

Loeber, R. and Stouthamer-Loeber, M. (1986) Family factors as correlates and predictors of juvenile conduct problems and delinquency. In M. Tonry and Morris, N. (eds), *Crime and Justice vol. 7* (pp. 29–149). University of Chicago Press.

Loper, A. B. and Cornell, D. G. (1996) Homicide by girls. *Journal of Family and Child Studies*, *5*, 321–33.

McCord, J. (1982) A longitudinal view of the relationship between paternal absence and crime. In J. Gunn and D. P. Farrington (eds.), *Abnormal Offenders, Delinquency, and the Criminal Justice System* (pp. 113–28). Chichester: Wiley.

McDonald, C. D. and O'Laughlin, E. M. (1997) *Relational Aggression and Risk Behaviors in Middle School Students*. Poster presented at the bi-annual meetings of the Society for Research in Child Development. Washington, DC.

Morash, M. and Chesney-Lind, M. (1991) A reformulation and partial test of the power control theory of delinquency. *Justice Quarterly*, *8*, 347–76.

Morey, L. C. (1991) *The Personality Assessment Inventory: Professional manual*. Psychological Assessment Resources.

Pajer, K. A. (1998) What happens to "bad" girls? A review of the adult outcomes of antisocial adolescent girls. *American Journal of Psychiatry*, *115*, (7), 862–70.

Patterson, G. R., Reid, J. B. and Dishion, T. J. (1992) *Antisocial Boys: A Social Interactional Approach (vol. 4)*. Eugene, OR: Castalia.

Pettiway, L. E. (1997) *Workin' It: Women Living through Drugs and Crime*. Philadelphia: Temple University Press.

Phelps, R. J. *et al*. (1982) *Wisconsin Female Juvenile Offender Study Project Summary Report*. Wisconsin: Youth Policy and Law Center, Wisconsin Council on Juvenile Justice.

Poe-Yamagata, E. and Butts, J. A. (1996) *Female Offenders in the Juvenile Justice System: Statistics Summary*. Pittsburgh, PA: National Center for Juvenile Justice.

Richters, J. E. and Cicchetti, D. (1993) Mark Twain meets DSM-III-R: Conduct disorder, development, and the concept of harmful dysfunction. *Development and Psychopathology*, *5*, 5–29.

Robins, L. N. (1966) *Deviant Children Grown Up: A Sociological and Psychiatric Study of Sociopathic Personality*. Baltimore: Williams and Wilkins.

(1986) The consequences of conduct disorder in girls. In Olweus, D., Block, J. and Radke-Yarrow, M. (eds.) *Development of Antisocial and Prosocial Behavior: Research, Theories, and Issues* (pp. 385–409). New York: Academic Press.

Robins, L. N. and Price, R. K. (1991) Adult disorders predicted by childhood conduct problems: Results from the NIMH Epidemiologic Catchment Area Project. *Psychiatry*, *54*, 116–32.

Sampson, R. J. and Laub, J. H. (1994) Urban poverty and the family context of delinquency: A new look at structure and process in a classic study. *Child Development*, *65*, (2), 523–39.

Scudder, R. G., Blount, W. R., Heide, K. M. and Silverman, I. J. (1993) Important links between child abuse, neglect, and delinquency. *International Journal of Offender Therapy & Comparative Criminology*, *37*, (4), 315–23.

Shaw, C. and McKay, H. (1942) *Juvenile Delinquency and Urban Areas*. University of Chicago Press.

Simon, R. (1975) *The Contemporary Woman and Crime*. Washington, DC: National Institute of Mental Health.

Smith, C. and Thornberry, T. (1995) The relationship between childhood maltreatment and adolescent involvement in delinquency. *Criminology*, *33*, (4), 451–79.

Snell, T. L. and Morton, D. C. (1994) *Women in Prison*. Special report. Washington, DC: Bureau of Justice Statistics, US Deptartment of Justice.

Snyder, H., Finnegan, T. A., Nimick, E. H., Sickmund, M. H., Sullivan, D. P. and Tierney, N. J. (1989) *Juvenile Court Statistics 1985*. Washington, DC: US Department of Justice.

Snyder, H. N. and Sickmund, M. (1995) *Juvenile Offenders and Victims: A Focus on Violence*. Pittsburgh, PA: National Center for Juvenile Justice.

Sommers, I. and Baskin, D. (1992) Sex, race, age, and violent offending. *Violence and Victims*, *7*, 191–201.

Spaccarelli, S. (1994) Stress, appraisal, and coping in child sexual abuse: a theoretical and empirical review. *Psychological Bulletin*, *116*, (2), 340–62.

Stattin, H. and Magnusson, D. (1990) *Pubertal Maturation in Female Development*. Hillsdale, NJ: Erlbaum.

Steffensmeier, D. (1983) Sex-segregation in the underworld: Building a sociological explanation of sex differences in crime. *Social Forces*, *61*, 1010–32.

(1993) National trends in female arrests, 1960–1990: assessment and recommendations for research. *Journal of Quantitative Criminology*, *9*, 413–41.

Steffensmeier, D. and Allan, E. (1995) Gender, age, and crime. In J. Sheley (ed.) *Handbook of Contemporary Criminology*. New York: Wadsworth.

Gender and crime: toward a gendered theory of female offending. *Annual Review of Sociology*, *22*, 459–87.

Steffensmeier, D., Allan, E. and Streifel, C. (1989) Development and female crime: a cross-national test of alternative explanation. *Social Forces*, *68*, 262–83.

Synder, H. N. and Finnegan, T. A. (1987) *Delinquency in the United States*. Washington, DC: Department of Justice.

Szapocznik, J. and Coatsworth, J. D. (1999) An ecodevelopemental framework for organizing the influences on drug abuse: a developmental model of risk and protection. In M. Glantz and C. R. Hartel (eds.) *Drug Abuse: Origins and Interventions*. Washington DC: American Psychological Association.

Szapocznik, J., Gorman-Smith, D., Coatsworth, J. D. and Tolan, P. (1998) *Families, Ecodevelopment, and Drug Abuse Prevention*. Unpublished manuscript.

Triplett, R. and Myers, L. (1995) Evaluating contextual patterns of delinquency: Gender based differences. *Justice Quarterly*, *12*, 59–79.

Tolan, P. H. and Guerra, N. (1994) *What Works in Reducing Adolescent Violence: An Empirical Review of the Field.* Center for the Study and Prevention of Violence. Boulder, CO: University of Colorado.

Tolan, P. G., Guerra, N. and Kendall, P. C. (1995) An developmental-ecological perspective on anti-social behavior in children and adolescents: Toward a unified risk and intervention framework. *Journal of Consulting and Clinical Psychology*, *63*,(4), 579–84.

Warr, M. (1998) Life course transitions and desistance from crime. *Criminology*, *36* (2), 183–216.

Wassermann, G. A. and Miller, L. (1998) The prevention of serious and violent juvenile offending. In R. Loeber and D. Farrington (eds.), *Serious and Violent Juvenile Offenders: Risk Factors and Successful Interventions.* (pp. 197–247). Thousand Oaks, CA: Sage.

Wellman, N. E. and Crick, N. R. (1998) *Relational and Physical Aggression and Social-Psychological Adjustment in a College Sample.* Unpublished manuscript, University of Minnesota.

Werner, E. (1992) The children of Kauai: resiliency and recovery in adolescence and adulthood. *Journal of Adolescent Health*, *13* (4), 262–68.

Werner, E. E. and Smith, R. S. (1992) *Overcoming the Odds: High Risk Children from Birth to Adulthood.* Ithaca, NY: Cornell University Press.

Widom, C. S. (1989) Child abuse, neglect and violent criminal behavior. *Criminology*, *27*, 251–71.

Widom, C. S. and White, H. R. (1997) Problem behaviours in abused and neglected children grown up: Prevalence and co-occurrence of substance abuse, crime and violence. *Criminal Behaviour and Mental Health*, *7*, (4), 287–310.

Wikstrom, P. H. and Loeber, R. (2000) Do disadvantaged neighborhoods cause well-adusted children to become adolescent delinquents? A study of male juvenile serious offending, individual risk and protective factors, and neighborhood context. *Criminology*, *38*, (4), 1109–42.

Zingraff, M. T., Leiter, J., Myers, K. A. and Johnson, M. C. (1993) Child maltreatment and youthful problem behavior. *Criminology*, *31*, (2), 173–202.

Zoccolillo, M. (1993) Gender and the development of conduct disorder. *Development and Psychopathology*, *5*, 65–78.

Zoccolillo, M., Pickles, A., Quinton, D. and Rutter, M. (1992) The outcome of childhood conduct disorder: Implications for defining adult personality disorder and conduct disorder. *Psychol. Med.*, *22*, 971–86.

Zoccolillo, M. and Rogers, K. (1991) Characteristics and outcome of hospitalized adolescent girls with conduct disorder. *Journal of the American Academy of Child and Adolescent Psychiatry*, *30*, 973–81.

10 Economic costs and benefits of primary prevention of delinquency and later offending: a review of the research

Brandon C. Welsh

Introduction

In recent years, in the United Kingdom and other industrialised countries, there has been a growing interest on the part of governments and other stakeholders in the economic costs and benefits of the early prevention of antisocial behaviour. Rising criminal justice costs, a greater understanding of the economic impacts of crime and fiscal cut-backs are just some of the issues that have prompted this attention. However, investments in effective delinquency and criminality prevention programmes have not kept pace with this level of interest, and investments remain extremely small in comparison with government spending on criminal justice strategies (Waller and Welsh, 1999). This chapter provides some evidence for moving beyond this passive interest.

This chapter is concerned with the primary prevention of delinquency and later offending. Primary prevention focuses on preventing these behaviours before any signs of them become evident. Essentially, it aims to influence positively the early risk factors or 'root causes' of delinquency and later offending, typically through broad-based strategies. Some of the major causes or risk factors include: growing up in poverty, living in poor housing, inadequate parental supervision and harsh or inconsistent discipline, parental conflict and separation, low intelligence and poor school performance, and a high level of impulsiveness and hyperactivity (Farrington, 1996). Secondary prevention, which is given some mention here, is distinguished from primary prevention through its targetted interventions at older children and adolescents who show signs of antisocial behaviour or other related risk factors (e.g. substance abuse, delinquent peers).

Reviews of proven and promising delinquency and criminality prevention programmes (e.g. Hurley, 1995; Mulvey, Arthur and Reppucci, 1993; Tolan and Guerra, 1994; Wasserman and Miller, 1998; Yoshikawa, 1994; Zigler, Taussig and Black, 1992; Tremblay and Craig, 1995) often make passing reference to the monetary savings that have been achieved by reduced criminal offending and other improved life course outcomes. Very little attention has been paid, however, to what these economic payoffs actually mean for the prevention of delinquency and later offending. This chapter attempts to explore in some detail this meaning by reviewing primary prevention studies that have been evaluated from an economic perspective.

The purpose of this chapter is not to determine which of the reviewed studies provides the best economic return on investment. Certainly, the small number of studies, not to mention the varied methodological rigour of the economic evaluations, would render such an exercise pointless. Instead, this chapter aims to report on what is known about the economic efficiency of the primary prevention of delinquency and later offending. As a background to this review, this chapter reports on some of the aggregate economic costs of crime and victimisation, and discusses some of the key issues in the economic analysis of crime prevention programmes.

Criminological, psychological, health and medical literatures throughout the western world were searched for published studies on the primary prevention of antisocial behaviour that had been evaluated using economic analysis techniques. Studies that had not carried out full economic evaluations to enable an assessment of the programme's efficiency were included if they presented sufficient cost and benefit data. To supplement the archival research phase, contacts were made with leading researchers and practitioners working in the fields of crime prevention and welfare economics in an effort to identify unpublished or in-press studies.

The chapter is divided into five main parts. The first part discusses some of the issues in studying the costs of crime and victimisation, and reports on some of the costs of crime in England and Wales and the United States. The second part overviews the techniques and methodological issues of economic analysis. The third part reviews studies of primary prevention programmes which have measured the outcome of delinquency or later offending, and have been evaluated using economic analysis techniques or have presented sufficient cost and benefit data. The fourth part summarises the findings of the economic analyses of the reviewed studies, and the fifth part brings together the main conclusions and identifies priorities for research.

Economic costs of crime and victimisation

Research on the costs of crime has received a great deal of attention of late, particularly in the industrialised countries of Australia (Walker, 1992, 1995), Canada (Brantingham and Easton, 1998; Spigelman, 1996;

Welsh and Waller, 1995), England and Wales (Home Office Standing Conference on Crime Prevention, 1988) and the United States (Cohen, Miller and Rossman, 1994; Mandel, Magnusson, Ellis, DeGeorge and Alexander, 1993; Miller, Cohen and Wiersema, 1996). This research has, for the first time, provided full monetary estimates for the impact (public and private) of a country's violent and property crime levels.

One is left to speculate about the reasons for this current surge in research activity on the costs of crime. Certainly, the fiscal climate of government cut-backs and down-sizing throughout the western world has played a role. Heightened public interest in crime and the political priority it has received of late has perhaps fuelled this alternative view of the impact of crime. The usefulness of quantifying the costs of crime is, however, more clear. Some of the reasons include: the ability to combine statistics on different crimes into a single, readily understood metric; guidance in resource allocation; and the creation of base-line data to carry out economic analyses of crime reduction programmes and policies (Miller, Cohen and Rossman, 1993, 186).

Monetising crime has also served to draw a greater level of awareness to populations seen as more vulnerable to crime and victimisation (e.g. women and children) (Greaves, Hankivsky and Kingston-Riechers, 1995; Kerr and McLean, 1996; Miller *et al.*, 1996), those at greater risk of criminal offending (e.g. youth) (Cohen, 1998; Miller, Fisher and Cohen, 2001; Potas, Vining and Wilson, 1990), specific types of crimes (e.g. auto theft and homicide) (Field, 1993; Miller *et al.*, 1993), certain sectors in society (e.g. businesses) (van Dijk and Terlouw, 1996), and commodities used in the commission of crimes (e.g. firearms) (Cook, Lawrence, Ludwig and Miller, 1999; Gabor, Welsh and Antonowicz, 1996).

For the purposes of monetising the full impact of crime, a comprehensive classification scheme of the areas in which costs are incurred is necessary. For their study of the costs of interpersonal crime in the United States, Mandel *et al.* (1993) identified costs as falling into one of six categories: (i) criminal justice system (police, courts and corrections); (ii) private security (alarms, private guards and security systems); (iii) urban decay (lost jobs and relocation of residents – urban flight); (iv) property loss (stolen goods); (v) medical care (treating crime victims); and (vi) shattered lives (pain, suffering and lost quality of life of crime victims and their families).

Although this classification scheme is by no means exhaustive (many would argue that it is impossible to quantify all of the costs of crime), it takes into account the vast range of public and private costs. Most importantly, it accounts for the full impact of crime on victims – an area that has, until recently, been non-existent in research on the costs of crime. In the United States, Miller *et al.* (1996) found that intangible losses to crime victims (pain, suffering, and lost quality of life) were more than three times tangible or out-of-pocket expenses (medical care, lost wages, and victim assistance programmes). Costs of crime in England and Wales and the United States are reviewed below. (For England and Wales, costs of crime are presented in English pounds and American dollars. At the time of writing, one American dollar was worth approximately £0.63.)

Costs of crime in England and Wales

The most comprehensive work to date to estimate the costs of crime in England and Wales was carried out by the Home Office Standing Conference on Crime Prevention (1988). Although the group stopped short of providing a 'global total' for the costs of crime in the country, its report presented detailed estimates for a wide range of costs to crime victims and for crime management. 'Unofficially, the quantifiable figures were thought by the working party to be comparable to the costs of running the entire National Health Service (£18bn in 1988)' ($28.6 billion) (*Today*, 1988, cited in Utting, Bright and Henricson, 1993, 67).

Like most countries, in England and Wales the most consistently collected data set on the costs of crime is for the government response to crime. In fiscal year 1993/94, public expenditure on the criminal justice system reached £9.4 billion ($14.9 billion), with the police accounting for the largest portion, 64 per cent, or £6.0 billion ($9.5 billion) (Barclay, 1995). Not included in this total is government spending on crime prevention, which in its widest sense (inclusive of all government departments) cost £241.3 million ($383.0 million) (Barclay, 1995). In fiscal year 1994/95, government compensation paid to victims of violent crime through the Criminal Injuries Compensation Board came to £175.4 million ($278.4 million); administration costs were an additional £17.5 million ($27.8 million) (Criminal Injuries Compensation Board, 1996).

The British Crime Survey (BCS) regularly collects information on various costs of crime to individual victims. Expressed as net losses (sum of property and damage losses, and lost earnings, minus property recovered or compensated for), the 1992 BCS found that in 1991, residential burglary, theft and damage cost £495 million ($785.7 million) and theft of and from vehicles cost £775 million ($1,230.2 million) (Mayhew, Aye Maung and Mirrlees-Black, 1993).

Costs of crime in the United States

Mandel and his colleagues (1993) estimated that the cost of violent and property crime in the United States in 1992 reached $425 billion. This cost includes: criminal justice system, $90 billion; private security, $65 billion; urban decay, $50 billion; property loss, $45 billion; medical care, $5 billion; and shattered lives, $170 billion, or 40 per cent of the total.

Recent research by Miller *et al.* (1996) has estimated that the full impact of crime on victims (tangible and intangible losses) in the United States costs $450 billion annually. Of this total, violent crime (including drunk driving and arson) accounts for $426 billion, while property crime accounts for $24 billion. Adding the excluded costs of criminal justice, private security and urban decay (a total of $205 billion) to this revised estimate of the costs of crime to victims, brings the full annual cost of violent (including drunk driving and arson) and property crime in the United States to $655 billion.

Key issues in the economic analysis of prevention programmes

Economic analyses (or economic evaluations) of programmes to prevent delinquency and later offending are rare. This paucity of research is common to many other prevention and intervention areas, such as child and adolescent mental health (see Knapp, 1997) and substance abuse (see Bukoski and Evans, 1998; Plotnick, 1994; Rajkumar and French, 1997).

Economic analysis can be described as a tool which allows choices to be made between alternative uses of resources or alternative distributions of services (Knapp, 1997, 11). Many criteria are used in economic analysis. The criterion most commonly associated with economic analysis is efficiency, which is the focus throughout this chapter. In short, the measurement of efficiency involves 'aggregating all the gains and losses from a programme in such a way that the net gain from one programme can be compared to that of an alternative' (Barnett and Escobar, 1987, 389). From this, the most economically efficient programme can be identified. What cannot be identified from an economic analysis, however, is the fairness or equity in the distribution of the services available (e.g. Are those persons most in need of the services receiving them?). This decision, as noted by Barnett and Escobar (1990), must be left to the values of the policy-makers.

Techniques of economic analysis

Cost-benefit (or benefit-cost) analysis and cost-effectiveness analysis are the two most widely used techniques of economic analysis. The majority of the reviewed studies in this chapter utilise the technique of benefit-cost analysis. Cost-offset analysis, which is more of a quasi-economic analysis technique is often classified incorrectly as a benefit-cost analysis. This technique simply compares costs incurred with costs saved (Knapp, 1997). The predominant distinguishing feature between benefit-cost and cost-effectiveness analysis is the comprehensiveness of assessment of programme outcomes. Barnett and Escobar (1987, 1990) describe cost-effectiveness analysis as an incomplete benefit-cost analysis. The incompleteness in cost-effectiveness analysis is that no attempt is made to estimate the monetary value of effects produced (benefits), only of programme resources used (costs). Benefit-cost analysis, on the other hand, values in monetary terms both costs and benefits.

Economic analysis framework

An economic analysis is a step-by-step process, which follows a standard set of procedures. In the case of benefit-cost analysis, all of the following six steps are carried out. For cost-effectiveness analysis, the estimation of the monetary value of benefits in step (iii) is omitted and step (v) is consequently omitted. The six steps of economic analysis are as follows: (i) define the scope of the analysis; (ii) obtain estimates of programme effects; (iii) estimate the monetary value of costs and benefits; (iv) calculate present value and assess profitability; (v) describe the distribution of costs and benefits (an assessment of who gains and who loses, e.g. programme participants, government/taxpayers, crime victims); and (vi) conduct sensitivity analyses (Barnett, 1993, 143). It is beyond the scope of this chapter to discuss each methodological step, but interested readers should consult the excellent reviews and applications of this methodology in the context of early childhood intervention programmes by Barnett (1993, 1996) and Barnett and Escobar (1987, 1990).

Two other key features of economic analysis require brief mention. First, an economic analysis is an extension of an outcome evaluation, and is only as defensible as the evaluation upon which it is based. Weimer and Friedman (1979, 264) recommended that economic analyses be limited to programmes that have been evaluated with an 'experimental or strong quasi-experimental design'. The most convincing method of evaluating crime prevention programmes is the randomised experiment (Farrington, 1983, 1997). Second, there are many perspectives that can be taken in measuring programme costs and benefits. Some benefit-cost analyses adopt a society-wide perspective which includes the major parties that can receive benefits or incur costs, such as government or taxpayer, crime victim, and programme participant. Other analyses may take a more narrow view, focusing on one or two of these parties. In reporting on the benefit-cost findings of the studies reviewed here, we have taken the middle-of-the-road approach, by reporting on, as far as possible, a combined government/taxpayer and crime victim perspective.

Review of studies

This section reviews primary and secondary prevention studies that have measured effects on delinquency and later offending, and have carried out some form of economic evaluation or have presented cost and benefit data. Additionally, to be included in this review, the outcome evaluation had to be based on a 'real-life' programme. That is, programme outcomes were neither assessed using statistical modelling techniques alone nor hypothesised on the basis of case study data, but rather employed research designs with the capacity to control for threats to internal and external validity, such as experimental and quasi-experimental designs. This resulted in a number of well known statistical modelling studies (e.g., Donohue and Siegelman, 1998; Greenwood, Model, Rydell and Chiesa, 1996; van Dijk, 1996, 1997) not being included in the present review. (For a discussion of these types of studies, see Welsh, Farrington and Sherman, 2001; for a summary of key findings of these studies, see Welsh and Farrington, 2000.) Secondary prevention studies are deserving of inclusion in this review on the grounds that there is a paucity of research on the economic efficiency of criminality prevention in general.

A review of the literature in the western world turned up six primary and three secondary prevention studies. In the layout of this review and in Table 10.1, which provides a summary of the studies reviewed, the secondary prevention studies appear at the end. A tenth study which carried out an economic evaluation (Coopers and Lybrand, 1994), the only one found in the United Kingdom, was not included because it was not an evaluation of programme effects. Instead, it assessed how many crimes would *need* to be prevented for the programme to be cost-effective.

Seven of the nine studies involved some form of economic analysis; the other two (Earle, 1995; Lally, Mangione and Honig, 1988) provided only cost and/or benefit data, one of which (Earle, 1995) enabled a crude estimation of its economic impact on public spending. All of the studies were carried out in North America; eight in the United States and one in Canada (Jones and Offord, 1989). At the start of treatment, subjects ranged in age from pre-birth to 18 years, with five of the nine studies commencing prior to the formal school years. The studies manipulated a host of risk factors, including family support, planning and environment, parenting, nutrition, education, cognitive development and behavioural problems. In the majority of the programmes, interventions were administered in the home. Length of treatment ranged from ten weeks to five years. In the majority of the studies, the follow-up period (the period of time in which programme effects were evaluated after the intervention had ended) to assess outcomes equalled or exceeded 16 months; in two studies there was no formal follow-up. The methodological rigour of the nine studies was very high, with three of the studies employing random assignment to experimental and control conditions.

The layout of the review of studies and accompanying table borrows from the schema used by Tremblay and Craig (1995) in their comprehensive review of developmental crime prevention. Summaries of the studies have provided information on research design and methodology, outcome evaluation findings and economic analysis findings.

Prenatal/Early Infancy Project

The Prenatal/Early Infancy Project (PEIP) was carried out in the semi-rural community of Elmira, New York, in the late 1970s to early 1980s. The programme was designed with three broad objectives: (i) to improve the outcomes of pregnancy; (ii) to improve the quality of care that parents provide to their children (and their children's subsequent health and development); and (iii) to improve the women's own personal life course development (completing their education, finding work and planning future pregnancies) (Olds *et al.*, 1993, 158).

Design and method

The programme enrolled 400 women prior to their 30th week of pregnancy. Women were recruited if they had no previous live births and had at least one of the following high-risk characteristics prone to health and developmental problems in infancy (85 per cent had at least one of the characteristics): under 19 years of age (47 per cent), unmarried (62 per cent) or poor (61 per cent). Twenty-four per cent possessed all three risk characteristics.

The women were randomly assigned to one of four treatment conditions. In the first condition (N = 90) no services were provided during pregnancy. Screening for sensory and developmental problems took place at ages one and two, and was provided in all four treatment conditions. Women in the second condition (N = 94) were provided with transportation vouchers to attend regular prenatal and child visits to physicians. Women in the third condition (N = 100), in addition to the free transportation, received nurse home visits during pregnancy on average once every two weeks, and those in the fourth condition (N = 116) received the same services as those in the third, but also received continued nurse home visits until the children reached the age of two. Three major activities were carried out during the home visits: (i) parent education

Table 10.1 *Summary of primary and secondary prevention studies*

Study author and location	Age at intervention	Context of intervention	Duration and type of intervention	Initial sample size	Evaluation design	Follow-up[a] and results[b]	Benefit-cost ratio[c]
Olds *et al.* (1997, 1998), Prenatal/Early Infancy Project, Elmira, New York	Prenatal	Home	2 years; T1 = parent education, parent support, community support, family planning, T2 = T1 minus postnatal home visits, C = 2 conditions not receiving home visits (screening services and free transportation to clinic)	400 mothers: T1 = 116, T2 = 100, C = 184	Randomised experiment	Immediate outcome (T1 versus C): mothers: child abuse and neglect+, discipline+; children: developmental quotient+ 13 years (T1 versus C): mothers: child abuse and neglect+; higher risk mothers: arrests and convictions+, social service use+; children (of higher risk mothers): arrests+	2 years follow-up: higher risk sample = 1.06, whole sample = 0.51 13 years follow-up: higher risk sample = 4.06, lower risk sample = 0.62

Lally *et al.* (1988), Syracuse University Family Development Research Project, New York	Prenatal	Home, day care	5 years; parent training, education, nutrition, health & safety, mother-child relationship	156 children: T = 82, C = 74	Before-after, experimental-control	Immediate outcome: cognitive functioning 0, social-emotional functioning+ 10 years: delinquency+, social behaviour+, school achievement (girls)+, school attendance (girls)+	Not measured
Seitz *et al.* (1985), Yale Child Welfare Research Programme	Prenatal	Home, day care	2.5 years; education, day care, community support, pediatric care, parent training	36 children: T = 18, C = 18	Before-after, experimental-control	10 years: mothers: education+, SES+, parenting style+; children: antisocial behaviour+, school attendance+, academic achievement 0, IQ 0	Not measured

(cont.)

Table 10.1 (*cont.*)

Study author and location	Age at intervention	Context of intervention	Duration and type of intervention	Initial sample size	Evaluation design	Follow-up[a] and results[b]	Benefit-cost ratio[c]
Schweinhart *et al.* (1993), Perry Preschool Programme, Ypsilanti, Michigan	3–4 years	Preschool, home	1–2 years; preschool intellectual enrichment, parent education	123 children (72 boys, 51 girls): T = 58, C = 65	Randomised experiment (stratified assignment)	9–10 years: delinquency+, school achievement+, cognitive functioning 0 14 years: police arrests+ 22 years: police arrests+, school achievement+, social service use+, educational achievement+	9–10 years follow-up: 2.48 14 years follow-up: 3.00 22 years follow-up: 7.16
Jones and Offord (1989), Participate & Learn Skills, Ottawa, Canada	5–15 years	Public housing	32 months; non-school, skill development	905 children (all age-eligible children in two public housing sites)	Before-after, experimental-control	16 months: police arrests+, self-concept+, pro-social skills+, community integration+	2.55

Hahn (1994, 1999), Quantum Opportunities Programme, five sites in US	15 years (average)	Community-based agency, home	4 years; education, skill development	250 youths: T = 125, C = 125	Randomised experiment	6 months: police arrests+, school achievement+, social services use+	3.68
Lipsey (1984), Los Angeles County Delinquency Prevention Programme	<15 years (average)	Community-based centre	10 weeks; family counselling, academic tutoring, employment training	7,637 youths (all in programme)	Before-after, experimental-control and before-after (no control)	Immediate outcome: police arrests+	1.40
Long *et al.* (1981), Job Corps, multiple sites in US	18 years (average)	Residential-based centre	n.a.; vocational training, education, health care	5,100 youths: T = n.a., C = n.a.	Before-after, experimental-control, with matching	18 months (average): police arrests+, substance abuse+, school achievement+, employment+	1.45

[a] The period of time in which program effects were evaluated after the intervention had ended.

[b] 0 = no intervention effects; + = desirable intervention effects.

[c] Expressed as a ratio of benefits to costs in monetary units (national currencies).

Notes: T = treatment group; C = control group; n.a. = not available.

about influences on fetal and infant development; (ii) the involvement of family members and friends in the pregnancy, birth, early care of the child and in the support of the mother; and (iii) the linkage of family members with other health and human services (Olds *et al.*, 1993,158).

Analyses focused primarily on comparisons between combined treatment conditions one and two (control group) and treatment condition four (programme group). Conditions one and two (not visited by a nurse during pregnancy or infancy) were grouped together because no differences between the two groups were observed in the use of the free transportation service for prenatal and child visits to physicians. Condition three was excluded as few lasting benefits were observed for nurse home visits during pregnancy relative to infancy (condition 4). Rates of attrition up to the age of two varied from 15 per cent to 21 per cent. There were no differences in attrition across the four treatment conditions. Forty-six non-white women were excluded from the statistical analyses due to the methodological limitations that a small sample size would present in cross-classifying race with other variables (Olds *et al.*, 1986).

Results

Compared to the control group, the programme group showed impressive results across a range of indicators. The most striking finding was a 78.9 per cent reduction in state-verified cases of child abuse and neglect during the first two years of the child's life for those at greatest risk in the programme group compared to their control counterparts (4 per cent versus 19 per cent) (Olds *et al.*, 1986). However, an evaluation of the programme during the two year period immediately following the completion of the intervention (Olds *et al.*, 1994) found that the desirable effects on child abuse and neglect were attenuated. Some of the key desirable findings included: (i) 32 per cent fewer emergency room visits among programme group children by age two; (ii) 80 per cent greater participation in the workforce among low income, unmarried programme group women by year four; and (iii) 43 per cent fewer subsequent childbirths among low income, unmarried programme group women by year four (Olds *et al.*, 1993).

Thirteen years after the completion of the programme, fewer treatment compared to control mothers for the sample as a whole were identified as perpetrators of child abuse and neglect (29 per cent versus 54 per cent), and, for the higher risk sample, fewer treatment mothers in contrast to the controls had alcohol or substance abuse problems or were arrested (Olds *et al.*, 1997). At the age of 15, children of the higher risk mothers who received the programme reported fewer arrests than their control counterparts (Olds *et al.*, 1998).

Economic analysis

Benefit-cost analyses were carried out to measure the effects of nurse visitation on government spending when the children were four and 15 years old. The same treatment conditions were compared as above.

The average per family cost of the two year programme was $3,246 (in 1980 US$) for the sample as a whole ($4,067 for programme group minus $821 for control group) and $3,133 for the higher risk sample ($4,113 for programme group minus $980 for control group). In other words, nurse visited families (treatment condition 4) were allocated between 4.2 and 5.0 times more programme spending than families receiving only screening and free transportation (treatment conditions 1 and 2 combined). Two years after the completion of the programme, per family savings (benefits) to governmental agencies reached $1,772 for the sample as a whole and $3,498 for the higher risk sample. After discounting, these figures were $1,664 and $3,313, respectively. The benefit-cost ratio was a desirable 1.06 ($3,313 divided by $3,133) for the higher risk sample, meaning that for each dollar that was invested in the programme, the public received $1.06 in return. For the sample as a whole, the benefit-cost ratio was an unfavourable 0.51 ($1,664 divided by $3,246), or a net loss of $0.49 for each dollar invested.

Of government savings to the higher risk sample ($3,313 per family), the largest portion (56 per cent) was attributed to reductions in Aid for Dependent Children (AFDC) payments. Reductions in Food Stamps accounted for 26 per cent of the savings; Medicaid, 11 per cent; and increases in tax revenue, 5 per cent. Fewer cases of child abuse and neglect among the programme group compared to the control group accounted for only 3 per cent of the government savings (to Child Protective Services), or approximately $100 per family.

An external benefit-cost study of the Elmira programme by RAND (Karoly *et al.*, 1998) at thirteen years post-intervention, which measured programme effects on childrens' delinquency and mothers' life course development, found a favourable benefit-cost ratio of 4.06 for the higher risk families and an unfavourable ratio of 0.62 for the lower risk families.

To test the generalisability of the findings of the Elmira study, currently two urban replications are underway: one in Memphis, Tennessee (Kitzman *et al.*, 1997), and the other in Denver, Colorado. Economic analyses are planned for both.

Hawaii Healthy Start

Hawaii Healthy Start began in July 1985 as a state-funded, single site demonstration project to prevent child abuse and neglect using a home visitation model similar to Olds and his colleagues (1986). After a successful trial, the programme was expanded considerably. Healthy Start is now a state-wide programme operating through thirteen sites. In fiscal year 1995, it had an annual budget of more than $8 million (Earle, 1995). Its goals are four-fold: (i) to reduce family stress and improve family functioning; (ii) to improve parenting skills; (iii) to enhance child health and development; and (iv) to prevent child abuse and neglect (Earle, 1995, 3).

Design and method

Over a four-year period (July 1987 to June 1991), 1,353 high risk families were enrolled in Healthy Start. Another 901 high risk families were served by the programme, but received less intensive home visiting services. The latter group was excluded from the evaluation reported on by Earle (1995). The majority of families were enrolled in the programme soon after delivery of the child. Around 10 per cent of the families were enrolled prenatally.

Families were recruited into the programme if, at postpartum screening of the mother and follow-up assessment with the mother (and father if present), using standardised instruments, it was determined that there was a high risk for child abuse and neglect. No data were presented on the risk characteristics of the sample under study. Socio-demographic analysis of the 1994 Healthy Start intake (2,800 families) provides a picture of the typical families served. Families were more often young (under 24 years of age), had a low income (50 per cent on welfare), had a history of substance abuse (38 per cent), had a history of domestic violence (43 per cent) and were homeless or living in temporary, overcrowded conditions (22 per cent). Sixty-five per cent of the women were single.

The programme employed an experimental-control design with before-after measures. A control group was established from an equal number of high-risk families (1,353). For the first six to twelve months postpartum, programme group families received weekly home visits carried out by para-professionals. Two major activities were carried out during the home visits at this time: (i) parent education (e.g. for feeding, washing, and the baby's early stages of development); and (ii) development of an individual family support plan to receive services from Healthy Start and other community service agencies (Earle, 1995).

Assessments of development (bonding of mother to infant and identification of developmental problems) also took place during home visits.

To identify problems in child development, mothers were administered a series of 'Infant/Child Monitoring Questionnaires' at four, eight, 12, 16, 20, 24, 30, 36 and 48 months. These questionnaires covered such areas as communication and motor, adaptive and personal-social skills. Further assessments were used to determine if home visits could be reduced up to a minimum of one every three months.

Results

The only comparable outcome measure reported by Earle (1995) is child abuse and neglect. At the end of the four-year intervention period, the rate of child abuse among programme group families was less than 1 per cent (0.7 per cent); the rate of child neglect was 1.2 per cent. Evaluators used a combined abuse/neglect (CAN) rate. For the programme group, the CAN rate was 1.9 per cent. For the control group, the CAN rate was 5.0 per cent. The difference in the CAN rate between the two groups (3.1 per cent) represented approximately forty-two cases of child abuse and neglect prevented over four years, or just over ten per year.[1]

Economic analysis

Although an economic analysis was not carried out by the author, limited cost and benefit data were presented, enabling a crude estimation of the programme's monetary impact. It was estimated that an annual budget of $349,000 was needed to provide home visitation services to 140 families per year. It was estimated that it cost child protection services $30,000 ($15,000/case/year at an average time of 2 years) for each case of child abuse or neglect. Over the course of the four-year intervention period, 42 fewer cases of child abuse and neglect occurred among the 1,353 programme families compared to their control counterparts. This represented a saving of $1.3 million. If we assume that the cases of child abuse and neglect occurred in the first year of the programme, something that is corroborated throughout the literature (see e.g. National Commission of Inquiry into the Prevention of Child Abuse, 1996), this one area could be seen as reducing annual programme costs to $2.1 million ($3.4 million[2] minus $1.3 million), or $1,552 per family.

Dividing total benefits ($1.3 million) by total costs ($3.4 million) produces an undesirable benefit-cost ratio of 0.38. In other words, for each dollar invested in the programme, only $0.38 was recouped in savings from reduced child abuse and neglect. It is important to reiterate that this represents a crude estimate of the programme's potential monetary value. At present, two randomised control evaluations are underway to provide a more empirical assessment of the programme's effectiveness, and for one of them – being carried out by Johns Hopkins School of Medicine – a full benefit-cost analysis is planned.

Syracuse University Family Development Research Project

The Syracuse University Family Development Research Project took place in the City of Syracuse, New York, and involved children born between 1969 and 1971. Its aim was to bolster family and child functioning through a comprehensive intervention strategy which focused on parent contact, with child care as supplementary (Lally *et al.*, 1988).

Design and method

The programme employed an experimental-control design with before-after measures. The programme group consisted of eighty-two children. A matched control group of seventy-four children was established when programme children reached three years of age. Families coming from extremely disadvantaged backgrounds were recruited into the Syracuse programme in the last trimester of pregnancy. In addition to low socio-economic status, characteristics of the programme mothers included: (i) having less than a high school education; (ii) having no work or a semi-skilled work history; (iii) being a teenager (mean age of 18 years); and (iv) being a single parent (over 85 per cent) (Lally *et al.*, 1988).

Beginning prenatally, programme mothers were provided with a range of educational and health services. Following birth, trained para-professionals provided weekly home visits to assist mothers (and other family members) with issues of child-rearing, family relations, employment and community functioning. Children were provided with four and a half continuous years of enriched child care (fifty weeks a year), commencing with five half days a week at six to fifteen months and, thereafter, with five full days a week until the age of sixty months.

Sample children were assessed at around 15 years of age, ten years after the completion of the programme. Due to sample attrition, the analyses reported on by Lally *et al.* (1988) included sixty-five programme families (those who had completed the programme) and fifty-four control families, or 76 per cent of the families who were part of the study sample at programme onset. No differences were found between the programme and control groups from the time of the completion of the intervention to the ten-year follow-up.

Results

The strongest programme effects were found in the area of juvenile delinquency, as defined by involvement in the juvenile justice system.

Compared to the control group, programme group children at ages ranging from 13 to 16 were only a quarter as likely to have been processed as probation cases by the county probation department (6 per cent versus 22 per cent), and the severity of offences and degree of chronicity was much higher amongst control group children.

Other key findings were found for school performance and attendance. According to school record data, mostly from seventh and eighth grades, programme girls were found to have statistically significantly higher academic performances than their control counterparts: 0 per cent versus 16 per cent failing school, and 76 per cent versus 47 per cent achieving a 'C' or better average. No differences were found for school functioning among the boys. School attendance, as measured by having more than twenty absences in the third and fourth year assessments, was also higher among programme girls than control girls: 14 per cent versus 50 per cent (third year), and 0 per cent versus 31 per cent (fourth year). Again, no differences were found among the boys.

Economic analysis

An economic analysis was not carried out. Researchers focused instead on a limited number of costs associated with youth encounters with the justice system: court processing, placements administered by the county probation department (foster care and non-secure and secure detention) and probation supervision.

Total costs of the programme group's (N = 65) involvement with the justice system was estimated at $12,111, while the control group (N = 54) amassed costs totalling $107,192. The estimated cost per programme child was $186, and per control child was $1,985. Very little can be said about how these savings would measure up to the costs of running the programme and other costs and other potential monetary benefits. At the very least, it could be said that if the programme's effects on delinquency are sustained during the late teenage and early adult years, the programme offers to save substantial governmental expenditure on the juvenile and adult justice systems.

Yale Child Welfare Research Programme

The Yale Child Welfare Research Programme was carried out in a low socio-economic inner-city area in the northeastern part of the US between 1968 and 1970. Its aim was '"to help disadvantaged young parents to support the development of their children and to improve the quality of family life"' (Provence and Naylor, 1983, 3, cited in Seitz, 1990, 84).

Design and method

The programme employed an experimental-control design with before-after measures. The programme group consisted of eighteen children from seventeen impoverished families. Women were recruited during pregnancy if they had no previous live births (the additional child was born during the programme and was added to the programme group), had no mental illness or physical handicap and the child possessed no known biological handicaps. A matched control group of eighteen children from eighteen families was recruited at the completion of the intervention period.

The programme began prenatally and ended at thirty months postpartum. It involved four main interventions. First, professional home visits were provided to assist with short-term (e.g. reduce physical dangers) and long-term (e.g. reaching career goals) family problems, and link families to community services. Second, pediatric care services were provided to the mother and child, decreasing in intensity from birth to infancy. Children received from thirteen to seventeen examinations. Emphasis was placed on educating parents to observe their child's health. Third, each child attended an enriched day care programme which focused on the child's emotional and social development for, on average, 13.2 months. Fourth, regular developmental examinations were carried out with the child, with the parent present, using standardised instruments.

The children were assessed at around the age of 12.5 years, ten years following the completion of the programme. Due to sample attrition and missing data, Seitz and her colleagues' (1985) analyses are presented for fifteen programme and fifteen control group families.

Results

Compared to control group families, programme families fared better in a host of categories, including the mothers achieving significantly more years of education (beyond high school), smaller family size and a greater period of time between births and greater socio-economic status, defined as being self-supporting or having full-time employment (87 per cent versus 53 per cent) (Seitz *et al.*, 1985).

For the children, differences were not apparent between the programme and control group (data were available for fourteen matched pairs) in tests for IQ or academic achievement. However, teacher interview data showed that 'control boys were likely to show aggressive, acting-out, pre-delinquent behaviour serious enough to require such actions as placement in classrooms for emotionally disturbed children or suspension from school' (Seitz, 1990, 86). Other differences between programme and control group children included a higher absenteeism rate for control children and a greater need for remedial and supportive school services by control boys over their programme counterparts.

Economic analysis

The authors did not carry out a complete benefit-cost analysis. However, monetary estimates were provided for resources used (costs) and some programme effects (benefits), using 1982 US dollars. The total per family cost of the programme for the full intervention period was estimated at $20,000. Estimations of benefits were limited to reduced use of social assistance and decreased remedial and supportive school services (only for boys: eleven matched pairs) for the follow-up year only, $30,000 and $10,000, respectively. Reduced reliance on social assistance was attributed to the increased employment on the part of programme group mothers.

Total benefits accrued from the programme group compared to the control group equalled $40,000 ($30,000 plus $10,000) per year. In other words, in one year the fifteen control group families consumed $40,000 more in public resources than their programme group counterparts. If this conservatively estimated trend were to continue, still not accounting for cumulative potential benefits from birth to the year prior to this assessment, the programme would be paid off in just over six additional years. In the words of Seitz *et al.* (1985, 389), 'the project currently appears to be paying itself off at the rate of at least two families per year'. In a detailed review of the Yale programme's ten-year follow-up findings, Barnett and Escobar (1987) found that the programme's estimated economic value could have been increased had a complete benefit-cost analysis been done.

Perry Preschool Programme

The Perry Preschool Programme started in 1962 in Ypsilanti, Michigan, is perhaps the most well known longitudinal study in the western world that has rigorously charted the effects of early childhood intervention. The principal hypothesis of the programme was that 'good preschool programs can help children in poverty make a better start in their transition from home to community and thereby set more of them on paths to becoming economically self-sufficient, socially responsible adults' (Schweinhart, Barnes and Weikart, 1993, 3).

Design and method

Prior to the start of the programme, 123 children aged three to four years were randomly assigned to either a programme group that received the preschool programming (N = 58) or a control group that did not (N = 65). The sample consisted of seventy-two boys and fifty-one girls. Families were recruited if they had low socio-economic status and their children showed low intellectual performance. Some of the characteristics of the sample families at the time of recruitment included: 40 per cent unemployment, 49 per cent collecting social assistance, 47 per cent single-headed households and low high school completions (11 per cent for men; 21 per cent for women).

The main intervention strategy involved high quality, active learning preschool programming administered by professional teachers for two years (thirteen children received one year). Preschool sessions were one-half day long and were provided five days a week for the duration of the thirty-week school year. The educational approach taken focused on supporting the development of the children's cognitive and social skills through individualised teaching and learning. Weekly home visits were also carried out by the teachers to provide parents with educational information and to enable them to take an active role in their child's early education. The sample has been most recently assessed at the age of 27 years, or twenty-two years post-intervention. Sample attrition was exceedingly low at this follow-up stage: only 4.9 per cent.

Results

At age 27, compared to the control group, programme group participants displayed a number of benefits across a range of pro-social functioning indicators. At this assessment, programme group participants had statistically significantly fewer police arrests, with the mean number of life-time arrests being 50 per cent lower for programme group participants compared to controls (2.3 versus 4.6). Also, fewer programme group members were judged to be chronic offenders (five or more arrests) compared to controls (7 per cent versus 35 per cent).

Other statistically significant outcomes realised by the programme group compared to the control group, at age 27, included: (i) higher monthly earnings (with 27 per cent versus 7 per cent earning $2,000 or more per month); (ii) higher percentages of home ownership (36 per cent versus 13 per cent) and second-car ownership (30 per cent versus 13 per cent); (iii) a higher level of schooling completed (with 71 per cent versus 54 per cent completing 12th grade or higher); and (iv) a lower percentage receiving social services at some time in the previous 10 years (59 per cent versus 80 per cent) (Schweinhart *et al.*, 1993, xv).

Economic analysis

A comprehensive benefit-cost analysis of Perry found that the programme's effects translated into substantial savings for both the programme group participants and the public (taxpayers/crime victims). In the economic analysis performed by Barnett (1993), reference to programme effects includes the programme's measured effects based on data through age 27 years and the programme's projected effects based on data beyond age 27 years. This combined measure is what gets reported throughout the literature. In both scenarios (measured and projected), benefits per programme participant far outweighed costs per programme participant. Also, as reported throughout the literature, programme benefits take into account only those that are accrued to the public (taxpayers/ crime victims); benefits received by the individual programme participant are not included.

Total public costs were estimated at $12,356 (in 1992 US$) for each participant. Programme costs were estimated from two categories: explicit, basic operating costs, which included instruction, administration and support staff, overheads, supplies and psychological screening; and implicit, capital costs, which took into account the school district classrooms and other facilities used by the programme (Barnett, 1993).

Total public benefits were estimated at $88,433 for each participant. The greatest benefits were from savings to the justice system ($12,796) and crime victims ($57,585). Savings to the justice system alone covered costs. Participants' arrest and incarceration histories were used to estimate savings to the main components of the criminal justice system: police, prosecutor's office, court, prison and probation. Savings to crime victims were estimated in a two-step process. First, participants' arrest histories were linked with national data on the ratio of arrests to crimes committed, which provided an estimate, by age, of the number and type of crimes committed by programme group participants. Second, these crime estimates were then combined with previously developed estimates of crime-specific victim costs (Cohen, 1988, 1992), which produced estimates of victim costs from crimes committed by programme group participants at each age (Barnett, 1993, 160). Crime-specific victim costs were not limited to out-of-pocket or direct monetary losses (e.g. lost property or wages), as is usually the case in such calculations. Also taken into account, where applicable, were the costs of crime associated with lost quality of life (e.g. pain and suffering), as well as the risk of death. (For an excellent discussion of these costs, see Cohen, 2000, 2001.)

The other benefits received by the public for each preschool participant included: higher educational output and reduced schooling costs, $6,287; revenue generated from taxes on increased earnings, $8,847; and reduced reliance on welfare, $2,918. Dividing total public benefits per participant ($88,433) by total public costs per participant ($12,356) produced a highly desirable benefit-cost ratio of 7.16. In other words, the pubic received $7.16 for every dollar invested in the programme.

Participate and Learn Skills

The Participate and Learn Skills (PALS) programme was implemented in a public housing community in Ottawa, Canada, in the early 1980s. It had two main objectives: (i) to advance the participating children toward higher non-school, skill development levels (e.g., sport and cultural activities); and (ii) to integrate children from the public housing community into the larger community (Jones and Offord, 1989, 739).

Design and method

The study employed an experimental-control group design with before–after measures to assess the effects of the community-based intervention. One public housing project served as the no-treatment control group and another received the intervention. The control site was not equivalent to the experimental site. The two projects were the largest in size that were under the management of the city housing authority and had comparable socio-demographic characteristics: (i) on average there were 417 children between the ages of 5 to 15 years at the programme site and 488 at the control site; (ii) children were distributed equally over gender and ages 5 to 15 years; (iii) approximately one-half of families relied on some form of social assistance for income and the other half were considered 'working poor'; and (iv) 56 per cent of households were headed by single parent mothers (Jones and Offord, 1989, 738–9).

In its first year (1980), the non-school, skill development programme offered free-of-charge forty courses in twenty-five different skill areas. Sports activities dominated (e.g. swimming, ice hockey). Others included music, arts and non-sport areas. Age-eligible children were recruited actively through direct contact, notices and follow-ups with those that did not participate in prior rounds of the programme. In the first year, the participation rate in at least one course among age-eligible children reached 70.8 per cent (228 of 322). In years two and three, the participation rate fell to 60.2 per cent and 49.0 per cent, respectively. The authors contend that the drop in participation was largely due to fewer courses being offered, as the number of children participating (322) remained fairly stable over the 32 months of the programme (Jones and Offord, 1989). The effects of PALS were assessed at the end of the programme (32 months) and again 16 months later.

Results

Children in the programme housing site fared better than their control counterparts on a range of measures. The strongest programme effect was found in the area of juvenile delinquency. For the duration of the programme, the monthly average of juveniles (in the age-eligible range) charged by the police was 80 per cent less (0.2 versus 1.0) at the experimental site compared to the control site. This statistically significant effect was diminished somewhat in the 16 months post-intervention: 0.5 juveniles charged per month at the experimental site compared to 1.1 juveniles charged at the control site.

Substantial gains were also observed in skill acquisition, as measured by the number of levels advanced in an activity, and integration in the wider community among experimental site children compared to those in the control site. Spill-over effects on participating children were found to be desirable (but not statistically significant) for self-esteem, but produced no change in behaviour at school or home.

Economic analysis

A benefit-cost analysis was carried out. Programme costs (operational and research) and immediate benefits for the intervention and follow-up phases were measured, using 1983 Canadian dollars (C$). The calculation of monetary benefits was limited to including only those areas where significant differences were observed between the experimental and control housing sites: fewer police charges against juveniles, reduced private security reports and reduced calls for fire department service. Altogether, potential savings (benefits) were estimated for four affected publicly-funded agencies: police, housing authority, community center and fire department.

Over the course of the 48 months, programme costs totaled C$258,694 and benefits were estimated at C$659,058. The city housing authority reaped the largest percentage of the benefits, 83.8 per cent or C$552,118. These benefits were due to the reduced demand for private security services in the experimental housing site relative to the control site. The next largest portion of the total benefits from the programme were accrued to the city fire department, C$88,416 (13.4 per cent). Monetary benefits accrued to the youth liaison section of the city police were relatively small, C$11,758 (1.8 per cent). Dividing the total benefits realised by the four public agencies (C$659,058) by the total cost of the programme (C$258,694) produced a desirable benefit-cost ratio of 2.55. In other words, for each dollar the public invested in the programme, the public received C$2.55 in return.

Quantum Opportunities Programme

The Quantum Opportunities Programme (QOP) was implemented as a demonstration programme in 1989 in five sites across the United States:

Philadelphia, Pennsylvania; Oklahoma City, Oklahoma; San Antonio, Texas; Saginaw, Michigan; and Milwaukee, Wisconsin. Beyond its many process aims, the QOP aimed to improve the life course opportunities of disadvantaged, at-risk youth during the high school years (Hahn, 1994, 1999).

Design and method

The sample consisted of 250 youths who were in the ninth grade of school. Youths were randomly assigned to either a programme group (N = 125) or a control group (N = 125). The sample sizes in each of the five sites were identical (N = 50), with an equal number in both the programme and control groups.

The two groups were equally matched in their level of disadvantage. Some of the high-risk characteristics included: 70 per cent lived with one parent, 45 per cent had repeated at least one grade in school and 84 per cent were receiving some form of public assistance (e.g. welfare). The programme lasted four years or up to grade 12 (the completion of high school) and was designed around the provision of three 'quantum opportunities': (i) educational activities (e.g. peer tutoring, computer-based instruction, homework assistance); (ii) service activities (e.g. volunteer with community projects); and (iii) development activities (e.g. curricula focused on life and family skills, and college and career planning) (Hahn, 1994).

Each of these opportunities was guaranteed for up to 250 hours each year for the duration of the programme. This guarantee was not limited to youths attending school, but also extended to those who dropped out, transferred or moved away from their original neighbourhood.

Cash and scholarship incentives were offered to students for work carried out in the three programme areas (education, service and development) to provide short-run motivation for school completion and future academic and social achievement. Cash incentives started off at $1.00 per hour and rose to $1.33 per hour, and $100 bonuses were provided upon completion of 100 hours of programming. Staff received cash incentives and bonuses for keeping youths involved in the programme.

Early on in the demonstration project, the Milwaukee site was dropped due to difficulties in programme implementation and participant follow-up. For the four sites remaining, attrition was very low at six months post-programme follow-up. Data were collected for 88 per cent of the programme group and for 82 per cent of the control group.

Results

The programme achieved a number of significant effects. Compared to the control group, QOP group members were: (i) more likely to have graduated from high school (63 per cent versus 42 per cent); (ii) more likely to be enrolled in some form of post-secondary education (42 per cent versus 16 per cent); (iii) less likely to have dropped out of high school (23 per cent versus 50 per cent); (iv) less likely to have been arrested (17 per cent versus 58 per cent);[3] and (v) less likely to have had children (24 per cent versus 38 per cent) (Hahn, 1994).

The last effect was deemed particularly important because of the high costs to the US government for the provision of health and welfare services to teenage mothers (Hahn, 1994). Olds *et al.* (1988, 1436) note that teenage mothers are at high risk of dropping out of school, having rapid successive pregnancies and becoming dependent on welfare. Children of teenage mothers are placed at greater risk of various health and developmental problems, and for unmarried teenage mothers these problems are magnified.

The evaluation also showed that fewer programme members relied on public assistance compared to their control counterparts. Additionally, in the six month follow-up, a greater number of programme members were found to have performed some form of community service compared to the controls: helped with a community project (21 per cent versus 12 per cent); volunteered as a tutor, counsellor or mentor (28 per cent versus 8 per cent); and given time to a non-profit, charitable, school or community group (41 per cent versus 11 per cent). Post-secondary enrollment (in two or four-year degree programmes) was also found to be higher among programme members than controls (55 per cent versus 24 per cent).

Economic analysis

A benefit-cost analysis of the programme revealed substantial benefits for both the participating members and the public. Costs of the programme for each participating member over the four years were $10,600. Total costs came to just over $1.1 million.

Programme effects valued in monetary terms (benefits) were limited to gains in education and fewer children. Excluded were potential economic benefits from reduced criminal activity, reduced dependence on public assistance and services provided to the community. It was assumed that those enrolled in the two and four-year post-secondary degree programmes would complete the programmes. No other information was provided on how benefits were calculated, which seriously limits the confidence that can be placed in the economic analysis findings.

Table 10.2 shows the breakdown of the monetary benefits produced by the programme. The total cost of the programme per programme group member was estimated at $10,600 and the total benefits per programme group member were estimated at $39,037. Dividing benefits ($39,037)

Table 10.2 *Economic benefits of the Quantum Opportunities Programme*

Source	Impact per 100 members	Payoff per member	Payoff per 100 members
More high school	21	$63,253	$1,328,313
Graduates compared to dropouts			
More two-year degrees	10	$69,161	$691,610
Compared to high school graduates			
More four-year degrees	13	$134,140	$1,743,820
Compared to high school graduates			
Fewer children	14	$10,000	$140,000
Total			$3,903,743

Source: Hahn (1994,19)

by programme costs ($10,600) produces a desirable benefit-cost ratio of 3.68.

Los Angeles County Delinquency Prevention Programme

Thirteen projects spread throughout Los Angeles County, in the State of California, made up the LA County Delinquency Prevention Programme. The LA County programme intervened with more than 10,000 youths each year. Short-term developmental prevention techniques were employed to manipulate the risk factors of early delinquency and school behavioural problems of later criminal offending (Lipsey, 1984).

Design and method

The study employed two types of design to evaluate the effects of the programme: a non-equivalent control group design and a one-group (no control group) pre-post design. For the one-group pre-post design the sample consisted of 7,637 youths. These youths participated in the delinquency prevention programme over the course of an unspecified year. Youths were referred to the programme by several agencies: police, probation and schools. In some cases the youth's parents made the referrals. Close to 40 per cent of the programme clients were referred with no prior arrest record. For the most part, these clients were referred due to exhibiting behaviour problems in school. The remainder had arrest records; 46 per cent with one prior, and 14 per cent with multiple priors. The average age at treatment was just below 15 years.

Short-term (ten weeks) crisis intervention family counselling was the primary intervention. Lipsey, Mills and Plant (1982) reported that the typical client of the programme averaged a total of 7.0 hours of service. Other services included academic tutoring and employment training. The primary data source was police arrest records.

Results

Programme results presented by Lipsey (1984) drew upon findings of earlier studies of the LA County Delinquency Prevention Programme carried out by Lipsey and other researchers (Lipsey *et al.*, 1982). These studies found that the programme prevented one or more police contacts for approximately 15 per cent to 20 per cent of the clients who were referred at the time of arrest by the police. A small proportion of these clients had one or more arrests prior to that point. For the sample as a whole, accounting for those who did not have an arrest at the time of referral, Lipsey (1984) estimated the programme's success rate on the reduction of subsequent delinquency in the effect size range of .25 to .33, or roughly 12 to 16 percentage points.

Economic analysis

A fairly rigorous benefit-cost analysis was carried out. Programme costs included total budget costs and overhead and administration costs. Additional costs were incurred by the police and the juvenile justice system. Lipsey (1984) did not provide an estimate of the total cost of the programme; however, on the basis of the information provided (benefit-cost ratio and benefits per client) it was possible to estimate that the total cost per client was $2,130. Savings to the police and the juvenile justice system from the prevention of 1.7 expected subsequent arrests per client was estimated at $2,982 per client. Dividing per client benefits ($2,982) by per client costs ($2,130) produced a desirable benefit-cost ratio of 1.40, which meant that for each dollar spent on the programme $1.40 was saved in the form of public expenditures on policing and the juvenile justice system.

Job Corps

The Job Corps was established in 1964 in the US as a federal training programme for disadvantaged, unemployed youths. Designers of the programme, the US Department of Labor, were hopeful that spin-off benefits in the form of reduced dependence on social assistance and a reduction in crime would be realised as a result of empowering at-risk youth to achieve stable, long-term employment opportunities. The programme is still active today. In fiscal year 1995, federal government funding for Job Corps reached $1.08 billion (The President's Crime Prevention Council, 1995).

Design and method

Long, Mallar and Thornton (1981) carried out an evaluation of the Job Corps programme using an experimental-control design with before-after measures, which matched Corps members who had been out of the programme for an average of eighteen months (maximum two years) and non-participating youths of similar age and socio-economic status. The sample as a whole included approximately 5,100 youths. Beyond generally being disadvantaged socio-economically and unemployed, the authors did not report on the specific make-up of the two cohorts. It is difficult to say whether this occurred because of poor matching, given the rigorous nature of the evaluation. It is assumed that the mean age at treatment mirrored the age group which Job Corps serves presently, 18 years.

Socio-demographic analysis of the 1991 Job Corps intake (approximately 70,000 youths) provides a picture of the typical youths served. Most were at high risk of substance abuse, delinquency and social assistance dependency. Two out of five youths came from families on social assistance, four out of five had dropped out of school and the average family income was $6,000 per year (Curtis, 1995), well below the poverty line for the time.

Job Corps' primary aim is to improve the employability of participants by offering a comprehensive set of services which principally includes vocational skills training, basic education and health care. At the time of the evaluation, the programme was residentially-based and featured classroom courses which provided the opportunity to obtain Graduate Equivalent Degrees, counselling and job training.

Results

The most significant findings of the programme group over the control group were increased job productivity (as measured by employment output during and following the programme) and reduced criminal activity. In the eighteen-month (average) follow-up period, Job Corps members were one-third less likely to have been arrested one or more times than non-participants and 75 per cent moved on to full-time study or a stable job where earnings were 15 per cent higher than non-participants who were employed (Eisenhower Foundation, 1990). Decreased dependency on social assistance was also realised by Job Corps participants compared to their control counterparts.

Economic analysis

A comprehensive benefit-cost analysis was carried out and reported in 1977 US dollars. Programme costs included budgeted operating expenditures and unbudgeted costs. Benefits were measured from two frames of reference: immediate programme effects on reduced consumption of public services by participants while in the programme, and post-programme effects on participants' long-term employability.

Job Corps yielded substantial net benefits for the public and individual Corps members. Total programme costs per Corps member came to $5,070; total benefits to society per Corps member came to $7,343. Reduced criminal activity per programme participant, as measured by reduced criminal justice costs, personal injury, property damage and value of stolen property, accounted for 28.8 per cent of the total benefits, or $2,112. Only programme participant output surpassed the benefits of reduced criminal activity to the public, $4,653 (63.4 per cent). For every dollar invested in Job Corps the public received $1.45 in return ($7,343 ÷ $5,070); $0.42 contributed by reduced criminal activity.

In 1994, the US Department of Labor initiated a four-year longitudinal-experimental study to assess the effectiveness and economic efficiency of the Job Corps programme (US Department of Labor, 1995). This will provide important information on the programme's ability to address crime and other social problems facing young people today.

Summary of economic analysis findings

This section summarises the economic analysis findings of the nine reviewed studies. Seven of the nine reviewed studies performed an economic analysis. For seven of the nine studies a benefit-cost ratio was calculated, either by the authors of the studies or this author.

Six of the seven studies for which a benefit-cost ratio could be calculated showed a desirable ratio. For these six studies the economic return on a one monetary unit investment ranged from a low of 1.06 to a high of 7.16. The one study that did not show a desirable benefit-cost ratio (Earle, 1995) was the study for which I carried out a crude economic analysis. For the five studies which began after birth and calculated a benefit-cost ratio, a desirable ratio was found for each, which ranged from 1.40 to 7.16.

By comparison, the two studies which began prenatally and calculated a benefit-cost ratio (Earle, 1995; Olds *et al.*, 1997) were found to have a rather low or undesirable monetary return for a one dollar investment; ranging from the Prenatal/Early Infancy Project just breaking even for the higher risk sample of mothers (1.06), to Hawaii Healthy Start showing an undesirable benefit-cost ratio of 0.38. The limited data on monetary benefits, age at treatment and length of follow-up undoubtedly contributed to their poor economic value.

For the five studies which began at birth or later, savings from reduced delinquency and criminality, as measured by less involvement with the justice system and costs avoided to victims of crime, accounted for a substantial proportion of the measured benefits. In the Perry Preschool study, for example, reduced offending accounted for 79.6 per cent of the total economic benefits, or $5.70 of the $7.16 produced on a one dollar investment. Some of the other benefits were realised from a reduced reliance on social assistance, increased output of the programme participants which generated increased tax revenue for the government, increased educational achievement which, in some cases, meant less use of remedial school services and reduced demand for publicly funded private security and emergency services.

For the two of the nine studies in which a benefit-cost ratio was not calculated (Lally *et al.*, 1988; Seitz *et al.*, 1985), one provided a limited economic analysis and the other presented cost data only. For the study by Seitz *et al.* (1985), benefits from reduced use of social assistance and decreased remedial and supportive school services were found to be paying-off per family programme costs at two families per year. A review of the study's findings by external researchers concluded that the programme's economic value could have been increased had a more complete benefit-cost analysis been carried out. For the study by Lally *et al.* (1988), the per child costs of the control group's involvement with the justice system were found to be over ten times the per child costs of the programme group.

Numerous methodological issues plague any comparison of programme evaluation findings. This is even more the case for comparisons of the findings of economic evaluations. In the studies that have been reviewed in this chapter different methodologies were employed to assess costs and benefits, different costs and benefits were examined and, in some cases, the recipients of the economic benefits, although mostly the taxpayer and crime victim, were based on varied theoretical assumptions. Equally important was the finding among all of the studies that programme benefits were calculated conservatively, while programme costs tended to be taken into account in full.

Conclusions and research priorities

As this chapter has shown, few primary (and secondary) prevention studies have measured the monetary value of programme effects and resources used. For those studies that have attempted to carry out an economic evaluation, such as a benefit-cost or cost-effectiveness analysis, only a handful have followed the rigorous methodology of economic analysis.

In the United Kingdom, even less is known about the economic efficiency of primary (and secondary) prevention programmes. A Home Office study which reviewed a range of early crime prevention programmes concluded that, 'There is little detailed evidence in the UK regarding the cost effectiveness of criminality reduction programmes' (Utting, 1996, 85). A more recent Home Office study (Nuttall, Goldblatt and Lewis, 1998) came to the same conclusion. As the present review has shown, there are, however, a number of examples of primary and secondary prevention programmes (in the United States) that have already initiated or are planning economic evaluations. Similarly, in the United Kingdom, economic evaluation research in this area is reported to be underway (Utting, 1996).

If more is to be learned about the individual and relative economic strength of the primary prevention of delinquency and later offending, and the implications this strategy holds for more effective and economically efficient crime reduction, three things must first take place. First, researchers and policymakers must play a greater role to ensure that programmes include, as part of the original research design, the provision for an economic evaluation. Prospective economic evaluations have many advantages over retrospective ones. As part of this, researchers must ensure that economic evaluations are not only rigorous, but are also comprehensive; that is, all resources used and all relevant programme effects need to be monetised. Second, greater use of experimental research designs, particularly randomised experiments, is needed. The stronger the outcome evaluation, the more confidence that can be placed in the findings of an economic evaluation. Third, funding bodies must be prepared to finance economic evaluation research. These are beginning to take place in the United Kingdom (see Dhiri, Goldblatt, Brand and Price, 2001).

It is also important that future research examine the effectiveness and economic efficiency of different types of primary prevention programmes, particularly over time. From the present review it is clear that programmes which produced substantial economic returns (benefits outweighing costs) were not limited to interventions implemented at one particular stage of the life course (e.g. infancy) nor one time frame when benefits started to accrue (e.g. long-term). Future research is also needed to identify which interventions work best with different populations.

Another important issue for future research in this area is the need for a standard set of criteria to measure monetary costs and benefits. In the present review, as in reviews of the costs and benefits of other crime prevention strategies (see Welsh and Farrington, 2000), there is the problem of non-comparable estimates of costs and benefits across the studies. An attempt to apply a standard criterion to all of the studies reviewed here was hampered by limited or missing information presented about key costs and benefits. This has important implications for comparing programmes' benefit-cost findings, as well as the potential economic standing of a prevention programme, which may play a role in whether or not funding is maintained.

Overall, it can be said that primary prevention is an economically efficient strategy to reducing delinquency and later criminal offending and improving the life course development of at-risk children and young persons and their families. Substantial and wide-ranging economic benefits (e.g. improved health, increased educational achievement, higher earnings, savings to the criminal justice system) are produced from the use of primary prevention programmes. Participating members of programmes, taxpaying citizens, government and potential victims of crime are indeed direct beneficiaries of the effects of primary prevention programmes.

NOTES

I wish to thank David Farrington and Mark Perfect for their helpful comments and suggestions on earlier drafts of this chapter.

1 It is unclear from the data presented by Earle (1995) at which point in time abuse and neglect were measured. Presumably, the 1,353 programme group families were enrolled at non-specific time intervals between July 1987 and June 1991. As the programme lasted four years, it is likely that only a small portion of the families had completed the programme.

2 $3.4 million was calculated by multiplying 1,353 (families) by the estimated annual per family cost of the programme ($349,000 ÷ 140 [families per year]).

3 This finding was not reported in Hahn (1994). It is from a separate study by Taggart (1995, cited in Greenwood *et al.*, 1996), which measured the total number of self-reported arrests over the four-year programme period.

REFERENCES

Barclay, G. C. (ed., 1995) *Digest 3: Information on the Criminal Justice System in England and Wales.* London: Research and Statistics Department, Home Office.

Barnett, W. S. (1993) Cost-benefit analysis. In L. J. Schweinhart, H. V. Barnes and D. P. Weikart, *Significant Benefits: The High/Scope Perry Preschool Study Through Age 27* (pp. 142–73). Ypsilanti, MI: High/Scope Press.

(1996) *Lives in the Balance: Age-27 Benefit-Cost Analysis of the High/Scope Perry Preschool Program.* Ypsilanti, MI: High/Scope Press.

Barnett, W. S. and Escobar, C. M. (1987) The economics of early educational intervention: A review. *Review of Educational Research*, *57*, 387–414.

(1990) Economic costs and benefits of early intervention. In S. J. Meisels and J. P. Shonkoff (eds.), *Handbook of Early Childhood Intervention* (pp. 560–82). Cambridge: Cambridge University Press.

Brantingham, P. J. and Easton, S. T. (1998) *The Costs of Crime: Who Pays and How Much? 1998 Update*. Vancouver, Canada: The Fraser Institute.

Bukoski, W. J. and Evans, R. I. (eds., 1998) *Cost-Benefit/Cost-Effectiveness Research of Drug Abuse Prevention: Implications for Programming and Policy*. NIDA Research Monograph 176. Washington, DC: National Institute on Drug Abuse.

Cohen, M. A. (1988) Pain, suffering, and jury awards: A study of the cost of crime to victims. *Law and Society Review*, *22*, 537–55.

(1992) A note on the cost of crime to victims. *Urban Studies*, *27*, 139–46.

(1998) The monetary value of saving a high-risk youth. *Journal of Quantitative Criminology*, *14*, 5–33.

(2000) Measuring the costs and benefits of crime and justice. In D. Duffee (ed.), *Criminal Justice 2000: Vol. 4. Measurement and Analysis of Crime and Justice* (pp. 263–315). Washington, DC: National Institute of Justice, US Department of Justice.

(2001) The crime victim's perspective in cost-benefit analysis: The importance of monetizing tangible and intangible crime costs. In B. C. Welsh, D. P. Farrington and L. W. Sherman (eds.), *Costs and Benefits of Preventing Crime* (pp. 23–50). Boulder, CO: Westview Press.

Cohen, M. A., Miller, T. R. and Rossman, S. B. (1994) The costs and consequences of violent behavior in the United States. In A. J. Reiss, Jr. and J. A. Roth (eds.), *Understanding and Preventing Violence: Vol. 4. Consequences and Control* (pp. 66–167). Washington, DC: National Academy Press.

Cook, P. J., Lawrence, B. A., Ludwig, J. and Miller, T. R. (1999) The medical costs of gunshot injuries in the United States. *Journal of the American Medical Association*, *282*, 447–54.

Coopers and Lybrand (1994) *Preventative Strategy for Young People in Trouble*. London: ITV Telethon/The Prince's Trust.

Criminal Injuries Compensation Board (1996) *Thirty-First Annual Report*. London: Her Majesty's Stationery Office.

Curtis, L. A. (1995) *The State of Families: Family, Employment and Reconstruction: Policy Based on What Works*. Milwaukee, WI: Families International.

Dhiri, S., Goldblatt, P., Brand, S. and Price, R. (2001) Evaluation of the United Kingdom's 'Crime Reduction Programme': Analysis of costs and benefits. In B. C. Welsh, D. P. Farrington and L. W. Sherman (eds.), *Costs and Benefits of Preventing Crime* (pp. 179–201). Boulder, CO: Westview Press.

Donohue, J. J. and Siegelman, P. (1998) Allocating resources among prisons and social programs in the battle against crime. *Journal of Legal Studies*, *27*, 1–43.

Earle, R. B. (1995) Helping to prevent child abuse – and future consequences: Hawaii Healthy Start. *Program Focus*, October. Washington, DC: National Institute of Justice, US Department of Justice.

Eisenhower Foundation (1990) *Youth Investment and Community Reconstruction: Street Lessons on Drugs and Crime for the Nineties*. Washington, DC: Author.

Farrington, D. P. (1983) Randomized experiments on crime and justice. In M. Tonry and N. Morris (eds.), *Crime and Justice: A Review of Research*: *Vol. 4* (pp. 257–308). University of Chicago Press.

(1996) *Understanding and Preventing Youth Crime*. York: Joseph Rowntree Foundation.

(1997) Evaluating a community crime prevention program. *Evaluation, 3*, 157–73.

Field, S. (1993) Crime prevention and the costs of auto theft: An economic analysis. In R. V. Clarke (ed.), *Crime Prevention Studies: Vol. 1* (pp. 69–91). Monsey, NY: Criminal Justice Press.

Forrester, D., Frenz, S., O'Connell, M. and Pease, K. (1990) *The Kirkholt Burglary Prevention Project: Phase II*. London: Home Office.

Gabor, T., Welsh, B. C. and Antonowicz, D. H. (1996) The role of the health community in the prevention of criminal violence. *Canadian Journal of Criminology, 38*, 317–33.

Greaves, L., Hankivsky, O. and Kingston-Riechers, J. (1995) *Selected Estimates of the Costs of Violence Against Women*. London, Canada: Centre for Research on Violence Against Women and Children.

Greenwood, P. W., Model, K. E., Rydell, C. P. and Chiesa, J. (1996) *Diverting Children from a Life of Crime: Measuring Costs and Benefits*. Santa Monica, CA: RAND.

Hahn, A. (1994) *Evaluation of the Quantum Opportunities Program (QOP): Did the Program Work?* Waltham, MA: Brandeis University.

(1999) Extending the time of learning. In D. J. Besharov (ed.), *America's Disconnected Youth: Toward a Preventive Strategy* (pp. 233–65). Washington, DC: Child Welfare League of America Press.

Home Office Standing Conference on Crime Prevention (1988) *Report of the Working Group on the Costs of Crime*. London: Home Office.

Hurley, J. (1995) *Delinquency Prevention Works*. Washington, DC: Office of Juvenile Justice and Delinquency Prevention, US Department of Justice.

Jones, M. B. and Offord, D. R. (1989) Reduction of antisocial behaviour in poor children by nonschool skill-development. *Journal of Child Psychology and Psychiatry, 30*, 737–50.

Karoly, L. A., Greenwood, P. W., Everingham, S. S., Houbé, J., Kilburn, M. R., Rydell, C. P., Sanders, M. and Chiesa, J. (1998) *Investing in Our Children: What We Know and Don't Know about the Costs and Benefits of Early Childhood Interventions*. Santa Monica, CA: RAND.

Kerr, R. and McLean, J. (1996) *Paying for Violence: Some of the Costs of Violence Against Women in B.C.* Victoria, Canada: Ministry of Women's Equality.

Kitzman, H., Olds, D. L., Henderson, C. R., Hanks, C., Cole, R., Tatelbaum, R., McConnochie, K. M., Sidora, K., Luckey, D. W., Shaver, D., Engelhardt, K., James, D. and Barnard, K. (1997) Effect of prenatal and infancy home visitation by nurses on pregnancy outcomes, childhood injuries, and repeated childbearing: A randomized controlled trial. *Journal of the American Medical Association, 278*, 644–52.

Knapp, M. (1997) Economic evaluations and interventions for children and adolescents with mental health problems. *Journal of Child Psychology and Psychiatry, 38*, 3–25.

Lally, J. R., Mangione, P. L. and Honig, A. S. (1988) The Syracuse University family development research program: Long-range impact of an early intervention with low-income children and their families. In D. Powell (ed.), *Parent Education as Early Childhood Intervention: Emerging Directions in Theory, Research and Practice* (pp. 79–104). Norwood, NJ: Ablex.

Lipsey, M. W. (1984) Is delinquency prevention a cost-effective strategy? A California perspective. *Journal of Research in Crime and Delinquency, 21*, 279–302.

Lipsey, M. W., Mills, J. I. and Plant, M. A. (1982) *1981 Los Angeles County Youth Services Network Evaluation.* Claremont, CA: Claremont Graduate School Center for Applied Social Research.

Long, D. A., Mallar, C. D. and Thornton, C. V. D. (1981) Evaluating the benefits and costs of the Job Corps. *Journal of Policy Analysis and Management, 1*, 55–76.

Mandel, M. J., Magnusson, P., Ellis, J. E., DeGeorge, G. and Alexander, K. L. (1993) The economics of crime. *Business Week* (December 13), 72–75, 78–81.

Mayhew, P., Aye Maung, N. and Mirrlees-Black, C. (1993) *The 1992 British Crime Survey.* London: Research and Statistics Department, Home Office.

Miller, T. R., Cohen, M. A. and Rossman, S. B. (1993) Victim costs of violent crime and resulting injuries. *Health Affairs, 12*, 186–97.

Miller, T. R., Cohen, M. A. and Wiersema, B. (1996) *Victim Costs and Consequences: A New Look.* Washington, DC: National Institute of Justice, US Department of Justice.

Miller, T. R., Fisher, D. A. and Cohen, M. A. (2001) Costs of juvenile violence: Policy implications. *Pediatrics, 107(1)*, electronic journal.

Mulvey, E. P., Arthur, M. W. and Reppucci, N. D. (1993) The prevention and treatment of juvenile delinquency: A review of the research. *Clinical Psychology Review, 13*, 133–67.

National Commission of Inquiry into the Prevention of Child Abuse (1996) *Childhood Matters: Report of the National Commission of Inquiry into the Prevention of Child Abuse*: *Vol. 1.* London: The Stationery Office.

Nuttall, C., Goldblatt, P. and Lewis, C. (eds., 1998) *Reducing Offending: An Assessment of Research Evidence on Ways of Dealing with Offending Behaviour.* London: Research and Statistics Directorate, Home Office.

Olds, D. L., Eckenrode, J., Henderson, C. R., Kitzman, H., Powers, J., Cole, R., Sidora, K., Morris, P., Pettitt, L. M. and Luckey, D. (1997) Long-term effects of home visitation on maternal life course and child abuse and neglect: Fifteen-year follow-up of a randomized trial. *Journal of the American Medical Association, 278*, 637–43.

Olds, D. L., Henderson, C. R, Chamberlin, R. and Tatelbaum, R. (1986) Preventing child abuse and neglect: A randomized trial of nurse home visitation. *Pediatrics, 78*, 65–78.

Olds, D. L., Henderson, C. R., Cole, R., Eckenrode, J., Kitzman, H., Luckey, D., Pettitt, L. M., Sidora, K., Morris, P. and Powers, J. (1998) Long-term effects of home visitation on children's criminal and antisocial behavior: 15-year follow-up of a randomized controlled trial. *Journal of the American Medical Association, 280*, 1238–44.

Olds, D. L., Henderson, C. R. and Kitzman, H. (1994) Does prenatal and infancy nurse home visitation have enduring effects on qualities of parental caregiving and child health at 25 to 50 months of life? *Pediatrics, 93*, 89–98.

Olds, D. L., Henderson, C. R., Phelps, C., Kitzman, H. and Hanks, C. (1993) Effects of prenatal and infancy nurse home visitation on government spending. *Medical Care, 31*, 155–74.

Olds, D. L., Henderson, C. R, Tatelbaum, R. and Chamberlin, R. (1988) Improving the life-course development of socially disadvantaged mothers: A randomized trial of nurse home visitation. *American Journal of Public Health, 78*, 1436–45.

Plotnick, R. D. (1994) Applying benefit-cost analysis to substance use prevention programs. *International Journal of the Addictions, 29*, 339–59.

Potas, I., Vining, A. and Wilson, P. (1990) *Young People and Crime: Costs and Prevention.* Canberra: Australian Institute of Criminology.

Rajkumar, A. S. and French, M. T. (1997) Drug abuse, crime costs, and the economic benefits of treatment. *Journal of Quantitative Criminology, 13*, 291–323.

Schweinhart, L. J., Barnes, H. V. and Weikart, D. P. (1993) *Significant Benefits: The High/Scope Perry Preschool Study Through Age 27.* Ypsilanti, MI: High/Scope Press.

Seitz, V. (1990) Intervention programs for impoverished children: A comparison of educational and family support models. *Annals of Child Development, 7*, 73–103.

Seitz, V., Rosenbaum, L. K. and Apfel, N. H. (1985) Effects of family support intervention: A ten-year follow-up. *Child Development, 56*, 376–91.

Spigelman, M. (1996) *Money Well Spent: Investing in Preventing Crime.* Ottawa, Canada: National Crime Prevention Council.

The President's Crime Prevention Council (1995) *Preventing Crime and Promoting Responsibility: 50 Programs that Help Communities Help Their Youth.* Washington, DC: US Government Printing Office.

Tolan, P. H. and Guerra, N. G. (1994) Prevention of delinquency: Current status and issues. *Applied and Preventive Psychology, 3*, 251–73.

Tremblay, R. E. and Craig, W. M. (1995) Developmental crime prevention. In M. Tonry and D. P. Farrington (eds.), *Building a Safer Society: Strategic Approaches to Crime Prevention* (pp. 151–236). Chicago: University of Chicago Press.

US Department of Labor (1995) *Job Corps Annual Report: Program Year 1994.* Washington, DC: Author.

Utting, D. (1996) *Reducing Criminality Among Young People: A Sample of Relevant Programmes in the United Kingdom.* London: Research and Statistics Directorate, Home Office.

Utting, D., Bright, J. and Henricson, C. (1993) *Crime and the Family: Improving Child-Rearing and Preventing Delinquency.* London: Family Policy Studies Centre.

van Dijk, J. J. M. (1996) Assessing the costs and benefits of crime control strategies. Unpublished manuscript. The Hague: Ministry of Justice.

(1997) Towards a research-based crime reduction policy: Crime prevention as a cost-effective policy option. *European Journal on Criminal Policy and Research, 5*, 13–27.

van Dijk, J. J. M. and Terlouw, G. J. (1996) An international perspective of the business community as victims of fraud and crime. *Security Journal, 7*, 157–67.

Walker, J. (1992) Estimates of the costs of crime in Australia. *Trends and Issues in Crime and Criminal Justice*, 39. Canberra: Australian Institute of Criminology.

(1995) Estimates of the costs of crime in Australia: Revised 1995. Paper prepared for the Commonwealth Law Enforcement Board.

Waller, I. and Welsh, B. C. (1999) International trends in crime prevention: Cost-effective ways to reduce victimization. In G. Newman (ed.), *Global Report on Crime and Justice* (pp. 191–220). New York: Oxford University Press.

Wasserman, G. A. and Miller, L. S. (1998) The prevention of serious and violent juvenile offending. In R. Loeber and D. P. Farrington (eds.), *Serious and Violent Juvenile Offenders: Risk Factors and Successful Interventions* (pp. 197–247). Thousand Oaks, CA: Sage.

Weimer, D. L. and Friedman, L. S. (1979) Efficiency considerations in criminal rehabilitation research: Costs and consequences. In L. Sechrest, S. O. White and E. D. Brown (eds.), *The Rehabilitation of Criminal Offenders: Problems and Prospects* (pp. 251–72). Washington, DC: National Academy of Sciences.

Welsh, B. C. and Farrington, D. P. (2000) Monetary costs and benefits of crime prevention programs. In M. Tonry (ed.), *Crime and Justice: A Review of Research*: *Vol. 27* (pp. 305–61). Chicago: University of Chicago Press.

Welsh, B. C., Farrington, D. P. and Sherman, L. W. (eds., 2001) *Costs and Benefits of Preventing Crime*. Boulder, CO: Westview Press.

Welsh, B. C. and Waller, I. (1995) *Crime and Its Prevention: Costs and Benefits*. Ottawa: Department of Criminology, University of Ottawa.

Yoshikawa, H. (1994) Prevention as cumulative protection: Effects of early family support and education on chronic delinquency and its risks. *Psychological Bulletin*, *115*, 28–54.

Zigler, E., Taussig, C. and Black, K. (1992) Early childhood intervention: A promising preventative for juvenile delinquency. *American Psychologist*, *47*, 997–1006.

11 Conclusions and the way forward

David P. Farrington and Jeremy W. Coid

Current knowledge about antisocial behaviour

In the past thirty years, a great deal has been learned about adult antisocial behaviour, as shown in the chapters of this book. It is known that most types of antisocial behaviour tend to be inter-related, in the sense that people who commit one type have an elevated probability of also committing other types. Hence, it is plausible to assume the existence of an antisocial syndrome, and that most types of antisocial acts basically reflect the same underlying theoretical construct, which might be termed an 'antisocial personality'. However, less is known about the development of the antisocial syndrome, and especially about developmental sequences of antisocial acts, or the extent to which one type of act facilitates or is a stepping stone to other types. Also, little is known about the developmental course of careers of antisocial behaviour: about ages of onset, probability of persistence or escalation, frequency of different acts at different ages, duration of problems, or ages of desistance.

Many research projects focus on only one type of antisocial act, such as crime or drug use. More researchers should aim to measure a wide variety of different types of acts and hence the full antisocial syndrome. While precise definitions of antisocial personality disorder (APD), and cut-off points between normal and pathological, change over time, the constituent acts are well known. They include property crimes, violent crimes, drug use, heavy drinking, drunk or reckless driving, sexual promiscuity or risky sex behaviour, divorce/separation or unstable sexual relationships, spouse or partner abuse, child abuse or neglect, an unstable employment history, debts, dependence on welfare benefits, heavy gambling, heavy smoking, and repeated lying and conning. Associated personality features include impulsiveness and a lack of planning, selfishness and egocentricity, callousness and a lack of empathy, a lack of remorse or guilt feelings, low frustration tolerance and high aggressiveness.

There is a great deal of continuity and stability over time in antisocial behaviour, but also a great deal of change in absolute levels of behavioural manifestations. Conduct disordered children have a relatively high probability of becoming antisocial adults, suggesting that the antisocial syndrome typically arises in childhood and persists into adulthood. However, there are many dropouts: most conduct disordered children do not develop adult APD, for example. The boundary between childhood and adulthood is artificial, since there is no sign of discontinuity at age 18. There is also intergenerational transmission of antisocial behaviour from parents to children (see chapter 4 by Terrie Moffitt and Avshalom Caspi), and antisocial behaviour is highly concentrated in certain families and individuals. However, little is known about the precise mechanisms that underlie this intergenerational transmission.

As the title suggests, this book is primarily concerned with adult antisocial behaviour rather than with APD or psychopathy. This is because far more is known about risk factors for, and early prevention of, adult antisocial behaviour. A key issue is whether APD and psychopathy are different in kind or in degree from antisocial behaviour in general. To the extent that the differences are primarily in degree, all the findings in this book about early prevention of antisocial behaviour will apply to APD and psychopathy as well. However, to the extent that the differences are primarily in kind, this will not necessarily be true.

Risk and protective factors

Prevention methods should be based on knowledge about risk and protective factors. Numerous risk factors have been identified for different types of antisocial behaviour, but there has been insufficient research on risk factors for the antisocial syndrome in general or for APD or psychopathy. It is unclear how far risk factors are the same for all types of antisocial acts. Important risk factors include conduct disorder, hyperactivity-impulsivity-attention deficit, low intelligence and attainment, inconsistent or harsh discipline, poor parental supervision, divorce/separation of parents, and socio-economic deprivation (see chapter 3 by Rolf Loeber, Stephanie Green and Benjamin Lahey). However, little is known about the influence of these risk factors on different stages of antisocial careers such as onset, persistence, escalation, duration or desistance, or about the independent, interactive or sequential effects of risk factors.

Little is known about precise causal mechanisms that might link risk factors and antisocial behaviours, and relatively little is known about protective factors that are not merely at the opposite end of the scale to a risk factor (see chapter 5 by Friedrich Lösel and Doris Bender). More research is needed on the effects of life events (e.g. getting married, getting a job, moving house) on the course of development of antisocial behaviour, using within-individual analyses in which each person is followed up before and after the life event (Farrington, 1988). Similarly, more research is needed on whether risk factors for antisocial behaviour are similar or different for males and females (see chapter 9 by Deborah Gorman-Smith and Moffitt *et al.*, 2001) and for the major racial and ethnic groups (Farrington, Loeber and Stouthamer-Loeber, 2003).

Early prevention

As pointed out in chapter 2 by Jeremy Coid, a key choice is between primary prevention targeted on the whole community and secondary prevention targeted on high risk children and families. Both approaches have advantages and disadvantages. An advantage of secondary prevention is that scarce treatment resources can be targeted on the people who are most in need. However, a disadvantage of secondary prevention is that identifying children and families as high risk may have stigmatising effects and may prejudice co-operation from the community.

It might perhaps be argued that primary prevention is likely to be most useful in preventing adult antisocial behaviour, while secondary prevention may be most useful in preventing adult syndromes of APD and psychopathy. However, research is needed to investigate this, and in chapter 2 Jeremy Coid argued that primary prevention might be useful in both cases.

Most is known about the primary prevention of adult antisocial behaviour, and that is the main concern of this book. A number of promising methods of preventing types of antisocial behaviour have been identified, including intensive home visiting in pregnancy and infancy, preschool intellectual enrichment programmes, parent training, interpersonal skills training, peer influence resistance strategies and anti-bullying programmes in schools (see chapters 6, 7 and 8). Multiple component programmes that include several of these elements seem particularly promising. All of these individual programmes could be implemented within the wide-ranging *Communities that Care* strategy (Hawkins and Catalano, 1992) described in chapter 1 by David Farrington. However, there have been few well-designed evaluations of these programmes, especially in relation to APD or psychopathy, and the effectiveness of *Communities that Care* has not yet been established.

Advancing knowledge about the effectiveness of prevention

In order to investigate the effectiveness of early prevention techniques, randomised experiments are needed. Few such experiments have been carried out in Great Britain. Most of the randomised experiments on the early developmental prevention of delinquency reviewed in chapter 1 by David Farrington were carried out in North America. Randomised experiments should be carried out in Great Britain to evaluate the effectiveness of intensive home visiting in pregnancy and infancy, preschool intellectual enrichment programmes, parent training, interpersonal skills training, peer influence resistance strategies and school-based programmes, in preventing adult antisocial behaviour, APD and psychopathy.

Unfortunately, it would take many years for the effects of early prevention techniques on adult antisocial behaviour, APD or psychopathy to be determined. However, the effects on earlier outcomes leading to adult antisocial behaviour (e.g. childhood and adolescent antisocial behaviour) could be determined more quickly. One possible strategy would be to investigate the impact on adult antisocial behaviour only if there was an impact on earlier outcomes, but that would exclude the possibility of detecting delayed effects. It would also be highly desirable to carry out a cost-benefit analysis of any intervention, to establish whether its monetary benefits exceed its monetary costs (see chapter 10 by Brandon Welsh). Also, it would be desirable to collect additional data on adult antisocial behaviour in the landmark early intervention projects described in chapter 1 by David Farrington.

It is particularly important to evaluate the additional effectiveness of early prevention programmes in reducing later APD and psychopathy. Where randomised experiments cannot be carried out, quasi-experimental evaluations should be conducted, attempting as far as possible to exclude alternative explanations of observed effects (Shadish *et al.*, 2002). Systematic reviews of the literature on the effectiveness of early prevention in reducing adult antisocial behaviour, APD and psychopathy should also be completed.

Goals of prevention programmes

Greater clarity is required regarding the goals of prevention programmes. This is not simply a matter of improving outcome measures. Many of the studies reviewed in this book were not specifically designed to reduce future delinquent and criminal behaviour, although many had this serendipitous outcome. We must emphasise that when designing future evaluations, a wide range of antisocial behaviours should be included, and these measures should be appropriate to the life-stage of the subjects. But it is equally important to be clear about what it is that the intervention ultimately hopes to achieve in terms of behavioural reduction. For example, is the intervention designed to reduce the overall level of antisocial behaviour across an entire sample of subjects randomised to receive the intervention (a population effect)? Or is the goal to reduce the level of antisocial behaviour in a previously identified, high-risk subgroup (a targeted effect)?

An intervention might hope to achieve both a population and targeted effect. For example, subjects chosen for a study might be representative of the larger population but subsequent analyses may reveal whether those considered at high risk are more or less likely to respond to the intervention than low-risk subjects. Problems of statistical power might be overcome by oversampling high-risk children. Such an approach is essential to provide better information on whether high-risk children, specifically those with conduct disorder, are likely to benefit from interventions that benefit the population as a whole. It is also important to establish which interventions they benefit from most, and to what degree. It may ultimately become apparent that high-risk children do not respond, or that the response is not adequate to justify the time, effort and cost involved. Research efforts should then move towards improved screening to identify high-risk children, including subgroups, and the development of tailored programmes targeted to meet their special needs.

Although a small number of individuals are responsible for a disproportionate amount of antisocial behaviour (see chapter 2 by Jeremy Coid), the population approach may ultimately lead to a greater reduction of antisocial behaviour in the general population with greater overall benefits in cost reduction. A reduction in less frequent, but more serious, behaviours which are more likely to be demonstrated by high-risk individuals may not be achievable. The public may be less impressed by a reduction in more common behaviours such as vandalism and car theft than by less substantial reductions in robbery and serious assault. The importance of cost savings may not be a priority shared by all parties. Investigators should therefore be entirely clear at the outset regarding their goal of intervention in view of the differing expectations of sponsors of research, policy-makers, politicians and the public. These can change over time.

Retrospective studies

In order to advance knowledge about early risk factors for APD or psychopathy, a retrospective case-control study could be carried out, comparing adults suffering from APD or psychopathy with controls. Both groups could be interviewed to assess the true extent of their antisocial behaviour, and to obtain retrospective information about their development over time and their early risk and protective factors. Additional information could be obtained from records and informants (e.g. partners, relatives or friends). This design has the advantage of producing speedy results, but the severe disadvantage is that retrospective information is often flawed (unless it can be corroborated by records). But this design is particularly useful when studying rarer outcomes such as APD or psychopathy.

Prospective longitudinal studies

The best way of advancing knowledge about the development of antisocial careers, and about risk and protective factors for onset, persistence, escalation, duration and desistance, would be to carry out a prospective longitudinal survey. Ideally, such a survey should begin at birth (or with pregnant women) with a representative sample from the population, but this type of survey would take a generation to produce findings about adult antisocial behaviour and in any case might not yield a significant number of highly antisocial individuals. In order to maximise the yield of antisocial people, it might be advisable to sample high-risk areas disproportionally.

Other types of longitudinal surveys also have attractions. For example, a follow-up of aggressive conduct disordered children aged 8 might be useful in identifying protective factors that influence why some conduct disordered children do not become antisocial adults. A follow-up of a sample of antisocial teenagers aged 18 might be useful in identifying factors that influence improvement and desistance and in determining how far it is possible to predict future antisocial careers. In both cases, it would be advisable to follow up control samples as well.

Use of existing longitudinal studies

One obvious method of obtaining speedy information in a prospective longitudinal survey would be to collect additional data on a wide variety of adult antisocial acts in an existing survey that started some years ago. Additional data would be particularly valuable in a survey based on an inner-city sample (to maximise the yield of adult antisocial behaviour), with a large sample of at least several hundreds, with extensive data about numerous different risk and protective factors, beginning in childhood and adolescence, and with repeated information from several different data sources (e.g. the subjects themselves, parents, peers, teachers and records).

Leading longitudinal studies on delinquency, substance use, sexual behaviour and mental health problems that began with childhood samples are reviewed in Loeber and Farrington (2001, appendix C). For example, there are three British studies based on urban samples that should be followed up throughout adulthood. These are the Cambridge Study in Delinquent Development, which is a follow-up of 411 boys originally aged 8–9 (Farrington, 2002); the Newcastle 1000-family study, which is a follow-up of 1142 children from birth (Kolvin *et al.*, 1990); and the Inner London study of 1689 children originally aged 10 (Rutter, 1981). Ideally, these samples should be followed up both in records and through repeated interviews.

New follow-ups of existing studies have many advantages in producing speedy results but also have disadvantages. The measures originally used may be outdated or may not address key modern theories or risk and protective factors that are now considered important. It may be difficult to locate subjects last studied many years ago and attrition rates may be high. There may also be disadvantages arising from the attempt to use a study to serve a purpose for which it was not originally designed.

High-risk longitudinal studies

In order to advance knowledge about development and risk factors for APD or psychopathy, a prospective longitudinal survey could follow up both a representative sample and a high risk sample, or alternatively an 'enriched' community sample. For example, a random sample of children in an inner city could first be screened using a risk assessment device. All high risk children and a fraction of the remainder could then be followed up, as in the Pittsburgh Youth Study (Loeber *et al.*, 1998). This design has the advantage of maximising the yield of the most antisocial people but also making it possible to draw conclusions about the whole community.

A number of risk assessment devices have been developed for use with young children. For example, the EARL-20B (Augimeri *et al.*, 2001) is an early assessment risk list for boys under 12 thought to be at risk of engaging in future antisocial behaviour. These risk assessment devices need to be studied in longitudinal surveys to determine how successful they are in predicting adult antisocial behaviour, APD and psychopathy, with special reference to sensitivity, specificity, false positive and false negative rates (Verhulst and Koot, 1992, p.49).

The accelerated longitudinal-experimental design

Ambitiously, all key questions about epidemiology, development, risk and protective factors, and prevention effectiveness could be tested in one large-scale project containing a number of different elements. This could be achieved within *Communities that Care* by adding on the follow-up of various age cohorts to the basic intervention design. However, an alternative strategy is to begin with an accelerated longitudinal design and plan to implement prevention experiments within this design.

An accelerated longitudinal design is one in which multiple overlapping cohorts are followed up. For example, four cohorts could be followed up simultaneously: the first from birth to age 6, the second from age 6 to age 12, the third from age 12 to age 18 and the fourth from age 18 to age 24. By linking up the cohorts, information about development from birth to age 24 could be obtained in only six years, instead of twenty-four years (Farrington, Ohlin and Wilson, 1986; Tonry, Ohlin and Farrington, 1991). Further cohorts could be added, for example from age 24 to age 30, and from age 30 to age 36, to obtain information about development over an even wider age range. However, in this chapter we will focus on obtaining information about development and prevention from birth to the mid-twenties.

Different measures of antisocial behaviour would be used in the four cohorts and should facilitate linking them up. In the youngest cohort (up to age 6), the focus should be on measuring childhood conduct problems and disruptive school behaviour. These should be measured initially at age 6 in the next youngest cohort, but then early delinquency and substance abuse should be measured up to age 12. These should be measured initially at age 12 in the next cohort, but then more serious types of offending, substance use, relationship and employment problems should be measured up to age 18. These should be measured initially at age 18 in the oldest cohort, followed by a wider range of antisocial behaviour, APD and psychopathy up to age 24. These measures should make it possible to trace developmental sequences of antisocial behaviour from infancy to adulthood.

In studying antisocial behaviour, it would be desirable to draw all cohorts from a high-risk area of a large city. Households could be sampled to determine which contained eligible individuals (i.e. at birth, age 6, age 12 or age 18). Ideally, the birth cohort would be obtained by sampling pregnant females in their second trimester of pregnancy. Each cohort could consist of a minimum of 500 males (to maximise the yield of antisocial people), except that the birth cohort could include 1000 live births (males and females). If resources could be obtained, the birth cohort could be followed up beyond the initial six-year period. Each person should be assessed at least once a year, with information collected from the subject (if not a baby), the mother and the teacher (during the years of compulsory education). For older cohorts, the first assessment should obtain retrospective information about development up to that age. This type of design has been implemented in Chicago (Harvard University, 2000).

The effectiveness of prevention techniques could be tested in each cohort after the subjects have been followed up for a few years (e.g. at about ages 3, 9, 15 and 21). In many ways, longitudinal and experimental studies have complementary strengths and weaknesses. The longitudinal study advances knowledge about the natural history of development and about the importance of numerous risk and protective factors, but has difficulty in unambiguously demonstrating causal effects. Perhaps the best method of demonstrating causal effects in a longitudinal study is through quasi-experimental analyses (Farrington, 1988). The experimental study unambiguously demonstrates causal effects but can only provide information about the importance of a small number of independent variables.

Results obtained in the first few years of the longitudinal follow-up, identifying key risk and protective factors, might be useful in choosing prevention methods. However, the main intervention at about age 3 could consist of a preschool intellectual enrichment programme combined with parent training. The main intervention at about age 9 could be interpersonal skills training combined with parent training. At about age 15, a school-based combination of interpersonal skills training and peer influence resistance training could be applied. At about age 21, interpersonal and employment skills training and peer influence resistance training could be effective. The main outcome measures would vary in each cohort, from childhood conduct problems in the youngest cohort to adult antisocial behaviour, APD and psychopathy in the oldest.

Putting research into practice

One of the key questions for clinical practice in the future is the extent to which the results of prevention experiments reviewed in this book can be successfully integrated into service-delivery systems and their effectiveness maintained. Three hurdles would have to be overcome. First, not all professionals are trained to administer the techniques which may produce the most future benefit. Second, not all professionals necessarily perceive themselves as 'responsible' for administering these interventions. And third, there is no organisation which currently has the overall responsibility for co-ordinating programmes designed to intervene with children for the purpose of preventing later antisocial behaviour. Responsibility is currently scattered across a range of service agencies, each with firmly demarcated boundaries. Jeremy Coid in chapter 2 has argued that the public health model might be successfully applied in the future. However, it could also be argued that responsibility might be more appropriately placed within the field of criminal justice, or with government departments with responsibility for public protection.

Nationally and locally, there is no agency in Great Britain whose primary mandate is the prevention of crime and antisocial behaviour. For example, the very worthwhile intervention programmes being implemented by Youth Offending Teams are overwhelmingly targeted on detected offenders. Therefore, a national agency should be established with a primary mandate of fostering and funding the prevention of crime and antisocial behaviour.

This national agency could provide technical assistance, skills and knowledge to local agencies in implementing prevention programmes, could provide funding for such programmes, and could ensure continuity, co-ordination and monitoring of local programmes. It could provide training in prevention science for people in local agencies, and could maintain high standards for evaluation research. It could also act as a centre for the discussion of how policy initiatives of different government agencies influence crime and associated social problems. It could set a national and local agenda for research and practice in the prevention of crime, drug and alcohol abuse, mental health problems and associated social problems. National crime prevention agencies have been established in many other countries, such as Sweden (Ministry of Justice, 1997; Wikström and Torstensson, 1999).

The national agency could also maintain a computerised register of evaluation research and, like the National Institute of Clinical Excellence, advise the government about effective and cost-effective prevention programmes. Medical advice is often based on systematic reviews of the effectiveness of health care interventions organised by the Cochrane Collaboration and funded by the National Health Service. Systematic reviews of the evaluation literature on the effectiveness of criminological interventions should be commissioned and funded by government agencies (see Farrington and Petrosino, 2001).

The prevention of crime and antisocial behaviour also needs to be organised locally. In each area, a local agency should be set up to take the lead in organising risk-focused prevention. In Sweden, two-thirds of municipalities have local crime prevention councils. The local prevention agency could take the lead in measuring risk factors and antisocial behaviour in local areas, using archival records and local household and school surveys. It could then assess available resources and develop a plan of prevention strategies. With specialist technical assistance, prevention programmes could be chosen from a menu of strategies that have been proved to be effective in reducing crime in well-designed evaluation research. This would be a good example of evidence-based practice.

Conclusions

This book brings together available knowledge about risk and protective factors and the effectiveness of early prevention methods for adult antisocial behaviour. However, it also reveals important gaps in knowledge, especially about risk factors and early prevention methods for APD and psychopathy. In this chapter, we have suggested ways of advancing knowledge about these topics, especially using new longitudinal and experimental studies.

There are many reasons why it is advantageous to implement experimental interventions within longitudinal studies. The impact of interventions might be better understood in the context of pre-existing trends or developmental sequences. Prior longitudinal data can establish baseline measures to verify the equivalence of people in different experimental conditions, and to estimate the impact of attrition from different experimental conditions. In addition, it can help to investigate interactions between types of people (and their prior histories) and types of interventions. Subsequent longitudinal data can assess the short-term and long-term impact of the intervention in changing people, and the developmental sequences linking short-term and long-term effects.

In practice, most experimental interventions have been designed to test the effectiveness of a technology (e.g. parent training) rather than to test causal hypotheses (e.g. about the effect of different methods of parenting). Including experimental interventions in longitudinal studies encourages use of the experimental results to draw conclusions about causal effects on antisocial behaviour (Robins, 1992). Also, it is more economical to carry out both longitudinal and experimental studies with the same individuals than with different individuals, providing that the two studies do not seriously interfere with each other.

In choosing interventions, there is a tension between selecting multiple component programmes that have a greater probability of changing people but create difficulty in identifying the precise 'active ingredient', and single component programmes with lesser impact but more clear-cut interpretation. Our preference is for multiple component programmes, as the available evidence suggests greater probability of a successful impact in preventing adult antisocial behaviour (Wasserman and Miller, 1998). If a multiple component programme proved to be effective, it is always possible to carry out subsequent experiments designed to disentangle the effects of the different components.

The accelerated longitudinal-experimental design described above is in some sense a 'space shuttle' within which many separate questions about epidemiology, development, risk and protective factors, and prevention effectiveness could be investigated. Once the study got off the ground, it would be flexible enough to include many different sub-studies and yield results relatively quickly. We believe that the time is ripe to mount a major initiative such as this in order to significantly advance knowledge about the causes and prevention of adult antisocial behaviour, APD and psychopathy in the new millennium. Whilst not a substitute, it should also inform a new generation of prospective, long-term, longitudinal studies which are also required.

REFERENCES

Augimeri, L. K., Koegl, C. J., Webster, C. D. and Levene, K. S. (2001) *Early Assessment Risk List for Boys (EARL-20B) Version 2*. Toronto: Earlscourt Child and Family Centre.

Farrington, D. P. (1988) Studying changes within individuals: The causes of offending. In M. Rutter (ed.) *Studies of Psychosocial Risk* (pp. 158–83). Cambridge University Press.

(2002) Key results from the first forty years of the Cambridge Study in Delinquent Development. In T. P. Thornberry and M. D. Krohn (eds.) *Taking Stock of Delinquency* (pp. 137–83). New York: Kluwer/Plenum.

Farrington, D. P., Loeber, R. and Stouthamer-Loeber, M. (2003) How can the relationship between race and violence be explained? In D. F. Hawkins (ed.) *Violent Crimes: Assessing Race and Ethnic Differences* (pp. 213–37). Cambridge University Press.

Farrington, D. P., Ohlin, L. E. and Wilson, J. Q. (1986) *Understanding and Controlling Crime*. New York: Springer-Verlag.

Farrington, D. P. and Petrosino, A. (2001) The Campbell Collaboration Crime and Justice Group. *Annals of the American Academy of Political and Social Science, 578*, 35–49.

Harvard University (2000) *Project on Human Development in Chicago Neighborhoods: 2000 Annual Report*. Cambridge, MA: Harvard University.

Hawkins, J. D. and Catalano, R. F. (1992) *Communities that Care*. San Francisco: Jossey-Bass.

Kolvin, I., Miller, F. J. W., Scott, D. M., Gatzanis, S. R. M. and Fleeting, M. (1990) *Continuities of Deprivation?* Aldershot: Avebury.

Loeber, R. and Farrington, D. P. (2001, eds.) *Child Delinquents: Development, Intervention and Service Needs*. Thousand Oaks, CA: Sage.

Loeber, R., Farrington, D. P., Stouthamer-Loeber, M. and van Kammen, W. B. (1998) *Antisocial Behavior and Mental Health Problems: Explanatory Factors in Childhood and Adolescence*. Mahwah, NJ: Erlbaum.

Ministry of Justice (1997) *Our Collective Responsibility: A National Programme for Crime Prevention*. Stockholm: National Council for Crime Prevention.

Moffitt, T. E., Caspi, A., Rutter, M. and Silva, P. A. (2001) *Sex Differences in Antisocial Behaviour*. Cambridge University Press.

Robins, L. N. (1992) The role of prevention experiments in discovering causes of children's antisocial behavior. In J. McCord and R. Tremblay (eds.) *Preventing Antisocial Behavior* (pp. 3–18). New York: Guilford.

Rutter, M. (1981) Isle of Wight and Inner London studies. In S. A. Mednick and A. E. Baert (eds.) *Prospective Longitudinal Research* (pp. 122–31). Oxford University Press.

Shadish, W. R., Cook, T. D. and Campbell, D. T. (2002) *Experimental and Quasi-Experimental Designs for Generalized Causal Inference*. Boston: Houghton Mifflin.

Tonry, M., Ohlin, L. E. and Farrington, D. P. (1991) *Human Development and Criminal Behavior*. New York: Springer-Verlag.

Verhulst, F. C. and Koot, H. M. (1992) *Child Psychiatric Epidemiology: Concepts, Methods and Findings*. Newbury Park, CA: Sage.

Wasserman, G. A. and Miller, L. S. (1998) The prevention of serious and violent juvenile offending. In R. Loeber and D. P. Farrington (eds.) *Serious and Violent Juvenile Offenders: Risk Factors and Successful Interventions* (pp. 197–247). Thousand Oaks, CA: Sage.

Wikström, P.-O. H. and Torstensson, M. (1999) Local crime prevention and its national support: Organisation and direction. *European Journal on Criminal Policy and Research*, *7*, 459–81.

Index

Made in the USA
Charleston, SC
16 December 2010